OXFORD COMMENTARIES ON INTERNATIONAL LAW

General Editors: *Professor Philip Alston*, Professor of International Law at New York University, and *Professor Vaughan Lowe*, Chichele Professorof Public International Law in the University of Oxford and Fellow of All Souls College, Oxford.

Sub-Series:

OXFORD COMMENTARIES ON THE GATT/WTO AGREEMENTS

General Editor: *Professor Robert Howse*, Professor of International Law at the University of Michigan.

The WTO Agreement on Safeguards

The WTO Agreement on Safeguards

A Commentary

ALAN O. SYKES

Frank & Bernice Greenberg Professor of Law,
University of Chicago

OXFORD
UNIVERSITY PRESS

This book has been printed digitally and produced in a standard specification in order to ensure its continuing availability

OXFORD
UNIVERSITY PRESS

Great Clarendon Street, Oxford OX2 6DP
United Kingdom

Oxford University Press is a department of the University of Oxford. It furthers the University's objective of excellence in research, scholarship, and education by publishing worldwide. Oxford is a registered trade mark of Oxford University Press in the UK and in certain other countries

First published 2006
Reprinted 2013

Published in the United States of America by Oxford University Press
198 Madison Avenue, New York, NY10016, United States of America

British Library Cataloguing in Publication Data
Data available

Library of Congress Cataloging in Publication Data
Data available

ISBN 978-0-19-927740-7

Acknowledgements

My interest in the law and policy of safeguard measures dates to my time as an associate at the Washington, D.C. law firm of Arnold & Porter, where I had the opportunity to work extensively on domestic safeguards investigations. I learned immensely from the excellent lawyers on those teams, including Bob Herzstein, Patrick Macrory, Claire Reade, Larry Schneider, and Tom Wilner. My experiences with these marvelous colleagues led me to pursue international trade law as an academic career. The University of Chicago Law School provided me with the opportunity to develop this interest. The opportunity was greatly enhanced by an invitation from John Jackson and Bill Davey to join them on their international trade casebook, on which we still collaborate, and for which I have been the primary draftsman of the chapter on safeguard measures in the last two editions. Most recently, I have benefited from extensive discussions of safeguards issues within the group of Reporters for the American Law Institute project on Principles of World Trade Law. I thank my co-reporters, Kyle Bagwell, Gene Grossman, Henrik Horn, Rob Howse, Petros Mavroidis, Damien Neven, Bob Staiger, and Joseph Weiler for their innumerable ideas and insights, as well as Henrik, Petros, and ALI Director Lance Liebman for offering me the opportunity to participate in the project. I am as always grateful to my wife Maureen for encouraging me to live the life of the mind, at some significant opportunity cost no doubt. I also wish to thank my collaborators at Oxford University Press, John Louth, Rebecca Smith, Darcy Ahl, and Caroline Quinnell, for their help in producing the final manuscript.

To Maureen, Maddie and Sophie

Preface

The term "safeguard measures" refers to certain forms of trade intervention by national governments to address the injurious effects of import surges on import-competing industries. Trade intervention for this purpose has been subject to discipline under the law of the General Agreement on Tariffs and Trade (GATT) since its inception in 1947, principally through Article XIX of the original GATT. During the Uruguay Round of GATT negotiations, which culminated with creation of the World Trade Organization (WTO) in 1994, discipline over safeguard measures was elaborated and deepened through a new WTO Agreement on Safeguards.

Safeguard measures, and the international law surrounding their use, raise important and interesting questions for scholars, policymakers and practicing lawyers. From a legal perspective, both GATT Article XIX and the Agreement on Safeguards contain numerous ambiguities and puzzles. Some of the most fundamental concepts are undefined or vaguely defined. Other central requirements of the treaty text raise logical conundrums that have no straightforward solution. The first and primary objective of this book is to analyze thoroughly the legal requirements relating to safeguard measures, with special focus on the aspects of the treaty text that have been in the past, or are likely to be in the future, a subject of legal dispute. In the process, the book thoroughly reviews the safeguards cases that have made their way through the WTO dispute resolution process to date (May 2006), and organizes the jurisprudence issue-by-issue.

From the standpoint of scholars and policymakers interested in the economics of international trade and its effects on general economic welfare, important normative questions arise about the use of safeguard measures. A second objective of this book is to consider the social utility of such measures, and to ask whether they can be justified on some principled economic (as opposed to purely political) basis.

From the perspective of scholars interested in political science and political economy, the WTO safeguard mechanism represents a variant of a treaty "escape clause"—that is, treaty authority to deviate from negotiated commitments under specified circumstances. Such escape clauses are reasonably common in international legal arrangements, and have been a subject of significant academic attention. The third objective of this book is to explore the role of safeguard measures in the WTO system from a political economy perspective, in search of a positive account of their design and structure.

The plan of the book is as follows. Chapter 1 reviews the genesis and history of safeguard measures in the GATT system, and the developments that led to political support for a new Agreement on Safeguards. It briefly highlights the important features of the Agreement, and provides some basic statistics on the use of safeguard measures to date in the WTO system. Chapter 2 considers the economics of safeguard measures. It thoroughly reviews the academic commentary on safeguards policy, addressing issues of efficiency, distribution, and political economy. Chapter 3 begins the core legal analysis, with a focus on background rules and principles of the WTO dispute resolution system. Chapter 4 addresses the procedural obligations imposed on national authorities by the Agreement on Safeguards. Chapters 5–8 then consider the key substantive prerequisites for safeguard measures—the "unforeseen developments" requirement, the increased quantities requirement, the serious injury test, and the causation requirement. Chapter 9 addresses the permissible scope and duration of safeguard measures. Chapter 10 then considers the disciplines on "grey-area" measures and related points. A brief conclusion follows. For the convenience of the reader, I have also included several appendices, containing the pertinent WTO treaty text, the current national legislation of the United States and the European Communities, the current status of notifications to the WTO Committee on Safeguards regarding national legislation, notifications to the Committee since the inception of the WTO concerning the use of safeguard measures by national authorities, and a listing of safeguard measures currently in place.

Contents

Table of WTO Panel and AB Reports

Short Title	Full Case Title and Citation	Page Reference
Argentina—Footwear	Panel Report, *Argentina—Safeguard Measures on Imports of Footwear*, WT/DS121/R, as modified by the Appellate Body Report WT/DS121/AB/R	77–78, 81, 91, 103–105, 107–109, 124, 126–29, 143, 150, 151–52, 167, 175–77, 192, 222, 227–29, 233
Argentina—Peaches	Panel Report, *Argentina—Definitive Safeguard Measure on Imports of Preserved Peaches*, WT/DS238/R	33, 105, 114–15, 129, 155, 174, 217
Chile—Agricultural Products	Panel Report, *Chile—Price Band System and Safeguard Measures Relating to Certain Agricultural Products*, WT/DS220/R	33, 129, 143–44, 154, 183
Chile—Edible Oils	*Chile—Provisional Safeguard Measure on Mixtures of Edible Oils*, WT/DS226	33
Chile—Fructose	*Chile—Definitive Safeguard Measure on Imports of Fructose*, WT/DS278	33
Chile—Sugar	*Chile—Safeguard Measures on Sugar*, WT/DS228	33
Chile—Sugar	*Chile—Safeguard Measures and Modifications of Schedules Regarding Sugar*, WT/DS230	33
EC—Asbestos	Appellate Body Report, *EC—Measures affecting Asbestos and Asbestos-Containing Products*, WT/DS135/AB/R	140

Short Title	Full Case Title and Citation	Page Reference
Slovakia—Sugar	*Slovakia—Safeguard Measure on Imports of Sugar*, WT/DS235	33
Turkey—Textiles	Appellate Body Report, *Turkey—Restrictions on Imports of Textile and Clothing Products*, WT/DS34/AB/R	234, 235, 236
United States—Brooms	*United States—Safeguard Measure Against Imports of Broom Corn Brooms*, WT/DS78	33
United States—Cotton Yarn	Appellate Body Report, *United States—Transitional Safeguard Measure on Combed Cotton Yarn from Pakistan*, WT/DS192/AB/R	141
United States—DRAMs	Appellate Body Report, *United States—Countervailing Duty Investigation on Dynamic Random Access Semi-conductors (DRAMS) from Korea*, WT/DS296/AB/R	80, 83, 84
United States—Lamb	*United States—Safeguard Measures on Imports of Fresh, Chilled or Frozen Lamb Meat from New Zealand and Australia*, WT/DS177&178/AB/R	33, 79, 80, 83, 105, 111, 113–14, 144–45, 148–49, 152–53, 155, 181–83, 195, 201, 207
United States—Line Pipe	*United States—Definitive Safeguard Measures on Imports of Circular Welded Carbon Quality Line Pipe from Korea*, WT/DS202	33, 52, 96, 99, 105, 127–28, 183, 196, 201, 213–16, 218, 222, 225–26, 230, 232–36, 239, 242–43, 247
United States—Steel	*United States—Definitive Safeguard Measures on Imports of Certain Steel Products*, WT/DS248–49, 251–54, 258–59/AB/R	33, 75, 80–82, 105, 115–17, 130–31, 134, 146–48, 184–85, 189, 193, 197, 209, 230–31, 243, 253

Short Title	**Full Case Title and Citation**	**Page Reference**
United States—Steel Wire Rod	*Definitive Safeguard Measures on Imports of Steel Wire Rod and Circular Welded Carbon Quality Line Pipe*, WT/DS214	33
United States—Wheat Gluten	Panel Report, *United States—Definitive Safeguard Measures on Imports of Wheat Gluten from the European Communities*, WT/DS166, as modified by the Appellate Body Report WT/DS166/AB/R	33, 82, 83, 89–90, 92–95, 99, 105, 127, 149–50, 177–79, 181–82, 195, 201, 207, 214, 229–30, 234, 239, 247

Table of GATT/WTO Documents

(Bold page numbers indicate material reproduced in full.)

Table of Other International Instruments and Legislation

(*Bold page numbers indicate material reproduced in full.*)

EUROPEAN

INTERNATIONAL

UNITED STATES

U.S. ITC Decisions

List of Abbreviations

CCFRS	certain carbon flat-rolled steel
COGS	costs of goods sold
DSU	Dispute Settlement Understanding
FFTJ	fittings, flanges, and tool joints
GATT	General Agreement on Tariffs and Trade
GNP	gross national product
ITC	International Trade Commission
ITO	International Trade Organization
MERCOSUR	Southern Cone Common Market (ES: Mercado Común del Sur)
MFA	Multifiber Arrangement
NAFTA	North American Free Trade Agreement
WTO	World Trade Organization

Chapter 1

THE EVOLUTION OF SAFEGUARD MEASURES IN THE WTO/GATT SYSTEM: AN OVERVIEW

The law of safeguards measures in the WTO/GATT system originates with Article XIX of the original GATT. With the creation of the WTO in 1994, Article XIX was supplemented, but not replaced, by the Agreement on Safeguards, so that safeguard measures must now comply with both sets of obligations.

This chapter reviews the evolution of safeguards policy in the history of the WTO/GATT system, from its origins in the preparatory work for GATT to the modifications in law and practice that accompanied the WTO Agreement on Safeguards. It stresses the deficiencies in the original structure of GATT Article XIX that became glaring with the passage of time, the drift of the GATT system away from formal reliance on GATT-legal safeguard measures toward "grey-area" substitutes, and the resulting effort to restore legal discipline over protection for troubled industries during the Uruguay Round through negotiations that led to the Agreement on Safeguards. The chapter also affords an introduction to the basic legal obligations of GATT Article XIX and the Agreement on Safeguards, with more detailed analysis of particular legal issues to follow in Chapters 3–10.

A The Genesis of the Safeguards Concept in the Pre-GATT Era

The impetus for GATT came from two related developments. First, the economic decline that began in the United States in 1929 brought a protectionist response in the form of the Tariff Act of 1930 (popularly known as the Smoot-Hawley tariff). The United States raised its tariff rates dramatically, with average tariffs on dutiable imports increasing from 29.5% in 1921 to 53.2% in 1931.[1] U.S. trading partners retaliated, and the early 1930s witnessed a substantial decline in world trade as a consequence of higher tariffs and economic recession. The mistake in policy was recognized by the new Roosevelt administration, which persuaded the Congress to pass the Reciprocal Trade Agreements Act of 1934. That Act authorized the President to negotiate international agreements for the reciprocal reduction of tariffs, an authority that was periodically renewed through 1948. Negotiations under the 1934 Act initially proceeded on a bilateral basis, yielding 32 bilateral agreements by 1945.[2] The United States (and no doubt others) found the bilateral approach increasingly unsatisfactory, however, and shifted its emphasis in 1945 toward the negotiation of a multilateral trading arrangement.[3]

The second development was World War II, and the perception that weak economic conditions had contributed importantly to the advent of military conflict. As the noted economist Richard Cooper has put it, "[t]he seeds of

[1] See Jackson, Davey and Sykes (2002), p. 5. [2] Id., p. 80.
[3] See Jackson (1969).

World War II, both in the Far East and in Europe, were sown by Hoover's signing of the Smoot-Hawley tariff."[4] Even before the end of the war, the Allied nations began to plan for new institutions to enhance global economic stability. The monetary side of the problem was addressed by the Bretton Woods conference in 1944, which conceived what would become the International Monetary Fund and the International Bank for Reconstruction and Development (the World Bank). The trade dimension was left to a series of additional conferences that took place between 1946 and 1948. At the first meeting of the United Nations Economic and Social Council in 1946, a U.S. resolution was adopted calling for the commencement of multilateral efforts to draft a charter for a new international trade organization. Thereafter, at a series of conferences in London, New York, and Geneva, delegates worked on two documents—a tariff reduction agreement, which came to be known as the General Agreement on Tariffs and Trade, and a charter for the International Trade Organization (ITO).

Work on the GATT and ITO proceeded in parallel, with the anticipation that the GATT would serve as the initial "agreement" on tariff reduction, while the ITO would serve as the "institution" to administer and enforce it and its successors.[5] The focus in drafting the GATT was on the negotiated tariff reductions associated with the tariff "bindings" of Article II, but the drafters also included numerous provisions addressing other matters, such as protectionist policies that might be substituted for tariffs and undermine the tariff commitments. Still other provisions addressed ways to amend, modify, or renegotiate the agreement.

In the latter regard, while seeking a renewal of his negotiating authority under the Reciprocal Trade Agreements Act in 1945, the Congress confronted the U.S. President with concerns about possible injury to U.S. industries as a result of trade concessions. The President responded by promising the Congress that he would insist on an "escape clause" in future trade agreements, akin to the one that had been inserted in the U.S.–Mexico trade agreement of 1942. An Executive Order requiring an escape clause in future agreements issued in 1947.[6] The escape clause in the U.S.–Mexico agreement read as follows:

If, as a result of unforeseen developments and of the concessions granted on any article enumerated and described in the Schedules annexed to this Agreement, such article is

[4] Cooper (1987), pp. 291–92.

[5] In this section I draw heavily on the history provided by Jackson (1969).

[6] See Exec. Order No. 9382 of February 25, 1947, 3 C.F.R. §624 (1947).

being imported in such increased quantities and under such conditions as to cause or threaten serious injury to domestic producers of like or similar articles, the Government of either country shall be free to withdraw the concession, in whole or in part, or to modify it to the extent and for such time as may be necessary to prevent such injury.[7]

During the course of subsequent negotiations over GATT and the ITO charter, U.S. representatives urged the inclusion of an escape clause modeled on the U.S.–Mexico clause. The delegates to the London conference in 1946 agreed in principle to the U.S. proposal, although they continued to quibble over the wording of the clause. A final decision to include an escape clause in GATT was reached at the New York conference in 1947, and Article XIX was drafted even as work continued on a somewhat different version of an escape clause to be included in the ITO charter. As shall be seen below, the resemblance between Article XIX and the escape clause in the U.S.–Mexico agreement is striking.

What happened subsequently owed to two quirks in U.S. law. First, the authority of the President under the Reciprocal Trade Agreements Act was to expire in 1948, and its renewal was by no means certain. That authority went beyond mere authorization to negotiate, and included the capacity to accept an agreement on behalf of the United States and to "proclaim" its legal effect under U.S. law. The negotiators of GATT were anxious to ensure that it should take effect before this authority expired. Second, because U.S. accession to the ITO entailed membership in a new international organization, it was believed that the President could not enter the ITO on the basis of his authority to accept "agreements"—an additional act of Congress was believed necessary to approve U.S. accession.

In the face of these constraints on the U.S. administration, negotiators concluded the GATT in 1947. Negotiations on the ITO charter continued, with the understanding that it would be submitted to the U.S. Congress for approval in due course. "Definitive" application of the GATT would await the creation and approval of the ITO, but in the meantime, a number of nations, including the United States, agreed to apply the GATT "provisionally" in accordance with a Protocol of Provisional Application. Upon the execution of the Protocol by a satisfactory number of nations, the GATT was accepted and "proclaimed" into U.S. law by President Truman. Other nations likewise accepted and applied GATT through the Protocol.

As negotiators had feared in 1947, however, protectionist sentiment in the U.S. Congress was on the rise. When the ITO charter was eventually

[7] Reciprocal Trade Agreement with Mexico, December 23, 1942, art. XI, 57 Stat. 833 (1943).

submitted for approval, the Congress balked, and in 1950 the President gave up further efforts to secure approval of the charter. Without the participation of the United States, the ITO never came into being. The GATT remained in force, "provisionally" applied,[8] but the institution that was expected to enforce and administer it did not exist. The subsequent history of GATT involved a slow transformation from an "agreement," with no institutional staff or superstructure, into a *de facto* institution for the governance of world trade. The original vision of the GATT, as a mere part of a broader institution, was not realized until the creation of the WTO in 1994.

Because of the Protocol of Provisional Application, however, the treaty text of GATT had legal force after 1947, and its "escape clause"—Article XIX—governed the use of safeguard measures until 1994. A close look at its provisions is now in order, along with brief consideration of some related GATT provisions.

B The GATT Agreement

1 Mechanisms for Adjusting the GATT Bargain Over Time

To place GATT Article XIX in perspective, note that it is but one of several mechanisms for adjusting the GATT bargain in the face of changing circumstances. Negotiation and renegotiation are a permanent fixture of the WTO/GATT system, and are governed by a number of different GATT articles. The authority for "unilateral" changes in policy may also be found in a number of places.

Large scale multilateral negotiations, aimed at a general lowering of tariffs and trade barriers, have come to be known as negotiating "rounds." The last *successful* round was, at this writing, the Uruguay Round, which created the WTO. These negotiations are authorized by GATT Article XXVIIIbis, which provides that the contracting parties may sponsor them "from time to time."

In addition, new members enter the WTO/GATT system on a regular basis. Under the "most-favored-nation" principle of GATT Article I, all members are entitled to the benefits of tariff concessions negotiated with others "immediately and unconditionally." Not surprisingly, existing

[8] Probably the most important consequence of provisional, rather than definitive, application was the presence of a "grandfather clause" in the Protocol that allowed nations to maintain certain prior inconsistent legislation. See Jackson (1969).

members are unwilling to extend these benefits to new members for free—accession to membership thus requires an often extended negotiation between the prospective member and existing members over the terms of accession, including the tariff bindings to be applied by the new member. These negotiations are governed by GATT Article XXXIII.

Apart from the major negotiating rounds and the accession negotiations, GATT members can renegotiate or modify their tariff commitments pursuant to three lines of authority. Article XXVIII(1) provides for a period of renegotiation over the modification of tariff schedules every three years. Article XXVIII(5) allows parties to reserve their rights to modify their tariff schedules outside of these regular windows. Finally, Article XXVIII(4) allows "special circumstances" negotiations authorized by the contracting parties, an authorization that has usually been forthcoming on request. As a practical matter, therefore, WTO/GATT members have the opportunity to reopen negotiations over prior tariff concessions at almost any time. All of these negotiations are to include any "contracting party with which such concession was initially negotiated" and any other contracting party determined by the contracting parties to have a "principal supplying interest." Any contracting party proposing to withdraw a trade concession through this process is encouraged to reach a mutually satisfactory agreement with the affected parties, which can include compensatory trade concessions on other goods.

Depending on the concession in question, efforts to reach a mutually agreeable arrangement may fail. In the event of such a failure, Article XXVIII(3) permits a party seeking to withdraw or modify a concession to do so nonetheless. Adversely affected trading partners may then withdraw "substantially equivalent concessions initially negotiated with" that party. Thus, the Article XXVIII procedure effectively allows GATT members to raise tariffs above a negotiated tariff binding, and allows such an increase even if the member in question is unable to secure the permission of other members through offers of compensation, albeit subject to a prospect of retaliatory withdrawal of concessions bounded by the concept of "substantial equivalence."

Yet another mechanism for adjusting obligations is the "waiver" pursuant to Article XXV(5). In "exceptional circumstances," the contracting parties may waive an obligation imposed on a particular GATT member by a two-thirds vote of at least half of the contracting parties. The waiver authority has been used on a number of occasions.

Two other provisions (aside from Article XIX) allow GATT members to take unilateral action that would otherwise violate GATT obligations. Article

XII concerns measures to address balance of payments difficulties. It is structured as an exception to the prohibition on quantitative restrictions (quotas) in Article XI, and permits limits on the quantity or value of imports by a party "necessary to forestall the imminent threat of, or to stop, a serious decline in its monetary reserves or, in the case of a contracting party with very low monetary reserves, to achieve a reasonable rate of increase in its reserves." This provision has regularly been used (or abused) by various nations claiming a shortage of hard currency.

Finally, with particular reference to developing countries, Article XVIII concerns measures affecting imports "to implement programmes and policies of economic development designed to raise the general standard of living of their people." It sets up somewhat more lenient procedures for the withdrawal of concessions to "promote the establishment of a particular industry" (infant industry protection in the parlance of economics), as well as to protect the balance of payments.

It should now be apparent that if a GATT member becomes dissatisfied with the consequences of a negotiated trade concession, quite a number of avenues may be open to modify it. The safeguard mechanism of Article XIX is but one of them, and it is important to be clear on what it adds to the arsenal. I thus turn to a careful examination of Article XIX.

2 The Design of Article XIX

GATT Article XIX is entitled "Emergency Action on Imports of Particular Products," and governs what came to be known in GATT parlance as a safeguard measure. Its full text may be found in Appendix 1.

The title and structure of Article XIX suggest how it fits into the broader mosaic of devices for adjusting the GATT bargain. The reference to "emergency" conditions in the title indicates that action under Article XIX was intended to address exigent circumstances, circumstances that perhaps cannot wait for the next negotiating round or the next regular window for negotiation under Article XXVIII. The circumstances addressed by Article XIX involve "serious injury" or threat thereof to a domestic industry. Such injury may be quite unconnected to any of the other specific bases for intervention elsewhere under GATT (balance of payments or development issues). And, although injury to a particular industry might be addressed by "special circumstances" renegotiations under Article XXVIII(4), tariff changes pursuant to Article XXVIII are permanent unless revisited in a subsequent negotiation. Article XIX, by contrast, contemplates the temporary withdrawal or modification of concessions, "for such time as may be necessary to prevent or remedy such injury." Finally, as shall become clear below, Article XIX ultimately allows an importing nation to take action regardless of whether it is able to secure the permission of affected trading partners, and is thus quite unlike a waiver which requires a favorable vote.

The requirements of Article XIX may be broken into three groups of obligations for purposes of discussion: (a) rules regarding the prerequisites for the use of a safeguard measure; (b) rules limiting the scope and nature of a safeguard measure; and (c) rules regarding the procedure to be followed prior to implementing such a measure and the rights of adversely affected GATT members to be compensated for the effects of a safeguard measure, or to "retaliate." Consider each in turn.

The Prerequisites. The key prerequisites for safeguard measures are contained in paragraph 1(a):

> If, as a result of unforeseen developments and of the effect of the obligations incurred by a contracting party under this Agreement, including tariff concessions, any product is being imported into the territory of that contracting party in such increased quantities and under such conditions as to cause or threaten serious injury to domestic producers in that territory of like or directly competitive products, the contracting party shall be free, in respect of such product, and to the extent and for such time as may be necessary to prevent or remedy such injury, to suspend the obligation in whole or in part or to withdraw or modify the concession.

A comparison of this paragraph with the escape clause of the 1942 U.S.–Mexico agreement (set out above) shows striking similarities, although the two are not identical.

It is clear from the text that a party wishing to use a safeguard measure must have experienced "increased quantities" of imports of some product. For this reason, Article XIX is often characterized as a device for addressing "import surges." Although the text is not clear on the point, an early GATT working party[9] concluded that "increased quantities" could be found either in absolute terms, or relative to domestic production (i.e., an increased import market share).[10]

To determine whether an increase is present, of course, some baseline must exist against which to assess whether any increase has occurred. The text

[9] In the GATT system, "working parties" were formed to study various issues of law and policy, including matters in dispute at times. They consisted of representatives of interested GATT members.

[10] See WTO, Guide to GATT Law and Practice, Vol. I, at 518 (Geneva: 1995) (hereafter cited as GATT Analytical Index).

does not specify the baseline precisely, but it suggests two possibilities—the point in time at which the "unforeseen developments" arose that contributed to the increase, and the point when there were "obligations incurred" that contributed to the increase.

The "unforeseen developments" and "obligations incurred" are not merely pertinent to selecting a baseline for imports, however, but the increased quantities of imports must *result* from these two factors. This requirement raises a number of immediate puzzles. What types of events count as "unforeseen developments?" When can an event that seems unlikely at some point in time nevertheless be "foreseen," or is "unforeseen" equivalent to "unlikely?" With respect to whom must the development have been unforeseen—the industry harmed by increased imports, officials in its government, or someone else? At what point in time must the development have been "unforeseen?" What does it mean to say that the increased imports must be caused by *both* "unforeseen developments" and "obligations incurred?"

Although the text is not a model of clarity, it perhaps had a natural interpretation during the early days of GATT. In 1947, GATT members had just concluded a negotiation in which they accepted a number of new "obligations," including tariff bindings on many products, and other general restrictions on their trade policies (such as the prohibition on quotas in GATT Article XI). One may imagine that the trade negotiators made these commitments to modify their trade policies in the shadow of general expectations about how the modifications would affect domestic industries in their home countries and, in particular, how much industrial dislocation would result from them. They were aware that their foresight was imperfect, however, and recognized that some obligations might lead to much more serious dislocation than they anticipated because of factors that were, roughly speaking, "unforeseen." Unexpected dislocation might be expected to produce stiff political pressure for some remedial action, and the negotiators through Article XIX preserved the flexibility to withdraw a concession temporarily to address that pressure. On this interpretation, the baseline against which to establish an increase in imports was the import level prior to the conclusion of GATT in 1947. Any increase that served as a predicate for safeguard action must also have been plausibly attributable to changes in trade policy that resulted from the original GATT bargain. And not just any increase would suffice—it had to be more dramatic than anticipated by the GATT negotiators, and in that sense also attributable to an "unforeseen development." The relevant actors for purposes of determining what was "foreseen" were the GATT negotiators, and the time frame for considering what was "foreseen" was the time of the original GATT negotiations. Whatever the merits of this reading, it becomes problematic in a number of ways with the passage of time. Those issues will be addressed in Section C.

Paragraph 1(a) contains a further prerequisite to a safeguard measure. The increased imports in question must "cause or threaten serious injury to domestic producers . . . of like or directly competitive products." This phrase too raises a number of interpretive questions. What is meant by "serious injury"—what degree of dislocation in an industry will suffice? Is the focus on price, output, profits, employment, or some combination of these or other factors? How is the requirement of "cause" to be determined—what if a variety of factors are afflicting an import-competing industry, such as recession or labor strikes, concurrently with greater import competition?

Questions also arise regarding the set of domestic producers that must be examined for evidence of serious injury (or threat thereof). The relevant producers are those who produce "like or directly competitive products." These terms are not defined in Article XIX or elsewhere in GATT, although the term "like product" in particular is used in a number of places. Jackson (1969) concludes that the term has no fixed meaning, although in general "likeness" requires quite a high degree of similarity between the products. The inclusion of the phrase "directly competitive" is clearly intended to convey the possibility that the injured producers may produce products that are insufficiently similar to be considered "like," but that are nevertheless close enough substitutes to be affected importantly by increased import competition.

All of these interpretive issues involving the prerequisites for safeguard measures under Article XIX survive today, albeit with some further wrinkles introduced by the Agreement on Safeguards and WTO Appellate Body decisions applying it. I will return to all of them in detail in later sections.

Before proceeding, note that paragraph 1(b) contains parallel prerequisites for safeguard measures to address injury caused to countries that receive trade preferences from an importing country, and who are seriously injured or threatened by increased imports from a third country into the importing country that grants the preference. To clarify, suppose that country X grants some trade preference to country Y (perhaps X and Y have a free trade agreement, or Y is the beneficiary of a developing country preference allowable under the Generalized System of Preferences). Suppose further that country X makes a GATT concession to country Z on the same products that it imports from Y. As a result, an unexpected increase in imports from Z to X occurs, resulting in displacement of the imports from Y into X, and causing serious injury or threat to Y's producers of like or directly competitive products. Paragraph 1(b) authorizes X to suspend the concession to Z that resulted in this state of affairs, *if* country Y so requests. This provision proved to be of extremely little importance in GATT practice, however, and I will not address it further.

Permissible Measures. Safeguard measures under Article XIX are not limited to the suspension of negotiated tariff concessions. Paragraph 1(a) makes clear that the increased quantities of imports may result from other obligations as well, and that it is permissible to suspend such obligations in addition to modifying or withdrawing a tariff concession. An obvious candidate for suspension aside from a tariff concession is Article XI, which generally prohibits quantitative restrictions.

As a practical matter, however, it is unlikely that a nation would resort to Article XIX in the absence of a tariff binding applicable to the imported product in question. Without a binding, the imported nation would be free to raise its tariff to any level it desires, and could address the import surge in that fashion without the need to modify or suspend any GATT obligation.

A question arises as to whether there are any limitations on the nature of the obligations that may be modified or suspended pursuant to Article XIX. One obligation that has been a particular issue in this regard is the most-favored-nation obligation of GATT Article I. In the face of an import surge, could an importing nation invoke Article XIX to justify discriminatory tariffs or quotas that restrict imports from some trading partners to a much greater extent than others? In modern parlance, this question raises the issue of "selectivity" in safeguard measures. Much more will be said about that issue in connection with analysis of the Agreement on Safeguards in Chapter 9. I note here only that Jackson (1969) reviewed the preparatory work on Article XIX at length, and concluded that the drafters of Article XIX did not intend to allow discriminatory safeguard measures.[11] He argues on that basis that safeguard measures under GATT were required to comply with the most-favored-nation principle.

Paragraph 1(a) contains some other important limitations on safeguard measures found in the phrase "to the extent and for such time as may be necessary to prevent or remedy such injury." The limitation on the "extent" of a safeguard measure makes clear that it cannot go beyond what is necessary to address the actual or threatened "serious injury" attributable to the import surge—Article XIX is not an excuse to impose an arbitrarily large amount of

[11] See also GATT Analytical Index, Vol. I, pp. 518–20.

protection. The task of implementing this limitation in a meaningful way is not an easy one. Article XIX gives no hint as to how importing nations are to go about quantifying the injury done by the import surge so as to ensure that the "extent" of a safeguard measure does not exceed what is permitted.

Likewise, the duration of a safeguard measure is limited to the period "necessary" to avoid or remediate the actual or threatened injury. It is not obvious how one is to determine the duration of "such time as may be necessary" to abate the problem. If an importing nation argues that the conditions tending to serious injury are persistent, can it use Article XIX to justify protection that is *de facto* permanent? The general view within the GATT system was that safeguard measures should be "temporary,"[12] but crisp principles to limit their duration never evolved.

Finally, a question arises whether a measure under Article XIX must be limited strictly to the modification or withdrawal of a prior concession. That is, consider an industry that at one time had an import quota of x units on imports, and a tariff of t on imports. The quota was eliminated pursuant to GATT Article XI, and the tariff was bound at a lower rate under GATT Article II. If the importing nation wishes to use a safeguard measure, is it limited to a tariff of t or a quota of x, or can it impose more stringent restrictions? Can it perhaps impose measures other than tariffs or quotas? Whatever the proper reading of Article XIX on this question, GATT practice clearly involved the use of more stringent barriers, or alternative barriers, in some cases.[13]

Consultation, Compensation and Retaliation. Article XIX(2) requires written notice to the GATT contracting parties "as far in advance as is practicable" before the implementation of any safeguard measure, followed by an opportunity for adversely affected GATT members to consult on prospective measures. Measures may be implemented provisionally before consultation in "critical circumstances" where delay might cause irreparable damage.

The objective of paragraph 2, although the text does not say so explicitly, is to encourage the affected parties to reach a mutually satisfactory arrangement for "compensation" prior to the withdrawal of a concession under Article XIX. Compensation can in principle take any form that is congenial—parties harmed by a safeguard measure could be compensated with foreign aid, for example, or a concession on a diplomatic matter completely unrelated to trade. In practice, however, nations facing a prospect

[12] See GATT Analytical Index, Vol. I, p. 522.
[13] See GATT Analytical Index, Vol. I, pp. 522–23.

of safeguard measures against their exports ordinarily seek trade concessions on other exports to restore the balance of concessions.

Of course, a nation that employs a safeguard measure may have little incentive to offer significant compensation unless some adverse consequence follows from a failure to compensate. Accordingly, paragraph 3(a) addresses circumstances where "agreement among the interested contracting parties with respect to the action is not reached." In that event:

> the contracting party which proposes to take or continue the [safeguard] action shall, nevertheless, be free to do so, and if such action is taken or continued, the affected contracting parties shall then be free, not later than ninety days after such action is taken, to suspend . . . the application to the trade of the contracting party taking such action . . . substantially equivalent concessions or other obligations under this Agreement the suspension of which the CONTRACTING PARTIES do not disapprove.

In short, failing an agreement on compensation, the nation proposing to use a safeguard measure may nevertheless proceed with it, but adversely affected trading partners may "retaliate" with the suspension of "substantially equivalent concessions" as long as the GATT membership as a whole does not disapprove.

The threat of retaliation motivated GATT members to negotiate seriously over compensation following a decision to employ a safeguard measure. The negotiations were sometimes successful as the next section will indicate, but not always. The credibility of the retaliatory threat may have played a role in that regard—if the nation(s) disadvantaged by a safeguard measure were large enough to threaten trade retaliation that would significantly injure the nation that had taken the measure, the latter nation would seemingly have more reason to be forthcoming in compensation negotiations. I am not aware, however, of any systematic study of this issue.

Note that while the prevailing view in GATT was that safeguard measures should adhere to the most-favored-nation principle, retaliation was discriminatory.[14] Only the nation employing the safeguard measure would be the subject of retaliatory action. A similar asymmetry arose between compensation and retaliation—compensatory trade concessions by the nation using a safeguard measure had to extend to all GATT members because of the most-favored-nation obligation of Article I.

The remainder of paragraph 3 dealt with two more minor points. First, in the event that the safeguard measure was taken on behalf of an exporting

[14] See GATT Analytical Index, Vol. I, p. 527.

nation receiving a preference [the case envisioned by paragraph 1(b) noted above], retaliatory measures could be directed at the exporting nation that had requested the measure rather than the nation that had taken the measure. Second, just as importing nations could take provisional safeguard measures without prior consultation under "critical circumstances," paragraph 3(b) authorized exporting nations to suspend their own concessions without prior consultation if necessary to remedy any serious or threatened injury caused by a safeguard measure against their exports. Thus, for example, if country A imposed a new tariff on exports of some product from country B pursuant to Article XIX, and country B's export industry suffered serious injury as a result, then country B could take emergency measures to help its industry without prior consultation. Both of these provisions appear to have been of little significance in practice.

C GATT Practice Under Article XIX and the Rise of Grey-Area Measures

We now turn to an examination of safeguard actions in practice under the GATT system. As shall be seen, the evolution of GATT practice was soon at odds with the design of Article XIX, increasingly so with time. Some of the textual prerequisites for safeguard measures came to be ignored, and eventually the GATT system drifted away from formal reliance on Article XIX altogether. The result was a political movement to restore and enhance discipline over safeguard measures, which culminated in the WTO Agreement on Safeguards.

1 Formal Reliance on Article XIX During the GATT Years

Article XIX requires GATT members employing safeguard measures to provide notice to the GATT membership. The GATT Analytical Index lists a total of 150 notifications of actions under Article XIX during the history of GATT (through January 1, 1995).[15] The most frequent users of Article XIX were Australia, the United States, Canada and the EEC, collectively accounting for over two-thirds of the notifications by all GATT members. Of course, some actions covered far greater trade volumes than other actions, so that a simple head count of notifications may paint a misleading picture as

[15] GATT Analytical Index Vol. I, pp. 539–59.

to which nations employed safeguard measures to the greatest extent based on the affected quantity of trade. Nevertheless, the general picture is one in which safeguards under GATT were largely a tool of developed economies.

The compendium in the Analytical Index provides some information about the role of compensation and retaliation in the system as well, although it would appear to be quite incomplete on this front. It indicates that compensation negotiations were successful in 20 cases or so, although a disproportionate number of these cases occurred early in the history of GATT. Retaliation pursuant to Article XIX(3) is reflected in the compendium only a handful of times, although it was threatened in a number of other cases. For the great bulk of cases, there is no indication of any compensation or retaliation, which may reflect incompleteness of information rather than their absence.

The time pattern of notifications is also interesting. The first 19 notifications occurred during the 1950–59 decade. From 1960–69, there were 35 notifications. Another 47 notifications occurred from 1970–79, while only 37 notifications occurred during 1980–89. The remaining 12 notifications occurred during 1990–94. The general trend was thus toward increasing formal reliance on Article XIX during the 50s, 60s and 70s, with diminished reliance toward the end of the GATT system during the 80s and 90s. This numerical trend must be seen against a background in which both GATT membership and the volume of trade were generally growing fairly steadily, so that the reduced reliance on Article XIX toward the end of the GATT system is in fact perhaps somewhat more dramatic than the number of notifications standing alone might indicate.

It would be incorrect to infer that renewed protection for industries harmed by import competition was on the wane toward the end of GATT, however, because GATT members often turned to measures outside the formal ambit of Article XIX that were never "notified" as Article XIX actions. Because these measures may have been taken without regard to whether the prerequisites for safeguard action under Article XIX had been met, and because they were usually not notified as Article XIX actions, they came to be known as "grey-area" measures. Their growth will be considered in subsection 5 below.

2 Safeguards Practice in Context: The GATT Dispute Settlement System

To understand the evolution of GATT practice under Article XIX, it is essential to understand how the system functioned more generally, and in particular to appreciate the limitations of its dispute settlement system. Note first that GATT had no central enforcer of its obligations, akin to a prosecutor. Breaches of the rules would only come to the attention of the system as a "dispute" if a member nation chose to complain about the conduct of another nation.

Even when a GATT member brought a dispute to the membership as a whole, its capacity to address the dispute was limited. In the early days of GATT, dispute resolution was largely a matter of negotiation and conciliation, much more so than "adjudication." Disputes would be addressed during regular meetings of the GATT membership (in the GATT "Council"), and would sometimes be referred to "working parties," which consisted of representatives of interested nations taking direction from their respective governments. Whether at a meeting of the membership or within a working party, each party to the dispute would present its views. If, at the conclusion of the process, no agreement had been reached, nothing would happen as a practical matter in most instances. Article XXIII of GATT did permit the contracting parties acting collectively to authorize an aggrieved party to suspend concessions in response to a breach of the agreement, but that authority was exercised only once in the history of GATT.[16]

Beginning in 1955, the practice began of referring disputes to groups of experts, known as "panels," which consisted of ostensibly impartial individuals acting in their individual capacity (as distinguished from acting as a representative of their government). These panels began to function somewhat like courts, rendering decisions on the merits of cases and producing written opinions. Their decisions did not automatically have the force of "law" in the GATT system, however, but instead required "adoption" by the GATT membership to become binding. GATT practice evolved to require "consensus" before any panel report could be adopted, which amounted to a unanimity rule. Thus, the adoption of panel decisions could be "blocked" by a single nation, including the losing party in the dispute. For a time, although this was changed toward the end of GATT, a disputant could also block the referral of a dispute to a panel altogether.

For these reasons, the dispute settlement system was quite imperfect, particularly on contentious issues, and departures from the rules were not systematically policed. Nations could deviate from their commitments with little ado unless another nation complained, and could respond to complaints by blocking the dispute process from producing a legally binding result.

[16] See Jackson (1997).

Against this backdrop, GATT members departed importantly from the rules laid down by Article XIX in a number of respects to be discussed below. Formal disputes relating to Article XIX were few and generally did not proceed beyond discussions within the GATT Council. One early dispute popularly known as the *Hatter's Fur* case—involving an Article XIX action by the United States—was referred to a working party, but was quite inconclusively resolved.[17] Aspects of this working party report will be discussed in several subsequent chapters.

3 Textual Obsolescence: The "Unforeseen Developments" Clause

As noted, Article XIX required that the increased quantities of imports which serve as a predicate for a safeguard measure result from "unforeseen developments and of the effect of the obligations incurred by a contracting party," an obligation that I term the "unforeseen developments clause." This requirement was quite comprehensible in the early days of GATT. New concessions were made in 1947, and the possibility arose that such concessions might result in an unexpected import surge. Article XIX was designed to address these "unforeseen" and perhaps politically awkward consequences of the original GATT bargain.

But how does one interpret these requirements of Article XIX in an agreement that is still in force after many years? Consider first the unforeseen developments notion, and imagine an import surge some decades after the entry into force of GATT. Could any such surge have been "foreseen" given the passage of so much time? By whom and at what instant in time might it have been "foreseen?" How are the answers affected by the fact that GATT negotiations are ongoing, with new negotiating "rounds" every decade or so? Does each round "reset the clock" on what is foreseen, or only if a new concession is made during the round? The phrase "unforeseen developments" no longer has a straightforward interpretation in an agreement that lasts for decades rather than a few years, and that is characterized by ever changing commitments.

Likewise, consider the requirement that the import surge result from "obligations incurred," and again imagine an import surge thirty or forty years after the entry into force of GATT. Could it plausibly be said that such a surge resulted from the "obligations incurred" if those obligations were

[17] See GATT/CP/106, report adopted on 22 October 1951, GATT/CP.6/SR.19, Sales No. GATT/1951–3.

incurred decades earlier, or does the lack of proximity in time between the concession and the import surge militate against any finding of a causal link between them as suggested in Jackson (1969)? How does one determine what portion, if any, of a surge is attributable to a particular GATT obligation? How is the analysis to be modified when a product has been the subject of a sequence of GATT concessions over time? Can an importing nation argue that any import surge for a product covered by a tariff binding is the result of "obligations incurred" because, absent the binding, the importing nation could and would have raised its tariff to eliminate the surge?

These questions have no obvious answers, and certainly the text of Article XIX offers no help. A few of the conceptual issues were addressed by the working party report in the *Hatter's Fur* case, but that dispute arose in 1951 before most of the issues raised by the passage of time had crystallized. No subsequent attention was paid to these questions within the dispute settlement process.

Instead, GATT practice evolved over time toward ignoring the requirements of the unforeseen developments clause. See McGovern (1986). At least some national laws governing the use of safeguard measures in domestic law made no mention of them. For example, Section 201 of the U.S. Trade Act of 1974, which remains the basis for the authority to use safeguard measures under U.S. law, merely requires the U.S. International Trade Commission (ITC) to determine "whether an article is being imported into the United States in such increased quantities as to be a substantial cause[18] of serious injury, or the threat thereof." [See Appendix 3.] There is no requirement that increased quantities of imports result from factors that are "unforeseen" or that they result from GATT obligations. No formal complaint was ever brought about this feature of U.S. law, nor am I aware of any substantial objection to it informally. European legislation likewise makes no mention of the unforeseen developments requirement. [See Council Regulation (EC) No. 3285/94, reproduced in Appendix 4.]

Such a development is an understandable consequence of the difficulties in giving content to the unforeseen developments clause of Article XIX in a long-lived agreement, coupled with the limited ability of the GATT system to give new interpretations to a deficient text. But as shall become immediately apparent, the absence in practice of a requirement akin to the unforeseen developments clause raised other difficulties for the

[18] A "substantial cause" is a "cause that is important and not less than any other cause." 19 U.S.C. para 2252(b)(1)(B). [See Appendix 3]. Chapter 7 will explore the differences between this test and the test for causal connection under Article XIX and the Agreement on Safeguards.

implementation of Article XIX by GATT members, difficulties that are quite fundamental.

4 The Causation Conundrum

Under Article XIX as originally drafted, it was not enough that an unforeseen import surge resulted from a trade concession. The import surge had to go on to cause or threaten serious injury. Although the inquiry into causation may be difficult as a practical matter, the logic of the inquiry was nevertheless reasonably clear in Article XIX. The unforeseen import surge, resulting from the trade concession, had to be responsible for serious injury. Within this framework, the causal or "exogenous" variable is the trade concession, and the "increased quantities" of imports are those resulting from that concession. Likewise, the level of imports prior to the trade concession serves as a baseline against which to measure the "increase." To establish causation, one then asks whether, in the absence of the trade concession and its unforeseen consequences for import competition, serious injury (or threat thereof) would have been averted. If so, then the unforeseen import surge "caused" the injury.

But now imagine reading out the first clause of paragraph one, as GATT members began to do in practice years ago. Then, one must simply have "such increased quantities (of imports) . . . as to cause or threaten serious injury." The baseline for the "increase," import levels prior to some trade concession, is no longer specified. Further, the "increased quantities" of imports themselves seemingly become the causal variable in the analysis, as there is no longer any background trade concession to which the "increased quantities" are themselves attributable.

Two considerable problems arise as a result. First, how does one now determine whether there are "increased quantities" of imports at all—against what baseline is the increase to be measured? In a growing global economy with fixed or declining trade barriers, the long-term trend in imports for many products will tend to be upward. Over shorter periods of time, import volumes can fluctuate due to a variety of economic factors. Without the first clause of Article XIX, it is entirely unclear how to determine whether the increased quantities requirement is met.

Second, and more fundamental, how can one treat increased quantities of imports as a causal or exogenous variable? Chapter 8 will explore this issue at considerable length, and at this stage I simply hope to make the reader aware of the basic conceptual problem. Economic theory suggests that the *quantity* of imports will be determined by the forces of supply and demand, just like the quantity of production by domestic firms.[19] The causal factors within the economic framework are the determinants of domestic supply, domestic demand, and import supply. Domestic demand is affected by such things as domestic consumer tastes and incomes; domestic supply by the domestic costs of inputs into production and the state of available production technology; and import supply by the parallel factors affecting supply and demand in other countries. The quantity of imports is a *result* of the interaction of these factors, and not a causal variable at all. Indicators of injury in the import-competing industry (such as falling prices, production or employment) are also the *result* of the same set of forces of supply and demand that determine the quantity of imports. Against this backdrop, the question "did increased quantities of imports cause serious injury to a domestic industry?" is highly problematic.

To offer a rough analogy, imagine that a player in a game of pocket billiards hits the cue ball, which strikes the 8-ball and the 12-ball simultaneously and causes each to roll into one of the pockets on the table. In ordinary language, the "cause" of this series of events is the external force applied to the cue ball, and it would make little sense to inquire instead whether the "cause" of the 12-ball rolling into one pocket was the 8-ball rolling into another pocket (or vice-versa). Yet, when one asks the question whether increased quantities of imports caused serious injury to the domestic industry, one is asking much the same sort of illogical question.

In short, changing practice in the GATT system, which dispensed with the first clause of Article XIX, rendered the causal inquiry conceptually deficient. This problem did not stop GATT members from purporting to establish compliance with the causation requirement of Article XIX(1)(a) as Chapter 8 will indicate, but one can certainly wonder whether the resulting decisions under national law comported with the intent of the GATT drafters. And because formal challenges to safeguard measures were few and did not result in any written decisions aside from the working party report in the *Hatter's Fur* case, there was no opportunity for the dispute resolution process under GATT to weigh in with any clarifying suggestions. The dearth of disputes owed, in part, to another important development—the rise of grey-area

[19] In the simplest of supply and demand diagrams without international trade, and under conditions of competition, the intersection of the supply curve with the demand curve determines both equilibrium price and production. The quantity produced is not a causal variable in this framework, but rather is the result of the underlying determinants of the position of the supply and demand curves.

measures and the decreasing formal reliance on Article XIX within the GATT system.

5 Prelude to the Uruguay Round: Grey-Area Measures and Their Critics

Quite aside from the puzzles raised by the textual prerequisites for safeguards action, Article XIX presented some mundane practical issues for nations wishing to protect their troubled industries. The first relates to the selectivity issue noted earlier. In some cases, the primary source of intensified import competition was only one or two exporting nations. If Article XIX indeed required safeguard measures to be applied on a most-favored-nation basis as most commentators argued, however, and if importing nations complied with that principle, a formal safeguard measure might restrict trade with a number of other suppliers whose exports had perhaps remained quite stable. Those nations in turn could pursue their rights to compensation or retaliation. Hence, a formal safeguard measure could embroil importing nations in thorny negotiations with supplier countries that were not even perceived to be an important source of the "problem." There was thus some natural pressure to prefer trade restrictions that targeted the most successful exporting nations and left the rest alone.

This preference could be all the more pronounced if the more successful exporting nations were in a poor position to "retaliate" for a safeguard measure, and thus in a poor bargaining position in negotiations over compensation. Imagine, for example, an industrialized nation (say, the United States) that had long imported a particular good from another industrialized nation (say, the European Community) and also produced that good domestically. Later, a newly industrialized nation (say, Malaysia) develops the capacity to produce the good, and its exports to the United States rise dramatically over some fairly short period of time, while the U.S. industry suffers a serious decline. A formal safeguard measure, restricting imports from Europe and Malaysia proportionately, would lead to a credible threat of retaliation by Europe and necessitate substantial compensation to avoid it. If the measure could be aimed only at Malaysia, by contrast, it might well suffice to achieve the level of protection desired for the U.S. import-competing industry, while Malaysia because of its smaller size and more limited imports from the United States might have few viable options for retaliation and little leverage in negotiating compensation. With this background, one can readily understand why some importing nations might have preferred to limit their "safeguard" measures to imports from "upstart" competitors, often newly industrialized nations.

A second practical problem with formal reliance on Article XIX is that its prerequisites for safeguard measures might not be satisfied in a given instance, despite considerable domestic political pressure to take some action against imports. The legal details can become quite a bother to political officials in such cases, producing further pressure for them to step outside of the system and pursue an alternative policy.

Because of these pressures (and perhaps others), importing nations began to negotiate arrangements outside of GATT to address the problems faced by troubled industries. These were generally bilateral agreements, covering only one or perhaps a few major suppliers. Typically, the government of the exporting country(ies) would be asked to agree on quantitative export limitations. These limits could be administered either by the exporting country or the importing country, using export/import licenses or some other device to monitor the quantity of trade. Various terms were used to refer to these agreements, including "voluntary restraint agreements," "voluntary export restraints," and "orderly marketing arrangements." All of these come under the rubric of "grey-area" measures, falling outside the formal provisions of GATT.[20]

The reader may wonder why exporting nations would have agreed to such measures. One answer is that in some instances, exporting nations (or their exporting firms) may have actually benefited from them. Restrictions on imports into a particular market tend to raise the price to the consumers of imports in that market—indeed, that is the *raison d'être* of protectionist measures generally. Not only domestic firms benefit from the price increase, but the entity that collects the price increment on imported goods will also benefit, other things being equal. When quantitative restrictions or "quotas" are used to restrict imports, the price increment will be collected by the entity that holds the right to import under the quota—that entity can purchase (or manufacture) the good in question at the prevailing price (or cost) in the exporting country, and then resell the good at the artificially high price induced by the quota in the importing country. This increment between the price or cost of the good in the country of exportation, and the artificially high price in the country of importation, is termed a "quota rent" by economists. Grey-area measures could be structured to give these quota rents to exporters (as by giving each exporting firm a share of the quota and allowing it to sell for as much as the market will bear in the importing country), or to give them to the government of the exporting nation (as by

[20] To be sure, such agreements were sometimes negotiated as part of a formal Article XIX measure as well—the U.S. statute, for example, specifically authorizes the President to negotiate orderly marketing agreements as a safeguard measure. See 19 U.S.C. para 2253(a)(3)(E).

conferring the rights to export on the government, which can then sell them to its exporters for a price that captures the quota rent). When grey-area measures were so structured, the exporting country would face a tradeoff between the losses associated with a lower *quantity* of exports due to the import restriction, and the gains associated with a higher *price* for each unit exported. Depending on the circumstances, the gain in the price (and profit) per unit exported could more than offset the lost profits on the units that were no longer exported because of the restriction. If so, the exporting nation came out ahead, and it is no mystery that it would agree to such an arrangement. In effect, it participated in a scheme to cartelize the importing country's market, and was cut in on a share of the cartel profits.

Given the protestations by exporting nations often associated with the advent of grey-area measures, however, it would be a mistake to suppose that exporting nations systematically came out ahead. The other reason why they may have agreed to the measures is that the perceived alternative may have been worse. For example, an importing nation could threaten, as an alternative to a negotiated grey-area measure, to take action under Article XIX. As noted, some exporting nations may have been in a poor position to retaliate, and thus to obtain much leverage in negotiations over compensation. Furthermore, the importing nation could suggest that an action under Article XIX would be structured so as *not* to confer any quota rents on exporting nations—the measure could simply employ a higher tariff on imported goods rather than a quota, so that the importing nation itself captured the increment in price on the imported goods as tariff revenue. Other sorts of explicit or implicit threats by the importing nation can be imagined as well, all of which would have confronted the exporting nation with bleak prospects should it balk at a request for a grey-area measure.

Bhagwati (1988) likewise reports that many grey-area measures were preceded by more formal actions under national trade laws. The restraints on Japanese automobile imports into the United States negotiated during the Carter administration were preceded by an (unsuccessful) safeguard action under U.S. law. Restraint agreements covering steel and semiconductor imports into the United States were preceded by a spate of antidumping and countervailing duty actions under U.S. law. Grey-area measures were thus in some instances a way for exporting nations to "settle" expensive litigation against them, litigation that on the whole may have threatened even more trade restrictive measures. For this reason as well, exporting nations often viewed grey-area measures as the lesser evil.

Complete data on the use of grey-area measures in the GATT system are lacking, largely because they were outside the system by design and were not systematically reported or notified, but the available information does suggest that the growth of grey-area measures was dramatic in the latter years of GATT. Some striking statistics were compiled by the GATT Secretariat. As of early 1991, 24 formal Article XIX measures were in effect within GATT.[21] At the same time, 284 known export restraint agreements were in effect. These agreements covered a wide array of products, with 15 or more agreements each affecting trade in agricultural products, textiles and clothing, steel, electronics, motor vehicles, footwear, and machine tools.[22] Many of the restraint agreements lasted for many years. A GATT report on 249 arrangements in force as of late 1989 notes that 36 were introduced prior to 1975, and another 39 between 1975 and 1979.[23]

These numbers do not include the restrictions on textiles and clothing trade that evolved under the so-called Multifiber Arrangement (MFA). The MFA began with a short-term arrangement on textile trade at the instance of the United States in the early 1960's. It was extended and eventually expanded to envelop 40 countries, including nine developed importing nations and 31 developing exporting nations, and survived in some form until the end of GATT. The MFA provided for overall quantitative limits on textile and clothing imports, within which importing nations would negotiate bilateral restraint agreements with supplier countries. See Jackson (1997).

The proliferation of grey-area measures attracted the attention of economists, who noted their potential to undo much of what GATT had accomplished to liberalize trade. The economists also undertook to quantify the cost of some of these measures to importing nations. To offer just a few examples from this considerable literature, Cline (1990) estimated the impact on the U.S. economy of textile and apparel limits under the MFA. He concluded that the added annual cost to American consumers for each domestic job saved from elimination in the apparel industry was approximately US$82,000, and that the cost per job saved in the textile industry was approximately US$135,000. These amounts were, of course, far in excess of the total wages earned by typical workers in those industries. Tarr

[21] GATT, Council Overview of Developments in International Trade and the Trading System. Annual Report by the Director General, C/RM/OV/2 (12 April 1991), p. 8.

[22] Id. p. 17, Appendix Table 1.

[23] GATT, Council Overview of Developments in the International Trading Environment, Annual Report of the Director General, C/RM/OV/1 (12 June 1991), p. 18, Appendix Table 2.

(1989) estimated the total annual costs to U.S. consumers from quotas in the automobile, steel and textile industries at roughly US$20.9 billion. These figures also roughly reflected net costs to the U.S. economy because the quota rents associated with protective measures were earned by exporting nations under these arrangements. See also Tarr and Morkre (1984); Trebilcock, Chandler and Howse (1990). Smith and Venables (1991) noted a further cost associated with grey-area measures in imperfectly competitive industries, namely, the cost associated with a loss of competitive discipline on domestic firms, which they estimate to have been quite significant as a result of grey-area measures in the European automobile market.

Although grey-area measures were negotiated outside the GATT system, they did not completely escape attention in its dispute resolution process. Exporting countries targeted by such measures occasionally argued before the GATT Council that they violated various GATT rules, including the Article XI prohibition on quantitative restrictions, the Article XIII rules regarding nondiscriminatory administration of quantitative restrictions, and Article XIX.[24] Chile filed two complaints relating to grey-area measures affecting European imports of apples. The EEC had negotiated restraint agreements with several other apple suppliers, but had failed to conclude an agreement with Chile. When it took action against Chilean imports nonetheless, Chile complained that such action violated GATT nondiscrimination obligations, and received favorable GATT panel rulings.[25] The EEC later filed a successful complaint relating to the "Semiconductor Agreement" between the United States and Japan, which the EEC claimed was illegally affecting the prices charged by Japanese exporters to European customers.[26]

As the GATT membership entered the Uruguay Round negotiations, an alliance began to develop between exporting nations that had been aggrieved by the proliferation of grey-area measures, and certain trade policymakers concerned about their growing protectionist impact. Stewart (1993) reports the basic negotiating position of the various players. Not surprisingly, developing and Pacific Rim countries as a group sought to end the selective use of grey-area measures (often against them), and to bring a strong nondiscrimination principle to bear on all safeguard measures, formal or informal. The United States, interestingly, expressed concern that the uncontrolled use of grey-area measures was leading to excessive protectionism, and

[24] See GATT Analytical Index Vol. I, p. 532.

[25] See EEC—Restrictions on Imports of Apples from Chile, L/5047, adopted on 10 November 1980; EEC—Restrictions on Imports of Dessert Apples—Complaint by Chile, l/6491, adopted on 22 June 1989.

[26] See Japan—Trade in Semi-Conductors, l/6309, adopted on 4 May 1988.

supported efforts to redirect GATT members toward formal reliance on Article XIX. Canada generally supported the U.S. position.

Other nations were more ambivalent about reform. Japan recognized that although it had been targeted by grey-area measures frequently, some of its industries reaped huge profits because of them (capturing the quota rents). European countries generally preferred to maintain flexibility in the use of safeguards, including the flexibility to act selectively.[27]

Although there was no consensus at the outset, the likely direction of reform, if any was to occur, was nevertheless clear. The prevalence of discrimination in formal or informal safeguards policy, and the rise of grey-area measures, were the primary concerns of GATT members who saw the system as "broken."

D Introduction to the Safeguards Agreement

The WTO website reports that the Agreement on Safeguards "was negotiated in large part because GATT Contracting Parties increasingly had been applying a variety of so-called 'grey-area' measures."[28] The preamble to the Agreement thus recites the members' desire to "clarify and reinforce the disciplines of GATT 1994, and specifically those of its Article XIX, to re-establish multilateral control over safeguards and eliminate measures that escape such control."

The centerpiece of the Agreement is a flat prohibition of new grey-area measures, coupled with a mandatory phasing out of existing measures by the end of calendar year 1999. Going forward, all measures involving "any emergency action on imports" must comply with Article XIX and the Agreement. The Agreement introduces considerable restraint on selectivity, although it did not altogether prohibit it. The Agreement also does a great deal on other fronts to elaborate the requirements of Article XIX, both substantively and procedurally.

This section provides an introduction and overview to the important provisions of the Agreement on Safeguards. Subsequent chapters will, of course, consider particular obligations in much more detail. For present purposes, it will suffice to reproduce the thoughtful summary of the agreement prepared by the WTO:[29]

[27] See Stewart (1993), pp. 1761–66.

[28] See <http://www.wto.org/english/tratop_e/safeg_e/safeint.htm>, visited January 30, 2006.

[29] Id.

The Agreement consists of 14 articles and one annex. In general terms, it has four main components: (1) general provisions (Articles 1 and 2); (2) rules governing Members' application of new safeguard measures (i.e., those applied after entry into force of WTO Agreement (Articles 3–9)); (3) rules pertaining to pre-existing measures that were applied before the WTO's entry into force (Articles 10 and 11); and (4) multilateral surveillance and institutions (Articles 12–14).

General provisions

Coverage of the Agreement

Article 1 establishes that the SG Agreement is the vehicle through which measures may be applied pursuant to Article XIX of GATT 1994. That is, any measure for which the coverage of Article XIX (which allows suspension of GATT concessions and obligations under the defined "emergency" circumstances) is invoked, must be taken in accordance with the provisions of the SG Agreement. The Agreement explicitly does not apply to measures taken pursuant to other provisions of GATT 1994, to other Annex 1A Multilateral Trade Agreements, or to protocols and agreements or arrangements concluded within the framework of GATT 1994. (Art. 11.1(c))

Conditions for Application of Safeguard Measures

Article 2 sets forth the conditions (i.e., serious injury or threat thereof caused by increased imports) under which safeguard measures may be applied. It also contains the requirement that such measures be applied on an MFN basis.

Rules governing new safeguard measures (applied after entry into force of the WTO Agreement)

Investigative Requirements

New safeguard measures may be applied only following an investigation conducted by competent authorities pursuant to previously published procedures. Although the Agreement does not contain detailed procedural requirements, it does require reasonable public notice of the investigation, and that interested parties (importers, exporters, producers, etc.) be given the opportunity to present their views and to respond to the views of others. Among the topics on which views are to be sought is whether or not a safeguard measure would be in the public interest. The relevant authorities are obligated to publish a report presenting and explaining their findings on all pertinent issues, including a demonstration of the relevance of the factors examined. The Agreement also contains specific rules for the handling of confidential information in the context of an investigation.

Factual Basis for Determination of Serious Injury or Threat Thereof

The Agreement defines "serious injury" as significant impairment in the position of a domestic industry. "Threat of serious injury" is threat that is clearly imminent as shown by facts, and not based on mere allegation, conjecture or remote possibility. A "domestic industry" is defined as the producers as a whole of the like or directly competitive products operating within the territory of a Member, or producers who collectively account for a major proportion of the total domestic production of those products.

In determining whether serious injury or threat is present, investigating authorities are to evaluate all relevant factors having a bearing on the condition of the industry, and are not to attribute to imports injury caused by other factors. Factors that must be analyzed are the absolute and relative rate and amount of increase in imports, the market share taken by the increased imports, and changes in level of sales, production, productivity, capacity utilization, profits and losses, and employment of the domestic industry.

Application of Measures

Safeguard measures may only be applied to the extent necessary to remedy or prevent serious injury and to facilitate adjustment, within certain limits. If the measure takes the form of a quantitative restriction, the level must not be below the actual import level of the most recent three representative years, unless there is clear justification for doing otherwise. Rules also apply as to how quota shares are to be allocated among supplier countries, as to compensation to Members whose trade is affected, and as to consultations with affected Members.

The maximum duration of any safeguard measure is four years, unless it is extended consistent with the Agreement's provisions. In particular, a measure may be extended only if its continuation is found to be necessary to prevent or remedy serious injury, and only if evidence shows that the industry is adjusting.

The initial period of application plus any extension normally cannot exceed eight years. In addition, safeguard measures in place for longer than one year must be progressively liberalized at regular intervals during the period of application. If a measure is extended beyond the initial period of application, it can be no more restrictive during this period than it was at the end of the initial period, and it should continue to be liberalized.

Any measure of more than three years duration must be reviewed at mid-term. If appropriate based on that review, the Member applying the measure must withdraw it or increase the pace of its liberalization.

Under critical circumstances, defined as circumstances where delay would cause damage that would be difficult to repair, provisional measures may be imposed. Such measures may be in the form of tariff increases only, and may be kept in place for a maximum of 200 days. In addition, the period of application of any provisional measure must be included in the total period of application of a safeguard measure.

Repeated application of safeguards with respect to a given product is limited by the Agreement. Ordinarily, a safeguard may not be applied again to a product until a period equal to the duration of the original safeguard has elapsed, so long as the period of non-application is at least two years.

Nonetheless, if a new safeguard measure has a duration of 180 days or less, it may be applied so long as one year has elapsed since the date the original safeguard measure was introduced, and so long as no more than two safeguard measures have been applied on the product during the five years immediately preceding the date of introduction of the new safeguard measure.

Concessions and Other Obligations

In applying a safeguard measure, the Member must maintain a substantially equivalent level of concessions and other obligations with respect to affected exporting Members. To do so, any adequate means of trade compensation may be agreed with the affected Members. Absent such agreement, the affected exporting Members individually may suspend substantially equivalent concessions and other obligations. This latter right cannot be exercised during the first three years of application of a safeguard measure if the measure is taken based on an absolute increase in imports, and otherwise conforms to the provisions of the Agreement.

Developing Country Members

Developing country Members receive special and differential treatment with respect to other Members' safeguard measures, and with respect to applying their own such measures. A safeguard measure shall not be applied to low volume imports from developing country Members, that is, where a single developing country Member's products account for no more than 3 percent of the total subject imports, as long as products originating in those low-import-share developing country Members collectively do not exceed 9 percent of imports.

In applying safeguard measures, developing country Members may extend the application of a safeguard measure for an extra two years beyond that normally permitted. In addition, the rules for re-applying safeguard measures with respect to a given product are relaxed for developing country Members.

Rules governing pre-existing measures (applied before the WTO's entry into force)

Pre-existing measures imposed pursuant to GATT Article XIX that were in effect at the time of the WTO Agreement's entry into force are to be terminated no later than eight years after they were first applied, or five years after the entry into force of the WTO Agreement, whichever comes later.

Pre-existing "grey area" measures that were in effect at the time of the WTO's entry into force are to be brought into conformity with the SG Agreement or phased out—pursuant to timetables to have been presented to the SG Committee by 30 June 1995—within four years of the WTO's entry into force (i.e., by December 31, 1998). Although all Members had the right to an exception with respect to a single specific measure, whereby they would have had until December 31, 1999 for the required phase-out, no Member other than the EC (whose single exception is contained in the Annex to the Agreement itself) exercised this option.

Multilateral surveillance and institutions

Multilateral oversight of the use of safeguard measures is conducted through notification requirements, as well as through the creation of a Committee on Safeguards charged with reviewing safeguard notifications, among other duties.

Members are required to notify the Committee of initiations of investigations into the existence of serious injury or threat and the reasons therefore; findings of serious injury or threat caused by increased imports; and decisions to apply or extend safeguard measures. Such notifications are required to contain the relevant information on which the decisions are based.

Members are required, before applying or extending a safeguard measure, to provide an adequate opportunity for consultations with Members who have substantial interests as exporters of the product. The aims of such consultations shall include review of information as to the facts of the situation, exchanging views on the proposed measures, and reaching an understanding as to maintaining a substantially equivalent level of concessions and obligations.

Provisional measures must be notified before being applied, and consultations must be initiated immediately after such measures are applied.

The results of consultations, mid-term reviews of measures taken, compensation, and/or suspension of concessions, must be notified immediately to the Council for Trade in Goods through the Safeguards Committee by the Member concerned.

Members are obligated to notify their own laws, regulations and administrative procedures to the Committee, as well as their own pre-existing Article XIX and grey area measures. Members also are entitled to counternotify other Members' relevant laws and regulations, actions, or measures in force. Members are not obligated to disclose confidential information in their notifications.

The Committee's role generally is to monitor (and report to the Council for Trade in Goods on) the implementation and operation of the Agreement, to review Members' notifications, and to make findings as to Members' compliance with respect to the procedural provisions of the Agreement for the application of safeguard measures, to assist with consultations, and to review proposed retaliation.

Consultations and disputes arising under the Agreement are to be conducted in accordance with Articles XXII and XXIII of GATT 1994 as elaborated by the Dispute Settlement Understanding.

Subsequent chapters, beginning with Chapter 3, will return to most of these features of the Agreement, often in great detail. Before proceeding, however, I offer a brief overview of WTO developments thus far under the Agreement on Safeguards.

E Safeguard Measures to Date in the WTO

As noted above, WTO members are obligated to notify the Committee on Safeguards of their pertinent legislation, and of any action taken pursuant to Article XIX and the Safeguards Agreement. This information is collected in an annual report from the Committee on Safeguards to the WTO Council for Trade in Goods. In addition, the WTO website provides up-to-date information on all disputes within the system.

1 Notified Legislation and Procedures

Article 3.1 of the Agreement provides that safeguard measures may only be applied following an investigation "pursuant to procedures previously established and made public in consonance with Article X of GATT 1994." Article 12.6 further provides that members must "promptly notify" the Committee on Safeguards of their "laws, regulations and administrative procedures relating to safeguard measures." The conjunction of these two provisions suggests that no member may take a safeguard measure without prior notification of the procedures for a safeguards investigation to the Committee on Safeguards.

The Committee's 2005 report[30] documents the status of these notifications. See Appendix 5. A total of 48 members (counting the 25 Member States of the European Communities as only 1 member) have notified the Committee that they indeed have laws, regulations or procedures in place. This list includes most of the major trading nations, including Australia, Brazil, Canada, China, the European Communities, India, Indonesia, Japan, Korea, Mexico, Pakistan, Thailand, and the United States. A total of 45 members have notified the Committee that they do *not* have any laws, regulations or procedures for the use of safeguards. Most of these are small trading nations, but the list includes a few sizeable players such as Malaysia and Singapore. Finally, 30 members have not yet notified the Committee as to whether or not they have pertinent laws, regulations, or procedures, most of these being small developing nations.

The Table in Appendix 5 provides the WTO document numbers for each notification. The reader may obtain details of the notified legislation from those documents. I include the current legislation in force for the United States—Section 201 of the Trade Act of 1974 et seq.—in Appendix 3. Appendix 4 contains the current generally applicable legislation for the EU, Council Regulation (EC) No 3285/94 of 22 December 1994.

2 Provisional or Definitive Measures Undertaken

Pursuant to the notifications required by the Agreement,[31] the Committee also reports on all safeguard investigations initiated under national law, and on provisional and definitive safeguard measures imposed. These notifications

[30] WTO, Report (2005) of the Committee on Safeguards to the Council for Trade in Goods, G/L/761, 8 November 2005.

[31] The information in this section was compiled from the annual reports of the Committee on Safeguards to the Council for Trade in Goods for the years 2000–2005. The WTO document numbers are G/L/409, G/L/494, G/L/583, G/L/651, G/L/703, and G/L/761.

are collected in Appendix 6, which covers all measures notified to date since the inception of the WTO.

From the entry into force of the WTO Agreement through November 3, 2005, national authorities initiated (and reported to the Committee) a total of 145 safeguard investigations. The United States initiated 10 investigations while the European Communities initiated four and Japan initiated three. India was a particularly frequent user of the investigative process, with 16 investigations.

Provisional measures, used for "critical circumstances where delay would cause damage which it would be difficult to repair" and limited to 200 days in duration, were imposed in 47 cases. Definitive measures were imposed in a total of 76 cases. As of November 3, 2005, 31 definitive safeguard measures remained in place, and 15 investigations were ongoing without any definitive measure yet having been imposed.

The overall pattern reflects a considerable return to formal reliance on Article XIX within the system. Grey-area measures were all to have been terminated by the end of 1999, and as best one can determine compliance with this obligation seems to have been largely satisfactory. No WTO dispute has been filed thus far over the alleged maintenance of a grey-area measure, although the reports of the Committee make occasional reference to the issue being raised informally.

3 Safeguard Measures in the Dispute Resolution System

As noted, formal disputes over safeguard measures during the years of GATT were rare. The only written dispute report pertaining to safeguard measures during the GATT era was the *Hatter's Fur* report of 1951. The paucity of formal disputes owed partly to the rise of grey-area measures, and partly to the weaknesses of the GATT dispute settlement mechanism, which could be "blocked" by any party from reaching a conclusion.

The creation of the WTO changed the dispute resolution system in a way that eliminated "blocking." If initial consultations fail to resolve a dispute, complaining parties have a right to a dispute panel and a subsequent appeal if desired. The final decision of the panel or, if that is appealed, the Appellate Body, is automatically binding on the parties ("adopted" by the WTO membership) absent a consensus of the membership to reject the findings (which has not happened to date). The prospect of a definitive outcome to the dispute process has encouraged WTO members to use it.

The return to formal reliance on Article XIX within the WTO system sparked by the Safeguards Agreement has been accompanied by a significant amount of litigation. As of August 2005, eighteen dispute cases were initiated (which entails a formal request for consultations by the complaining WTO member). In nine of these cases, the measure in question was eventually terminated before the process reached the stage of a panel report.[32] In one case, the measure remains in place but the dispute process appears to have stopped short of the panel stage.[33] Eight of the cases proceeded to a panel and resulted in the issuance of a panel report,[34] and six of those decisions were appealed resulting in an Appellate Body Report.[35]

In all eight of the cases that resulted in a panel and/or Appellate Body decision, the complaining nation prevailed on multiple grounds. As subsequent chapters will make clear, the jurisprudence that has emerged from these cases makes it exceedingly difficult for WTO members to employ safeguard measures in a way that will withstand legal challenge. Of course, many measures are not challenged as the statistics above indicate, and even a challenged measure can remain in place during the litigation process. It would thus be an overstatement to say that the decisions to date sound a death knell for safeguard measures in the WTO system, but they certainly make them more difficult to employ for any length of time greater than that necessary for a complaining nation to obtain a favorable dispute ruling.

The remainder of this book will focus extensively on the legal issues relating to the use of safeguards within the system, both in the treaty text and in the Appellate Body jurisprudence to date, and on broader policy questions regarding the proper role of safeguards in the system. To set the stage for consideration of the central policy issues, the next chapter turns from the history of safeguard measures to a survey of their economics.

[32] These cases are Chile—Edible Oils, DS226; Chile—Fructose, DS278; Chile—Sugar, DS228 & 230; EC—Steel, DS260; EC—Salmon, DS326 & 328; Hungary—Steel, DS/159; Slovakia—Sugar, DS235; United States—Brooms, DS78; and United States—Steel Wire Rod, DS214.

[33] Ecuador—Fibreboard, DS303.

[34] These cases were Argentina—Footwear, DS121 & 123; Argentina—Peaches, DS238; Chile—Agricultural Products DS207; Korea—Dairy Products, DS98; United States—Lamb, DS177 & 178; United States—Circular Welded Caron Quality Pipe, DS202; United States—Steel, DS248, 249, 251, 252, 253, 254, 258, 259 & 274; and United States—Wheat Gluten, DS166.

[35] The two panel reports not appealed came in Argentina—Peaches and Chile—Agricultural Products (safeguards portion not appealed).

Chapter 2

ECONOMIC POLICY CONSIDERATIONS

My goal in this book is not simply to illuminate the legal issues associated with safeguard measures, but to explore the rationale for safeguard measures in the WTO/GATT system, and the related policy debate over the proper role of safeguard measures. These issues are primarily economic ones, blended with what one might also term the "political economy" of the system. This chapter surveys the economic and political economic literature bearing on safeguards, and offers thoughts on the outstanding issues.

From a positive standpoint, the central question is why did the drafters of GATT and of the Uruguay Round accords see fit to include safeguard measures in the GATT and WTO systems? In particular, what constructive role did the negotiators see for temporary protection, in response to import surges, when the import-competing domestic industry was seriously injured (or threatened with serious injury)? A convincing positive account for safeguard measures in the system must address all elements of the legal prerequisites for safeguards. On the normative side, the central question is whether safeguard measures have a principled justification grounded in economic efficiency, distributive equity, or something else. Here, too, the answer must pay close attention to the circumstances under which safeguard measures are permitted. Unfortunately, I cannot promise definitive answers to any of these questions in this chapter, only an exploration of possibilities.

As noted in the Preface, I do not assume any prior background in economics on the part of the reader. Thus, I will begin in Section A with a quite basic treatment of the economics of international trade and trade protection. I recommend that readers with a background in international economics skip this section, and proceed directly to Section B which focuses more narrowly on the economics of safeguard measures, and what I term the "conventional" arguments for them—restoring the competitiveness of a beleaguered industries, easing the process of structural adjustment, and compensating the "losers" from trade liberalization. Section C then offers an alternative perspective on safeguard measures grounded in political economy. This perspective, I believe, serves better than the traditional arguments to explain the presence of safeguards in the WTO system, and offers an interesting and somewhat agnostic perspective on their normative value.

A The Basic Economics of International Trade and Protectionism

Economist and Nobel Laureate Paul Samuelson once wrote, "There is essentially only one argument for free trade or freer trade, but it is an exceedingly powerful one, namely: Free trade promotes a mutually profitable division of labor, greatly enhances the potential real national product of all nations, and makes possible higher standards of living all over the globe."[1] If this argument is right, why interfere with free trade using safeguard measures?

[1] Paul A. Samuelson (1973) *Economics*. 9th ed., p. 692.

Do the industries that qualify for safeguard protection somehow represent an exception to the normative case for free trade? Why did the drafters of GATT and now the WTO include in their agreement the authority for safeguard measures? This section lays a foundation for discussion of these questions, starting with the basic case for free trade to which Samuelson refers.

The case can be presented in varying ways, but perhaps the simplest is to focus on the effect that trade has on prices, and to trace the attendant effects on the well being or "welfare" of citizens in trading nations. I will offer a basic "partial equilibrium" exposition of these effects here. For readers interested in a more sophisticated "general equilibrium" treatment, one good source is Dixit and Norman (1980).

The change in prices in each country due to trade will have two components. Once a country begins exporting a good, it faces higher demand for that good because foreign demand has now been added to domestic demand. Typically, the price of the exported good will tend to rise as a result. Reciprocally, when a country begins importing a good, it faces greater supply of that good in the face of its fixed domestic demand. The price of the imported good (and its domestic counterpart) will typically fall. As shall be seen, the normative case for free trade rests on the notion that each of these two phenomena (falling price of imported goods and rising price of exported goods) confers a net gain on trading nations. To understand why it is helpful to introduce two additional concepts—consumer surplus and producer surplus.

Consumer surplus exists when consumers are able to purchase something for a price that is less than the value they place on it. For example, imagine that a consumer is willing to pay up to $1.00 for a 12-ounce Coca-Cola—that is, the consumer considers herself indifferent between parting with a dollar and obtaining the Coca-Cola, or retaining the dollar to use on something else. If this consumer can purchase the Coca-Cola for $0.60, however, she considers herself clearly better off, and prefers to go through with the transaction than to forego it. The consumer surplus from the transaction can be conceptualized as the difference between the maximum willingness-to-pay for the good (here, $1.00), and the price actually paid (here, $0.60)—$0.40 on these numbers.[2]

This amount can be approximated by an area under the demand curve in a standard economic diagram. Figure 2.1 depicts a demand curve for some arbitrary good, which slopes downward from left to right. As the price declines (the variable on the vertical axis), more consumers find it attractive to purchase

[2] One could also define it with reference to the consumer's minimum price for parting with the good in question. For further discussion see Varian (1992), Chapter ten.

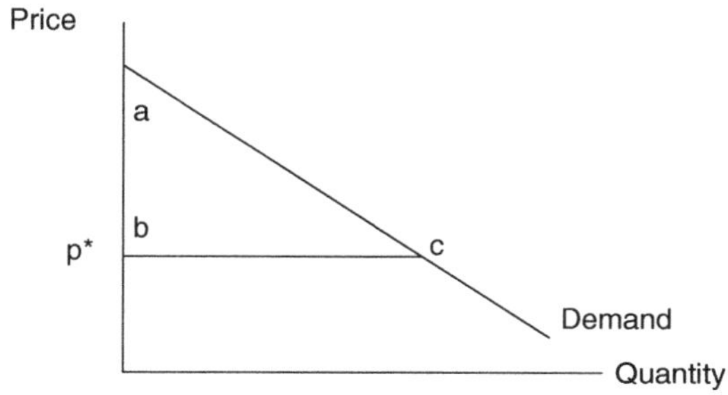

Figure 2.1 Consumer Surplus

the good and the quantity that they will buy increases (the variable on the horizontal axis). One can loosely think of each point on the curve as representing an individual consumer, and as denoting the maximum amount that the consumer will pay to obtain the good. Now suppose that the prevailing market price is p*. Each consumer located on the demand curve above and to the left of a horizontal line drawn at p* then has an opportunity to buy the good for less than their maximum willingness-to-pay, and will earn consumer surplus equal to the difference between that amount (given by their position on the demand curve) and p*. The total consumer surplus in the market is thus equal to the sum of the consumer surplus for all these individuals.

It is possible to show using calculus methods that the amount of consumer surplus in this market is approximated by the area under the demand curve and above the prevailing price, i.e., the area represented by triangle *abc*.[3]

Producer surplus will be a more straightforward concept to those without economic backgrounds. It is simply the profit earned by producers in a market—the difference between revenue and cost for each producer, summed over all of the producers. It can also be seen in a simple economic diagram. Figure 2.2 depicts a "supply" curve for some arbitrary good (the notion of a supply curve implicitly assumes that the industry producing the good is "competitive"). Each point on the supply curve denotes the amount of production that the industry will deliver at the corresponding price. In a competitive industry, producers will supply their output up to the point where the price no longer covers their incremental or "marginal" cost of additional output.

Thus, each point on the supply curve also represents the marginal cost of incremental production at that quantity level. Total profit will equal the

[3] For complicated reasons, this area is only an approximation, although it will often be a pretty close one. The classic treatment of the issue is Willig (1976).

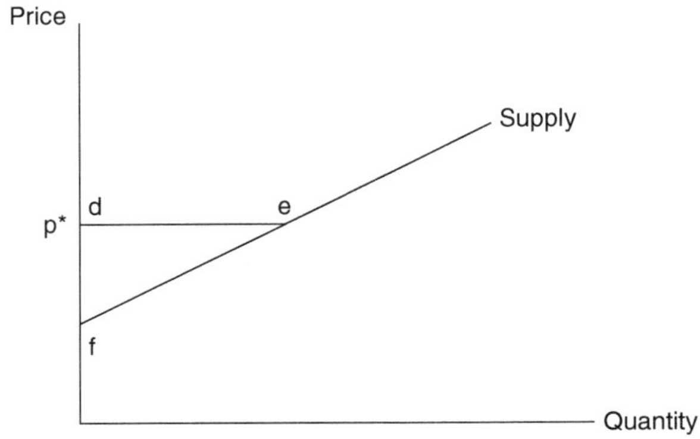

Figure 2.2 Producer Surplus

difference between the prevailing price and the marginal cost of each unit of output up to the total amount produced at the prevailing price. It can again be shown by calculus methods that this profit is equal to the area above and to the left of the supply curve and below a horizontal line drawn at the prevailing price. At the prevailing price of p* in the Figure, therefore, producer surplus is equal to the area of the triangle *def.*

Note that the notion of producer surplus as "profit" is slightly misleading, as that phrasing implies that producer surplus is earned entirely by firms. In fact, producer surplus may also be captured by workers or the suppliers of other factors of production such as land. To the degree that a worker in a particular job earns a wage that exceeds what the worker could earn elsewhere, for example, that part of the wage too is producer surplus.

With this background, we can now examine further the normative economic argument for free trade. When trade occurs, prices will be affected as noted above. In the market for a good that a country imports, prices will tend to fall, which benefits consumers in that market but harms domestic producers of competing goods. In the market for a good that a country exports, prices will tend to rise, which benefits domestic producers of the exported good but harms domestic consumers of that good. To make the argument that the nation benefits on balance from trade, one must have some basis for aggregating these effects and deciding whether the net impact is favorable or unfavorable. The conventional way to do so is simply to add up the effects of the price changes on consumer and producer surplus in each market, thus presupposing as a normative matter that all such surplus should receive equal "weight."

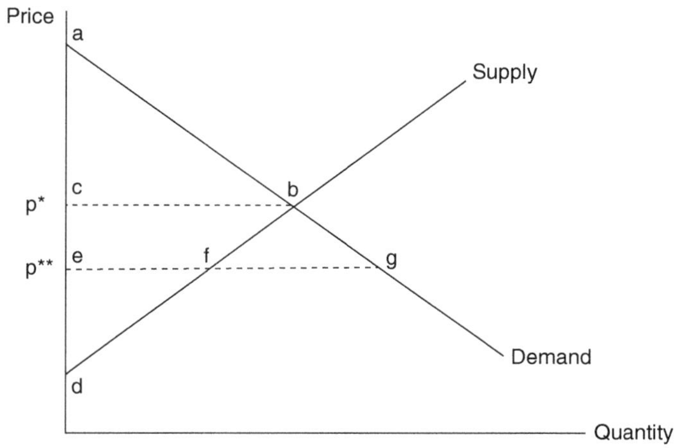

Figure 2.3 Effect of Trade in Market with Imports

Proceeding in this fashion, consider first a market in which trade results in imports that compete with the products of domestic firms, lowering prices. Suppose first, and counterfactually, that the influx of imports causes prices of the good in question to fall, but has no impact on the quantities purchased by domestic consumers or produced by domestic producers. On this counterfactual assumption, there is no net change in the sum of producer and consumer surplus. All consumers receive a benefit equal to the drop in price on what they were already purchasing, while all domestic producers incur a loss of revenue and profit equal to the drop in price multiplied by their initial quantity of production. The sum of the two effects is a complete wash. Now note that *in actuality*, the gain in consumer surplus will be greater than in this counterfactual, because when prices fall, some new consumers will come into the market and earn surplus on their purchases (the market moves farther down the demand curve). Likewise, the loss to domestic producers is smaller than in the counterfactual, because they will reduce their output and cushion the loss of profits by cutting back production to the point where price once again covers their marginal costs (domestic producers move back down the supply curve until the point where the lower price again covers marginal cost). After consumers and producers adapt to the price reduction, therefore, the sum of producer and consumer surplus must increase.

Figure 2.3 illustrates this argument, which for some arbitrary good depicts the demand curve of consumers in the importing country and the supply curve of domestic producers. For simplicity, we will assume that imported and domestic goods are fungible, although that is in no way necessary to the essential argument. The price in "autarky"—without any international trade—is p*, determined by the intersection of the domestic supply and demand curves. At that price, consumer surplus is given by the area *abc*, and producer surplus by the area *bcd*. After the opening of trade and import competition, price falls to p**. The difference between the quantity demanded at that price and the amount supplied by domestic producers is the quantity of imports.

At the new price level, consumer surplus rises to an amount given by the area *aeg*, while domestic producer surplus falls to an amount given by the area *def*. It is apparent that consumers gain more than domestic producers lose, however, with the net gain given by the area of the triangle *bfg*. The net gain in the sum of consumer and producer surplus is also termed a *welfare* gain, or an *efficiency* gain.

Now consider a market in which the nation in question is an exporter, and where the opening of trade causes prices to rise. The reason for the existence of net gains in such a market is symmetrical to the analysis of the import market. When prices rise, there would be no change in the sum of producer and consumer surplus if, counterfactually, consumers all bought the same amount of the good and producers all produced the same amount. But producers can and will do better by expanding output, moving up the supply curve and earning more surplus. Consumers can and will cut their losses by buying less of the good and shifting their purchases to something else that earns surplus. The net effect is positive, as Figure 2.4 illustrates. Initial

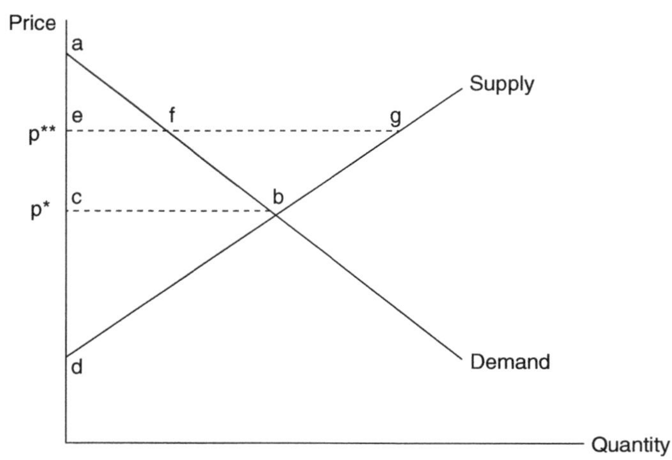

Figure 2.4 Effect of Trade in Market with Exports

consumer surplus at the autarky price p^* is given by the area *abc*, and producer surplus is given by *bcd*.

When price increases to p^{**}, the difference between the quantity demanded and the quantity produced by domestic producers is exported. Consumer surplus declines to the area *aef*, while producer surplus grows to *deg*. The net gain in the sum of consumer and producer surplus is given by the triangle *bfg*. Here too, trade produces an efficiency gain.

Figures 2.3–4 assume that markets are competitive. There is a further benefit from trade in markets that are not. If the domestic industry is imperfectly competitive (the extreme case being a monopoly), and uses its market power to set price above marginal cost when it does not face international competition, the initial sum of producer and consumer surplus will be lower than depicted. The advent of import competition can then reduce the market power of domestic firms and reduce or eliminate the loss of aggregate surplus due to the exercise of market power.

In sum, the normative economic case for "free or freer trade" in Samuelson's phrasing rests on the view that it yields net gains to trading nations, in the form of an increase in the aggregate producer and consumer surplus in the economy. An immediate corollary of this argument, subject to some qualifications that I will note in a moment, is that government intervention to reduce trade flows, including restrictions on imports, will impose net losses on an economy. For example, with reference to Figure 2.3, one can imagine that the movement from the autarky price p^* to the price p^{**} occurs because the government removes some prohibitive barrier to trade, such as a prohibitively high tariff or a zero quota. Conversely, if we suppose that the price p^{**} is the price that arises with "free trade," it seems that any government policy which restricts imports and causes price to rise above p^{**} will impose net losses on the economy—as price rises toward p^*, the net gains from trade given by triangle *bfg* must steadily shrink.

This last proposition is subject to a few qualifications. Thus far, we have considered the effect of trade on consumer and producer surplus, but there is another type of "surplus" in play when governments influence trade through tariffs—"government surplus" or, in simpler terms, tariff revenue. When governments capture some of the surplus in a market through tariff revenue, is it possible that a tariff can increase total surplus? The answer is "no" for a "small" country, and "yes" for a large country. By "small," economists mean a country that is not large enough to influence the price of the things that it imports from abroad by altering the quantity of those imports. It is an international "price taker." A "large" country, by contrast, can affect the

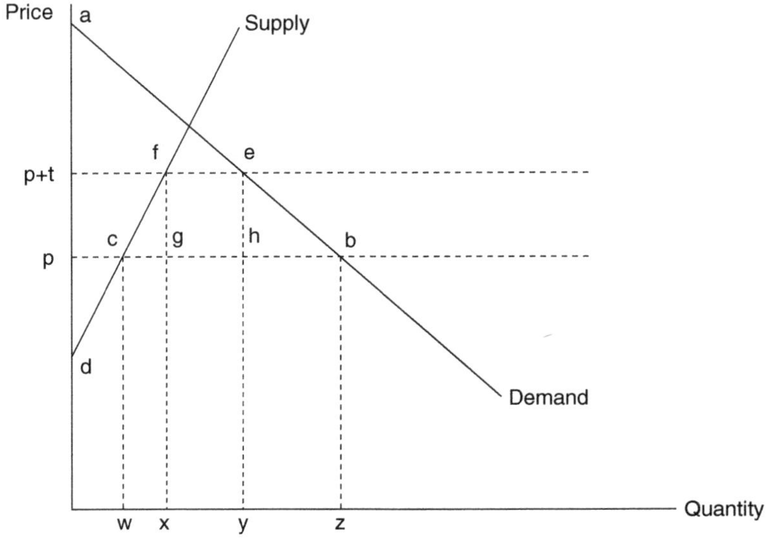

Figure 2.5 Effect of a Tariff—Small Country Case

price that it pays for imports by manipulating the quantity that it buys. Such a country has a degree of buyer power or "monopsony power" that it can exploit through tariff policy.

Figure 2.5 depicts the small country case. With open trade, the importing nation can obtain all that it wishes to import at the fixed price p. Consumer surplus is given by the area of the triangle *abp*, while producer surplus is given by the area *cdp*. If the government then imposes a tariff in the amount t, price to consumers in the market will rise to $p + t$—foreign suppliers will not lower their price even if the quantity imported declines (in effect, the supply curve for imports is horizontal at p). After the tariff, consumer surplus declines to the area $ae(p + t)$, while producer surplus increases to the area $df(p + t)$.

Government tariff revenue also appears in the diagram. Note that the quantity of imports falls as a result of the tariff from an amount z-w to an amount y-x. Each unit imported results in revenue for the government of t, and so the total revenue is $t(y\text{-}x)$. That amount is simply the area of the rectangle *efgh*. Accordingly, when one examines the sum of consumer surplus, producer surplus and government revenue before and after the tariff, it is apparent that total surplus declines by the sum of the two triangles *cfg* and *beh*. The first triangle represents the loss due to the expansion of domestic

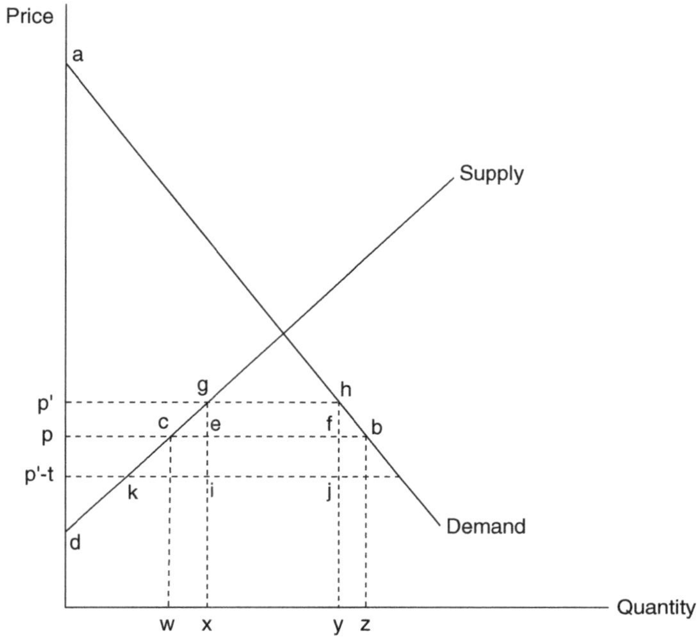

Figure 2.6 Effect of a Tariff—Large Country Case

production above the quantity *w*—domestic marginal costs above that quantity exceed the price at which the good can be bought from abroad. The second triangle represents the loss of consumer surplus to consumers who are priced out of the market when price rises from p to p + t.

If the importing nation is large, the analysis changes in an important way. In Figure 2.5, the full cost of the tariff is passed along to domestic consumers because foreign sellers will not reduce their price even when the quantity imported declines. But if the tariff leads foreign sellers to reduce price and absorb part of the tariff, then some of the government revenue generated by the tariff comes at the expense of foreign producer surplus rather than domestic consumers. From the perspective of the importing country, therefore, which perhaps cares not at all about the surplus lost by foreigners, the tariff is less harmful and may even be beneficial.

Figure 2.6 illustrates the point. The price before the tariff is *p*, yielding an initial consumer surplus of *abp* and domestic producer surplus of *cdp*. A tariff is imposed in the amount *t*, but because the importing country is large, foreign sellers will reduce their prices as the quantity purchased from them declines. The new equilibrium price is *p'*, and the net price to foreign sellers is now $p' - t$, which is less than p because of the price reduction by foreign sellers. Consumer surplus falls to *ahp'*, while domestic producer surplus rises to *dgp'*. The quantity of imports is the difference between demand and domestic supply, and falls as a result of the tariff from $z - w$ to $y - x$. Tariff revenue of t per unit on imports of $y - x$ is equal to the area of the rectangle *ghji*. Comparing the sum of consumer surplus, producer surplus and government revenue before and after the tariff, there is a loss in the form of the triangles *ceg* and *bfh* analogous to the loss triangles in Figure 2.5. Here, however, there is also a surplus gain in the form of tariff revenue equal to the rectangle *efji*. This amount represents the surplus extracted from foreign sellers who have lowered their price from p to $p' - t$ as a result of the tariff. The net effect on surplus, therefore, depends on whether the gain *efji* exceeds the sum of the losses *ceg* and *bfh*. On inspection, the diagram as drawn suggests that the net effect is a gain in surplus.

The result in Figure 2.6 relates closely to what has come to be known in economics as the theory of the "optimal tariff." It is possible to show that a "large country" can always increase its aggregate national surplus by imposing an appropriate tariff on imports to exploit its monopsony power.[4] See Krugman and Obstfeld (2003). Beyond a certain point, however, the effect of raising tariffs turns negative even for large countries, often at fairly low tariff rates. In general, the size of the optimal tariff depends on the "elasticity of import supply" from abroad. This concept captures the slope of the supply curve for imports (which is not drawn in the preceding diagrams but is implicit in the analysis).

In Figure 2.5, the implicit import supply curve is horizontal, or "perfectly elastic." The small importing nation can import all that it wishes at the price p. For Figure 2.6, the implicit import supply curve is fairly "inelastic"—it slopes upward fairly steeply. For that reason, when the tariff is imposed and the quantity imported declines, foreign sellers reduce their price fairly substantially as they move down and to the left on their supply curve. In general, the optimal tariff is higher, the more *inelastic* is the import supply curve.

It is important to recognize that the "optimal tariff" from the importing country's perspective does *not* increase global economic surplus—quite the contrary. The gain to the importing country in Figure 2.6 comes from the price reduction by foreign sellers, so that the importing nation's gain is from

[4] A symmetric point can be made regarding export tariffs by large countries—a nation with market power as a seller can use tariffs to raise its welfare by extracting surplus from foreign consumers.

the foreigners' perspective a loss, and from the global perspective a wash. Indeed, the net impact on global surplus of a tariff is assuredly negative in general because it induces production by less efficient firms, and prices some consumers out of the market protected by the tariff. Optimal tariffs are thus a "beggar-thy-neighbor" policy that may increase surplus for the importing nation viewed in isolation, but reduce the welfare of trading partners and reduce total global surplus.

Moreover, the pursuit of optimal tariffs by one country may invite its trading partners to do the same if they are also "large." The resulting state of affairs may leave all nations worse off than if they eschewed such policy. This observation afforded an early theory of the function of trade agreements—if nations behaved so as to maximize their national surplus, they might be tempted to charge optimal tariffs when acting unilaterally, but might determine that a mutual agreement to forbear from such behavior would make them better off collectively. Modern trade theorists have refined this perspective on trade agreements as shall be seen in subsequent sections of this chapter.

In addition to the theory of the optimal tariff, the normative case for free trade requires an additional, general caveat relating to the so-called *market failure* problem. As an example, suppose that a nation suffers from a severe problem with air pollution, which is causing substantial health problems in the population. Assume that most of the pollution is caused by automobiles. The pollution problem is called a market failure problem because the users of automobiles do not take account of the harm that their air pollution imposes on others, and there is no "market" in which those who would benefit from reduced pollution can offer to pay polluters to abate their polluting activities. The nation responds to the situation by imposing a substantial tariff on imported automobiles, which causes all prices in the automobile market to rise and leads to fewer vehicles on the road and less pollution. Might the surplus associated with the resulting improvement in health offset the losses otherwise associated with the tariff? The answer is yes.

Market failures may come in many forms besides pollution. The modern learning on *strategic trade*, for example, focuses in part on industries where production generates a positive benefit to the economy that firms cannot capture in their revenue stream, and that hence will be undersupplied because of this market failure. For example, suppose that firms in a particular industry generate knowledge that diffuses to other local firms and enhances their efficiency. This may occur as employees change jobs, or simply hear about the work going on elsewhere. Examples of such local knowledge spillovers may arise in high technology industries, such as the cluster of firms in Silicon Valley. The firms that create this knowledge spillover will have a difficult time charging for it, and hence their value to the economy exceeds the value that they can capture in prices for their goods or services. Economic theory predicts that such an industry will end up being "too small" from a social perspective. To the extent that such an industry is confronted by import competition, one way to induce it to expand is to protect it from competition, as by imposing a tariff. See generally Krugman (1986).

Does the existence of market failures substantially undermine the case for "free or freer" trade? The general view among economists is that they do not, because intervention in trade is generally not the best way to address them. Consider the example of pollution once again. A tariff on imported automobiles may help reduce automobile purchases and pollution, but it distorts production decisions by inducing consumers to shift some of their purchases to more costly or lower quality domestic automobiles. A uniform tax on all automobiles, or on gasoline, or uniform emissions controls, can address the pollution problem directly without distorting consumer choice. Likewise, in an industry with knowledge spillovers, a tariff causes a loss of consumer surplus as we have seen, which might be averted by a more direct inducement to industry expansion in the form of a government subsidy (assuming that the tax to raise the money for a subsidy is less of a source of economic distortion than the tariff). A classic reference on the proposition that trade intervention is generally not an ideal response to market failure is Johnson (1971).

The final caveat to the normative case for open trade is perhaps an obvious one, although it raises subtle issues to which the discussion will return in subsequent sections. Although trade yields net gains in surplus to trading nations, why is aggregate surplus the touchstone for what is normatively appealing? It is not obvious that a dollar of surplus to a consumer of widgets, or a dollar of surplus to a firm producing gadgets (or maybe to its workers) should all "count" the same in deciding whether the nation as a whole is better or worse off as a result of trade. Perhaps some workers or consumers are more needy than others, or for some other reason more deserving of additional "surplus." It may be appropriate for nations to worry not only about the aggregate surplus form trade, therefore, but also about its impact on the distribution of wealth. The question whether distributional considerations offer a persuasive justification for certain forms of intervention in trade will receive further attention below.

B Basic Economics of Safeguard Measures: Efficiency and Distribution

With the general case for free trade (and its caveats) in mind, we now turn to safeguards policy and the protection of troubled industries. The central question is the following: Do industries beleaguered by unanticipated increases in import competition, and that qualify for safeguard measures under GATT Article XIX, somehow stand as a principled exception to the argument for open trade? This section will suggest that the answer is likely no, and will in the process review several (mostly unsatisfactory) arguments for safeguard measures that have been advanced through the years.

1 The Economic Consequences of Safeguard Measures: A First Cut

The conventional economic argument for free trade set out above rests on "static" analysis, in that it simply compares the situation in equilibrium before and after the opening of trade. The "dynamic" transition between policy regimes is not explicitly considered. In actuality, of course, changes in trade policy will necessitate a dynamic adjustment process for affected firms. Exporting firms that gain new market access opportunities must expand their production, hire more workers, and learn how best to take advantage of sales opportunities in new or more open markets. Likewise, import-competing firms faced with greater import competition must adjust to falling prices, often by curtailing production and reducing their workforce. Workers in such industries may have to search for new jobs, and perhaps even retrain themselves for a new industry.

The transition to a more open trading system thus brings new prosperity to exporting firms, and a potentially difficult period of contraction for import-competing firms. These observations, while surely correct, do not undermine the basic economic case for free trade (at least the efficiency-based case for free trade—distributional concerns will be addressed in due course). Just as consumers in an importing nation gain more than import-competing firms lose in the eventual equilibrium following reduced trade barriers, so too will they tend to gain more during the transition to the new equilibrium (subject to some caveats below). In well-functioning markets, falling prices due to import competition will add more to consumer surplus than they detract from producer surplus. A simple inspection of Figure 2.3 above, for example, will suggest that the triangle representing the net gain from trade expands steadily as price falls from p^* to p^{**}. A symmetrical argument (based on Figure 2.4) applies to exporting industries, and suggests that the net gains from increased export opportunities grow steadily as prices rise from p^* to p^{**}.

Within this framework, what is the effect of a safeguard measure? Such measures retard the growth of imports in industries subject to them, and interfere with the decline of prices in those industries. Thus, as a first approximation, safeguard measures reduce or eliminate the net gains from more open trade in the import-competing industries, and reduce or eliminate the net gains to the affected exporting nations.[5]

Note a few caveats. The first relates to the earlier discussion of the optimal tariff and to the difference between Figures 2.5 and 2.6. If the importing nation that imposes a safeguard measure is "large," and if the measure imposed is a tariff, then it is conceivable (but by no means certain) that the importing nation may experience a net economic gain through the exploitation of its monopsony power. The tariff revenue generated by the tariff may come substantially at the expense of foreign exporters who reduce prices in response to it, rather than at the expense of domestic consumers.

For two reasons, however, the possibility that a safeguard measure in the form of a tariff may yield net gains to a large importing nation does not supply an economic justification for the protection of "injured" industries in general, or for safeguard measures in particular. First, and most obviously, this possible consequence of the safeguard measure from the importing nation's perspective has nothing to do with the (injured) condition of the import-competing industry in question, but with the importing nation's monopsony power in the industry. Any benefits from the safeguard measure are in this sense only coincidentally related to the circumstances in which safeguard measures are legally permissible under the law. Second, as noted in Section A, the economic loss to trading partners from the imposition of a tariff by a "large" nation generally exceeds any gains to the importing country. Policies that enhance the economic welfare of one trading nation at the expense of the trading community at large may well be tempting in an environment in which trading nations do not cooperate. Ideally, however, the very function of a trade agreement such as GATT or the Uruguay Round

[5] The effect may be even more troublesome in some industries. Durling and Prusa (2003) argue that in some instances, notably the steel industry, safeguard measures have the effect of shifting profits from some domestic firms to others wastefully. They suggest that steel tariffs on certain basic steel products used as inputs by non-integrated domestic firms raised their costs and shifted business toward integrated domestic firms that do not rely on imported inputs.

accords is to constrain or eliminate self-regarding protectionist policies for the mutual benefit of all signatories. Hence, the mere fact that protection may at times afford economic gains to an importing country hardly provides an economic justification for safeguards measures under GATT or the WTO. Rather, an appealing justification, if one exists, must rest on the proposition that safeguards actions afford net gains to signatories in the aggregate.

A similar caveat relates to the discussion in Section A regarding market failures and, in particular, to the strategic trade rationale for protection. If the industry protected by a safeguard measure fits the strategic trade paradigm,[6] so that its presence yields positive spillovers to the rest of the economy that the firms in the industry do not capture in their revenue streams, it is possible that the industry may contract excessively in response to import competition from the importing nation's perspective. Protection may then enhance the economic welfare of the importing nation. But again, any benefits from such a policy would be largely coincidental in relation to the circumstances in which safeguard measures are permitted under the law, and may come at the expense of trading partners. Also, other policies (such as subsidies to domestic firms) would likely dominate trade protection as indicated in Section A.

Finally, the reader may well have noted that the economic effect of a safeguard measure is not always confined to the industry in which it is imposed. As Chapter 1 noted, the possibility of retaliation follows the imposition of some safeguard measures, as does the possibility of negotiated trade compensation. Safeguard measures will also tend to affect exchange rates—by reducing the demand for imports, they reduce the demand for foreign currency and cause the domestic currency to appreciate. Economic analysis of safeguards policy must take these possibilities into account.

The first possibility—retaliation—plainly worsens the economic picture. If safeguard measures beget retaliation, then the benefits of more open trade are lost in multiple industries.

[6] Industries may also fit the strategic trade framework if they contain firms that can exercise monopoly power, and can extract monopoly profits from foreign consumers. The strategic trade literature notes how protection for such firms can in some cases benefit an importing country by shifting profits to its firms at the expense of foreign firms. See Helpman and Krugman (1989). This too is an altogether unconvincing basis for safeguard measures, because once again the gains would be only coincidentally related to the condition of the import-competing industry, and would come at the expense of other trading partners. Moreover, troubled and declining industries are particularly unlikely to fit this framework—firms with the capacity to extract monopoly profits are likely to be prosperous and successful.

By contrast, the possibility of compensation softens the economic impact of a safeguard measure. If new trade restrictions in one industry are coupled with relaxed trade restrictions in another, the net impact on economic welfare may be small or even positive. This possibility does not make out much of a case for safeguard measures, however, for two reasons. First, even when compensation is agreed upon, the net impact of safeguard measures will be quite uncertain, and there can be no basis for assuming that it will be positive. Second, in practice, compensation arises rather infrequently. Indeed, the new Agreement on Safeguards was designed to reduce the use of compensation as indicated in Chapter 1 and as will be discussed further in Chapter 9.

Finally, the exchange rate effect of safeguard measures does nothing to strengthen the case for them. From the importing nation's perspective, other import-competing industries will become somewhat more competitive, while exporting industries become less competitive. The effects are reversed from the perspective of trading partners. The net impact on an otherwise well-functioning trading system, however, is adverse for the reasons given in Section A.

As a first cut, therefore, the standard economic case for open trade also makes a case against the use of safeguard measures. Such measures will often harm importing and exporting countries alike (focusing on aggregate consumer and producer surplus in each), and in the few instances where they may benefit importing nations, the benefits are only coincidentally related to the legal prerequisites for safeguard measures and will come at the expense of trading partners. Only if trade compensation were routinely coupled with safeguard measures would there be any basis for optimism that their net (efficiency) impact is potentially benign, but compensation has been the exception rather than the rule in practice. Based on the analysis to this point, it is difficult to see a constructive role for safeguard measures, or to understand why GATT or WTO members would have elected to permit them.

But we have yet to consider a number of arguments for safeguard measures that have been advanced through the years, some of which may well have occurred to the reader. I will divide these arguments into two general categories—the "conventional" arguments for safeguard measures found in older literature and to some degree in national and international legal texts, and the more modern "political economy" explanations for safeguards.

2 Conventional Arguments for Safeguard Measures

Perhaps the most often invoked arguments for safeguard measures are those recited in U.S. national legislation creating the authority for safeguard measures under domestic law. Section 201 of the U.S. Trade Act of 1974 provides that if an industry exhibits the conditions of injury contemplated by Article XIX,[7] the President shall take "appropriate and feasible" action that he determines will "facilitate efforts by the domestic industry to make a positive adjustment to import competition." A "positive adjustment" occurs, according to the statute, when the domestic industry "is able to compete successfully with imports after [safeguard measures] terminate" or "experiences an orderly transfer of resources to other productive pursuits," and when "dislocated workers in the industry experience an orderly transition to productive pursuits." The statute thus authorizes safeguard measures when the President determines that one of two goals will be advanced—restoring the competitiveness of the domestic industry, or facilitating its structural adjustment ("orderly contraction"). Related to the notion of orderly contraction is the suggestion that safeguard measures may serve to redistribute income toward needy individuals displaced by import competition. This section examines these ideas carefully.

(a) Restoring Competitiveness

Industries petitioning for safeguard measures under national law routinely argue that temporary protection will enable them to restore their competitive position. Protection will do so, ostensibly, by providing the industry with a period of higher profits, enabling it to invest in new technology and modern equipment that will subsequently allow it to compete successfully in the international marketplace. The implicit source of net gains to the international community (and to the importing nation) lies with the eventual emergence of efficient competitors. The premise is that the protected industry will in time lower its costs of production to the point that protection is no longer necessary to its survival, and that the eventual savings in production costs (or perhaps the elimination of distortions attributable to monopoly power that would otherwise exist) will more than offset the short-term inefficiencies that arise during the period of protection.

This argument is problematic for several reasons. First, it relies on the questionable assumption that governments can accurately identify, and will choose to protect, only those industries that can become "competitive" (or "competitive again" in the case of declining industries). That set of industries is likely much smaller than the set of "seriously injured" industries, for the

[7] The U.S. statute is not fully congruent with Article XIX in several respects, as will be discussed in later chapters.

simple reason that competitiveness can be quite difficult to change. Many industries beleaguered by import competition can do nothing about the problem, and will face the same difficulties anew after protection is lifted. Politically organized industries may nevertheless seek and obtain trade protection, irrespective of the impact that it is likely to have on long-term competitiveness, because of the short-term profits that it brings.

Second, even if governments were able to identify appropriate candidates for assistance and would properly exclude poor candidates, protection is not necessarily the best way to provide such assistance. Direct loans or subsidies to the troubled industry are in theory superior to protection, unless such measures entail sufficiently higher administrative costs. Loans or subsidies to cover periods of losses can be as effective as protection in enabling an industry to become "competitive," but they do not introduce the deadweight loss attributable to the protection-induced distortion of prices.

Finally, and most importantly, government intervention to restore competitiveness is simply unnecessary, at least in countries with reasonable access to private capital markets. Private lenders will finance efforts to become "competitive" as long as the returns from such investments justify the apparent risk. Their unwillingness to do so is a strong signal that the investment is not justified, and there will often be little basis for governments to second-guess the judgment of the capital markets.

To be sure, if the industry in question generates some external economy that individual firms in the industry cannot capture (the strategic trade type of spillover noted previously), the social returns to investment in the industry will exceed the private returns. But other policy instruments, such as loans and subsidies, are still preferable in theory to protection. Further, the strategic trade argument for protection only applies to a narrow class of industries that generate substantial spillovers, while safeguard measures may be used in any industry. For all of these reasons, the suggestion that safeguard measures are useful for restoring the competitiveness of failing industries is not terribly persuasive.

(b) Orderly Contraction and Structural Adjustment

The Preamble to the Agreement on Safeguards refers to "the importance of structural adjustment," and as noted U.S. law makes much of the notion that safeguards can facilitate an orderly transition of resources to other pursuits. This section and the next consider the economic soundness of these justifications for safeguards as well as related arguments that safeguards are part of a sensible policy for the redistribution of income in the face of trade-related dislocation.

Beyond question, protection can slow the rate of industrial contraction in response to import competition, or end contraction altogether. But such delay is ordinarily an economic vice, not a virtue. Industries contract because the price that they can command for their goods and services is insufficient to cover their costs. They respond by moving down their supply curves (recall Figure 2.3) until their costs have fallen to the point that price again covers costs (as costs fall or prices rise due to the diminution of supply). In well-functioning markets, this process is economically desirable, because when prices do not cover the costs of inputs, it is preferable for those inputs to be employed elsewhere. The reason, put simply, is that inputs will be made available to firms in a competitive market at any price that equals or exceeds their "opportunity cost," the price that those inputs can command in their best alternative use. Then, if the owners of the necessary inputs—whether land, capital equipment, labor, or raw materials—collectively require a price to supply them that exceeds the value of the additional output they will ultimately produce, it follows that those inputs collectively are more valuable in alternative uses. It is economically inefficient to discourage their redeployment to those uses.

In the transition to an alternative use, of course, some inputs may spend a period of time unemployed, or may remain unemployed forever. The laid-off worker will have to search for another job, or may decide to stop working altogether in preference for leisure time. A closed factory may never reopen. But again, in well-functioning markets, there is nothing inefficient about such developments. The worker who is unemployed while searching for another job makes an efficient investment in the search, trading off the costs of additional search time against the expected benefits of a better compensation package or a more attractive work environment. The worker who exits the labor force altogether does so efficiently because the value of leisure to that worker exceeds the returns to working at the available wage. The factory that closes permanently does so efficiently because it cannot operate at a level where the price it can command for its output exceeds its costs of production.

The reader may question a key premise in this analysis—that markets are well-functioning, so that a decision by an input supplier to exit an industry reflects the existence of greater returns elsewhere. To be sure, if inputs can earn *more* in the industry that is contracting than they can elsewhere, or can produce something in that industry that is more valuable than they can produce elsewhere, it is no longer desirable for them to exit the industry. But why would this happen? If the input is more valuable in its current deployment, why is it not offered enough to induce it to stay there?

Such "market failures" are sometimes thought to arise, particularly in labor markets. Indeed, John Maynard Keynes' famous analysis of the business cycle in his *General Theory of Employment, Interest and Money* rested heavily on the notion of "sticky wages"—wage rates that do not adjust downward appropriately when economic conditions decline, causing workers to be laid off and unemployed when it would be better for them to retain their existing jobs at a lower wage rate. One potential source of sticky wages is unionization. Unions can negotiate for wages that exceed competitive levels, and allow union members to earn significantly more than they can elsewhere. When industry conditions deteriorate, unions may resist wage cuts that would save jobs, even though some of their membership may be laid off and left with substantially inferior employment opportunities. Another possible source of sticky wages, suggested by some of the literature on job search and unemployment, is that workers may become overoptimistic about their employment prospects elsewhere. This is most likely to occur during a cyclical downturn, when workers' information about opportunities elsewhere may become out of date in a way that leads to excessive optimism. See Alchian (1970). Sticky wages can also result from government safety net programs (such as welfare and unemployment insurance), which in effect subsidize unemployment and make it more attractive than it would be in an idealized market.

For the above reasons, and perhaps others, wages may resist downward adjustment during periods of industrial contraction, and workers may become unemployed or accept drastically reduced wages elsewhere (the $30/hr steel worker who takes a minimum wage job at McDonald's), even though it would be preferable from an economic standpoint for the workers to have remained in their original positions at a reduced wage. If this phenomenon occurs with some regularity, might it provide an economic justification for the goal of "orderly contraction," and perhaps offer an economic rationale for safeguard measures to facilitate it?

Sykes (1990) and Horn and Mavroidis (2003) consider this possibility at some length. Both suggest that safeguard measures may afford a "second-best" solution to the problem of inefficient unemployment or underemployment arising from labor market failures. But this argument for safeguards has many caveats, and in the end may be so limited as to become unconvincing. First, as implied by the statement that safeguards are "second-best," trade protection is quite likely an inferior policy instrument for addressing labor market failures, for the reasons developed in Section A. Direct intervention in the market that is functioning imperfectly—here, the labor market—can address the problem of wage stickiness without introducing the economic costs of protection. An employment subsidy, for example, can serve this purpose.

Second, safeguards may make the problem of labor market failure worse. If workers know that they are more likely to obtain protection when they resist wage concessions and precipitate sizeable unemployment problems, then a policy of protecting industries exhibiting such problems may exacerbate the wage stickiness.

Third, recall that under Article XIX, protection for "injured" industries is to be temporary, limited to the period of "serious injury." The argument for temporary protection as a response to inefficient unemployment has little force if it merely postpones dislocation to a future period. Such an outcome may be particularly likely where the "injury" to the protected industry is attributable to a decline in its competitiveness. Once protection is lifted, the unemployment problem may simply recur. For safeguard measures to be effective at ameliorating the problem one must imagine that the industry is allowed to contract gradually at a rate that allows its resources to avoid periods of unemployment or underemployment—perhaps the rate of job loss is limited to the rate at which new jobs for workers with comparable qualifications are opening up elsewhere. Horn and Mavroidis (2003). The difficulty with this approach to the implementation of safeguards, of course, is that it may be very difficult in practice for governments to calibrate safeguard measures so precisely. The information necessary to do so may not be readily available, and political forces may press for other degrees of protection in any event.

Fourth, taking a general equilibrium perspective on the effects of trade intervention, it is worth noting that trade intervention will shift the terms of trade through its effect on exchange rates. By reducing the demand for foreign currencies to buy imports, protection will cause the home-market currency to appreciate. As a result, overseas demand for domestic exports will decline and export industries will sell less. The possibility arises that the consequences of labor market failures may at least to some degree be shifted from a contracting import-competing industry to an array of contracting export industries in the same country.

Finally, even if the importing country would gain from a safeguard action, what of its trading partners? Will safeguard measures create unemployment among workers in those nations comparable to the reduction in unemployment in the importing nation, and simply shift unemployment from country to country? Once again, a convincing economic rationale for safeguard measures must explain how GATT and WTO signatories gain in the aggregate.

For these reasons, the argument that safeguards measures can efficiently alleviate unemployment in the presence of labor market distortions is problematic, or at least incomplete. We will return to these issues below when we consider the political economy of safeguards policy.

(c) Equity and Redistribution

The analysis above focuses on the efficiency implications of safeguard measures, much like the traditional case for free trade. But aggregate economic welfare is surely not the sole metric for assessing the wisdom of public policy. Governments routinely accept reductions in aggregate social wealth for the purpose of redistribution, and such policies enjoy significant popular support. Corden (1974) argues that much of trade policy can be understood as a concern for distributive outcomes, reflected in what he termed the "conservative social welfare function"—a principle that "any significant absolute reductions in real incomes of any significant section of the community should be avoided." Deardorff (1987) draws the connection between Corden's analysis and safeguards policy. Jackson (1997) also suggests that safeguard measures may serve to ease the adjustment problems faced by the "losers" in the process of trade liberalization. Is the "redistributive" case for safeguard measures a convincing one?

Plainly, an increase in import competition may cause firms in an importing country to contract or fail. Employees and their families may then suffer serious financial hardship that the citizenry may wish to ameliorate. But the hardships of unemployment and economic dislocation that result from import competition are no different in character from those that can result from domestic competition, technological change, or the vagaries of the business cycle. Hence, individuals who suffer financial reversals as a result of import competition arguably should enjoy no special entitlement to assistance, but rather should receive only the protection of whatever public safety net programs the government makes available to the citizenry as a whole.

One possible counterargument is that if economic dislocation results from trade concessions, it is somehow different from other dislocation because deliberate changes in policy are responsible for the hardship. Some writers have argued, for example, that the removal of trade barriers by the government undermines the legitimate reliance interests of domestic firms and workers who invested in physical and human capital on the assumption that prior trade policies would remain in place. See Jackson (1969). But there are serious difficulties with this argument. A wide range of government policy decisions about government spending, regulation of the workplace, monetary policy and other matters can cause serious economic dislocation, yet no entitlement to special assistance exists for those harmed by these actions. It is unclear why changes in the level of protection in a nation's trade policy should be treated differently. Indeed, the mere fact that some industrial interest group has succeeded in obtaining protection in the past hardly seems a sufficient basis for creating a permanent entitlement to that protection or for requiring compensation for its removal. Such an entitlement will only increase the expected returns to the pursuit of protection in the political arena, leading to more lobbying effort by those desiring protection and probably to greater protection in the first instance. Yet another serious objection is that safeguards measures in practice are at best quite imperfectly linked to situations in which dislocation is demonstrably related to any trade concession (more on that point in later chapters).

An alternative argument for special assistance to workers displaced by import competition is that such workers, if their skills are not readily transferable to other industries, may suffer a greater hardship than other displaced workers. When domestic firms fail as a result of competition from other domestic firms, for example, the demise of one domestic firm is typically accompanied by the expansion or creation of another domestic firm in the same line of business. Displaced workers may then have an opportunity to secure alternative employment that draws upon their existing skills and training, perhaps even in the same geographic area. In the case of workers displaced by import competition, by contrast, relocation abroad is often an unattractive option. Likewise, when workers are displaced by cyclical downturns in the domestic economy, they may at least anticipate that the displacement is temporary and that they will eventually be able to return to work in a position that draws upon their existing human capital. Workers displaced by import competition may have little hope of returning to work in the same industry. Instead, they may confront a choice between retraining themselves for a new line of work or accepting employment in unskilled positions. Thus, one might argue, special assistance is appropriate because the adverse economic consequences of import-related displacement for the worker and dependents are particularly acute.

But again, numerous objections may be offered. First, it is unclear whether the empirical premise of the argument is correct. Limited empirical evidence suggests that workers displaced by import competition do not necessarily spend a longer period of time unemployed or suffer a greater reduction in their incomes than do workers displaced by other causes. See Richardson (1982). Indeed, workers suffering permanent displacement due to import competition are seemingly no differently situated than workers displaced by technological change, workers who typically receive no special entitlement to aid.

Second, the distributive case for aid to workers displaced by import competition is weakened if they have already been "compensated." If the risk of displacement is known *ex ante*, such compensation may be built into wages. Related, the distributive case is weakened to the degree that threatened workers are already among the more affluent workers. "Workers whose skills are not readily transferable" are more or less by definition skilled workers, who will generally earn more than unskilled workers. Public aid to skilled workers may tend to benefit individuals who are considerably better off than the neediest members of society.

Third, just as conventional economic wisdom suggests that other policy instruments may be preferable to protection as a solution for any labor or capital market imperfections, so too it suggests that the hardship of economic dislocation is better alleviated through tools other than restrictive trade policies. Retraining programs and public employment agencies, for example, can often reduce periods of unemployment and move workers quickly to alternative positions in which their services can be utilized efficiently. Special "adjustment assistance" programs already provide added relocation and retraining assistance to workers displaced by import competition in some countries.[8] Economists have long maintained that such programs can reduce the hardships of economic dislocation at lower cost to the economy than protectionist policies. Indeed, these programs not only avoid the distortion of consumer prices that accompanies protection, but they also encourage the prompt movement of resources to higher-valued uses. Protection, by contrast, delays the efficient reallocation of resources. See generally Trebilcock, Chandler and Howse (1990); Hufbauer and Rosen (1986).

Finally, trade protection is an exceptionally clumsy method of redistribution. It raises prices in the protected industry, rather than targeting aid

[8] The United States, for example, has an elaborate statutory scheme in place for the provision of adjustment assistance. See 19 USC paras 2271–98.

directly to particular, needy individuals. Many of the benefits will be captured by comparatively wealthy and perhaps well-diversified stockholders in the companies that receive protection, or by workers who would have retained their jobs in the absence of protection. Other methods of redistribution can provide aid in a fashion much more targeted toward needy individuals. For all of these reasons, the redistributive argument for safeguard measures has limited persuasive force as well.

C Safeguard Measures from a Political Economy Perspective

If the "conventional" normative arguments for safeguard measures are not terribly convincing, as argued in Section B, can one articulate other reasons why the WTO system permits safeguard measures to curb the expansion of trade? This section offers some possible answers grounded in the modern economics of public choice, or "political economy" in the parlance of trade economists.

The political economy accounts of safeguards fall into roughly three categories. The first is the notion that the availability of safeguard measures affords a domestic political "safety valve" for protectionist pressures, deflecting them into an administrative process that ultimately affords less protection than would be put in place by the legislature absent the safety valve. The second is the suggestion that safeguard measures facilitate deviation from trade commitments when the political pressure to do so is intense, and when nations would otherwise "cheat" on commitments anyway to the detriment of the trading system in the long run. The third suggestion is that safeguard measures may be useful because they reduce the risk of trade concessions under conditions of political uncertainty, and thereby facilitate more of them. As shall become clear, I am most persuaded by the third line of argument, although all three positions are worthy of consideration.

1 The Domestic Safety Valve Hypothesis

One of the early political economy arguments for safeguards policy, developed from a U.S. perspective, focuses on a possible difference between administrative protection and legislative protection. Section 201 of the U.S. Trade Act of 1974 allows injured industries to appeal for temporary protection to the U.S. ITC, an independent agency, and subsequently to the

President, if the ITC finds that the statutory injury requirements have been met. It thus affords an alternative to direct protectionist legislation by the U.S. Congress. Several writers have argued that the limited protection available through administrative action under Section 201 may be less trade-restrictive than the Congressional action that might emerge if the administrative route were unavailable. For example, Barton and Fisher (1986) suggest that safeguards "can serve as a safety valve in the formulation of trade policy in a democratic society by relieving pressures that might result in even more extreme solutions from Congress." This justification for safeguard measures is also considered at length in Lawrence and Litan (1986) and in Jackson (1997). One can imagine the argument also being advanced in other national settings where the safeguard mechanism is created as an administrative alternative to conventional legislative or parliamentary action.

The argument proceeds from the notion that safeguard measures are temporary, while legislated protection may be permanent, thus making the administrative option preferable from a policy standpoint. Further, administrative protection is only permitted after a fact-finding agency finds evidence to justify it, such as the facts required to satisfy the statutory injury test under U.S. law. By creating such an administrative route to protection, the argument runs, legislators can deflect protectionist pressures into the administrative process where the fact-finding process will limit the number of beneficiaries of protection and ensure that protection is temporary.

Whatever the merits of the safety valve hypothesis as a justification for an administrative route to protection in a domestic political system such as that of the United States, however it affords a questionable basis for safeguards in the WTO system. Article XIX and the Agreement on Safeguards allow WTO members to avoid their tariff bindings (and other WTO obligations) under specified circumstances. If the putative policy goal is to create obstacles to domestic interest groups seeking new or renewed protection, however, inescapable international commitments to eschew trade protection would seem helpful, which would themselves allow legislatures to "deflect" protectionist pressures by insisting that their hands were tied. By instead creating a "loophole" to international obligations limiting trade protection, Article XIX and the Agreement on Safeguards facilitate and encourage the pursuit of protection by import-competing interest groups.

Further, it is questionable whether the safety valve hypothesis is convincing even in a purely domestic context. Restated, the argument claims that the overall level of protection will fall if the government creates an administrative avenue for interest groups to obtain protection, even though the preexisting avenues for obtaining protection (direct legislation) have not been foreclosed. Yet, one must wonder why any interest group with the political muscle to obtain protection through the legislative route will settle for a lesser level of protection through the administrative route. It might be argued instead that the administrative route affords a device for some groups that lack the ability to mobilize the legislature to obtain protection anyway. The creation of a new administrative route to secure protection, without restricting the other legal devices for protection, seemingly lowers the costs of obtaining protection and might well increase the level of protection in the end. For these reasons, the core premise of the safety valve hypothesis—that safeguard measures diminish protection by channeling pressure away from greater legislative protection toward lesser administrative protection—seems unconvincing.

2 Safeguard Measures and "Cheating"

Bagwell and Staiger (1990, 2002, 2005) argue that the function of a safeguard mechanism in the WTO/GATT system is to legalize behavior that might otherwise count as "cheating" and cause the system to unravel. Rosendorff and Milner (2001) make a very similar argument, positing that an "escape clause" in a trade agreement is a device for permitting limited cheating on the agreement in the face of domestic political pressure to do so, while preserving the opportunity for long-term cooperation. I will focus here on the Bagwell/Staiger version of this argument. To explain it, some background on their general theory of trade agreements is required.

Bagwell and Staiger posit that trade agreements exist to address the external harms that national trade policy decisions impose on their trading partners. When a government intervenes in trade, as by imposing a tariff, trading partners will suffer to some extent as long as the importing nation is at all "large." Then, trade restrictions will lower the prices received by foreign exporters and harm them (recall the distinction between Figures 2.5 and 2.6 above). When "large" nations choose their trade policies without any cooperation over them (policy choices in "noncooperative" or "Cournot-Nash" equilibrium in economic parlance), they ignore this harm done to trading partners. The resulting policy equilibrium can be improved upon through trade agreements—Country A will be willing to modify its trade policies that harm exporters in country B, for example, in exchange for reciprocal promises by Country B to modify policies that harm country A's exporters.

Trade agreements require an enforcement mechanism, however, and no central authority exists to compel adherence to them. Instead, they must be "self-enforcing." That is, parties will adhere to them only to the degree that they fear losing the benefits of the agreement if they cheat and other parties retaliate. One well-known retaliatory strategy for sustaining cooperation over time is known to game theorists as the grim strategy—if a party cheats, other parties discontinue cooperation and revert to the behavior that they find desirable in the absence of cooperation. In a repeated interaction of indefinite duration, such a strategy can support cooperation over time as long as the parties to the agreement are adequately "patient" (have low enough discount rates regarding the future) and thus value the future gains from cooperation more than the short-term gains from cheating. See, for example, Rasmussen (2001).

Bagwell and Staiger suggest that trade agreements operate in this fashion. Parties to trade agreements move as far as they can toward maximizing their mutual welfare, subject to the constraint that the agreement remain self-enforcing. Cooperation is sustained by a mutual threat to revert to Cournot-Nash behavior, sacrificing the gains from cooperation in the future should cheating be detected in the present.

A temptation to "cheat" arises in their framework because nations are "large." By raising tariffs above agreed levels, importing nations can extract economic surplus from foreign exporters. The degree to which surplus can be extracted depends, among other things, on the volume of trade with particular exporters. The more that exporters sell to an importing country, the more the importing country can extract from them by raising tariffs above agreed levels.

A role for safeguard measures arises in this framework if there are temporary shocks to trade flows. Consider a change in economic conditions that causes a surge in imports. As import volume increases, the gains from cheating increase for the importing nation because a higher tariff will yield more revenue and more surplus extracted from foreign exporters. The prospect of a breakdown in cooperation in the future may no longer suffice to deter cheating, and as a result cheating may occur, and parties may invoke the grim strategy. To avert this prospect, it may be in the interest of the parties to a trade agreement to permit temporary deviation from tariff commitments in response to temporary import shocks. The role of a safeguard clause in the agreement is essentially to define what would otherwise be "cheating" as a permissible deviation, thereby allowing temporary responses to import surges while preserving the long-term benefits of cooperation once the shock abates.

Bagwell and Staiger write from a positive perspective, but their analysis has normative implications as well. Their theory suggests that trade agreements would eventually collapse due to cheating and retaliation following short-term import surges without a safeguard mechanism in place. It is essential in their framework for nations to be able to deviate temporarily from commitments if long-term cooperation, and the benefits of freer trade associated with it, are to be realized.

Although Bagwell and Staiger's account of safeguards is clever and rigorous, it too seems to have some difficulties explaining the structure of safeguard rules in practice. First, nothing in their theory makes the condition of the import-competing industry relevant to the use of safeguard measures—only a sufficient increase in imports would seem to be required for the temptation to "cheat" to arise. Yet, as Chapter 1 indicated and as subsequent chapters address further, the requirement of injury to an import-competing industry is central to the prerequisites for safeguards under WTO law.

Second, and related, their theory suggests that temporary safeguard measures are a sensible response to temporary import surges. In practice, however, safeguard measures are often used to afford temporary protection to industries that are in permanent decline, where there is no reason to suppose that the increase in imports is "temporary."

Third, their analysis suggests that a temptation to cheat arises when import volumes surge, so that higher tariffs can extract more surplus from foreign exporters. Yet, in practice, safeguard measures are permissible when imports are declining as long as their market share is rising.

Fourth, the history of trade protection for declining industries is replete with instances in which nations confronted with import surges employed unauctioned quantitative restrictions as protective measures. Indeed, grey-area measures typically had this characteristic. Such measures generally confer the rents from protection (quota rents) on foreign exporters. If the motivation for protection was to exploit the enhanced possibilities for terms of trade gains created by an import surge, however, policies that confer those gains on foreigners do not seem sensible. History suggests, therefore, that protection for declining industries is often motivated by a desire to protect them *per se*, and not by the collateral terms of trade gains that appropriate tariff increases (or auctioned quotas) might realize.

Finally, it is not clear that safeguards are needed to address the problem of "cheating" in a system with a well-functioning dispute resolution system and calibrated retaliation such as that of the WTO. In such a system, "cheating" is policed directly by the retaliation process, which also provides an alternative to the grim strategy and prevents the agreement from unraveling when one party cheats on a modest scale. For these reasons, I question whether Bagwell and Staiger offer a fully persuasive account of safeguard measures under WTO law.

3 The Contractarian Perspective: *Ex Ante* vs. *Ex Post* Protection

In his seminal early work on GATT, Kenneth Dam suggests almost in passing that "the presence of [Article XIX] encourages cautious countries to enter into a greater number of tariff bindings than would otherwise be the case."[9] In other words, Dam suggests that the opportunity to impose safeguard measures *ex post* leads to more trade concessions *ex ante*. This suggests the kernel of both a positive explanation and a normative justification for safeguard measures, which is developed at length in Sykes (1991), building on Hillman (1982) and Baldwin (1982). The analysis draws heavily on economic learning about the design of optimal contracts, and thus may be termed a "contractarian perspective" on safeguards. See Srinivasan (2005). It also draws on the modern public choice literature and its analysis of rent-seeking behavior by special interest groups.

(a) Some Preliminaries: Basic Lessons from Public Choice Theory

A substantial literature now exists on the political economy of trade policy, particularly in democracies. The theory of public choice suggests that policymaking under democratic government depends on the interplay of special interest forces in the political "marketplace." Buchanan and Tullock (1962): Olson (1965). There is little reason to expect the democratic process systematically to yield "efficient," "equitable," or otherwise "correct" outcomes by any idealized criterion for measuring the success of policy. Rather, elected officials will pursue their political self interest. They will "supply" policy initiatives to interest groups that "demand" them, with the currency of the political marketplace in the form of votes, campaign contributions, and the like. Ultimately, well-organized groups—those most adept at lobbying and most capable of "paying" for policy initiatives—will have their interests vindicated, while diffuse, poorly organized interest groups will not see their interests served very effectively.

[9] Dam (1970) at p. 99.

For this reason, elected officials are likely to concern themselves more with the impact of trade policy on producer interests than on consumer interests. Individual firms in import-competing or export-oriented industries often have much to gain from specific trade policy measures. They will often find it in their interest individually or collectively through trade associations to lobby for favorable trade initiatives. In contrast, the number of consumers in many industries is large and the amount at stake for each consumer on a given trade issue is often quite small. The costs to each consumer of acting individually in an effort to influence the political process will often exceed the potential gains. The task of organizing consumers to act collectively through some form of association will also often be greater than any potential organizer is willing to pay. In the end, trade policy decisions will tend to be dominated by producer interest groups.

This proposition does not imply, however, that protectionist interests will always triumph, because certain powerful producer lobbies have an interest in an open trading system. Downstream industries that use imported input products, for example, benefit directly from reduced protection with respect to those inputs. Exporting industries can also benefit considerably from reduced protection at home if that reduction is coupled with reciprocal trade concessions in foreign markets to which they export.[10] Large multinational companies also often prefer a liberal trading regime, as they frequently import from and export to foreign affiliates. These interest groups favoring more open trade will align themselves against the import-competing producer groups who favor trade protection. The intensity of producer interests on each side—free trade and protectionist—will determine the policy outcome.

This line of analysis immediately suggests why trade agreements systematically *liberalize* trade rather than restrict it. When nations set policy on their own, export interests have a somewhat limited stake in opposing trade protection—they worry about it only to the degree that they fear foreign retaliation against their exports, or currency appreciation that would render them less competitive. These effects are diffused across all export industries, and they may well fail to organize in a manner that allows them to weigh in effectively against protectionist initiatives in one or a few industries. When

[10] In fact, exporters can gain from trade liberalization even without reciprocal concessions. Reduced protection for the home market will increase the demand for imports and thus for the foreign currency necessary to buy them. The home-market currency will then depreciate relative to foreign currencies, with the result that home-market exports become more competitive in world markets.

nations negotiate over trade policy, by contrast, exporter interest groups see an opportunity for their governments to pursue specific trade concessions that would benefit their industry by securing better access to foreign markets. Export interest groups thus participate more extensively and effectively when trade negotiations arise, and their presence pushes the political equilibrium toward greater liberalization.

The intensity of protectionist pressure from import-competing interest groups is also variable. Indeed, conventional wisdom holds that the intensity with which producer interests lobby for protection increases as their financial condition worsens. Casual empiricism offers many bits of confirming evidence. The great increase in protectionism in the 1930s, initiated by the Smoot-Hawley Tariff act of 1930 in the United States, followed the beginning of the Great Depression. In more modern times, the most protected industries seem to be the ones that have the greatest difficulties competing in international markets—industries that are declining over time and that can credibly claim that protection is necessary to their survival. Clear examples in the United States include the carbon steel, footwear, and textile and apparel industries.

There are several reasons why declining industries will often represent the best organized and most effective lobbies for protection. First, political officials may be more willing to support protection for an industry facing severe difficulties when they can justify it to their constituents by appealing to the hardship faced by dislocated workers. Producer interest groups, aware of this fact, will increase their lobbying efforts as the likelihood of success increases. Second, when an industry confronts financial difficulties, the returns from productive activity within the industry may decline relative to the returns from lobbying for protection, causing a reallocation of resources toward lobbying. See Magee and Young (1987). A third possible explanation is that the value of protection to an industry is greater when times are hard. In a prosperous industry, an increase in prices attributable to protection may attract further entry into the industry by new firms, and the gains may be competed away as a result to a large extent. In a declining industry, by contrast, the rate of return to new investment in the industry will typically be below the competitive return that investors require before they will make new investments. An increase in price due to protection can then increase the rate of return without attracting new entrants into the industry who would compete away the gains. Hillman (1982). Consequently, industries that obtain protection can retain the gains for a longer period of time (until their physical capital depreciates), and will invest more to secure protection.

(b) Positive Implications

Sykes (1991) combines these lessons from the public choice literature with the literature on optimal contracting to develop a formal model that suggests a role for safeguard measures in trade agreements. The central results of the model have ready intuitive explanations. The analysis begins with the premise that political officials in each country seek to maximize their political welfare. They enter into trade negotiations for the purpose of exchanging trade concessions that make them mutually better off—to achieve a political Pareto improvement in the language of economics. The notion that optimal agreements achieve the Pareto frontier for the parties to them is a familiar one in the optimal contracting literature. See Shavell (1980). Roughly speaking, negotiators on each side will agree to reciprocal concessions as long as the political support that they lose from their domestic import-competing industries is smaller than the political support that they gain from their domestic exporting industries. They will also agree to additional legal terms that yield "net" political benefits, in the sense that the value to one party exceeds the cost to another in a political sense.[11]

The negotiating process is complicated by the fact that the future is uncertain. Negotiators cannot perfectly forecast the effects of trade concessions, and may face the possibility of economic shocks that render concessions more or less burdensome politically than anticipated. What is the best response to such uncertainty? One option would be to make all concessions irrevocable nevertheless, and then to agree to all reciprocal concessions that have positive *expected* value. Sykes (1991) shows, however, that the negotiators can do better than that by including a safeguard clause in their agreement.

Intuitively, the safeguard clause permits political officials to "take back" concessions that prove unduly burdensome from a political standpoint after uncertainty resolves. It is similar in its function to *force majeure* clauses in ordinary contracts, or to other contractual provisions that excuse performance when it becomes excessively costly. It is well-known in the contracts literature that when the cost of performance to one party exceeds the benefits

[11] More formally, one can model the optimal contracting problem as one in which the utility of one negotiator is maximized subject to the constraint that the utility of all others achieves some fixed value. The solution to this formal problem will define points on the parties' Pareto frontier. For any such point, a "shadow price" exists that allows the units of utility for each negotiator to be converted into the same units for purposes of comparison. Optimal contract terms have the property that their net impact on the utility of all negotiators, summed across all parties using the appropriate shadow prices for each of them, is positive.

of performance to the other, it is in their mutual interest to agree that performance is excused. This situation is sometimes termed "efficient breach," although if the bargain expressly provides for it then no "breach" actually occurs.

In what states of the world will trade negotiators agree to allow the safeguard clause to be invoked (when is breach "efficient")? Here, we circle back to the public choice literature, which suggests that declining industries suffering substantial dislocation will often lobby the hardest for trade protection. For such import-competing industries, domestic political officials will be under particularly acute pressure to intervene in trade. The observation that such industries will work hard to secure protection, however, does not suffice to establish that deviation from agreed concessions is efficient, because the effects on officials in exporting countries must also be taken into account. Accordingly, when will the revocation of concessions impose comparatively modest political costs abroad, so that the gains to officials in the importing country can "outweigh" the losses to officials in the exporting country? The public choice analysis suggests a possible answer here as well—*prosperous* exporting industries may tend to produce less political outcry following renewed protection because they can weather it without serious dislocation themselves, and because they may anticipate that their period of prosperity will be temporary anyway due to the prospect of competitive entry. Putting these observations together, the implication is that a safeguard clause will allow concessions to be revoked when the import-competing industry is suffering severe dislocation, and when the exporting industry that would be harmed by revocation is prosperous.

The reader will perhaps note a parallel between the analysis here and the essential contours of GATT Article XIX. Article XIX permits parties to revoke concessions when the a trade concession unexpectedly results in "serious injury" or threat thereof to an import-competing industry, but only in the presence of "such increased quantities" of imports as to be causally responsible for that injury. Putting aside the meaning of causation for now, safeguard measures are allowed when the import-competing industry is suffering serious dislocation, and when the exporting industry has expanded its sales considerably. The expansion of sales by exporters is likely to be positively correlated to some, perhaps considerable, degree with their prosperity. Thus, one might argue, Article XIX allows a safeguard measure when, roughly, the import-competing industry is doing unexpectedly badly, and the exporting industry is doing unexpectedly well, much as the theory suggests.

The mapping between the theory and Article XIX is not perfect, however, to be sure. For example, this account of safeguards has some difficulty explaining why an increase in the market share of imports, without any absolute increase in imports, should be sufficient for a safeguard action.

One must also concede that this line of argument rests on an empirical conjecture regarding the political benefits of protection for declining industries in importing nations versus the political costs of that protection abroad. Grossman and Mavroidis (2005) express some skepticism regarding this conjecture, noting that export industries may have quasi-fixed factors of production that earn rents over an extended period of time (for example, owners of prime farm land may capture substantial rents from farm exports that are not eroded by competitive entry because comparable farm land is unavailable). They are surely right that some export industries have such quasi-fixed factors of production and that, other things being equal, those industries will offer greater political objection to the advent of any new protection abroad. Likewise, it is certainly possible in a given instance that the political costs to officials in exporting nations from a safeguard measure may "outweigh" the political benefit to officials in the importing nation for this reason, and that even a measure satisfying the terms of Article XIX may be politically "inefficient."

The possibility that Article XIX may not produce politically "efficient" results in all cases does not, in my view, detract fatally from the contractarian explanation for it. Article XIX is admittedly a crude device for promoting joint political welfare due to the costs of writing and enforcing a more sophisticated bargain. The question is not whether it functions perfectly, but whether it can yield net political benefits on average to the trading community. For the reasons given above, the political benefits to protecting industries suffering serious dislocation from intensified import competition are often great, and the attendant political costs abroad are plausibly more modest on average. This account of the function of safeguard measures stands alone among political economy explanations, in my view, in offering a rationale both for the presence of safeguard measures in the WTO/GATT bargain, and for the basic structure of Article XIX that requires both increased import competition and *serious injury* or threat to an import-competing industry.

Two further remarks are in order. First, the optimal contracting literature suggests that renegotiation of the bargain is an alternative mechanism for dealing with situations in which the benefits of performance have changed, and "efficient breach" may be desired. Why not simply let a party suffering from an unexpectedly burdensome commitment renegotiate at that time to "buy" their way out from under it? The primary difficulty with renegotiation as an alternative to a safeguard clause in an agreement like GATT is the "hold-up problem." GATT has always had many signatories (now approaching 150), and if a party wishing to revoke a concession had to secure the advance permission of every other party affected by it, a difficult negotiation could result. Parties would posture and "hold out" for more "compensation" before agreeing to allow the concession to be revoked, and the negotiation could drag on for a long time. The safeguard rules in Article XIX have always allowed GATT signatories to take a safeguard measure without securing advance permission if necessary. Indeed, GATT Article XXVIII (the basic renegotiation article) is similar in this regard.

Second, safeguard measures under GATT are supposed to be *temporary*. Yet, the conditions that produce severe dislocation in an import-competing industry need not be and, as noted previously, safeguard measures have regularly been used to protect industries suffering from long-term competitive decline. Why, then, are safeguard measures limited in duration? One answer is that when nations wish to revoke a concession permanently, the GATT provides another avenue—Article XXVIII. Nations can choose that route when permanent modifications in the bargain are desirable. In addition, even when an industry is suffering long-term decline, the demand for protection need not persist. If protection is limited so that it does not raise prices to the point of attracting new investment in the protected industry, the declining industry will naturally contract as its physical and human capital depreciates. Temporary protection, perhaps phased down as the industry contracts, can address the most acute political pressure for protection without creating new constituents for it.

The theory of safeguards developed here has a variety of additional implications for the structure and operation of a safeguard mechanism, including implications for the rules of compensation and retaliation, and for the analysis of causation in safeguard cases. These will be considered in later chapters.

(c) Normative Implications

The contractarian perspective on safeguards adds an interesting normative twist, which relates back to the suggestion by Kenneth Dam that a safeguard mechanism facilitates trade concessions. A formal demonstration of the points to follow may be found in Sykes (1991), but again the key points are quite intuitive.

Suppose that the function of a safeguard mechanism is indeed to permit political officials to "take back" concessions that prove unduly burdensome politically, at least when the political costs to trading partners are more modest. How does that affect their willingness to make trade concessions in the first instance? Clearly, the opportunity to avoid a concession when it proves exceptionally burdensome reduces the riskiness of making concessions. Trade officials can go ahead and agree to them, knowing that if an adverse shock occurs they can be withdrawn. From the perspective of a party *making* a concession, therefore, a safeguard mechanism makes it more attractive and should increase that party's willingness to agree to the concession.

Of course, the prospect that a concession may be revoked is unfortunate from the perspective of the party *receiving* the concession. Once this issue is taken into account, can we be sure that a safeguard mechanism facilitates concessions? Might it reduce their value to the beneficiary more than it increases their value to the party making the concession, and actually reduce the value of trade agreements?

The answer is no, *if* the safeguard mechanism is properly designed. As long as the safeguard mechanism permits the revocation of concessions only when revocation is "efficient," all parties will benefit from it, and will be more willing to make concessions. The reason is that each party to a trade agreement both makes and receives concessions. If each knows that they can revoke burdensome concessions as long as revocation imposes only modest costs on trading partners (it is "efficient"), both will be better off than they would be if concessions were irrevocable. Likewise, to the extent that some pairs of reciprocal concessions would be unattractive under a rule of irrevocability because they would have negative expected value to negotiating officials, a safeguard mechanism can tip the balance and give the concessions positive expected value.

In short, Kenneth Dam was essentially right. A properly designed safeguard mechanism, which limits safeguard measures to cases where they are politically efficient, will make reciprocal trade concessions more attractive to all parties. As a result, more trade concessions will be made, and the result will be greater trade liberalization *ex ante*. This observation suggests an important normative justification for safeguard measures.

Two related considerations cut in the other direction, however, so that the normative case for safeguards in this framework becomes an uneasy one. First, although a safeguard mechanism may result in greater trade liberalization *ex ante*, it obviously also produces additional trade protection *ex post*.

The net effect on the level of protection and openness of trade over trade is not obvious as a theoretical matter. It is also difficult to assess as an empirical matter, since we cannot know exactly what concessions would have been foregone *ex ante* in the absence of a safeguard mechanism.

Second, as implied by the above discussion, the safeguard mechanism is only useful for facilitating concessions if it limits safeguard measures to cases where they are politically efficient. Even if it is intended to do so, it can be abused. And if parties employ safeguard measures opportunistically, the *ex ante* value of reciprocal concessions can be reduced rather than enhanced. If safeguards are to serve the purpose of facilitating concessions, therefore, it is important that parties to trade agreements anticipate their use only under appropriate circumstances. To this end, agreements must be written in a fashion that allows safeguard measures only in proper circumstances. As subsequent chapters will suggest, neither Article XIX nor the Agreement on Safeguards appear to accomplish this objective very well, and the decisions by WTO dispute panels and the Appellate Body do little to improve on matters. Before returning to these issues, however, some background on the WTO dispute resolution process is in order.

Chapter 3

PRELIMINARY ISSUES IN WTO SAFEGUARDS DISPUTES: BURDEN OF PROOF, STANDARD OF REVIEW, AND THE "RECORD"

Like all legal systems, the WTO dispute resolution system must confront a number of procedural issues, as well as quasi-procedural questions such as what standard of review to apply in deciding whether the decisions of national authorities comply with WTO law. A complete discussion of these issues is beyond the scope of this book, but it is useful to address a few important principles that routinely have an impact on WTO safeguards disputes.

A The Burden of Proof

Legal systems commonly place the "burden of proof" on the party that puts forward a claim. The burden of proof is conceptually important in close cases—if the adjudicator finds the evidence on both sides in equipoise, the party with the burden of proof will lose. Further, the burden of proof is frequently coupled with a burden to come forward with evidence, sometimes known as a burden of production. Unless the party putting forward a claim also produces evidence to support it, the responding party may say nothing and still prevail.

If the burden of proof initially rests with the complaining party, the respondent may nevertheless bear a burden of proof with respect to certain issues. Legal systems frequently afford certain "affirmative defenses" to the violation of certain obligations, and the responding party often bears the burden of proof as to any affirmative defense.

The GATT system embraced this general approach long ago, and placed the initial burden of proof on the party that alleges a violation of GATT obligations. If that party carried its initial burden, it made out its *prima facie* case, forcing the responding party to afford an effective rebuttal of some element(s) of the *prima facie* case, or else to invoke an applicable exception to the GATT obligation in question. When the responding party relied on an exception to defend behavior that was otherwise a violation, it was viewed as relying in effect on an affirmative defense, as to which it had the burden of proof.

For example, a complaining party might have alleged that a GATT member's domestic tax legislation discriminated between like domestic and imported goods in violation of the GATT national treatment obligation. If the complaining party presented evidence of such discrimination, the *prima facie* case was established. The respondent party could rebut the *prima facie* case by showing that prohibited discrimination did not, in fact, occur, or could invoke an exception to the national treatment obligation such as one contained in GATT Article XX. If the responding party relied on such an exception, it would have the burden of proof in showing that the exception was applicable.

This basic approach under GATT has carried over into the WTO generally, and into safeguards disputes in particular. In the first safeguard dispute to reach the panel stage of WTO dispute resolution, *Korea—Dairy*, the panel noted that the burden of proof rests with the complaining party. The complaining party establishes a *prima facie* case by offering evidence sufficient for the panel to conclude that pertinent provisions of GATT or the Agreement on Safeguards have been violated. A "*prima facie* case is one which, in the absence of effective refutation by the defending party, requires a panel, as a matter of law, to rule in favour of the complaining party presenting the *prima facie* case."[1] The Appellate Body later concurred that the burden of proof rests with the complaining party, and added that complaining parties must make their own

[1] Korea—Definitive Safeguard Measures on Imports of Certain Dairy Products, WT/DS98/R, para 7.24 (hereafter Korea—Dairy Panel).

case—a panel cannot do it for them by relying on legal theories or evidence that the complaining party did not put forward.[2]

These rulings imply that the obligations contained in GATT Article XIX and in the Agreement on Safeguards are primary WTO obligations, not exceptions to them. It is for this reason that the complaining member has the burden of proof. One can imagine that things might have evolved differently—it could be argued, for example, that the primary obligations are those contained in GATT Articles II and XI restricting the use of tariffs and quotas, and that safeguard measures are an allowed "exception" to those primary obligations more in the nature of an affirmative defense. An argument to that effect does not seem to have surfaced in the disputes to date, however, and it seems settled that the initial burden of proof rests with the complaining party on the issues that have thus far arisen under Article XIX and the Agreement on Safeguards.[3]

B The Standard of Review at the Panel Stage: What Degree of Deference to National Authorities?

Like certain other trade measures within the WTO system (such as anti-dumping duties), safeguard measures may be employed only after an investigation by national authorities determines that the prerequisites for safeguard measures under WTO law have been met. If another WTO member challenges a safeguard measure, it in effect alleges that the findings of the national authorities in their investigation are mistaken or in some other way inadequate to meet the requirements of WTO law. What weight or deference should a WTO dispute panel give to the findings of national authorities in deciding such cases? This question may be rephrased as asking

[2] Korea—Definitive Safeguard Measures on Imports of Certain Dairy Products, WT/D598/AB/R, paras 146–49 (hereafter Korea—Dairy AB).

[3] The panel report in United States—Steel does contain some language suggesting that the burden of proof may "shift" to the responding nation on certain issues after a *prima facie* case has been made by the complaining party. In particular, it suggests that once a case has been made that the substantive prerequisites for a safeguard measure under Article 4.2 of the Agreement on Safeguards have not been met, a presumption arises that the measure is broader than permissible under Article 5.1, shifting the burden of proof to the respondent nation under Article 5.1. United States—Definitive Safeguard Measures on Imports of Certain Steel Products, WT/DS248–49, 251–54, 258–59/R, para 10.29 (hereafter United States—Steel Panel). This proposition seems no more than a statement that once the *prima facie* case is made out, the respondent nation has a burden to rebut it, a burden that applies to all of the issues for which a *prima facie* case of violation has been made, including those as to which a presumption of violation arises based on a violation of a related provision.

what is the appropriate "standard of review" for panels to employ in assessing the soundness of findings by national authorities.

In establishing a standard of review, many legal systems treat legal findings and factual findings differently. Higher courts commonly afford little deference to the interpretation of the law by lower courts and administrative bodies, but often afford considerable deference to their findings on factual questions that they have directly investigated. The findings of national authorities in safeguard investigations can have both of these components. National authorities may expressly or implicitly interpret WTO law in reaching a conclusion that the requirements for safeguard measures have been met. They will also reach conclusions that are more "factual" in nature, such as a conclusion that a domestic injury is suffering "serious injury."

Perhaps unfortunately, WTO treaty text says remarkably little about the appropriate standard of review. The one notable exception is found in Article 17.5 of the WTO Antidumping Agreement, which provides that a panel must determine whether the national authorities' "establishment of the facts was proper and whether their evaluation of those facts was unbiased and objective." If these conditions are met, the panel must accept the factual determination even if the panel "might have reached a different conclusion." On issues of WTO law, Article 17.5 makes clear that national authorities must follow WTO law, properly interpreted. But when the Antidumping Agreement is subject to more than one "permissible interpretation," the decisions of national authorities shall be deemed in conformity with WTO law if they have embraced one of the permissible interpretations. The latter principle is somewhat akin to a principle of U.S. administrative law known as *Chevron* deference, which holds that (in some cases) an administrative agency's interpretation of a statute within its enforcement jurisdiction must be accepted by a reviewing court if it is a reasonable one.[4]

These principles in the Antidumping Agreement raise a host of interpretive questions, but their omission from other WTO agreements has led both panels and the Appellate Body to infer that the standard of review under other agreements is not necessarily the same. In articulating an alternative, the only treaty text of much relevance is Article 11 of the WTO Dispute Settlement Understanding (DSU), which states that "a panel should make an objective assessment of the matter before it, including an objective assessment

[4] Croley and Jackson (1996) offer a thoughtful and skeptical assessment of whether the *Chevron* principle is suitable for the resolution of cases under WTO law.

of the facts of the case and the applicability of and conformity with the relevant covered agreements."

The term "objective assessment" is hardly clear on its face and admits of varying interpretations. One reading might simply be that a panel is required to be unbiased, and that the concept of "objective assessment" says little about the standard of review. The Appellate Body held otherwise, however, in *EC—Hormones*, an early dispute under the WTO Agreement on Sanitary and Phytosanitary Measures. It stated that Article 11 provides the standard of review for cases other than those arising under the Antidumping Agreement. With regard to factual issues, an "objective assessment" is not equivalent to *de novo* review in the view of the Appellate Body—that is, the panel is not to reopen all of the factual issues raised by the case and make its own judgment. But "total deference" to the findings of national authorities is not appropriate either. The proper inquiry is somewhere in between, exactly where being somewhat unclear. On legal issues, the Appellate Body said only that panels should apply the customary rules of interpretation of public international law.[5] By implication, however, the panel owes little or no deference to the construction of WTO law adopted by national authorities (outside of the antidumping area). Panels should instead draw their own conclusions about the meaning of applicable treaty text using the customary rules of interpretation.

In the first safeguard case to proceed to a panel, *Korea—Dairy*, the panel followed *EC—Hormones*, and interpreted the standard of review as requiring it to determine "whether the [national authority] had examined all facts in its possession or which it should have obtained . . . and whether adequate explanation had been provided of how the facts as a whole supported the determination made."[6] In *Argentina—Footwear*, the panel elaborated the standard somewhat further, with particular reference to the question whether Argentina had established a proper linkage between increased imports and serious injury pursuant to Article 4.2 of the Agreement on Safeguards. The panel held that its task was essentially two-fold—to determine "whether the domestic authority has considered all relevant facts, including an examination of each factor listed in Article 4.2(a)," and "whether the published report on the investigation contains adequate explanation of how the facts support the determination made."[7]

On appeal, Argentina argued that the panel had given too little deference to the findings of national authorities under this standard. But the Appellate

[5] EC Measures Concerning Meat and Meat Products (Hormones), WT/DS26/AB/R, paras 116–19.

[6] Korea—Dairy Panel para 7.30.

[7] Argentina—Safeguard Measures on Imports of Footwear, WT/DS121/R, para 8.124 (hereafter Argentina—Footwear Panel).

Body agreed with the panel that it was proper to insist that the national authorities consider all relevant facts, including all those enumerated by the treaty text, and further to insist on "a reasoned explanation of how the facts supported their determination."[8]

This two-fold standard has come to prevail with regard to many issues in safeguard disputes. In *United States—Lamb*, the Appellate Body described it as having both a formal aspect and a substantive aspect. "The formal aspect is whether the competent authorities have evaluated 'all relevant factors.' The substantive aspect is whether the competent authorities have given a reasoned and adequate explanation for their determination."[9]

Both aspects raise some difficult questions. As to the first, how does one determine whether the national authority has "considered all the relevant facts"? It is easy enough to check whether the published report of the national authorities recites information pertinent to each factor enumerated in the treaty text. Is that sufficient to establish that each fact was properly "considered?" And what of other potentially "relevant facts" not enumerated in the treaty text—how does one identify them, and ascertain whether they have been properly considered? If a fact is not put in issue by a party to the investigation by national authorities, can it later be raised before the WTO as a "relevant fact" that was not "considered"?

In *United States—Lamb*, the most extensive treatment of the standard of review to date by the Appellate Body, some of these issues were addressed. *Lamb* stated that the inquiry into whether the authorities have considered all relevant factors is "not simply a matter of form, and the list of relevant factors to be evaluated is not a mere 'check list'... competent authorities must conduct a substantive evaluation of the 'bearing'... that the relevant factors have on the 'situation of the domestic industry.'"[10] Thus a mere recitation that a factor has been considered is not enough. Some greater degree of substantive evaluation must be evident, but exactly what?

Lamb also addressed the question of whether parties to WTO disputes could raise issues and arguments that were not made before the national authorities. I will say more about this issue in the next section, concerning the "record on review" and related issues.

The second aspect of the standard of review raises other hard questions. The panel is not to engage in *de novo* review, says the Appellate Body, yet it

[8] Argentina—Safeguard Measures on Imports of Footwear, WT/DS121/AB/R, para 121 (hereafter Argentina—Footwear AB).

[9] United States—Safeguard Measures on Imports of Fresh, Chilled or Frozen Lamb Meat from New Zealand and Australia, WT/DS 177&178/AB/R, para 103 (hereafter United States—Lamb AB).

[10] Id. para 104.

is to insist on a "reasoned explanation of how the facts supported [the] determination." What, exactly, is the difference? Clearly, the absence of *de novo* review precludes the panel from embarking on its own fact-finding mission to gather new evidence not before the national authorities. But in deciding whether the national authorities have provided a "reasoned explanation," is the panel not in effect deciding whether it finds the analysis of the national authorities persuasive?[11] If so, does that not amount to the panel "substituting its own judgment" for the judgment of national authorities in a fashion akin to *de novo* review? Or is the question for a panel instead something like whether "reasonable people" could possibly draw the conclusions put forth by national authorities, even if the panel disagrees with them?

The Appellate Body opinion in *United States—Lamb* also addressed these issues to a degree:

> We wish to emphasize that, although panels are not entitled to conduct a *de novo* review of the evidence, nor to *substitute* their own conclusions for those of the competent authorities, this does *not* mean that panels must simply *accept* the conclusions of the competent authorities. To the contrary, in our view, in examining a claim under Article 4.2(a), a panel can assess whether the competent authorities' explanation for its determination is reasoned and adequate *only* if the panel critically examines that explanation, in depth, and in the light of the facts before the panel. Panels must, therefore, review whether the competent authorities' explanation fully addresses the nature, and, especially, the complexities, of the data, and responds to other plausible interpretations of that data. A panel must find, in particular, that an explanation is not reasoned, or is not adequate, if some *alternative explanation* of the facts is plausible, and if the competent authorities' explanation does not seem adequate in the light of that alternative explanation. Thus, in making an "objective assessment" of a claim under Article 4.2(a), panels must be open to the possibility that the explanation given by the competent authorities is not reasoned or adequate.
>
> In this respect, the phrase "*de novo* review" should not be used loosely. If a panel concludes that the competent authorities, in a particular case, have *not* provided a reasoned or adequate explanation for their determination, that panel has not, thereby, engaged in a *de novo* review. Nor has that panel substituted its own conclusions for those of the competent authorities. Rather, the panel has, consistent with its obligations under the DSU, simply reached a conclusion that the determination made by the competent authorities is inconsistent with the specific requirements of Article 4.2 of the *Agreement on Safeguards*.[12]

[11] For further discussion of such issues, see Osech (2003).
[12] United States—Lamb AB paras 106–07.

The Appellate Body thus leaves panels considerable room to reject the reasoning of national authorities, on grounds that they have not "fully addressed the nature and complexities of the data," or that their explanation does not "seem adequate" in light of some possible alternative explanation. Subsequent chapters will make clear that the "reasoned and adequate explanation" requirement under the standard of review, as articulated in *Lamb*, has been used rather aggressively by panels to strike down findings by national authorities that the panels find less than fully convincing.

One recent decision outside of the safeguards area, however, found that a panel went beyond its mandate and came too close to an exercise in *de novo* review. In *United States—DRAMs*, a case under the Agreement on Subsidies and Countervailing Measures, the Appellate Body reversed a panel that had rejected a finding of subsidization by the U.S. Department of Commerce. It found that the panel had demanded too much of the individual pieces of evidence in the case, rather than looking at all the circumstantial evidence in its "entirety" as had the Commerce Department. The panel likewise refused to consider certain evidence in the agency record without a legal basis for excluding it, and incorrectly faulted the Commerce Department for being unaware of certain facts outside the agency record. As a consequence, "the Panel went beyond its role as the reviewer of the investigating authority's decision and, instead, conducted its own assessment, relying on its own judgement, of much of the evidence."[13] Although *Lamb* opens the door to aggressive scrutiny of the reasoning advanced by national authorities, *DRAMs* suggests that there are some limits to it, particularly if a panel errs in defining the "record" for its review, the subject of the section C.[14]

One final issue warrants brief mention. In *United States—Steel*, the United States argued that the standard of review for issues that arise under GATT Article XIX, such as the compliance of the responding nation with the "unforeseen developments" requirement of Article XIX(1)(a), is different from the standard applicable to issues arising under the Agreement on Safeguards. The Appellate Body squarely rejected that suggestion, holding that the standard was the same—a "reasoned and adequate explanation" was required in support of findings by national authorities under Article XIX as well.[15]

[13] United States—Countervailing Duty Investigation on Dynamic Random Access Semiconductors (DRAMS) from Korea, WT/DS296/AB/R, paras 180–90 (hereafter United States—DRAMS AB).

[14] For further discussion of the DRAMs case, see Becroft (2005).

[15] United States—Definitive Safeguard Measures on Imports of Certain Steel Products, WT/DS 248–49, 251–54, 258–59/AB/R, paras 273–80 (hereafter United States—Steel AB).

C The "Record" on Review and Related Issues

In determining whether national authorities have considered "all relevant factors," and whether they have provided a "reasoned and adequate explanation" for their findings, a question arises as to what body of materials a panel should consult to answer these questions—what makes up the "record" of the national investigation. A related question arises as to whether issues or evidence may be raised before a panel that were not clearly raised before the national authorities during their safeguards investigation.

Regarding the record, Article 3.1 of the Agreement on Safeguards requires an investigation by the "competent authorities" of WTO members prior to their use of safeguard measures. Further, "[t]he competent authorities shall publish a report setting forth their findings and reasoned conclusions reached on all pertinent issues of law and fact." Panels and the Appellate Body consistently look to this "published report" to provide evidence that the competent authorities have considered the relevant factors, and provided a reasoned and adequate explanation of their findings. In the first two safeguard disputes to proceed to a panel, *Korea—Dairy* and *Argentina—Footwear*, there was some wrangling over what constituted the published report of the competent authorities. In both instances the panel took account of certain documents that could be said to have been part of the basis for the deliberations of the competent authorities, and that had been submitted by the responding nation in the dispute. Going forward, however, there should generally be little dispute over what constitutes the "published report" as long as national authorities in the nations that employ safeguard measures take seriously their publication obligation and include everything on which their determination relies in what they deem to be the "published report."

Occasionally, however, national authorities may wish to supplement their initial "published report" when it subsequently appears deficient in some way. In *United States—Steel*, the original report by the U.S. ITC did not address the question of "unforeseen developments" under Article XIX(1)(a). Anticipating that this issue would arise before a WTO panel, the U.S. government asked the ITC to prepare a supplemental report assessing the existence of unforeseen developments. The complainants argued that the supplemental report should not be considered by the panel, but the panel was willing to assume "*arguendo*" that the supplemental report was part of the "published report" as long as it had been issued in timely fashion before the safeguard measures had been imposed.[16]

[16] United States—Steel Panel para 10.58.

A more difficult and contentious issue concerns efforts by complaining nations to raise new issues or evidence in dispute proceedings that were not raised before the national authorities during their investigation. One can readily imagine how, if the door to such tactics is open, nations may "sandbag" national authorities by hiding issues from them during the course of their investigation, only to raise them before a WTO dispute panel as the basis for a claim that the investigation by national authorities was deficient. For this reason, rules of procedure in domestic litigation systems commonly provide that a party waives its right to introduce evidence on appeal that it might have introduced at an earlier stage of the proceeding. Likewise, it is often impermissible to raise legal issues on appeal that were not raised and preserved earlier in the proceeding.

Two decisions by the Appellate Body in the safeguards area suggest, however, that it is at times permissible to raise new arguments and perhaps even new evidence in the dispute panel process. In *United States—Wheat Gluten*, the European complainants argued that the United States had failed to consider "all relevant factors" bearing on the question whether increased imports had caused or threatened serious injury pursuant to Article 4.2(a) of the Agreement on Safeguards. The panel concurred with the complainants that the "relevant factors" were not limited to those specifically enumerated in Article 4.2(a), but concluded that the only other relevant factors were those "clearly raised . . . by the interested parties in the domestic investigation."[17]

The Appellate Body disagreed. Pointing to the text of Article 4.2, which states that the "competent authorities shall evaluate all relevant factors," it held that the set of "relevant factors" was not necessarily limited to those put forward by interested parties in the investigation. "If the competent authorities consider that a particular 'other factor' may be relevant . . . their duties of investigation and evaluation preclude them from remaining passive in the face of possible shortcomings in the evidence submitted, and views expressed, by the interested parties." Yet, the Appellate Body also rejected the "European Communities' argument that the competent authorities have an open-ended and unlimited duty to investigate all available facts that might possibly be relevant."[18] This test under *Wheat Gluten* is a bit fuzzy, but taken literally it seemingly requires the complaining party in a WTO dispute to

[17] United States—Definitive Safeguard Measures on Imports of Wheat Gluten from the European Communities, WT/DS166/R para 8.69 (hereafter United States—Wheat Gluten Panel).

[18] United States—Definitive Safeguard Measures on Imports of Wheat Gluten from the European Communities, WT/DS166/AB/R paras 55–56 (hereafter United States—Wheat Gluten AB).

produce evidence that the competent authorities "considered" a factor to be potentially relevant even though it was not raised by any party to the investigation, and then proceeded to ignore it. This problem seems unlikely to arise very often, at least if national authorities avoid reference in their published report to concerns that they have declined to analyze.[19]

A more worrisome case from the perspective of national investigating authorities is perhaps *United States—Lamb*. The WTO dispute panel in *Lamb* refused to consider certain alternative explanations for the condition of the domestic industry put forward by New Zealand "to the extent that any of the alternative explanations . . . are in effect new analyses of the record evidence . . . [T]hese factual and legal arguments would be relevant to our review only to the extent that they were raised in the investigation."[20] The Appellate Body again disagreed, citing *Wheat Gluten*, and noting that just as national authorities may be required to go beyond the arguments raised by interested parties in an investigation, so too "panels are not limited to the arguments submitted by the interested parties to the competent authorities." The Appellate Body added, however, that the obligation to act in good faith under the Dispute Settlement Understanding implies that "WTO members cannot improperly withhold arguments from competent authorities with a view to raising those arguments later before a panel. In any event, as a practical matter, we think it unlikely a Member would do so."[21]

Notwithstanding the Appellate Body's optimism that WTO members would not attempt to sandbag national authorities by holding back arguments, or its optimism that a good faith obligation can police the problem, *Wheat Gluten* and *Lamb* create a serious potential difficulty for national authorities. Their published report must contain a "reasoned and adequate" explanation of their findings, including proper attention to "alternative explanations" of the facts. If a possible alternative explanation does not clearly surface until the panel stage of WTO dispute resolution, it seems

[19] In United States—DRAMs, the Appellate Body also made clear that the opportunity to raise new "factors" was limited to cases involving "an allegation that the agency failed to investigate sufficiently or to collect certain information." Otherwise, "a panel must limit its examination to the evidence that was before the agency during the course of the investigation, and must take into account all such evidence submitted by the parties to the dispute." United States—DRAMs AB para 187.

[20] United States—Safeguard Measures on Imports of Fresh, Chilled or Frozen Lamb Meat from New Zealand and Australia, WT/DS 177–78/R para 7.207 (hereafter United States—Lamb Panel).

[21] United States—Lamb AB paras 114–15.

quite unlikely that a "reasoned and adequate" treatment of the issue will be found in the published report. Whether this will become a significant issue in the future remains to be seen.

D The Standard of Review in the Appellate Body

When a panel decision is appealed to the Appellate Body, the standard of review is a conventional one, and will be familiar from most domestic systems of appellate litigation. On issues of law, the Appellate Body gives little or no deference to the panel's analysis, and conducts a *de novo* inquiry into the correctness of its conclusions about WTO law. On factual issues, the Appellate Body is highly deferential, and will rarely if ever overturn purely "factual" conclusions by a panel. Thus, in Appellate Body reports, the "issues on appeal" are invariably framed as legal rather than factual questions.

As any good appellate litigator knows, however, the line between the law and the facts is not always a bright one. An appellant can challenge the factual conclusions reached by a panel by framing the challenge artfully, as by suggesting that the panel failed to apply the correct "standard of review" in its analysis. The *United States—DRAMs* decision under the Subsidies Agreement, noted earlier, affords a good illustration. The panel rejected certain findings of subsidization by the U.S. Department of Commerce, thus concluding that U.S. countervailing duties were illegal under the Agreement on Subsidies and Countervailing Measures. The Appellate Body reversed the panel's finding that the evidence did not support the existence of subsidization, ruling that the panel had engaged in what amounted to *de novo* review. Such reversals of panels are not common, but do highlight that a proper framing of the issue on appeal can result in the reversal of what are essentially factual conclusions by a panel.

Chapter 4

PROCEDURAL OBLIGATIONS IN THE AGREEMENT ON SAFEGUARDS

The Agreement on Safeguards imposes a number of procedural obligations on national authorities. A failure to comply with these procedural rules can render national safeguard measures illegal under WTO law just as surely as any violation of the substantive rules. This chapter details the important procedural obligations, and also the role of the WTO Committee on Safeguards in monitoring the actions of national authorities.

A The Committee on Safeguards

The governance structure of the WTO system is organized into various councils and committees. Major decisions are the subject of the "Ministerial

Conference," which meets roughly every two years (the highly publicized meetings in Seattle and Doha, for example, were ministerial conferences). In the intervening periods, the governing body is the General Council, consisting of representatives of all WTO members. Operating under the guidance of the General Council are three other Councils focused on the major areas of substantive WTO obligations—the Council for Trade in Goods, the Council for Trade in Services, and the Council for Trade-Related Aspects Intellectual Property Rights. All of these bodies are open to the representatives of every WTO member.[1]

Article 13 of the Agreement on Safeguards establishes a "Committee on Safeguards," which reports to the Council for Trade in Goods. Like most WTO bodies, participation is open to any WTO member that wishes to serve.

The role of the Committee on Safeguards is to monitor compliance and implementation of the Agreement on Safeguards by national authorities. The Committee is the recipient of various notifications that national authorities must make (described below), and may at the request of any member investigate whether the substantive or procedural requirements of the Agreement have been met in connection with any safeguard measure or proposed retaliatory measure. The Committee is obligated to prepare an annual report to the Council for Trade in Goods "on the general implementation of [the Agreement on Safeguards] and make recommendations towards its improvement."[2] The reports are public documents and contain a great deal of useful information about the operation of the system.

B The Procedural Obligations of National Authorities

The Agreement on Safeguards imposes a wide range of procedural obligations on national authorities, obligations that in some cases go considerably beyond anything contained in the text of GATT Article XIX. In a number of cases, national authorities have been held to have violated these obligations. Note that the "remedy" for a violation of WTO obligations here as in other areas of WTO law is essentially the same regardless of the nature of magnitude of the violation—the dispute panel or the Appellate Body, as the case may be, will declare the measures at issue to be inconsistent with WTO law,

[1] See generally Agreement Establishing the World Trade Organization, Article IV.
[2] Agreement on Safeguards, Art. 13.1(a).

and recommend that they be eliminated or otherwise brought into conformity with treaty obligations. A safeguard measure may thus be declared illegal as a result of what might seem a rather minor infraction of the rules on a procedural matter of modest importance. All procedural obligations must thus be taken seriously.

The procedural requirements for safeguard investigations by national authorities have several elements. Many of them are simply due process requirements, aimed at affording interested parties an opportunity to participate meaningfully in proceedings that may lead to the adoption of a safeguard measure. Others relate to the limited obligation of WTO members to maintain the balance of concessions after they implement a safeguard measure, and to afford adversely affected members a reasonable chance to negotiate for compensation (see Chapter 10).

1 Advance Publication and Notification of Investigative Procedures

GATT Article X(1) requires that all "[l]aws, regulations, judicial decisions and administrative rulings of general application . . . pertaining to . . . requirements, restrictions, or prohibitions on imports . . . shall be published promptly in such a manner as to enable governments and traders to become acquainted with them." Article X(2) further requires that no measure restricting imports "shall be enforced before such measure has been officially published." The Agreement on Safeguards likewise provides in Article 2.1 that a "Member may apply a safeguard measure only following an investigation by the competent authorities of that Member pursuant to procedures previously established and made public in consonance with Article X of GATT 1994."

National authorities must not only publish their investigative procedures in an appropriate domestic forum, but pursuant to Article 12.6 of the Agreement on Safeguards they must also notify the Committee on Safeguards of their laws regulations and administrative procedures relating to safeguard measures "as well as any modifications made to them." The Committee includes such notifications as part of its annual report, thus providing further publicity of national laws and regulations to the WTO membership at large. Finally, should any WTO member fail to make the required notification to the Committee, another member may bring such failure to the attention of the Committee pursuant to Article 12.8.

2 Notification of Investigations

Members are obligated by Article 12.1(a) of the Agreement on Safeguards to notify the Committee on Safeguards "immediately" upon "initiating an investigatory process relating to serious injury or threat thereof and the reasons for it." This obligation has two elements—a timing or immediacy requirement, and a requirement as to the content of the notification.

In *Korea—Dairy*, the European Communities challenged the Korean notification to the Committee on Safeguards on both issues. The notification stated the date of the initiation of the investigation, and as to the "reasons for it" noted that a petition for safeguard measures had been filed by a domestic industry, and that imports had increased. The notification was transmitted to the Committee on Safeguards 14 days after the publication in Korea of the decision to initiate an investigation. Europe argued that the "reasons" were inadequate insofar as it failed to include any discussion of the other requirements for the use of a safeguard measure (serious injury and the like). It also argued that the two-week delay in transmitting the notification violated the immediacy requirement. The dispute panel rejected the first argument, noting that there was no detailed requirement as to the content of the notice in the treaty text, and concluding that the notice was sufficient to provide adequate information about the initiation of the investigation so that other WTO members could avail themselves of their right to participate. But the panel accepted the claim that Korea's notice was not "immediate,"[3] and was thus a violation of Article 12.1(a). The Appellate Body did not address this issue.

Much the same timing issue arose in *United States—Wheat Gluten*. The decision to initiate an investigation was made by U.S. authorities on October 1, 1997, but the notification to the Committee on Safeguards came 16 days later. The panel held that such notification was not "immediate," and the Appellate Body affirmed. It stated that compliance with this requirement should be assessed case-by-case, with attention to the burden involved in preparing the notification. The complexity of the notification was relevant, as was any need for language translation. But the goal of the immediacy requirement is to provide other members with the "fullest possible period to reflect upon and react to" a safeguards investigation. Because the U.S. notification was a simple one page document reflecting the information that

[3] Korea—Dairy Panel paras 7.130–34.

had been published in the U.S. Federal Register, the 16-day delay could not be justified.[4]

The rather strict approach to the "immediacy" requirement evident in these cases may be defended on the grounds that the parties adversely affected by safeguard measures often have quite limited time to prepare themselves to participate in safeguard investigations by national authorities. The import-competing industries seeking safeguard measures, by contrast, may plan their submissions well in advance, and indeed safeguard investigations are often initiated only following a formal petition by a domestic industry that it may have had many months to prepare. It is not implausible that even a few additional weeks of notice to trading partners may make a material difference in their ability to prepare their case satisfactorily.

3 Due Process Requirements for the Conduct of Investigations

Under Article 3.1 of the Agreement on Safeguards, a safeguards investigation "shall include reasonable public notice to all interested parties and public hearings or other appropriate means in which importers, exporters and other interested parties could present evidence and their views, including the opportunity to respond to the presentations of other parties and to submit their views, *inter alia*, as to whether or not the application of a safeguard measure would be in the public interest." Beyond the simple requirements of notice and opportunity to participate, an important element of this obligation is the "opportunity to respond" to arguments by opposing parties. A meaningful opportunity to respond requires that parties have effective notice of the arguments being put forth by others, along with some reasonable time to analyze and reply to them. Private (*ex parte*) contacts between interested parties and national authorities can raise an issue about the adequacy of opportunities to respond. Likewise, when an argument put forth by one party is based on confidential information, the ability of other parties to respond may be brought into question—I will say more about the general problem of confidential information below.

4 Publication Requirements Following an Investigation

Article 3.1 of the Agreement on Safeguards states that "[t]he competent authorities shall publish a report setting forth their findings and reasoned

[4] United States—Wheat Gluten AB paras 103–112.

conclusions reached on all pertinent issues of fact and law." This obligation is supplemented by Article 4, which pertains to the analysis of serious injury, threat of serious injury, and the causal connection to imports. Article 4.2(c) provides that "[t]he competent authorities shall publish promptly, in accordance with the provisions of Article 3, a detailed analysis of the case under investigation as well as a demonstration of the relevance of the factors considered."

As shall become clear in Section C of this chapter and in subsequent chapters, these publication requirements provide the legal "hook" for the enforcement of many of the substantive obligations of the Agreement on Safeguards. The published decisions of national authorities are subject to close scrutiny and form the "record" of the case for purposes of WTO review. The obligation to provide "reasoned conclusions" allows reviewing panels and the Appellate Body to find fault with decisions that fail to persuade them of their soundness.

For example, in *United States—Wheat Gluten*, the Appellate Body reversed a finding by the panel that the U.S. ITC investigation had given proper consideration to the profitability of the domestic industry, a factor enumerated in Article 4.2(a). During the investigation at the ITC, the respondents questioned the cost allocation assumptions that were used to generate profitability data for domestic producers. The ITC report simply stated that it had "carefully considered" and "reviewed" the cost allocation methodologies at issue. During the WTO panel proceeding, the panel asked the United States to clarify what the ITC had done in this regard, and was apparently satisfied with its responses. But the Appellate Body held that the panel had failed to apply the proper standard of review—the very fact that the panel had to ask the United States for clarifications implied that the published report itself did not contain a "reasoned and adequate" explanation for its conclusions.[5]

5 Notification Requirements Following an Investigation or a Decision to Apply a Measure

Article 12.1 and 12.2 of the Agreement on Safeguards provide in pertinent part:

1. A Member shall immediately notify the Committee on Safeguards upon:...
   (b) making a finding of serious injury or threat thereof caused by increased imports; and
   (c) taking a decision to apply or extend a safeguard measure.

[5] Id. paras 156–63.

2. In making the notifications referred to in paragraphs 1(b) and 1(c), the Member proposing to apply or extend a safeguard measure shall provide the Committee on Safeguards with all pertinent information, which shall include evidence of serious injury or threat thereof caused by increased imports, precise description of the product involved and the proposed measure, proposed date of introduction, expected duration and timetable for progressive liberalization. In the case of an extension of a measure, evidence that the industry concerned is adjusting shall also be provided. The Council for Trade in Goods or the Committee on Safeguards may request such additional information as they may consider necessary from the Member proposing to apply or extend the measure.

Like the notification requirement applicable upon the initiation of an investigation (Article 12.1(a)), these requirements have both a temporal element ("immediately notify"), and a content requirement. Here, the content requirement is more elaborate—to supply "all pertinent information," including the various items listed.

The phrase "all pertinent information" raises a question about the level of detail that must be contained in the notifications, and was at issue in *Korea—Dairy* and *Argentina—Footwear*, the first two safeguard cases to proceed through the dispute resolution system. In both cases, the European Communities argued that the notifications were deficient in detail. The European position was, in essence, that all of the information relied on by national authorities to make their determinations of increased imports, injury, causation and so on should be notified—that the notification requirement was co-extensive with the publication requirement under Articles 3.1 and 4.3. Both panels rejected the European position. The *Dairy* panel noted that if the drafters of the Agreement on Safeguards had desired to make the notification requirements co-extensive with the publication requirements, they could have used a simple cross reference. Both panels also noted that Article 12.2 specifically authorizes the Committee on Safeguards to request additional information, and inferred that this power would be unnecessary if all available information was required to be notified. The *Footwear* panel further noted that the function of notifications is to provide transparency about national processes, and to facilitate consultations—it was not necessary to these purposes in the panel's view for all information developed during an investigation to be notified.[6]

The Appellate Body addressed these issues in its *Korea—Dairy* decision and steered an intermediate course between the position of the panels and the

[6] Korea—Dairy Panel para 7.127; Argentina—Footwear Panel paras 8.298–300.

European Communities. It held that the requirement of "all pertinent information" pertaining to "evidence of serious injury or threat thereof caused by increased imports" must be interpreted with reference to Article 4, which lists factors that must be evaluated in assessing injury and causation. The requirement of "all pertinent information" thus encompasses, "at a minimum," information on all of the items enumerated in *both* Article 12.2 and Article 4.2. But the Appellate Body concurred with the panel that the notification requirement was not co-extensive with the publication requirement of Articles 3.1 and 4.2(c), and that members need not supply "all the details of the recommendations and reasoning to be found in the report of the competent authorities."[7] Thus, members must "address" all of the listed factors, "at a minimum," but the level of detail that they must provide is less than required in their published report, by some unspecified measure. Members seeking to comply with the "all pertinent information" requirement would be well-advised to err on the side of providing greater information rather than less, however, in as much as they must provide the information anyway in their published report.

A further issue arose as to the meaning of the notification requirement under Article 12.1(c), which arises upon "taking a decision to apply" a measure. Article 12.2 requires such notifications to contain a "precise description of . . . the proposed measure (and) proposed date of introduction." The panel in *Korea—Dairy* focused on this text, and decided that it implies an obligation to notify proposed measures once the government has decided on them internally. If the information on the proposed measure is not already contained in the prior notification pursuant to Article 12.1(b), a separate notification is required later as to the proposed measure (apparently pursuant to 12.1(c) in the view of the panel).[8] The Appellate Body did not review this finding.

Subsequently, in *United States—Wheat Gluten*, the European Communities argued from the text of Article 12.2 that the notification pursuant to Article 12.1(c) must occur *before* the safeguard measure is applied by national authorities. Otherwise, it was argued, meaningful consultations on the proposed measure, pursuant to Article 12.3 (discussed below), could not occur. The panel accepted this argument, holding that the 12.1(c) notification must occur prior to the implementation of a measure.[9] The Appellate Body reversed this finding. It insisted that the panel had confused

[7] Korea—Dairy AB para 109. [8] Korea—Dairy Panel para 7.120.
[9] United States—Wheat Gluten Panel paras 8.200–207.

the issue of timing under Article 12.1 with the issue of content under Article 12.2. The obligation to notify information about a proposed measure is plainly contained in Article 12.2, but it does not follow that the notification required by Article 12.1(c) must contain this content.[10] Following the logic to its conclusion, the Appellate Body ruling implies that information about the proposed measure may be a part of the 12.1(b) notification, or that it can be contained in a separate and subsequent notification (whether it occurs pursuant to 12.1(b) or (c) is unclear). Article 12.1(c) simply requires immediate notification of a decision to apply a measure, and a violation of that provision cannot be found solely because the notification does not occur prior to the application of a measure. But a violation of Article 12.1 *will* arise if a member fails to provide effective notice of a *proposed* measure at some stage of the process.

Finally, the immediacy requirement under Article 12.1(b) & (c) was at issue in both *Korea—Dairy* and in *United States—Wheat Gluten*. The *Dairy* panel found violations of the immediacy requirement under Article 12.1(b) and 12.1(c) based on delays of 40 days and 23 days respectively.[11] In *United States—Wheat Gluten*, the immediacy requirement of 12.1(b) was violated according to the panel by a 26-day delay. By contrast, the notification under Article 12.1(c), five days after the application of the measure, "might well satisfy the requirement of immediate notification."[12] The Appellate Body agreed that the five-day delay was acceptable, with notification coming one day after publication in the U.S. Federal Register, and four working days after the pertinent decision was taken.[13] What can fairly be said about the immediacy requirement is that a delay of more than a few days between a decision by national authorities and the notification to the Committee is problematic, at least absent some exceptional circumstances.

6 Consultation Requirements Prior to Application of a Measure

Article 12.3 provides:

A Member proposing to apply or extend a safeguard measure shall provide adequate opportunity for prior consultations with those Members having a substantial interest as exporters of the product concerned, with a view to, *inter alia*, reviewing the

[10] United States—Wheat Gluten AB paras 117–26.
[11] Korea—Dairy Panel paras 7.137, 145.
[12] United States—Wheat Gluten Panel paras 8.198–207.
[13] United States—Wheat Gluten AB para 129.

information provided under paragraph 2, exchanging views on the measure and reaching an understanding on ways to achieve the objective set out in paragraph 1 of Article 8.

The cross-referenced text of Article 8.1 states:

A Member proposing to apply a safeguard measure or seeking an extension of a safeguard measure shall endeavour to maintain a substantially equivalent level of concessions and other obligations to that existing under GATT 1994 between it and the exporting Members which would be affected by such a measure, in accordance with the provisions of paragraph 3 of Article 12. To achieve this objective, the Members concerned may agree on any adequate means of trade compensation for the adverse effects of the measure on their trade.

The Article 12.3 obligation to provide an opportunity for consultations arises when a member is "proposing to apply" a measure, which necessarily implies that the opportunity must occur prior to the implementation of the measure. The phrase "adequate opportunity for prior consultations," by contrast, is not terribly informative as to what is required. One may imagine that the "adequacy" of the opportunity may turn on several considerations. The amount of time permitted for consultation before a measure is applied is potentially important, as is the adequacy of the information supplied to members who seek consultations. One might also read into the "adequacy" requirement an obligation to negotiate in good faith.

With regard to the text of Article 8.1, the question arises as to what a member must do to comply with the requirement to "endeavour" to maintain substantially equivalent concessions. Does this too imply an obligation to negotiate in good faith? What would establish an absence of good faith? Must a member actually make an offer of compensation before applying a measure, even if it is rejected?

Some of these issues have arisen in cases to date, though important questions remain open. In *Korea—Dairy*, the European Communities argued that the opportunity to consult was inadequate because the Korean notifications omitted some of the "pertinent information." As noted above, the panel rejected the claim that Korea's notifications were incomplete as to their content (although they were not "immediate"), and went on to suggest that the opportunity for consultations might be "adequate" even if notifications are incomplete as long as subsequent exchange of information cures the problem. The panel emphasized that consultations in the case had occurred at length, had resulted in modification of the proposed measure, and had come close to resolving the dispute.[14] It thus found no violation of Article 12.3, a finding that was not addressed on appeal.

In *United States—Wheat Gluten*, the European Communities again argued that the opportunity for consultations was inadequate. It noted that the opportunity for consultations occurred before the United States had made available the details of the proposed measure. It further argued that the United States had not made a "genuine endeavour" to maintain equivalent concessions, and that it had "failed to demonstrate that it has actively and concretely offered adequate compensation and that compensation was rejected (or at least not accepted) by the Member concerned."[15] Europe argued further that a violation of Article 12.3 establishes a violation of Article 8.1 as well—the lack of an adequate opportunity for consultation establishes that the member proposing to apply the safeguard measure has not properly "endeavoured" to maintain the balance of concessions.

The panel seized on the fact that no opportunity for consultations was made available by the United States after the details of the final proposed measure became known, and found a violation of Article 12.3. Its finding was linked to its earlier finding that the notification under Article 12.1(c) should occur before the safeguard measure is applied.[16] The panel also accepted the argument of the European Communities that a violation of Article 12.3 sufficed to show a violation of Article 8.1.

As noted, the Appellate Body overruled the panel's interpretation of Article 12.1(c), but nevertheless concurred that the opportunity for consultations was inadequate. The basic obligation under Article 12.3 is to provide members with "sufficient information and time to allow for the possibility, through consultations, of meaningful exchange on the issues identified" in Article 12.3. This obligation includes a requirement that the member proposing to apply a safeguard measure provide "sufficiently detailed information on the form of the proposed measure, including the nature of the remedy." The Appellate Body noted that the consultations between the United States and the European Communities were conducted on the basis of the Article 12.1(b) notification, which did *not* contain important details about the proposed measure, such as the proposed numerical quota share for individual exporting members.[17] Consequently, a violation of Article 12.3 as well as Article 8.1 was established.

[14] Korea—Dairy Panel paras 7.146–53.

[15] United States—Wheat Gluten Panel paras 8.212–13.

[16] Id. para 8.219.

[17] United States—Wheat Gluten AB paras 136–42.

A similar issue arose in *United States—Line Pipe*. The United States held consultations with Korea based on its Article 12.1(b) notification, which did not contain details on the proposed measure. Those details were later disclosed in a press release some 17 days before the measure was applied. No subsequent consultations occurred. The United States argued that the 17 day window allowed Korea adequate time to seek further consultations if it so desired. The panel disagreed, focusing not on the length of the time period but on the adequacy of the press release as a means of communicating the details of the proposed measure. It found that some interested members might not know of the press release or have adequate ways to obtain a copy of it.[18]

On appeal, the United States stressed that Korea had in fact obtained a copy of the press release on the day that it was issued, and that the panel's concern for the adequacy of the press release as a way to communicate was misplaced given the facts of the case. The Appellate Body agreed that the emphasis of the panel was "misdirected," but found fault with the U.S. position for an alternative reason. It underscored its statement in *Wheat Gluten* that Article 12.3 requires a member to provide others with "sufficient time" for a "meaningful exchange." "It would not have been possible, in our view, for Korea to have analyzed the measure, considered its likely consequences, conducted appropriate consultations domestically, and prepared for consultations with the United States in so short a time."[19] The fact that Korea had not requested consultations within the 17-day window was not conclusive in the face of an inadequate opportunity to prepare. The Appellate Body thus affirmed, for a different reason, the finding that Article 12.3 had been violated.

Along the way, the Appellate Body also noted that the obligation to afford adequate opportunity for consultations includes an obligation to negotiate in good faith, citing the general good faith obligation found in Article 26 of the Vienna Convention on the Law of Treaties. Beyond this affirmation of the good faith obligation, however, the dispute process has yet to generate rulings on exactly what "good faith" requires under Articles 12.3 and 8.1.

7 Miscellaneous Notification and Consultation Requirements

I note in passing several other obligations that have yet to surface as important issues in dispute proceedings. The text of Article 12.3 requires

[18] Korea—Definitive Safeguard Measures on Imports of Circular Welded Carbon Quality Line Pipe from Korea WT/DS202/R, paras 7.313–14 (hereafter United States—Line Pipe Panel).

[19] Korea—Definitive Safeguard Measures on Imports of Circular Welded Carbon Quality Line Pipe from Korea WT/DS202/AB/R, paras 106, 111 (hereafter United States—Line Pipe AB).

consultations prior to the extension of a measure as well as its initial application (Chapter 9 will provide further discussion of the permissible duration of measures). Measures may only be extended if evidence is present that an industry is adjusting. Under Article 12.1(c). any decision to extend a measure must be notified to the Committee on Safeguards, and the "pertinent information" required by Article 12.2 includes evidence that the industry is adjusting.

Article 6, to be discussed briefly in Chapter 9, permits provisional safeguard measures in "critical circumstances." The authority in Article 6 is intended for cases in which the delays associated with imposing safeguard measures only after the process involving prior consultations would result in irreparable harm to the domestic industry. Provisional safeguard measures must be notified to the Committee prior to their implementation under Article 12.4. Consultations are required "immediately" after the measure is taken.

Finally, Article 12.5 requires members to notify to the Committee "immediately" the results of consultations under Article 12.3 and 12.4, any compensation agreed during those consultations, and any proposed retaliation relating to safeguard measures. And paralleling the requirement of Article 12.1(b), it requires members to notify the results of any review by national authorities regarding the extension of a measure.

8 The Issue of Confidential Information

Much of the information gathered in safeguard investigations, whether from domestic producers or from importers and exporters, is considered confidential by the company that supplies it. It may include detailed production, cost and pricing data, information about transactions with individual customers, and the like. The ability of national authorities to obtain such information may well turn on their ability to make a credible promise not to reveal it in any fashion that might allow it to reach competitors.

Accordingly, the Agreement on Safeguards acknowledges that confidential information may be present in safeguard investigations, and not only permits but requires national authorities to respect its confidentiality. The key provision is Article 3.2:

> Any information which is by nature confidential or which is provided on a confidential basis shall, upon cause being shown, be treated as such by the competent authorities. Such information shall not be disclosed without permission of the party submitting it. Parties providing confidential information may be requested to

furnish non-confidential summaries thereof or, if such parties indicate that such information cannot be summarized, the reasons why a summary cannot be provided. However, if the competent authorities find that a request for confidentiality is not warranted and if the party concerned is either unwilling to make the information public or to authorize its disclosure in generalized or summary form, the authorities may disregard such information unless it can be demonstrated to their satisfaction from appropriate sources that the information is correct.

Article 3.2 refers to the treatment of confidential information by the competent authorities of WTO members, but it is coupled with Article 3.1, discussed above, which requires the competent authorities to publish a report setting forth findings and "reasoned conclusions," and with Article 4.2(c), which requires the competent authorities to publish a "detailed analysis" of the injury and causation issues in accordance with Article 3.

An obvious potential tension arises—what if the publication of "reasoned conclusions" and "detailed analysis" would reveal confidential information? Article 4 of the Agreement on Safeguards requires, for example, analysis of factors such as sales, production, and profits in assessing the existence of serious injury. If an industry contains only one or a few firms, the publication of this information may be tantamount to the publication of individual data for the firms, data that they consider confidential.

National authorities have long been sensitive to this issue. The U.S. ITC, for example, redacts information from its published reports when, in the view of its staff, the publication of the information might reveal confidential information. Likewise, when ITC Commissioners make reference to confidential information in their analysis, that information is redacted from their opinions. Can such a published report by the "competent authorities" meet the obligation to supply "reasoned conclusions" when the information essential to the analysis is omitted? How can a dispute panel review the adequacy of the report in the face of such redactions?

The solution under U.S. law when ITC decisions are appealed to a domestic court is to release confidential information to appellate adjudicators, and to attorneys for both sides, under a "protective order" that provides severe penalties for inappropriate disclosure. That process works reasonably satisfactorily to allow all relevant parties access to confidential information for purposes of formulating their arguments, without serious danger of its disclosure to competitors or other inappropriate parties.

What is to be done, however, when the "appellate review" of sorts is conducted by a WTO dispute panel? Such panels are not in a position to issue protective orders or to enforce penalties for their violation.

In *United States—Wheat Gluten*, the European Communities argued that the redaction of confidential information from the U.S. ITC report was *by itself* a violation of Article 4, because no "detailed analysis" had been "published." The panel rejected this argument, noting that the prohibition on the publication of confidential information in Article 3.2, and the cross-reference to Article 3 in Article 4.2(c), gave the United States a basis for its omission of confidential information from published materials.

A deeper and more intractable question was raised by the refusal of the United States to provide the panel and the European Communities with certain confidential information that had been requested during the panel process. The United States was willing to supply the information to the panel only, but the panel rejected that proposal on the grounds that it amounted to an impermissible *ex parte* contact. The United States took the position that it could not disclose the information at issue to representatives of the European Communities, and that because of the nature of the data, it was impossible to index or summarize it in a way that preserved its confidentiality.[20] The panel was plainly not pleased with the U.S. position, but declined the European invitation to draw adverse inferences about all issues as to which information had been withheld.

On appeal, the European Communities argued that the panel had abused its discretion in refusing to draw adverse inferences. The Appellate Body "deplored the conduct of the United States" in refusing to supply information despite the best efforts of the panel to assure confidentiality, but held that the decision of a panel whether to draw adverse inferences was a matter of its discretion as a fact finder, and was not reversible on appeal.[21]

A similar issue arose before the panel in *United States—Line Pipe*. Korea and the panel made numerous requests for information that the United States considered to be confidential, and the United States provided some but not all of it in summary or indexed form. Korea asked, among other things, for a complete copy of the confidential ITC staff report collecting all of the data obtained in the investigation, but the United States refused to supply it. The panel ultimately concluded that it had sufficient information to perform its function without pressing the United States for further information,[22] and the matter did not arise on appeal.

One suspects that the issue has not been laid to rest, although it does not appear to have been a serious problem since *Line Pipe*. Panels have the ability

20 United States—Wheat Gluten Panel paras 8.10–25.

21 United States—Wheat Gluten AB para 168–76.

22 United States—Line Pipe Panel paras 7.2–11.

to establish procedures for dealing with confidential information, and it will certainly facilitate their review if all parties can agree to them. But it cannot be denied that the panels lack the power to punish misbehavior in the same way that a domestic court can punish the violation of a protective order, and hence there may always be some uneasiness on the part of national authorities when asked to make confidential information available to the representatives of other WTO member states.

Chapter 5

"UNFORESEEN DEVELOPMENTS" AND "THE EFFECT OF THE OBLIGATIONS INCURRED"

Recall the text of GATT Article XIX, paragraph 1(a):

If, as a result of unforeseen developments and of the effect of the obligations incurred by a contracting party under this Agreement, including tariff concessions, any product is being imported into the territory of that contracting party in such increased quantities and under such conditions as to cause or threaten serious injury to domestic producers in that territory of like or directly competitive products, the contracting party shall be free, in respect of such product, and to the extent and for such time as may be necessary to prevent or remedy such injury, to suspend the obligation in whole or in part or to withdraw or modify the concession.

The first clause conditions the use of safeguard measures on the presence of "unforeseen developments" and "the effect of the [GATT] obligations incurred," which must in turn produce imports in "such increased quantities and under such conditions" as to cause or threaten injury.

As explained in Chapter 1, the requirement that a GATT member using safeguard measures point to "unforeseen developments" and "the effect of [GATT] obligations" was taken seriously in the early days of GATT. Both issues are discussed in the 1951 working party report on the *Hatter's Fur* case, for example, a case that will be discussed at a number of points below. Over time, however, GATT practice evolved to the point that members no longer paid attention to these textual requirements. The U.S. statute authorizing safeguard measures under domestic law made no mention of these issues, for example, and the U.S. ITC which administers the law ignored them in its safeguard investigations. No GATT member ever brought a complaint.

By the time of the Uruguay Round, therefore, the "unforeseen developments" and "effect of the obligations incurred" requirements in Article XIX had become dead letters in GATT practice. Perhaps unsurprisingly, the WTO Safeguards Agreement makes no mention of them as well. The text corresponding to Article XIX(1)(a) in the Safeguards Agreement is Article 2.1, which simply states:

> A Member may apply a safeguard measure to a product only if that Member has determined, pursuant to the provisions set out below, that such product is being imported into its territory in such increased quantities, absolute or relative to domestic production, and under such conditions as to cause or threaten to cause serious injury to the domestic industry that produces like or directly competitive products.

The practice of ignoring the "unforeseen developments" and "effect of the obligations incurred" elements of Article XIX during the later years of GATT, and their omission from the otherwise parallel text in the Safeguards Agreement, hints that the Uruguay Round negotiators were content for them to remain dead letters. But the Safeguards Agreement does not formally supplant Article XIX. To the contrary, at the conclusion of the Uruguay Round, GATT members withdrew from the old GATT treaty and signed the new Uruguay Round agreements, which incorporated the text of the old GATT in GATT 1994. The text of Article XIX(1)(a) was not altered. Regardless of what the negotiators of the Safeguards Agreement may have had in mind, therefore, Article XIX(1)(a) remains a binding legal text. An argument can thus be made that the textual obligations of Article XIX and the Safeguards Agreement are cumulative, and that both apply to safeguard measures going forward. In the first safeguard cases to be brought into the WTO dispute resolution process, precisely such an argument was advanced by the European Communities.

A The Resurrection of Article XIX(1), First Clause

Of the disputes that have proceeded to the point of a formal ruling since the formation of the WTO, the first was brought by the European Communities in 1997 against measures in the Korean dairy industry. In 1998, the

European Communities brought another case against measures in the Argentine footwear industry. The European complaints alleged numerous violations of Article XIX and of the Safeguards Agreement in each case, but both alleged that the respondent countries had failed to comply with the first clause of Article XIX when implementing their safeguard measures. Europe argued in particular that the first clause of Article XIX requires national authorities to establish that import trends in the products under investigation result from unforeseen developments. It argued that the omission of the unforeseen developments requirement from the Safeguards Agreement is immaterial because the obligations of Article XIX and the Safeguards Agreement should be read cumulatively.

Korea and Argentina's first line of response was to suggest that the omission of the unforeseen developments requirement from the Safeguards Agreement creates a "conflict" between that Agreement and Article XIX. The general Interpretative Note to Annex 1a of the Agreement Establishing the WTO provides:

> In the event of conflict between a provision of the General Agreement on Tariffs and Trade 1994 and a provision of another agreement in Annex 1A to the Agreement Establishing the World Trade Organization (referred to in the agreements in Annex 1A as the "WTO Agreement"), the provision of the other agreement shall prevail to the extent of the conflict.

Neither of the dispute panels accepted the proposition that the mere omission of words found in Article XIX from the Safeguards Agreement was sufficient to create a "conflict," however, and hence this line of argument was unavailing.

Nevertheless, each panel in the end rejected the European position. The *Korea—Dairy* panel concluded that the reference to unforeseen developments in Article XIX was not intended as a binding legal obligation. Instead, it simply "explains why a provision such as Article XIX may be needed,"[1] in effect providing context to Article XIX without imposing any legal prerequisite to a safeguard measure. The panel was further comforted by the fact that its reading of Article XIX was supported by GATT practice, and by the omission of the unforeseen developments requirement from Article 2 of the Safeguards Agreement.

The *Argentina—Footwear* panel likewise emphasized the "express omission" of the "unforeseen developments" requirement from the Safeguards

[1] Korea—Dairy Panel para 7.45.

Agreement,[2] the fact that it was ignored in GATT practice and that "[i]t would be unrealistic to assume that the practice of non-enforcement of the unforeseen developments condition was unknown" to the drafters of the Safeguards Agreement. If they had wished to revive it, the panel argued, they would have done so expressly.[3] Thus, the panel concluded, compliance with the requirements of the Safeguards Agreement regarding the prerequisites for safeguard measures should also be deemed compliance with Article XIX—the Safeguards Agreement had effectively modified the rules to eliminate any requirement of unforeseen developments.

Europe appealed both decisions. The Appellate Body rulings in the two cases came down the same day, and are virtually identical on this particular issue.[4] The Appellate Body noted that the text of GATT 1994 is part of the Uruguay Round package that is binding on all members. Further, Article 11 of the Safeguards Agreement states that no member may take safeguard measures "as set forth in Article XIX of GATT 1994 unless such action conforms with the provisions of that Article applied in accordance with this Agreement." From this text, the Appellate Body inferred that the drafters of the Safeguards Agreement had specifically affirmed the continuing vitality of Article XIX. Article XIX and the Safeguards Agreement are thus to be read cumulatively, as Europe had argued. Further, a treaty interpreter "must give meaning and effect to all the terms of the treaty. An interpreter is not free to adopt a reading that would result in reducing whole clauses or paragraphs of a treaty to redundancy or inutility."[5] In the view of the Appellate Body, the panel decisions had the effect of reading the text of Article XIX, first clause, out of existence, in violation of this principle. Finally, as to the suggestion by the *Footwear* panel that the "express omission" of the unforeseen developments requirement from the Safeguards Agreement supported an inference that the drafters wished to eliminate it, the Appellate Body concluded that if the drafters "had intended to expressly omit this clause, [they] would and could have said so."[6]

With these twin decisions, the Appellate Body fully revived the first clause of Article XIX. In five safeguard disputes that have been brought since and that have resulted in a decision, complainants have argued that the national

[2] Argentina—Footwear Panel para 8.58.
[3] Id. para 8.66.
[4] See Korea—Dairy AB paras 68–92; Argentina—Footwear AB paras 76–98.
[5] Korea—Dairy AB para 80.
[6] Argentina—Footwear AB para 88.

authorities failed to comply with the unforeseen developments requirement. They have prevailed on the issue in four of five cases,[7] and in one case the issue was not reached for reasons of judicial economy.[8]

One can certainly quarrel with the legal soundness of the Appellate Body decisions on this issue. Given the uniform practice of ignoring Article XIX(1), first clause, during the latter years of GATT, and its omission from the Safeguards Agreement, one may well doubt that the drafters of the Uruguay Round Agreements had any intention of reviving the obligation. The suggestion by the *Footwear* panel that had the drafters wished to alter established GATT practice in this area, they would have done so with clarity, seems persuasive. The difficult interpretive issues that the clause raises in a long-lived agreement (to be considered below), which led in part to its eventual irrelevance in GATT practice, might also have been noted as a basis for letting it remain dormant.

Other commentators have also been quite critical of the Appellate Body decisions on this issue. See, for example, Lee (2005). Lee recounts the negotiating history of the Safeguards Agreement, *inter alia*, and argues that the omission of the unforeseen developments requirement was quite intentional—it was omitted, he suggests, because the European Communities and the United States argued that it was too restrictive and difficult to apply.

Lee also makes the point that other provisions of Article XIX were omitted from the Agreement on Safeguards which, if still applicable as the Appellate Body suggests, create some apparent contradictions. Most particularly, Article XIX(3)(b) authorizes immediate retaliation against provisional safeguard measures taken under Article XIX(2). Yet, as discussed in Chapter 10 below, Article 8(3) of the Agreement on Safeguards suspends the right of retaliation for the first three years of a safeguard measure, assuming certain conditions are met. If both principles are applicable "cumulatively," they appear to contradict. Although the conflict rule of the general Interpretative Note to Annex 1a of the Agreement Establishing the WTO can be invoked here, so that the rule in the Agreement on Safeguards will prevail on this particular point, the very existence of such a conflict does hint that the drafters of the Agreement did not intend to retain the separate principles of Article XIX.

In any event, the Appellate Body has given no indication of an intention to reverse its position. For now, it is incumbent on WTO members wishing to

[7] Argentina—Peaches, DS238; United States—Lamb, DS177 & 178; United States—Line Pipe, DS202; United States—Steel, DS248, 249, 251, 252, 253, 254, 258, 259 & 274.

[8] United States—Wheat Gluten, DS166.

employ safeguards to link the circumstances that justify them to "unforeseen developments," and to "the effect of the obligations incurred" under GATT. The remainder of this chapter will consider what these requirements entail as a practical matter.

With regard to the unforeseen developments requirement, a number of obvious questions arise. At what point in time must the events in question have been unforeseen—the time of the last tariff concession? What if the last concession on the product in question was decades ago—could anything today have been foreseen? What if the product has been the subject of numerous tariff concessions over time—are expectations associated with the last concession the only relevant ones? Did the entry into force of GATT 1994 "reset" the clock on expectations, even if tariff bindings remained unchanged? Whose expectations are relevant—the trade negotiators in each sector? How does one establish their expectations as an evidentiary matter? Or is the standard an objective one—what would a reasonable trade negotiator have expected? This list of questions is assuredly incomplete, and the Appellate Body has afforded only limited guidance regarding the answers.

Regarding "the effect of the obligations incurred," is it necessary to establish that a specific GATT commitment, on tariffs or otherwise, "caused" the import surge at issue? What if the last commitment was many years ago—could it possibly be the cause of recent developments? The Appellate Body has suggested an answer to these questions which, as shall be seen, renders the requirement to link import surges to "obligations incurred" a rather trivial one. I address this issue next because of the simplicity with which it has apparently been resolved, before proceeding to the much more thorny problem of operationalizing the unforeseen developments requirement.

B Establishing the "Effect of Obligations Incurred"

When Article XIX was negotiated in 1947, one can readily imagine why the drafters contemplated that safeguard measures should address "the effect of the obligations incurred" under GATT. Tariff concessions negotiated at the time might well have resulted in larger volumes of imports than anticipated. Under such circumstances, a clear causal link between the import surge and the recent trade concession would be apparent.

A linkage to the 1947 tariff concession was indeed considered important by the *Hatter's Fur* working party in 1951. It noted that the U.S. tariff concession on the hat bodies in question were "substantial," and documented a sharp rise in imports beginning in 1948 when the tariff concession went into effect.[9]

But what about an import surge five or ten years later? Or decades later? Suppose that no additional trade concessions had been negotiated in the interim, or that any new concessions were quite modest. Would the passage of time since the last important trade concession require an inference that the import surge was caused by something else? Under this view, the requirement to link import increases to "obligations incurred" could become an insuperable hurdle to the use of safeguard measures in industries where no recent, substantial trade concessions had been negotiated.

But there is an alternative view that allows Member States to argue that import surges are always attributable to GATT obligations, at least when tariffs have been bound and imports are already taxed at the bound rate. When an import surge occurs that triggers a desire to impose safeguard measures in an importing nation, that nation can plausibly argue that in the absence of the tariff binding, and in the absence of the GATT Article XI prohibition on quantitative restrictions, it would have responded to the import surge by raising trade barriers to reduce or eliminate it. In this sense, GATT obligations are always responsible for the import surge, and a linkage to "the effect of obligations incurred" can be established in any case where tariffs are bound and cannot be raised.

In both *Korea—Dairy* and *Argentina—Footwear*, the Appellate Body offered a construction of Article XIX that apparently tracks this latter view:

> With respect to the phrase "of the effect of the obligations incurred by a Member under this Agreement, including tariff concessions", we believe that this phrase simply means that it must be demonstrated, as a matter of fact, that the importing Member has incurred obligations under the GATT 1994, including tariff concessions. Here, we note that the Schedules annexed to the GATT 1994 are made an integral part of Part I of that Agreement, pursuant to paragraph 7 of Article II of the GATT 1994. Therefore, any concession or commitment in a Member's Schedule is subject to the obligations contained in Article II of the GATT 1994.[10]

[9] Report of the Intersessional Working Party on the Complaint of Czechoslavakia Concerning the Withdrawal by the United States of a Concession under the Terms of Article XIX, GATT/CP/106, March 27, 1951, paras 6–7 (hereafter Hatter's Fur Report).

[10] Korea—Dairy AB para 84; Argentina—Footwear AB para 91.

In this passage, the Appellate Body seems to be saying that it suffices to show that increased imports are due to "obligations incurred" if the member using safeguard measures can demonstrate that it has incurred obligations under GATT 1994, including tariff concessions. That showing should be possible in every case. It is difficult to imagine how a dispute could arise without a tariff binding in place, since a member with an unbound tariff could always raise it unilaterally without any need to rely on a safeguard measure.

Thus, the Appellate Body evidently does not require members to demonstrate that increased imports are attributable directly to any recent trade concession. Although the quoted passage might be subject to an alternative reading, it is noteworthy that in the disputes brought since *Korea—Dairy* and *Argentina—Footwear*, complainants have not raised the issue of compliance with the "obligations incurred" language of Article XIX. Rather, the focus has been entirely on the "unforeseen developments" language, to which we now turn.

C Establishing the Link to "Unforeseen Developments"

1 In General

In both *Korea—Dairy* and *Argentina—Footwear*, the Appellate Body offered some initial thoughts on the meaning of the unforeseen developments requirement.

> [W]e must examine these words in their ordinary meaning, in their context and in light of the object and purpose of Article XIX. We look first to the ordinary meaning of these words. As to the meaning of "unforeseen developments", we note that the dictionary definition of "unforeseen", particularly as it relates to the word "developments", is synonymous with "unexpected". "Unforeseeable", on the other hand, is defined in the dictionaries as meaning "unpredictable" or "incapable of being foreseen, foretold or anticipated". Thus, it seems to us that the ordinary meaning of the phrase "as a result of unforeseen developments" requires that the developments which led to a product being imported in such increased quantities and under such conditions as to cause or threaten to cause serious injury to domestic producers must have been "unexpected".[11]

Having stated that "unforeseen" is synonymous with "unexpected," the Appellate Body next embarked on a rather cryptic discussion of "conditions"

[11] Korea—Dairy AB para 84; Argentina—Footwear AB para 91.

for the application of a safeguard measure, as distinguished from "circumstances" that must be shown:

When we examine this clause—"as a result of unforeseen developments and of the effect of the obligations incurred by a Member under this Agreement, including tariff concessions . . ."—in its immediate context in Article XIX:1(a), we see that it relates directly to the second clause in that paragraph—"If, . . . , any product is being imported into the territory of that Member in such increased quantities and under such conditions as to cause or threaten serious injury to domestic producers in that territory of like or directly competitive products . . .". The latter, or second, clause in Article XIX:1(a) contains the three *conditions* for the application of safeguard measures. These *conditions*, which are reiterated in Article 2.1 of the *Agreement on Safeguards*, are that: (1) a product is being imported "in such quantities and under such conditions"; (2) "as to cause"; (3) serious injury or the threat of serious injury to domestic producers. The first clause in Article XIX:1(a)—"as a result of unforeseen developments and of the obligations incurred by a Member under the Agreement, including tariff concessions . . ."—is a dependent clause which, in our view, is linked grammatically to the verb phrase "is being imported" in the second clause of that paragraph. Although we do not view the first clause in Article XIX:1(a) as establishing independent *conditions* for the application of a safeguard measure, additional to the *conditions* set forth in the second clause of that paragraph, we do believe that the first clause describes certain *circumstances* which must be demonstrated as a matter of fact in order for a safeguard measure to be applied consistently with the provisions of Article XIX of the GATT 1994. In this sense, we believe that there is a logical connection between the circumstances described in the first clause—"as a result of unforeseen developments and of the effect of the obligations incurred by a Member under this Agreement, including tariff concessions . . ."—and the conditions set forth in the second clause of Article XIX:1(a) for the imposition of a safeguard measure.[12]

Thus, even if "unforeseen developments" are not a "condition" for the use of safeguard measures, they must nevertheless be demonstrated "as a matter of fact" before safeguard measures may be lawfully employed. The apparent rationale for this peculiar distinction between "conditions" and "circumstances" owes to the title of Article 2 of the Safeguards Agreement—"Conditions." Evidently, the Appellate Body did not wish to suggest that unforeseen developments were a "condition," since the list of "conditions" in Article 2 made no mention of them. But because they are required to be demonstrated "as a matter of fact," they are a condition for the use of safeguard measures for all practical purposes.

[12] Korea—Dairy AB para 85; Argentina—Footwear AB para 92.

How does a WTO member make the requisite factual showing that "unexpected" developments have led to circumstances in which a product "is being imported" such that the "conditions" of Article XIX are satisfied? The answer depends on the resolution of several other questions about the meaning of "unforeseen developments." In the remainder of this chapter, I will address these and other related questions to the extent that guidance is available.

In both *Korea—Dairy* and *Argentina—Footwear*, the Appellate Body noted that its reading of Article XIX, first clause, was consistent with the reasoning of the working party report in the *Hatter's Fur* case, which stated: ". . . 'unforeseen developments' should be interpreted to mean developments occurring after the negotiation of the relevant tariff concession which it would not be reasonable to expect that the negotiators of the country making the concession could and should have foreseen at the time when the concession was negotiated."

This passage suggests three things. First, the relevant point in time for the assessment of what is "unexpected" is the point in time at which the "relevant tariff concession" was negotiated. That point was easy to determine at the time of *Hatter's Fur*, of course, because there had been only one negotiating round in 1947. Many of the tariff concessions now in place within the WTO, however, were negotiated under GATT and are decades old. Many were also modified over a series of GATT negotiating rounds. In such instances, what is the relevant point in time for assessing expectations? One possible move in response to this question is to note that GATT members formally withdrew from the old GATT, and entered the new GATT 1994 at the inception of the WTO. This might be taken to have "reset the clock" on trade negotiations, and would at least provide an anchor for the assessment of expectations in the near term. With the passage of time and with additional negotiating rounds, however, the question of what is the "relevant tariff concession" might still resurface. I will say more about this issue below in connection with the discussion of the factual issues in various safeguard disputes.

A second implication of the quoted passage from *Hatter's Fur* is that the relevant actors for purposes of assessing what was "unexpected" are the trade negotiators for the country making the concession. Other actors are not the focus, whether in the private sector or on the other side of the negotiating table.

A third implication is that what was "unexpected" is an objective test. One does not inquire what was in fact foreseen by the relevant trade negotiators, but what they "could and should have foreseen at the time." This in turn implies that as an evidentiary matter, the focus is not on the testimony or recollection of negotiators, but on the information that was available to them at the time.

Regarding the procedural requirements for the showing of unforeseen developments, the Appellate Body has made clear that national authorities must identify them prior to the implementation of safeguard measures. In *United States—Lamb*, the United States argued before the dispute panel and Appellate Body that increased imports of lamb meat were attributable to certain unforeseen developments. But the U.S. ITC, which conducts safeguard investigations under U.S. law, did not address the existence of unforeseen developments in the report that it published prior to the implementation of the U.S. measures—U.S. law did not require such analysis as noted, and the Appellate Body reports in *Korea—Dairy* and in *Argentina—Footwear* had not yet been issued. The U.S. arguments regarding unforeseen developments thus appeared to be *ex post* rationalizations for the measures in question, rather than analysis that had informed the thinking of national authorities prior to the implementation of the measures. The Appellate Body concurred with the complainants that such *ex post* rationalizations were inadequate, and that a demonstration of unforeseen developments must be made before a safeguard measure is applied.[13] The Appellate Body noted that under Article 3.1 of the Safeguards Agreement, "competent authorities shall publish a report setting forth their findings and reasoned conclusions reached on all pertinent issues of fact and law." Because unforeseen developments must be demonstrated before a safeguard measure may be applied, the published report of the competent authorities must contain a "finding" or "reasoned conclusion" on unforeseen developments.[14]

2 Factual Issues in Individual Cases

This section reviews the few safeguard disputes to date that have seriously addressed the unforeseen developments requirement as a factual matter, with an eye toward ascertaining as much as possible about how a WTO member can fulfill the requirement in practice. As shall be seen, important issues remain unresolved. I will take the cases chronologically.

[13] United States—Lamb AB para 72.

[14] Id. para 76.

Hatter's Fur. Because the Appellate Body has cited the *Hatter's Fur* report with some implicit approval, I begin with that case even though it is a GATT case with no legal force in the WTO. The United States made a significant tariff concession in 1947 on women's hats and hat bodies. Imports began to rise dramatically in 1948 and the United States sought to withdraw the concession under Article XIX. Czechoslovakia complained that the conditions of Article XIX had not been met, and the dispute was referred to a "working party" (standard practice at the time) consisting of representatives of a number of GATT members (including the disputants).

The United States argued that the "unforeseen development" responsible for the import surge was a change in fashion shortly after the tariff concession that greatly favored a style of hats that were most cheaply produced abroad. Czechoslovakia argued essentially two things in response—that changes in women's fashion tastes are not unforeseeable in general, and further that the specific change in question was foreseeable in 1947 because it had already taken place in European fashion capitals, even if it had not spread to the United states.

The members of the working party, with the exception of the United States representative, agreed that a change in fashion was not an "unforeseen development" in itself. Nevertheless, the working party concluded (except for the Czechoslovak representative) that "United States negotiators in 1947 could not reasonably be expected to foresee that this style change . . . would, in fact, subsequently take place, and would do so on as large a scale and last for as long a period as it in fact did."[15] The style change favored labor intensive methods of production, and because of the tariff concession, U.S. producers were unable to compete effectively in the new environment. Thus, the working party concluded that the totality of the circumstances, and "particularly the degree to which the change in fashion affected the competitive situation," amounted to unforeseen developments within the language of Article XIX.[16]

Hatter's Fur suggests that an unforeseen change in demand patterns favoring imports over domestic goods may constitute the "unforeseen development" that justifies a safeguard measure. One might infer more generally that any substantial and unforeseen change in the competitive environment that substantially favors imports over domestic goods may qualify as an unforeseen development in principle, as long as it could not reasonably have been anticipated by the relevant trade negotiators at the relevant point in time.

[15] Hatter's Fur Report para 11. [16] Id. para 12.

United States—Lamb. As noted, the United States was held by the Appellate Body to have violated the unforeseen developments requirement in *Lamb* because the U.S. ITC did not address the issue in its published report. Nevertheless, at the panel stage of the dispute, the parties also joined issue on the merits of the unforeseen developments claims put forward by the United States *ex post*, and the panel had some interesting reactions to them.

The panel first addressed a conceptual question regarding precisely what must have been *caused* by the unforeseen developments. The complainants argued that, according to the text of Article XIX(1)(a), the unforeseen developments must be shown to have caused the surge in imports. Further, because a causal linkage must be drawn between unforeseen developments and import volumes, it follows that the increased imports *themselves* cannot be an unforeseen development—they must instead *result* from such a development.

The panel responded as follows:[17]

> The phrase concerning "unforeseen developments" in Article XIX:1 is grammatically linked to both "in such increased quantities" and "under such conditions". Rather than implying a two-step causation, we view this structure as meaning that while "unforeseen developments" are distinct from increases in imports *per se*, it may be sufficient for a showing of the existence of this "factual circumstance" that "unforeseen developments" have caused increased imports to enter "under such conditions" and to such an extent as to cause serious injury or threat thereof.

Here, the panel seemingly agreed with the complainants that a party cannot point to increased imports themselves as unforeseen developments (although it backtracked later as noted below). But it also rejected the notion that the unforeseen developments must cause the import surge. It is enough to show that the unforeseen developments lead imports to enter "under such conditions" as to cause or threaten injury.

One might question this reasoning on two grounds. First, what does it mean to say that unforeseen developments cause imports to enter "under such conditions" as to cause injury, yet under circumstances in which they are not also causally responsible for the increase in imports? Any development that allows imports to compete more effectively with domestically produced goods would also seem logically to lead to increased import volumes, *ceteris paribus*. Second, the text of Article XIX refers to situations in

[17] United States—Lamb Panel para 7.15.

which unforeseen developments lead to imports "in such increased quantities *and* under such conditions" as to cause or threaten injury. The panel's reading seemingly converts the "and" to "or." Thus, although the *Lamb* panel rejected the "two-step causation" reading of the unforeseen developments requirement, it is by no means clear that it was correct to do so. It is even less clear what the alternative reading means as a practical matter.

The panel then turned to the specific factual claims of unforeseen developments put forward by the United States. In particular, the United Sates argued that there had been an unforeseen change in competitive conditions owing to two factors: a change in the product mix of imports from frozen lamb meat toward fresh/chilled lamb meat (which made imports more directly substitutable for the predominantly fresh domestic product), and a change in the cut size of imported lamb meat (which had a similar effect). The complainants responded with two lines of argument. First, they suggested that the United States was impermissibly pointing to the imports themselves as the unforeseen development, an argument that the panel (somewhat mysteriously) rejected as equivalent to the "two-step causation" requirement.[18] Second, the complainants argued that the change in the mix of imports was a long-term trend that was apparent before the end of the Uruguay Round (the time of the "relevant tariff concession"), and that the shift had not been terribly substantial in any case. The panel ultimately held for the complainants on these issues, not because the U.S. position was logically flawed, but because the U.S. ITC had not explained clearly in its report how the two changes in the mix of imports had constituted "an unanticipated change that created conditions in which increased imports were causing or threatening to cause serious injury."[19]

The *Lamb* panel thus seems to accept in principle that a change in the nature of imported goods, allowing them to compete more effectively, may constitute the requisite unforeseen development. But it is incumbent upon the party employing safeguard measures to provide a reasoned analysis on such matters as the Appellate Body has emphasized. *Lamb* also suggests that the relevant point in time for measuring expectations (at least for now) is the conclusion of the Uruguay Round, supporting the notion that the conclusion of the Round "reset" the clock on all pre-existing GATT tariff concessions.

Argentina—Peaches. The panel decision in *Peaches*, which was not appealed, also addressed the question whether increased imports themselves

[18] Id. para 7.35. [19] Id. para 7.42.

could constitute the unforeseen developments required by Article XIX. After reviewing the text of Article XIX, the panel concluded that imports "in such increased quantities and under such conditions" must *result* from unforeseen developments, a phrasing which implies that "they must be two distinct things... The text of Article XIX:1(a) cannot support an interpretation that would equate increased quantities of imports with unforeseen developments."[20]

The panel, along with the disputants, also agreed that the central issue was what had been foreseen at the time of the Uruguay Round when the tariff concession on peaches was negotiated. In this connection, it noted that the level of world production and stocks—one of the ostensible "unforeseen developments" noted by Argentina—was only one percent higher at the time of the Argentine safeguard proceeding than it had been in the 1992–93 season during the Uruguay Round negotiations. A change of this modest degree "normally... could and should have been foreseen by the Argentine negotiators."[21] In this passage, the panel thus suggests that what is "foreseen" may be measured against past experience, and that events which do not deviate significantly from historical experience must ordinarily be deemed to be foreseen.

Otherwise, the *Peaches* report is fairly unremarkable. Much like the earlier panel reports, it concluded that the published report of the Argentine authorities failed to provide a reasoned showing as to how the purported unforeseen developments had been unforeseen at the appropriate point in time, and how they had resulted in the circumstances described in the second clause of Article XIX(1)(a).

United States—Steel. U.S. law has yet to be amended to require that increased imports result from unforeseen developments, and the initial ITC decision in the steel case in 2001 paid little heed to the issue. But prior to the imposition of the steel safeguard measures in March 2002, the United States Trade Representative requested additional information from the ITC regarding unforeseen developments, and received a supplemental report on that issue. Based in large part on this supplemental report, the United States argued before the dispute panel that four unforeseen developments had contributed to the influx of imports that had injured the U.S. steel industries (the case involved a wide range of products that were divided by the U.S. ITC into 27 distinct "industries"). The four developments were the Asian

[20] Argentina—Definitive Safeguard Measure on Imports of Preserved Peaches, WT/DS238/R, paras 7.17–18 (hereafter Argentina—Peaches Panel).

[21] Id. para 7.31.

financial crisis, the drop in demand for steel abroad due to the dissolution of the Soviet Union, the unexpected strength of U.S. economy and its demand for steel, and the persistent appreciation of the U.S. dollar.[22] Among other arguments, the complainants urged that none of these events were "unforeseen," and questioned whether they had resulted in increased imports sufficient to justify safeguard measures.

In assessing these issues, the panel began by noting that the parties agreed that "the point in time at which developments should have been unforeseen is that of the completion of the Uruguay Round."[23] Also, the standard for what is unforeseen has an "objective element"—"[t]he standard is not what the specific negotiators had in mind but rather what they could (reasonably) have had in mind."[24] The panel then allowed that the Asian financial crisis could constitute an unforeseen development "since it took place after the United States last negotiated its tariff concessions on the steel products covered by the investigation."[25] The same was true of the consequences for the steel market of the dissolution of the Soviet Union, even though the dissolution process had begun prior to the end of the Uruguay Round, because the economic consequences of the dissolution may not have been clear at that time. The ongoing strength of the U.S. economy and the U.S. dollar were harder to regard as unforeseeable, but the panel concluded that these factors were not viewed by the ITC as unforeseen developments in themselves, but simply circumstances that contributed to the increase in imports that resulted from the developments in Asia and the Soviet Union. Thus, the United States prevailed on the proposition that unforeseen developments had affected the steel market to some degree.

The panel held further, however, that Article XIX requires the unforeseen developments to have resulted in increased imports that cause serious injury or threat (in contrast to the *Lamb* panel which had rejected the "two-step causation" approach). It was on this issue that the United States failed to persuade the panel, in part because the ITC findings of injury were all contained in the original ITC report rather than its supplemental report—at no time prior to its affirmative injury findings did the ITC identify the increased imports that had resulted from the unforeseen developments at issue and analyze their impact on the domestic industry. Such analysis was required to be provided separately, according to the panel, for every line of steel products (every "industry") in which a safeguard measure was taken.[26]

[22] United States—Steel Panel para 10.40. [23] Id. para 10.74.
[24] Id. para 10.43. [25] Id. para 10.80. [26] Id. para 10.128.

Instead, the ITC had simply asserted in its supplemental report, after the original injury findings had been made, that unforeseen developments had affected the steel market in a general way. As the panel stated, "in light of the complexity of the matter, a more sophisticated and detailed economic analysis was called for."[27]

The Appellate Body affirmed the panel in most pertinent respects. In particular, it concurred with the panel in its apparent endorsement of the "two-step causation" reading of Article XIX that had been rejected by the *Lamb* panel: "To trigger the right to apply a safeguard measure, the [unforeseen] development must be such as to *result* in increased imports of *the product* ('such product') that is subject to the safeguard measure."[28] It also agreed that in a situation such as *Steel* where multiple "industries" were found to exist, a member proposing to invoke safeguards must demonstrate that unforeseen developments led to increased imports for each "industry" covered by a safeguard measure.[29] It likewise concurred that the ITC had failed to make such a showing with a "reasoned and adequate" explanation.[30]

The *Steel* panel's treatment of the unforeseen developments requirement is helpful in suggesting how to operationalize it in practice, but at the same time underscores that it is a potentially severe hurdle for any nation that seeks to employ safeguard measures. As to certain questions posed earlier in this chapter—unforeseen by whom? at what point in time?—the panel concurs with earlier panels that the relevant actors are trade negotiators, that the issue is what they could "reasonably" have foreseen, and that the relevant time is the point when the member seeking to use safeguards "last negotiated its tariff concessions on the . . . products covered by the investigation." The end of the Uruguay Round may be taken to have "reset the clock" on this latter issue.

In deciding whether events were "unforeseen" by the negotiators at the relevant time, the focus in the first instance will be on whether the events in question took place before or after the conclusion of the negotiations. One can thus imagine the rules here evolving in a manner that is roughly consistent with the rules in the "nonviolation" nullification and impairment cases—a presumption might arise that negotiators foresee the results of events that take place before the conclusion of negotiations, and do not foresee the results of events that take place later.[31] Further, as tariffs decline to

[27] Id. para 10.125. [28] United States—Steel AB para 314. [29] Id. para 319.

[30] Id. para 326.

[31] See Japan—Measures Affecting Consumer Photographic Film and Paper, WT/DS44/R, para 10.79.

lower levels and more and more time passes since the last tariff negotiation on many products, the set of "unforeseen" events will presumably expand and unforeseen developments should become easier to identify.

But the requirement of linkage between unforeseen developments and increased imports poses substantial analytical challenges. It is hardly clear what sort of "more sophisticated and detailed economic analysis" will suffice. Consider the steel case itself: By the panel's reasoning, the United states should have ascertained how much U.S. imports had increased, in each of 27 steel "industries," as a result of the Asian financial crisis and the drop in demand for steel inside the old Soviet Union. It should then have analyzed whether this increase caused or threatened to cause serious injury to the relevant industry. On the surface, such an analysis seems to call for something approaching a global general equilibrium model of each segment of the steel market, so that the effect of events in particular overseas markets such as Asia and the former Soviet Union can be simulated with precision. If that sort of analysis is indeed required, the time and expense involved could be enormous. The accuracy of such exercises is also subject to considerable doubt because the results often turn on controversial assumptions. And for many industries, the data necessary to estimate the parameters for such models will be lacking, and modelers would have little choice but to fall back on simulations that rest on seat of the pants guesses about relevant supply and demand elasticities, cross-elasticities of demand, and the like.

The alternative to such analysis is to rely on much less rigorous methods, such as the presence of simple correlations between the "unforeseen developments" and import volumes. If steel imports went up during the Asian financial crisis, for example, one might infer that the crisis was the "cause" (even though correlation and causation are hardly the same thing, as Chapter 8 will discuss at length). Perhaps a future reviewing panel will be satisfied with such an approach despite its deficiencies, but the question of what will suffice as a "reasoned and adequate explanation" of the linkage between unforeseen developments, increased imports and injury remains unclear.

Conclusion. The Appellate Body's revival of Article XIX(1)(a), first clause, was arguably a mistake as a legal matter. In any event, it creates a considerable hurdle for WTO members that desire to use safeguard measures, and important questions surrounding its implications are as yet unanswered. It is settled that what is "unforeseen" is to be measured with reference to the expectations of the members' trade negotiators, subject to an objective standard asking what they reasonably could have foreseen. The point in time at which expectations are to be evaluated is the time of the "relevant tariff concession," which for the moment appears to be the conclusion of the Uruguay Round when new and pre-existing tariff concessions were embodied in the national schedules of GATT 1994. Subsequent negotiating rounds will no doubt complicate the question of when the "relevant tariff concession" occurred.

Significant economic developments after the date of the "relevant tariff concession" may be deemed to have been unforeseen at the time, although perhaps not if they are similar enough to historical experience. Thus far, the cases suggest no limitation in principle on what sort of "development" can be relied on by national authorities—changes in demand or supply conditions at home or abroad that advantage imports all appear to be acceptable. As more time passes since the "relevant tariff concession," the likelihood that recent developments will have been "foreseen" at the time of the concession seemingly diminishes. This observation hints that the task of establishing that developments were "unforeseen" may become easier over time, at least in the absence of any new tariff concessions that reset the clock.

The primary obstacle to satisfying the unforeseen developments requirement may well be the task of linking the unforeseen developments to the import surge in the industry in question. The task of convincingly showing how particular unforeseen developments have produced increased imports (if indeed that is required as the steel panel held, and as the text of Article XIX suggests) is not an easy one in general, particularly if it is done rigorously. It remains to be seen how nations will attempt to meet this requirement, and whether their analytical approach will withstand scrutiny in the dispute process.

Chapter 6

THE INCREASED QUANTITIES REQUIREMENT

GATT Article XIX permits safeguard measures when, *inter alia*, a "product is being imported in such increased quantities and under such conditions as to cause or threaten serious injury to domestic producers." The parallel language in Article 2.1 of the Safeguards Agreement requires an appropriate determination by a WTO member that a "product is being imported into its territory in such increased quantities, absolute or relative to domestic production, and under such conditions as to cause or threaten serious injury to the domestic industry." Both texts make abundantly clear that imports in "increased quantities" are a prerequisite to safeguard measures. On this issue, the principal difference in the text of the Safeguards Agreement is to make explicit that an increase may occur either in absolute terms, or in their market share ("relative to domestic production"), an interpretation of Article XIX that emerged early during the course of GATT practice.[1]

This seemingly simple requirement is in fact the subject of much wrangling under both national and WTO law. Most fundamentally, to determine whether an "increase" has occurred, some baseline is required. Given the expansion of global trade, it will be the rare imported product that has not exhibited an "increase" against some historical baseline. Likewise, trading

[1] Support for this reading of Article XIX may be found in a 1948 working party report on Modifications to the General Agreement. See GATT Analytical Index, Vol. I, p. 518.

volumes are often volatile, and an artful selection of a recent baseline can often be made so that import volume or market share appears higher today. Because baselines can often be chosen that show either an increase or a decrease in imports, the parties to national and international proceedings regarding safeguard measures routinely fight over them.

A separate issue arises as to whether the increase in imports must achieve any particular magnitude. Is it enough, for example, that the absolute quantity of imports has risen from 10,000 units to 10,001? The treaty text makes reference not merely to "increased quantities," but to "such increased quantities." Is the inclusion of the word "such" meant to suggest that the increase must be substantial in some sense?

Finally, what is to be made of a case in which imports have risen steadily over a recent period of years, but declined somewhat quite recently? The treaty text refers to a product that "*is* being imported . . . in such increased quantities"—does this reference to current circumstances foreclose safeguard measures in the face of a current downtrend in imports? This chapter will address these and related questions, providing what guidance it can based on WTO decisions to date.

A The Baseline Issue During GATT

In the early days of GATT, the entry into force of the GATT in 1947 supplied a natural baseline against which to assess whether "increased quantities" were present. GATT Article XIX(1) refers to "increased quantities" that "result" from "unforeseen developments" and the "effect of [GATT] obligations." Those "obligations" first arose in 1947, and any "unforeseen developments" producing an import surge would have occurred subsequently. Accordingly, the *Hatter's Fur* working party of 1951 was clearly focused on the trends in imports during 1948, 1949, and 1950 as compared to their pre-GATT levels in 1946 and 1947.[2]

As Chapter 8 will emphasize, Article XIX also provided GATT members in the early days with an intelligible inquiry as to the causal prerequisite for safeguard measures. GATT "obligations" were expected to result in increased imports, but the increase might be greater and more injurious than expected due to "unforeseen developments." Thus, conceptually, the question was whether "unforeseen developments" following GATT concessions had *caused* imports to rise well above anticipated levels, in turn *causing* serious injury or threat.

[2] Hatter's Fur Report para 6.

With the passage of time, as Chapter 1 discussed, this basic structure of Article XIX became more difficult to apply. The problem was particularly evident as to the selection of the proper baseline for the assessment of "increased quantities." Additional negotiating rounds meant that on some products, multiple tariff concessions had been negotiated. If the date of the "obligations" supplied the baseline, which obligations were the pertinent ones? And if the pertinent tariff concession was many years earlier with a general expansion of trade in the interim, what was to be made of the fact that the increased imports requirement would be trivially satisfied in many cases due to the general growth in trade? Alternatively, perhaps the date of the "obligations" was not the proper focus, but the date of the "unforeseen developments" on the grounds that any increase in imports prior to that date was part of the bargain and not an appropriate basis for safeguard measures. But if so, we return to the difficult issues of the last chapter—exactly how does one identify unforeseen developments?

One can imagine that the GATT membership might have wrestled with these issues and somehow resolved them, but it did not. Instead, as Chapters 1 and 5 explored in detail, the "unforeseen developments" and "effect of the obligations incurred" requirements of Article XIX(1) became dead letters in GATT practice. As a result, neither requirement remained a viable touchstone for the selection of an import baseline, and GATT members moved toward other approaches.

The practice under U.S. law affords a useful illustration. U.S. law long ignored the "unforeseen developments" and "effect of the obligations incurred" elements of GATT Article XIX, and instead instructed the U.S. ITC to determine "whether an article is being imported into the United States in such increased quantities as to be a substantial cause of serious injury" or threat, without specifying in the statute any baseline against which to assess "increased quantities." The ITC wrestled with the baseline issue for some time.

Some ITC Commissioners employed an elastic conception of the proper baseline, searching for a time period that they believed was representative of long term trends rather than "abnormal economic conditions." The result might be a baseline extending back over a decade.[3] Others preferred the original approach of Article XIX, and looked to the time of the most recent trade concessions on the product in question to establish the baseline, which

[3] U.S. International Trade Commission, Stainless Steel and Alloy Tool Steel, Inv. No. TA-201–5, Pub. No. 756 (1976)(views of Commissioners Moore and Bedell). The case is also reported in 1 I.T.R.D. 5404 (1976).

often (though not necessarily) would have occurred during the last GATT negotiating round.[4] Still others emphasized the importance of making the baseline routine and predictable, and tended toward a somewhat arbitrary rule of thumb.[5] The latter view largely carried the day in the end, and it eventually became convention at the ITC to focus on the most recent five-year period for which data are available.[6] "Increased quantities" would be deemed to exist if imports had risen during that five-year window, although litigants remained free to argue that import trends during that period were for some reason unrepresentative of long-term trends.

As shall be seen below, other nations have mimicked the U.S. approach, selecting a standard "period of investigation," often five years. Investigations conducted on this basis by the United States or other WTO members have now come before the WTO dispute resolution process on several occasions.

B Baselines and "Increased Quantities" in WTO Disputes to Date

After the Appellate Body revived Article XIX(1), first clause, to insist anew on a linkage between "increased quantities" and "unforeseen developments" as well as the "obligations incurred," one might perhaps have expected the Appellate Body also to insist on attention to these issues in the selection of an import baseline, much as in the early days of GATT. For example, the Appellate Body might have suggested that the entry into force of GATT 1994 established a new baseline of "obligations" against which to measure the volume and market share of imports. Or it might have suggested that the date of the "unforeseen developments" can supply a baseline.

Interestingly, however, both dispute panels and the Appellate Body have declined to suggest that any particular baseline is required by the treaty text (even though one could certainly argue that Article XIX(1), first clause, provides a baseline). Yet, panels and the Appellate Body have often found fault with findings of increased imports by members applying safeguard measures, often in ways that directly or implicitly reject the member's own choice of a baseline. In the process, they have articulated a number of

[4] Id. (views of Commissioner Minchew).
[5] Id. (views of Commissioner Ablondi).
[6] See Jackson, Davey & Sykes (2002), p. 611.

Table 6.1 Total Imports of Footwear into Argentina, 1991–1996

	Quantity (million pairs)	Value (US$ millions)
1991	8.86	44.41
1992	16.63	110.87
1993	21.78	128.76
1994	19.84	141.48
1995	15.07	114.22
1996	13.47	116.61

Total imports/production

	by volume	by value
1991	12%	11%
1992	22%	24%
1993	33%	34%
1994	28%	36%
1995	25%	34%
1996	19%	28%

additional principles that members must follow in determining whether a product "is being imported" "in such increased quantities" as to permit the use of safeguards. This section reviews the pertinent rulings to date. I will take the decisions in chronological order, omitting those in which the increased imports question was not addressed by the panel. The next section summarizes the lessons to be derived from them, and offers a general critique.

Argentina—Footwear. Footwear was the first WTO case to delve seriously into the increased imports requirement. Argentine law specified that the period of investigation should be the most recent five full calendar years for which date were available (1991–95). The authorities gathered data for those years, and later added data for a sixth calendar year. I reproduce the data on import volumes and market share above in Table 6.1.[7]

Based on endpoint-to-endpoint comparisons for the years 1991–95, the Argentine authorities concluded that imports had risen both in absolute terms and relative to domestic production. Subsequent statements by the authorities further noted that imports in 1996 were above 1991 levels.[8]

[7] See Argentina—Footwear Panel paras 8.144, 8.151.

[8] Id. paras 8.145, 8.151.

The European Communities argued that the finding of increased imports was flawed for essentially two reasons. First, it suggested that Argentina's reliance on five years of data extended too far back into the past, and that a finding of increased imports must be based on more recent data. Second, it argued that a simple endpoint-to-endpoint comparison was improper, and that intervening (downward) trends in imports had not been properly considered by Argentina.

The panel rejected the first argument. It noted that the Agreement on Safeguards "is silent regarding the period of investigation," and that five years of historical data can be "quite useful."[9] It also found nothing in the treaty text to support the suggestion by the European Communities that only a "sharply increasing trend" at the end of the period of investigation would suffice for a finding of increased imports.

But the panel was persuaded by the second argument. It noted that findings based on simple endpoint-to-endpoint comparisons were highly manipulable, and depended on the choice of the base year. A base year of 1992, for example, would wipe out the apparent increase in total imports through either 1995 or 1996. The sensitivity of the analysis owed to the fact that imports declined during the intervening years after 1993. And for the panel, "if an increase in imports in fact is present, it should be evident both in an endpoint-to-endpoint comparison and in an analysis of intervening trends over the period." For support, it pointed to the requirement of "such increased quantities" in Article 2.1, suggesting that this phrase required an evaluation of the "full context" of any increase. In this regard, it noted that Article 4.2(a) of the Agreement on Safeguards requires members to evaluate the "rate and amount of the increase in imports" as part of their analysis of the causal link between imports and injury or threat. The panel took this reference to require an evaluation of intervening trends during the period of investigation. It also pointed to the steady decline in imports since 1993 as evidence that the decline was not a mere temporary reversal of an upward trend. It thus concluded that Argentina had failed to demonstrate "such increased quantities" as to satisfy Article XIX and the Agreement on Safeguards, because "it did not adequately consider the intervening trends in imports, in particular the steady and significant declines in imports beginning in 1994, as well as the sensitivity of the analysis to the particular end points of the investigation period used."[10]

[9] Id. para 8.166. [10] Id. para 8.276.

The Appellate Body affirmed this finding, agreeing that Articles 2.1 and 4.2(a) together necessitate a consideration of trends over the period of investigation and not just the endpoint-to-endpoint comparison: "[T]he rate and amount of the increase in imports in absolute and relative terms must be evaluated . . . [T]he competent authorities are required to consider the *trends* in imports over the period of investigation (rather than just comparing the end points)."[11] But the Appellate Body also called into question the panel's rejection of the notion that the most *recent* trends should be the focus of attention. "[W]e do not agree with the panel that it is reasonable to examine the trend in imports over a five-year historical period."[12] The Appellate Body insisted that the phrase "is being imported" in Article 2.1 "indicates that it is necessary for the competent authorities to examine recent imports, and not simply trends in imports during the past five years—or, for that matter, during any other period of several years."[13] It proceeded to state:

> In our view, the determination of whether the requirement of imports "in such increased quantities" is met is not a merely mathematical or technical determination. In other words, it is not enough for an investigation to show simply that imports of the product this year were more than last year—or five years ago. Again, and it bears repeating, not just *any* increased quantities of imports will suffice. There must be "*such* increased quantities" as to cause or threaten to cause serious injury to the domestic industry in order to fulfill this requirement for applying a safeguard measure. And this language in both Article 2.1 of the *Agreement on Safeguards* and Article XIX:1(a) of the GATT 1994, we believe, requires that the increase in imports must have been recent enough, sudden enough, sharp enough, and significant enough, both quantitatively and qualitatively, to cause or threaten to cause "serious injury".[14]

Thus, the Appellate Body insists that imports must have increased "recently." But how recently, and in what amount? The phrase "recent enough, sudden enough, sharp enough, and significant enough, both quantitatively and qualitatively, to cause or threaten to cause 'serious injury' " provides little guidance (as Chapter 8 will elaborate at length). The insistence on "not just any increase" but "such increased quantities" as to cause injury is equally unhelpful. Thus, although one can perhaps understand from an examination of Table 6.1 why Argentina's finding of increased imports made the panel and the Appellate Body uneasy, the Appellate Body decision in the case raises more questions than it answers.

[11] Argentina—Footwear AB para 129. [12] Id. para 130. [13] Id. para 130.
[14] Id. para 131.

One might also argue that both the panel and the Appellate Body to a degree collapsed the "increased imports" requirement with the required analysis of causation. As the panel acknowledged, Article 4.2(a) and its reference to the rate and amount of increased imports is concerned with factors to be considered in assessing causation. The Appellate Body decision might be taken to say that a member may not find "such increased quantities" at all unless the trends are such as to support an inference that imports are causing or threatening injury, thus collapsing the two inquiries. This issue resurfaces below in the discussion of the *Steel* dispute. The broader question of whether it is coherent at all to think of imports as a causal variable will be addressed at length in Chapter 8.

United States—Wheat Gluten. In *Wheat Gluten*, the United States had employed its standard five-year period of investigation and gathered import data for the years 1993 to 1997. Over that five-year period, imports had increased in absolute terms from 128 million pounds to 177 million pounds, as well as relatively to domestic production. The European Communities again challenged the finding, arguing primarily that the United States had relied excessively on and endpoint-to-endpoint comparison of data.

The panel rejected the European position, noting that imports (absolute and relative) had declined or remained flat during the early years of the period of investigation, but increased dramatically during the last two years (1996 and 1997). Because most of the increase was "recent," the panel agreed with the United States that increase in imports was "recent, sudden, sharp and significant" under the standard set forth by the Appellate Body in *Footwear.*[15] The panel's finding was not appealed.

United States—Line Pipe. In *Line Pipe*, the U.S. ITC gathered five years of data for calendar years 1994–98, and an additional six months of data for the first six months of 1999. It evaluated import trends over the five calendar years, and compared import levels in the first six months of 1998 (interim 1998) to the first six months of 1999 (interim 1999). It found that imports had risen rather steadily over the calendar years 1994–98. The absolute volume of imports declined from interim 1998 to interim 1999, but remained at "very high levels" compared to earlier years in the period of investigation. Imports relative to domestic production continued to rise from interim 1998 to interim 1999.

Korea challenged the finding of increased imports on essentially three grounds: (a) that the five (and one-half) year period of investigation was too

[15] United States—Wheat Gluten Panel paras 8.27–36.

long in light of the Appellate Body's emphasis on "recent" import increases; (b) that the U.S. ITC was required to compare the first six months of 1999 to the *last* six months of 1998 and not simply the first six months (a comparison that would have showed a decline in total imports and import share); and (c) that a finding of increased imports was impermissible in light of the decline in total imports acknowledged by the ITC to have occurred between interim 1998 and interim 1999.

The panel rejected all three claims. It found that the length of the period of investigation was reasonable in the absence of specific constraints in the treaty text, and in light of the fact that it in no way prevented the ITC from focusing closely on the most recent years. The comparison made between interim 1998 and interim 1999 (first six months in each case) was likewise defensible as the "standard practice" of the ITC in past cases, a practice that had evolved to eliminate possible distortions due to seasonal or cyclical fluctuations in trade flows. Finally, despite the decline in total imports between interim 1998 and 1999, they remained at high levels compared to earlier years, and an overall finding of increased imports was permissible.[16] The panel's finding was not appealed.

Chile—Agricultural Products. The Chilean safeguard measures covered several products, including edible vegetable oils, wheat and wheat flour. The Chilean Commission charged with the conduct of safeguard investigations issued "minutes" setting forth its findings on increased imports over the course of several paragraphs. The minutes recited various facts tending to support a finding of increased imports, but the panel found them insufficient.

For example, as to wheat flour, there was simply a finding that imports had "fluctuated," and that restrictions on trade in wheat might lead to a future increase in imports of wheat flour. Regarding edible oils, the Commission noted that total imports were "similar" from 1993 to 1997, increased by 23 percent in 1998, and then fell by 24 percent over the first ten months of 1999. Regarding wheat, the minutes noted a large increase in imports in 1999, and a slight increase in 1998 over 1997, but 1997 had witnessed a significant drop relative to 1996. Consequently, total imports in 1999 were apparently lower than in 1995 or 1996.

The panel held that the findings on each product were insufficient to meet the Appellate Body's standard in *Footwear*. The long term trends for each product presented at best a mixed picture. Further, the Chilean Commission had apparently relied to a degree in its findings on a *prospect* of future

[16] United States—Line Pipe Panel paras 7.183–214.

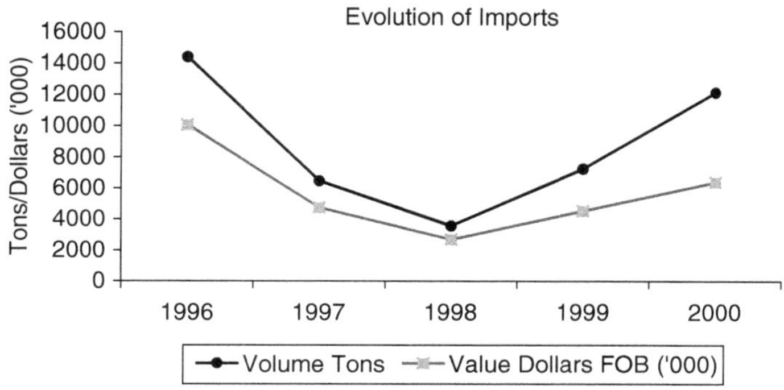

Figure 6.1 Evolution of Chilean Imports

increases in imports, and not simply on actual increases. The panel held that Article 2.1 requires actual increases in imports. Finally, the Commission had apparently omitted completely to analyze the ratio of imports relative to domestic production in its published report, as required by the Appellate Body in *Footwear*.[17] As noted, Chile did not appeal the panel's findings regarding its safeguard measures.

Argentina—Peaches. The key issue in *Peaches* may be seen readily in the above graph of total imports, which I reproduce from the panel report as Figure 6.1.[18]

The data cover a familiar five-year window. Total imports declined rather dramatically from 1996 to 1998 and then rose rather dramatically from 1998 to 2000, although not quite reaching their original levels.

In their published report, the Argentine authorities recited all of these facts, making clear that they had "considered" the early decline in imports in their analysis. Nevertheless, based on the developments in the most recent years, the authorities determined that the increased import requirements of Article 2.1 were satisfied. In so doing, Argentina sought to use prior WTO decisions offensively, noting that no specific baseline for the period of investigation could be found in the treaty text, and that the Appellate Body had emphasized the importance of "recent" trends. In Argentina's view, the sharp rise in imports since 1998 was enough.

The panel acknowledged the basis for the Argentine position in the prior cases, and conceded that the Argentine authorities "did at least acknowledge

[17] Chile—Price Band System and Safeguard Measures Relating to Certain Agricultural Products, WT/DS207/R, paras 7.150–162 (hereafter Chile—Agricultural Products Panel).

[18] Argentina—Peaches Panel para 7.44.

all the facts," including the data from 1996–98. Nevertheless, in the view of the panel, the Argentine authorities did not persuasively establish an increase in the total volume of imports given the historical data from earlier years—"they did not evaluate the increase from 1998 to 2000 in light of" the earlier data.[19] Further, the panel noted that the Argentine authorities had acknowledged that 1998 was a year affected by a poor harvest in the major exporting country, which caused imports to be abnormally low. The reliance on 1998 as a baseline was thus, for the panel, doubly suspect.

The general principle underlying the panel's finding is somewhat murky. Is the panel in effect saying that a recent upward trend in imports cannot suffice for a finding of increased imports when they remain below the levels of a few years earlier? Or that such a finding is insufficient at least when evidence is present that an intervening baseline year was one of unusually low imports? The panel itself would likely not characterize its holding either way. As with prior panels, the panel acknowledged that it was not to apply a *de novo* standard of review,[20] and that it simply required a "reasoned and adequate explanation" of the competent authorities' findings. The Argentine authorities had clearly considered all of the facts deemed relevant by the panel. The panel's decision is best read as a statement that even though the authorities had "considered" all the facts including the earlier import data, they did not persuasively articulate why their ultimate reliance on the most recent data was appropriate.

The Argentine authorities had also relied on an increase in imports relative to domestic production to support their finding. Here, the panel found that the analysis of the Argentine authorities was "sparse." The authorities did not expressly discuss the data for years prior to 1998, and relied heavily on the last few years of data in their analysis without explaining why. Again the panel found that the authorities had failed to provide a reasoned and adequate explanation for their determination.[21]

United States—Steel. The steel investigation covered a vast array of imported steel products. Ultimately, the U.S. ITC defined twenty-seven separate "industries" producing steel products within the scope of the investigation. For each of these industries, the ITC proceeded to determine whether imports had increased, and if so, whether increased imports were a substantial cause of serious injury or threat of injury as required by U.S. law. This analysis resulted in negative determinations for 15 industries, affirmative determinations for eight industries, and "divided" determinations (a 3–3 vote) for four

[19] Id. para 7.65. [20] Id. para 7.7. [21] Id. paras 7.70–79.

industries.[22] Under U.S. law, a negative determination by the ITC precludes any action by the President to impose a safeguard measure. Affirmative determinations and divided determinations are forwarded to the President for consideration of possible relief, along with remedial recommendations that the President is not bound to follow. President Bush then instituted ten distinct safeguard "measures" covering various steel products.

A complete review of the panel findings for all ten measures at issue would be unduly burdensome on both the reader and the author. Instead, I will be selective with the goal of showing the general approach of the panel to the increased imports issue.

The panel began with a review of general principles. Following the earlier Appellate Body decisions, the panel held "that the use of the present tense in the verb phrase 'is being imported' in both Article 2.1 of the Agreement of Safeguards and Article XIX:(1)(A) of the GATT 1994 indicates that it is necessary for the competent authorities to examine recent imports and that the increase in imports was 'recent'."[23] Further, "the emergency nature of safeguard measures calls for an assessment of whether imports increased suddenly so that the situation became one of emergency."[24] And finally, "[i]n light of the Panel's above conclusion that the competent authority must have determined that imports increased suddenly and recently, the Panel will generally focus its analysis on the situation of imports in the more recent period that preceded the end of the period of investigation."[25]

The panel then proceeded to examine the data on import trends for each of the ten product categories covered by the challenged measures. In most instances, the panel generated a graph representing the import volume and market share data over the five-year period of investigation employed by the ITC. Bearing in mind that the panel's focus was generally on the "more recent period that preceded the end of the period of investigation," the graph for each product category says much about how the panel came out in each case. I reproduce four of the graphs below for purposes of illustration:

For hot-rolled bar [Figure 6.2], the panel found that the ITC report did not contain a "reasoned and adequate" explanation of why imports had increased. The panel focused on the ITC's "failure to account for the most recent data from interim 2001 . . . The decrease from interim 2000 (1.34 million tons) to interim 2001 (952,392 tons) represented a decrease by 28.9%, whereas the increase in the year-to-year period before (1999 to 2000)

[22] USITC, Certain Steel Products, Inv. No. TA-201–73, (USITC Pub. No. 3479, December, 2001), Vol. I.

[23] United States—Steel Panel para 10.159.

[24] Id. para 10.166.

[25] Id. para 10.175.

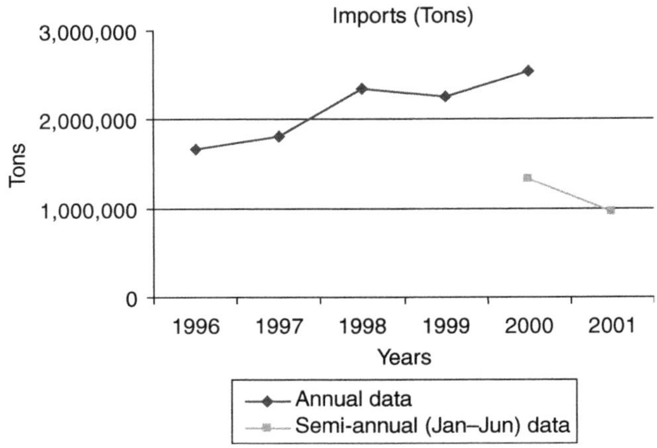

Figure 6.2 Hot-Rolled Bar

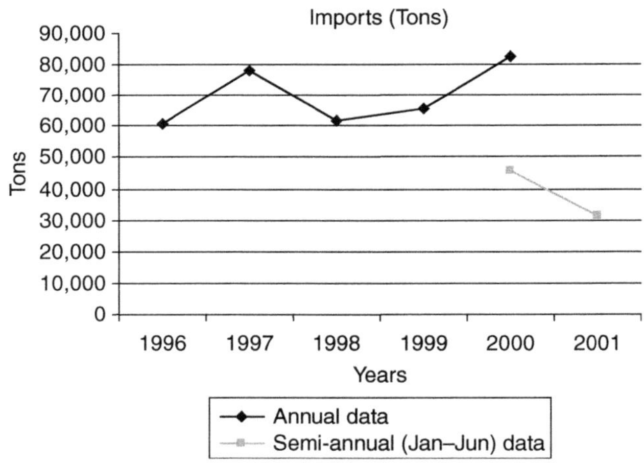

Figure 6.3 Stainless Steel Rod

that was characterized as 'rapid and dramatic' was merely 11.9%. In light of this decrease in the most recent period, the Panel does not believe that the trend of imports from 1996 to 2000 (an increase by 52.5%) is sufficient to provide a basis for a finding that, at the moment of the determination, hot-rolled bar 'is being imported in such increased quantities'."[26]

The analysis was similar in key respects for stainless steel rod [Figure 6.3]. The panel stated: "The USITC relied on the overall increase occurring between 1996

[26] Id. para 10.205.

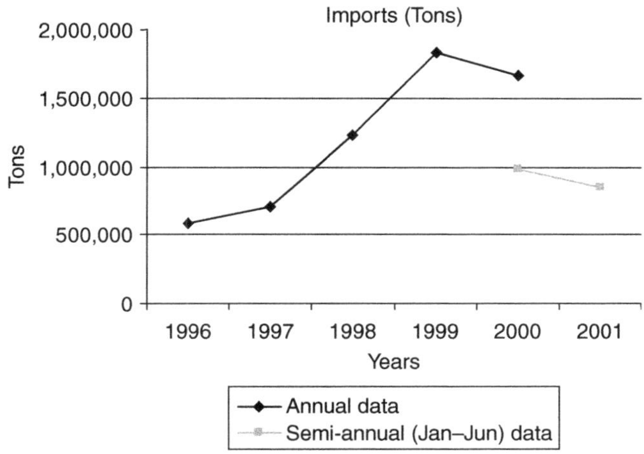

Figure 6.4 Rebar

and 2000, with the largest increase from 1999 to 2000 (25%). The decline between interim 2000 and interim 2001 was acknowledged, but the USITC did not give an explanation why it nevertheless found that there was an increase of imports in absolute numbers. This failure is particularly serious since this decrease (by 31.3%) was sharper than the preceding increase, and, as a matter of proportion, offset the increase of the two preceding years."[27]

For rebar [Figure 6.4], by contrast, the panel accepted the ITC finding of increased imports: "In light of the tripling of imports, the decrease over the last 18 months is not significant enough in order to stand in the way of a conclusion that rebar 'is being imported in such increased quantities' ."[28]

Likewise, as to stainless steel bar [Figure 6.5], the panel found that "in the light of the significant increase from 1999 to 2000 (19.3 percentage points), the decline by 3.3 percentage points from interim 2000 to interim 2001 is, contrary to what the European Communities has stated, insignificant. It simultaneously does not detract from a finding that imports, relative to domestic production, remain at high levels so that stainless steel bar 'is being imported in (such) increased quantities'."[29]

For two other product categories, tin mill products and stainless steel wire, the panel ruled that the United States failed to demonstrate the presence of increased imports because it had relied on the separate opinions of ITC Commissioners who had defined the relevant "industries" in different ways. For

[27] Id. para 10.267. [28] Id. para 10.225. [29] Id. para 10.254.

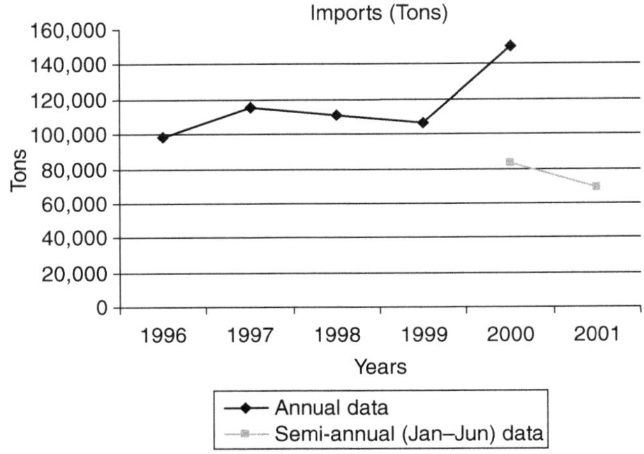

Figure 6.5 Stainless Steel Bar

example, some treated "tin mill products" as a separate industry, while another included tin mill products in a broader industry. The panel was of the view that the separate findings reached in such fashion could not collectively constitute a "reasoned and adequate" explanation for the finding of increased imports.

The Appellate Body concurred with the panel's findings on particular measures to the extent that they were challenged by the United States, except for the findings on tin mill products and stainless steel wire. The Appellate Body held that the findings of different Commissioners, who had defined the industries in varying ways, could in principle suffice, individually or collectively, as a "reasoned and adequate" explanation for a finding of increased imports.[30] It was unnecessary for the Appellate Body to complete the panel's analysis under the proper legal standard, however, because the safeguard measures for tin mill products and stainless steel wire were found to be illegal on other grounds.[31]

C Summary and Critique

Dispute panels scrutinize findings of "increased quantities" closely. National authorities *must* evaluate import data concerning both total imports and imports relative to domestic production. Neither the treaty text nor any dispute body has yet suggested any definitive guidelines for determining the

[30] United States—Steel AB paras 416, 429. [31] Id. para 431.

period over which data must be collected, but the five-calendar-year window that was previously standard practice in the United States appears to be acceptable. It is important for national authorities to acknowledge all prominent facts regarding trends in the data to demonstrate that they have been "considered," but mere "consideration" of the facts is not enough. The Appellate Body's focus on the phrase "is being imported" in GATT Article XIX and Article 2.1 of the Agreement on Safeguards has led it and subsequent panels to emphasize the need for "recent" increases in imports. The focus on the phrase "such increased quantities" has led to a *de facto* requirement that the recent increase also be substantial.

A member cannot simply choose any baseline that results in an endpoint-to-endpoint comparison reflecting an increase in imports. If a change in the baseline year can easily reverse that finding, the member may well have a difficult time establishing "increased quantities." Any evidence that the baseline period was an abnormally low period for imports is also an impediment to such a finding, as is any substantial downward trend in imports between the endpoints if the national authorities must rely on the low point of the downtrend as the baseline for the finding of a recent increase. A small, recent decline in imports is not fatal to the ability of a member to find increased quantities, however, if the general level of recent imports is nevertheless considerably above the levels of a few years earlier.

The textual genesis of these principles is clear from the preceding discussion, but do they make any sense as a policy matter? To answer that question, one requires some more general theory of the circumstances in which safeguard measures are appropriate, which returns us to the questions posed in Chapter 2—questions that have no definitive answer.

Nevertheless, one might question the great emphasis of the Appellate Body on "recent" data. The preamble to the Agreement on Safeguards emphasizes the importance of "structural adjustment." Article 7 of the Agreement provides that safeguard measures may be imposed for four years, with the possibility of an extension to eight years. Both the preamble and the potential duration of the measures are suggestive of the notion that safeguard measures exist in part to address economic or political pressures associated with industries suffering a long-term decline in competitiveness. If this is right, why should the opportunity to utilize safeguard measures turn more on "recent" import fluctuations rather than long-term import trends? For example, suppose that the market share of a domestic industry has declined slowly but substantially over a twenty year period, or suppose that it declined dramatically a few years ago but stabilized only in the most recent months or year. Is it obvious that the drafters of the Agreement on Safeguards would wish to exclude such an industry from the opportunity to secure safeguard measures? Does the Appellate Body's emphasis on "sudden," "sharp," and "recent" changes in import statistics do so?

Other aspects of the decisions seem more sensible. Certainly the concern for baseline manipulation, and the reluctance of the panels to accept simple endpoint-to-endpoint comparisons using an artfully chosen baseline, help to ensure that meaningful evidence of intensified import competition is present. Otherwise, strategic manipulation of the endpoint comparisons, perhaps coupled with strategic attention to the timing of safeguard investigations by national authorities, could reduce the "increased quantities" requirement to a near nullity.

Chapter 7

SERIOUS INJURY, THREAT AND INDUSTRY DEFINITION

Article 2 of the Agreement on Safeguards, closely paralleling the original language of GATT Article XIX, permits safeguard measures when a "product is being imported . . . in such increased quantities and under such conditions as to cause or threaten to cause serious injury to the domestic industry that produces like or directly competitive products." A WTO member proposing to employ safeguard measures must thus determine which domestic producers are members of the "industry," and demonstrate that they suffer from "serious injury" or a threat of such injury. In disputes over safeguard measures to date in the WTO, complainants routinely challenge findings of serious injury or threat by national authorities, and have challenged their definition of the "industry" on occasion as well. This chapter carefully reviews the guidance on these issues in the treaty text, and indicates why the findings of national authorities have often been found wanting.

A Defining the "Industry"

The Agreement on Safeguards provides limited guidance regarding the scope of the "industry." Article 4.1(c) simply states:

> [I]n determining injury or threat thereof, a "domestic industry" shall be understood to mean the producers as a whole of the like or directly competitive products operating within the territory of a Member, or those whose collective output of the like or directly competitive products constitutes a major proportion of the total domestic production of those products.

The text contains two general principles. First, the industry comprises the producers of "like or directly competitive products." These terms are not defined in the Agreement, nor are they defined elsewhere in WTO treaty text despite the fact that they appear in a number of places. Second, the industry includes the "producers as a whole" of these products, or at least those who produce a "major proportion." The text thus makes clear that injury findings may not be based on the condition of a small subset of the relevant producers, yet also indicates that not every single producer must be included in the analysis. The latter proviso is needed because it may be impractical to assemble data from every producer, particularly in industries with a large number of small producers.

The question of what products are "like or directly competitive" with imported products is often a contentious issue in safeguards investigations by national authorities. Domestic industries seeking safeguard measures will typically put forward a proposed definition of industry that maximizes their chances of prevailing on key issues in the case (such as on the existence of "serious injury"). Their opponents in the investigation will then seek to broaden or narrow the scope of the industry as befits their own assessment of the issues.

An example from a U.S. safeguard investigation in the 1980s illustrates the strategic issues that arise on both sides. U.S. producers of cedar home roofing products, known as "shakes" and "shingles," brought a petition before the U.S. ITC seeking safeguard measures against imports, almost all of which came from Canada.[1] The domestic petitioners suggested that all wood shakes and shingles are like or directly competitive, and that the domestic producers of those products constituted a single industry that had suffered serious

[1] U.S. International Trade Commission, Wood Shakes and Shingles, Inv. No. TA 201–56, Pub. No. 1826 (1986).

injury. The Canadian respondents responded with two arguments about the scope of the industry. First, they pointed to differences in various types of wooden shakes and shingles as a basis for suggesting that several different industries should be found to exist. This strategy was motivated by a belief that some of the proposed "industries" were not seriously injured, such as the producers of white cedar shingles. In the alternative, the respondents contended that the petitioners' proposed industry definition was too narrow, and should be expanded to include substitute roofing products such as asphalt shingles and roofing tiles. Here again, the respondents believed that the broader industry definition would yield an industry that was not seriously injured. The ITC ultimately accepted the petitioners' proposed definition and the petitioners prevailed in the case.

Industry definition is malleable in safeguard cases because the terms "like" and "directly competitive" are imprecise, and judgments about their application to individual cases are generally quite subjective. Nevertheless, some loose guidance for their application may be found in a number of WTO decisions.

1 General Guidance on the Meaning of "Like" and "Directly Competitive"

At the outset, it must be noted that the terms "like" and "directly competitive" are found in many parts of WTO treaty text outside the safeguards area. GATT Article I, for example, prohibits WTO members from applying discriminatory tariffs or other customs charges to imports of "like products" originating in the territories of member nations. GATT Article III prohibits internal taxes or other internal charges that discriminate between imported goods and "like" domestic products. Article III further prohibits differential internal taxes imposed "so as to afford protection" as between the taxed product and a "directly competitive or substitutable product" not similarly taxed. Article 2 of the Agreement on Technical Barriers to Trade imposes nondiscrimination obligations for technical regulations, again barring less favorable treatment of "like products." This list is by no means exhaustive.

Decisions outside the safeguards area may thus inform the interpretation of the phrase "like or directly competitive" under the Agreement on Safeguards. One must be cautious in drawing inferences from cases in other issue areas, however, because the Appellate Body has held that terms such as "like product" need not mean the same thing every time they are used in the treaty text.[2] Nevertheless, the cases elsewhere at least provide a useful starting point.

As to the general meaning of "like product," the Appellate Body has repeatedly looked to historical GATT practice in the area, and especially to a 1970 GATT working party report on border tax adjustments.[3] The *Border Tax Adjustments* working party stated:

> . . . the interpretation of the term ["like product"] should be examined on a case-by-case basis. This would allow a fair assessment in each case of the different elements that constitute a "similar" product. Some criteria were suggested for determining, on a case-by-case basis, whether a product is "similar": the product's end-uses in a given market; consumers' tastes and habits, which change from country to country; the product's properties, nature and quality.[4]

The *Border Tax Adjustments* report also suggested that a fourth consideration was important—the tariff classification of the products at issue.

In *European Communities—Asbestos*, the Appellate Body reviewed the *Border Tax* criteria, and then set forth its own restatement of them:

> We note that these four criteria comprise four categories of "characteristics" that the products involved might share: (i) the physical properties of the products; (ii) the extent to which the products are capable of serving the same or similar end-uses; (iii) the extent to which consumers perceive and treat the products as alternative means of performing particular functions in order to satisfy a particular want or demand; and (iv) the international classification of the products for tariff purposes.[5]

The first three of these considerations all seem to bear directly on the degree to which the products are substitutes for each other in economic parlance. Tariff classification may also be an indicator of substitutability, although many products that are not closely substitutable are classified under the same tariff headings to be sure.

The Appellate Body has had several opportunities to address the concept of "directly competitive" products as well. One clear implication of the treaty

[2] European Communities—Measures Affecting Asbestos and Asbestos-Containing Products, WT/DS135/AB/R (2001) (hereafter European Communities—Asbestos AB) held, in particular, that the concept of the "like product" was broader under GATT Article III(4) than under Article III(2).

[3] References to the Border Tax Adjustments analysis may be found, for example, in Japan—Taxes on Alcoholic Beverages, WT/DS8,10&11/AB/R (1996) (hereafter Japan—Alcoholic Beverages), and in European Communities—Asbestos AB.

[4] The original GATT report in question is Report of the Working Party on Border Tax Adjustments, BISD 18S/97 (1970), para 18.

[5] European Communities—Asbestos AB para 101.

text is that the set of directly competitive products is broader than the set of like products—that is, the degree of substitutability between them can be somewhat less. Beyond that general observation, however, the precise scope of "directly competitive" is fuzzy.

In *Japan—Alcoholic Beverages*, a case involving tax discrimination under GATT Article III(2), the Appellate Body upheld findings by a panel that linked the concept of "directly competitive" to the economic measure of "elasticity of substitution" or "cross-price elasticity of demand" (the latter being the preferred term among economists). The cross-price elasticity of demand is a measure of the extent to which the demand for one product changes in response to a change in the price of another product. If a small increase in the price of product *A* causes a large increase in the demand for product *B*, an inference would arise that the two products are closely substitutable (consumers respond to the price increase on *A* by switching their purchases to *B*). Such a situation would correspond to a high, positive cross-price elasticity of demand.

The Appellate Body went on to suggest, however, that the cross-price elasticity of demand was not "the decisive criterion." Rather, it agreed with the panel that "the decisive criterion in order to determine whether two products are directly competitive or substitutable is whether they have common end-uses, *inter alia*, as shown by elasticity of substitution." Thus, quantitative assessment of the degree of competition between products is simply one indicator, and no case has held that it is required.

In *Korea—Alcoholic Beverages*, another case under GATT Article III(2), the Appellate Body stated that "according to the ordinary meaning of the term, products are competitive or substitutable when they are interchangeable or if they offer, as the Panel noted, 'alternative ways of satisfying a particular need or taste'."[6] It also agreed with the panel that the apparent degree of competition between products might be distorted by protectionist measures that drive their prices apart, and allowed that a panel could look to the degree of competitiveness in other national markets for an inference about the degree of competition that would exist in the absence of such distortion.

Finally, *United States—Cotton Yarn* involved a transitional safeguard measure pursuant to the Agreement on Textiles and Clothing.[7] That Agreement defines the "domestic industry" using language nearly identical to the corresponding language in the Agreement on Safeguards, except that it employs the phrasing "like and/or directly competitive products." (Recall

[6] Korea—Taxes on Alcoholic Beverages, WT/DS75/AB/R para 115.

[7] United States—Transitional Safeguard Measure on Combed Cotton Yarn from Pakistan, WT/DS192/AB/R.

that the Agreement on Safeguards refers to "like or directly competitive".) The United States had made an injury finding relating to imports of cotton yarn based on its examination of the "industry" producing and selling cotton yarn on the open market in the United States. It excluded from the industry certain vertically integrated U.S. firms that produced cotton yarn for internal use and did not sell their yarn on the open market except in *de minimis* quantities. The exclusion of these firms was justified by the United States on the grounds that the imported yarn was not "directly competitive" with the yarn produced by vertically integrated U.S. companies—the products did not compete head-to-head in the marketplace. The panel rejected this proposition, and the Appellate Body affirmed. Among other things, the United States had conceded that the imported and domestic products were "like,"[8] and the Appellate Body concluded that all like products are of necessity directly competitive. It also noted a number of economic considerations supporting its determination, such as the fact that the price of imported yarn will affect the decision by domestic firms to produce yarn internally or to buy it on the open market, thus creating a degree of implicit competition between the imported product and captive domestic production.

In sum, the cases in other issue areas suggest that both "like" and "directly competitive" products are groups of products that are substitutable by end users. "Like" products are generally closer substitutes than products which are merely "directly competitive." Quantitative measures of substitutability—the cross-price elasticity of demand—are appropriate to consider in assessing the degree of substitutability, but not mandatory or decisive, and no numerical "cutoffs" have been suggested with respect to these measures. Qualitative assessment of factors indicating substitutability is permitted and common, as is consideration of tariff classification.

2 Industry Definition Issues in Safeguard Disputes to Date

Although complainants have raised questions about industry definition in a number of safeguards disputes, relatively little law has emerged on the

[8] Having made this concession, the United States was forced to adopt a somewhat strained construction of the industry definition criterion. Under the Agreement on Textiles and Clothing, the industry consists of the producers of like *and/or* directly competitive products—the United States argued that because of the and/or phrasing, it could define the industry based on either the group of like products *or* the group of directly competitive products. Thus, it insisted, it could choose to focus on directly competitive products alone, and leave out certain products that are nevertheless "like." The Appellate Body did not reach this issue, however, having held that the imported and domestic products were directly competitive in any event.

subject, in part because panels have sometimes exercised judicial economy to avoid these issues while deciding the case on other grounds. Nevertheless, four of the disputes to date raise issues worth noting.

I start with a comparatively minor point. In *Argentina—Footwear*, Argentina divided the footwear industry into several market segments for purposes of collecting data from its domestic industry. Some of this market segment data was presented in the report of the national authorities. The European Communities argued that, having gathered data separately by market segment, Argentina was obliged to establish injury and causation for each segment. The European Communities did not dispute, however, that footwear in the aggregate comprised a single group of like or directly competitive products. On this basis, the panel agreed with Argentina that injury and causation should be established for the footwear industry as a whole, and not for each market segment.[9]

The other cases of note raise questions that are harder and of quite broad importance. The first involves industries in which imports may have a competitive impact on multiple stages of processing in the importing nation. The second concerns the treatment of multi-product firms.

(a) *Imports and Prior Stages of Processing*

Economists often refer to "stages of processing" in an industry. This term conveys the idea that some final products are produced through a sequence of production processes. Consider steel products, for example—iron is first obtained from a mining operation, then transformed at a steel mill into steel, and perhaps later transformed through a finishing process into a variety of different steel products. The prior stages of processing are the "upstream" stages in relation to the subsequent "downstream" stages of processing. A question arises in some safeguard investigations whether upstream stages of processing may be included in the domestic industry competing with imports of a finished product.

In *Chile—Agricultural Products*, Chile had imposed safeguard measures based on a rather loose analysis of the industries in question. It apparently included wheat and wheat flour in the same industry, it included crude and refined vegetable oils in the same industry, and it based its injury finding regarding imported vegetable oils in part on evidence of harm to rapeseed growers (as distinguished from rapeseed oil producers). The dispute panel

[9] Argentina—Footwear Panel paras 8.135–37.

ruled that Chile had not adequately explained or justified its findings on any of these industry definition issues.[10]

A similar matter was raised in *United States—Lamb*, and addressed at much greater length in the dispute process. The U.S. safeguard measure involved imports of fresh, chilled, or frozen lamb meat. The U.S. ITC, following its own precedent in the safeguards area and in other areas (anti-dumping and countervailing duty cases), found that U.S. growers of live lambs were part of the domestic industry. It held specifically that the "like product" was lamb meat. But it also held that growers of live lambs are "producers" of lamb meat, relying on the fact that there is a "continuous line of production" from the raw to the processed product, and a "substantial coincidence of economic interest between the growers and the processors." Interestingly, the ITC did *not* hold that live lambs were directly competitive with imported lamb meat.

Australia and New Zealand challenged the industry definition, and the panel agreed with their position. A "producer" is someone whose operations "bring a thing into existence" said the panel, and a grower of live lambs does not produce lamb meat. The United States also sought to rely on the phrase "producers as a whole" of the like product in Article 4.1(c) of the Agreement on Safeguards, suggesting that lamb growers were among the "producers as a whole." The panel rejected this view as well, suggesting that the reference to producers as a whole was intended to ensure that data on the industry are representative, not to broaden its scope. The panel also relied on some pre-WTO GATT panel decisions in the subsidies area that were supportive of its views, and on the fact that proposals to change the treaty text during the Uruguay Round in response to those panel decisions were not adopted. Finally, the panel noted that even if some of the injury caused by an imported product is "passed back" to upstream producers of input products, injury should also in general be evident to the producers of the finished product that competes directly with the imports—by implication, a broadening of the "industry" is unnecessary for the importing nation to establish its right to use safeguard measures. Likewise, a safeguard measure based on injury to producers of the finished product will confer some benefits on upstream producers even if they are not included in the domestic "industry" for purposes of the injury analysis.[11]

The Appellate Body upheld the panel's findings, although it regarded the issue as somewhat more straightforward than the panel. The Appellate Body

[10] Chile—Agricultural Products Panel paras 7.141–49.
[11] United States—Lamb Panel paras 7.46–118.

emphasized that the industry can include only the producers of "like or directly competitive products." The U.S. ITC itself held that lamb meat was the "like product," and did not hold that live lambs and lamb meat were directly competitive. *A fortiori*, in the view of the Appellate Body, producers of live lambs are not part of the domestic industry. It added that the "continuous line of production" and "coincidence of interest" tests in U.S. law have no textual basis in WTO law. Finally, it concurred with the panel that the phrase "producers as a whole" in Article 4.1(c) is simply intended to ensure that the industry encompasses the bulk of domestic producers of the product(s) at issue, and does not permit the producers of products that are not "like or directly competitive" to be included in the industry.[12]

Thus, in the decisions to date in which national authorities have included upstream stages of processing in the domestic industry, the dispute process has ruled against them. But it has not entirely closed the door to the inclusion of upstream producers—could national authorities persuasively argue that upstream products are "directly competitive" with downstream products?

Consider the *Lamb* case as an illustration. On the one hand, it seems obvious that live lambs are not interchangeable with lamb meat by the end user. Few consumers will choose to purchase live lambs and slaughter them in the back yard in response to an increase in the price of lamb chops. If the focus is exclusively on the interchangeability of the products by end users, therefore, upstream products will almost invariably be excluded from the scope of what is "directly competitive".

On the other hand, there can be little doubt that import competition in the market for lamb meat can have a substantial effect on growers of live lambs. A fall in the price of imported lamb meat will force domestic packers of lamb meat to lower their prices to remain competitive, which in turn reduces what they will pay for domestic live lambs. The impact upstream will tend to be greater when the upstream product has no other significant use than to be transformed into the finished product that competes with imports, as is perhaps the case with live lambs. In this sense, imports of lamb meat can unquestionably have a dramatic *competitive impact* on the growers of lambs. Might it make sense to construe the notion of "directly competitive" products somewhat more broadly, to allow the inclusion of products on which import competition has a large competitive impact?

The *Lamb* panel is surely correct that even if the market consequences of increased competition from imported lamb meat are "passed back" to

[12] United States—Lamb AB paras 77–96.

growers to a degree, they will also be evident in some fashion at the level of the domestic packers who produce the lamb meat directly. If imported lamb meat is displacing domestic production, for example, production by packers should exhibit a decline, their prices will often exhibit decline, and so on. Yet, it is also possible that the primary impact on the profitability of domestic firms will be felt upstream. Simple price theory suggests that the impact of a decline in the price of the finished product will be transmitted upstream to a greater extent when the upstream product is inelastically supplied (as may well be the case with live lambs, at least in the short run, given that they have few alternative uses). One can also imagine contractual arrangements in which the price for the input product is tied to the price of the finished product in a way that transmits most of the impact of a price drop in the finished product to the input suppliers. Whenever most of the effects of a decline in price are "passed back" in the words of the Lamb panel, the producers of the finished product will find that their profitability is insulated to a significant degree from the effects of import competition. If so, perhaps they will not exhibit "serious injury," and may have little reason to expend resources in pursuit of safeguard measures.

In sum, therefore, the suppliers of upstream products may at times have a greater financial stake in trade policy with respect to downstream imports than the firms which actually produce the downstream products that compete directly with the imports. It is not implausible that for such cases, the drafters of a safeguards agreement might desire that upstream producers have standing to initiate a case, and that their financial condition should "count" in assessing whether "serious injury" is present.

From an economic perspective, therefore, one can argue either way on the question whether, at least in certain exceptional cases, upstream domestic input products should be deemed "directly competitive" with downstream imports. A final resolution of this issue must await further guidance from the Appellate Body.

(b) Multiproduct Firms

United States—Steel raised an array of interesting questions about the proper definition of industry. The dispute panel avoided them on grounds of judicial economy, and the issues consequently vanished in the appeal. I note some of them briefly here, however, because of their conceptual importance and the likelihood that they will recur.

The steel industry produces a wide array of finished products—steel slab, hot and cold-rolled steel sheet, flanges, tubes and pipes, and so on. These products are made from the same basic input product (steel), but the finished products are quite different from one another. A consumer who needs a pipe cannot substitute a slab; a consumer who needs flange cannot substitute steel sheet.

Recognizing the differences among various steel products, the U.S. ITC defined 27 separate "industries" during its investigation and analyzed each of them separately. Even so, some of the individual "industries" included products that were still quite different from one another. For example, one of the industries was defined as "certain carbon flat-rolled steel," which included various slab, plate, hot-rolled, and cold-rolled products. Another, "tin mill products," included various products coated with tin, chromium, or chromium oxides, having significantly different end uses. Among other things, the complainants in *Steel* argued that these industry definitions were impermissible because they encompassed many products that are not "like or directly competitive" with one another. The complainants thus argued, in effect, that the ITC should have defined and analyzed far more than 27 industries.

Several critical issues are in play here. The first is the most obvious one, emphasized by the complainants—when an industry is defined to include an array of products that do not in fact compete with each other, it is logically more difficult to draw inferences about the causal relation between import competition and developments in the domestic industry (the subject of the next chapter). If imports of cold-rolled sheet have become cheaper, for example, it seems unlikely that they could bear any causal connection to a decline in the domestic sales of steel slab.

But there are competing considerations, including the transaction costs of safeguard investigations. As the number of industries multiplies, the required analysis becomes more and more expensive and time consuming. In an investigation involving as many different end-products as *Steel*, these costs may become staggering if every type of product must be treated as originating in a separate industry.

Related, it may be nearly impossible to obtain reliable data on so many "industries." The category of "tin mill products" may have appeal as candidate for an "industry" not because all such products are substitutes for each other, but because they are all produced by tin mills. National authorities can perhaps obtain reliable data on output, profitability, and other measures of industrial health for domestic tin mills, but it may be extremely difficult to obtain useful data for each tin mill product separately. Among other things, profitability data by product would no doubt require complex cost allocation calculations, calculations that would likely rest on questionable and perhaps inevitably arbitrary assumptions. The problem is not limited to the steel industry, but is a generic one that arises with all multi-product firms. A concern for such data issues is one of the reasons why the ITC has not focused exclusively on consumer substitutability or "demand-side" considerations in its analysis—the situation on the "supply-side" has also factored into its industry definition decisions as well.

Steel raised, but did not resolve, the basic question of whether these supply-side issues are permissible considerations in defining the domestic "industry." The Appellate Body decisions to date, with their focus on what products are "interchangeable," do not suggest much room for these factors. The Appellate Body also stated squarely in *United States—Lamb*, that "the focus must be on the products, and their 'like or directly competitive' relationship, and not on the processes by which those products are produced."[13] But if that is the ultimate resolution of the matter, the ability of importing nations to employ safeguard measures in industries populated with multiproduct firms will be considerably impaired, for better or worse.

With reference to the *Border Tax* factors and the Appellate Body's restatement of them, some room for argument arises based on factor (i), physical characteristics. In an "industry" such as tin mill products, for example, the included products have certain physical similarities relating to the inputs used to produce them, even if they are not all substitutes for the end user. Likewise, tariff headings (factor (iv)) for steel products sometimes include products that are not substitutes for each other, although they do tend to divide products more finely than did the ITC. It remains to be seen whether industry definitions that rely primarily on such considerations can withstand scrutiny.

B "Serious Injury"

Import-competing industries may qualify for safeguard measures when they exhibit "serious injury" or a threat of such injury. This section will focus on current "serious injury," while the next will consider special issues that arise in threat cases.

The Agreement on Safeguards defines serious injury as "a significant overall impairment in the position of a domestic industry." Article 4.2(a) then states:

In the investigation to determine whether increased imports have caused or are threatening to cause serious injury to a domestic industry under the terms of this

[13] United States—Lamb AB para 95. The Appellate Body added a somewhat cryptic footnote to the effect that production processes might be appropriately considered if the issue is whether two articles are *separate products*—i.e., one assumes, whether two complementary goods that are sold bundled together must be treated as distinct products or not. Id. note 55.

Agreement, the competent authorities shall evaluate all relevant factors of an objective and quantifiable nature having a bearing on the situation of that industry, in particular, the rate and amount of the increase in imports of the product concerned in absolute and relative terms, the share of the domestic market taken by increased imports, changes in the level of sales, production, productivity, capacity utilization, profits and losses, and employment.

Thus, the treaty text affords a list of factors that national authorities "shall evaluate," among "all relevant factors of an objective and quantifiable nature," in making a judgment about whether an industry exhibits significant overall impairment.

The core standard of "significant overall impairment" is obviously imprecise and open to differing opinions and judgments. Nothing in the treaty text explains how the various factors are to be "evaluated," or how much weight each factor is to receive in the overall assessment. One might thus suppose that national authorities have wide discretion in their assessment of serious injury, and that the treaty text imposes few meaningful constraints on this aspect of their analysis. Nevertheless, findings of serious injury by national authorities have been found deficient with some regularity in WTO disputes.

The Appellate Body has stated on various occasions that "serious injury" is a tough standard to meet. In *United States—Lamb*, it remarked:

The standard of "serious injury" set forth in Article 4.1(a) is, on its face, very high. Indeed, in *United States—Wheat Gluten*, we referred to this standard as "exacting". Further, in this respect, we note that the word "injury" is qualified by the adjective "serious", which, in our view, underscores the extent and degree of "significant overall impairment" that the domestic industry must be suffering, or must be about to suffer, for the standard to be met. We are fortified in our view that the standard of "serious injury" in the *Agreement on Safeguards* is a very high one when we contrast this standard with the standard of "material injury" envisaged under the *Anti-Dumping Agreement*, the *Agreement on Subsidies and Countervailing Measures* (the "*SCM Agreement*") and the GATT 1994. We believe that the word "serious" connotes a much higher standard of injury than the word "material".[14]

In this passage, the Appellate Body offers a clear signal that findings of serious injury should be scrutinized closely, and dispute panels have for the most part taken a hard look at them.

[14] United States—Lamb AB para 124.

The earliest disputes addressed two arguable ambiguities in the text of Article 4.2(a). Both concern the obligation to consider all "relevant factors." First, must national authorities expressly evaluate every specifically enumerated factor in Article 4.2(a), or just those that the authorities consider "relevant?" In both *Korea—Dairy* and *Argentina—Footwear*, the dispute panels concluded that all of the enumerated factors must be considered in every case. The Appellate Body agreed in *Argentina—Footwear*, and affirmed the panel's finding that Argentina had violated Article 4.2(a) by failing to give due consideration to capacity utilization and productivity.[15]

The second issue is whether the list of enumerated factors in Article 4.2(a) is exhaustive of the set of "relevant factors." The Appellate Body decision in *Footwear* made clear that it is not—any other "relevant factor" must also be evaluated.[16] The decision left open the question of how national authorities are to identify other relevant factors, an issue which was later addressed in *United States—Wheat Gluten* in the context of causation analysis. I discuss that aspect of *Wheat Gluten* in the next chapter.[17]

The Appellate Body decision in *Footwear* also took pains to suggest that mere consideration of the various factors is not enough—"we do not believe that an evaluation of the listed factors in Article 4.2(a) is all that is required to justify a determination of 'serious injury'."[18] National authorities must demonstrate that the industry is exhibiting significant overall impairment:

> Obviously, any such evaluation will be different for different industries in different cases, depending on the facts of the particular case and the situation of the industry concerned. An evaluation of each listed factor will not necessarily have to show that each such factor is "declining". In one case, for example, there may be significant declines in sales, employment and productivity that will show "significant overall impairment" in the position of the industry, and therefore will justify a finding of serious injury. In another case, a certain factor may not be declining, but the overall picture may nevertheless demonstrate "significant overall impairment" of the industry. Thus, in addition to a technical examination of whether the competent authorities in a particular case have evaluated all the listed factors and any other relevant factors, we believe that it is essential for a panel to take the definition of "serious injury" in Article 4.1(a) of the *Agreement on Safeguards* into account in its review of any determination of "serious injury".[19]

[15] Argentina—Footwear AB para 136.

[16] Id. para 139.

[17] The holding in Wheat Gluten is simply that the national authorities have an affirmative obligation to investigate all relevant factors, and cannot limit themselves to considering factors clearly raised by the parties to the investigation.

[18] Id. para 138.

[19] Id. para 139.

This passage makes clear that no one factor is determinative in injury analysis, but also encourages panels to do more than simply verify that national authorities have considered a check list of factors. Precisely what a panel must do to properly "take into account" the definition of serious injury remains murky, however, and harks back to the question of the proper standard of review as discussed in Chapter 3.

Both the *Korea—Dairy* and *Argentina—Footwear* panels clearly did more than simply ask whether a factor had been nominally evaluated. Each held that although national authorities had considered data on certain factors, the data were not shown to be sufficiently representative of the industry as a whole. As a result, consideration of the factors at issue was not reasoned and adequate.[20] The *Footwear* panel also found that the national authorities had placed undue emphasis on comparisons of the data for the beginning and end of the period of investigation without adequate attention to intervening trends,[21] and that they failed to explain how an increase in the value of domestic production over the period of investigation was consistent with a finding of serious injury.[22] Several panels have raised similar sorts of questions about findings of threatened injury by national authorities, as the next section will indicate.

The general lesson is that national authorities must identify and coherently respond to arguments questioning the existence of serious injury. Conclusory dismissal of such arguments, or a failure to address them altogether in the published report, raises a considerable risk that a panel will find a lack of reasoned and adequate basis for the injury finding. National authorities must also make clear how the data on which they rely is reasonably representative of the domestic industry and address any concerns about its statistical soundness.

C Threat of Serious Injury

Article 4.1(b) of the Agreement on Safeguards defines threat of serious injury as follows:

"threat of serious injury" shall be understood to mean serious injury that is clearly imminent, in accordance with the provisions of paragraph 2. A determination of the

[20] See Korea—Dairy Panel paras 7.70–75, Argentina—Footwear Panel paras 8.218–25.
[21] Id. para 8.216. [22] Id. para 8.226.

existence of a threat of serious injury shall be based on facts and not merely on allegation, conjecture or remote possibility.

Several of the disputes to come before WTO panels have involved safeguard measures predicated on findings of threatened injury, and the analysis by national authorities has regularly been found lacking.

In *Argentina—Footwear*, the national authorities found a threat of serious injury in addition to current serious injury. But they did not conduct a serious, independent analysis of the threat issue. Likewise, the finding appeared to rest on a threat of increased imports rather than on actual increased imports. The panel held that findings of threat must be separately reasoned and justified, and further that a threat of increased imports cannot suffice—imports must have increased in actuality. These issues were not addressed on appeal.

A related issue arose in *United States—Line Pipe*. The U.S. ITC made a finding of "serious injury or the threat of serious injury" in its report. The somewhat unusual finding owed to the fact that three of six Commissioners found current serious injury, while two of the remaining Commissioners found threatened injury. Korea argued that such a finding was impermissible—it claimed that national authorities must make a finding of serious injury *or* threat, and suggested that the two were mutually exclusive. The panel accepted this proposition, but the Appellate Body reversed it. It ruled that the phrase "cause or threaten to cause serious injury" in Article 2.1 could be read to say that serious injury and threatened injury can exist concurrently. It thereby rejected the suggestion that a finding must be made of one or the other, but not both.[23] As a practical matter, the ruling allows a country like the United States, whose national authorities consist of six independent Commissioners, to base an injury finding on the collective opinions of the various Commissioners even though their findings are not all consistent.

The Appellate Body also addressed the standards for threat cases in *United States—Lamb*. The U.S. ITC did not find current serious injury in its investigation, but found a threat of serious injury based on "declines during the period of investigation in the domestic industry's market share, production, shipments, profitability and prices among other difficulties that the industry is facing."[24] As noted earlier in this chapter, the panel found that the ITC had defined the industry improperly by including growers of live lambs, but it proceeded to review the ITC finding of threat anyway, assuming

[23] United States—Line Pipe AB paras 134–77.

[24] U.S. International Trade Commission, Lamb Meat, Inv. No. TA-201–68 (April 1999) at I-21.

arguendo that the industry definition was proper. The panel concluded that the ITC had collected and analyzed data on all of the relevant factors in the treaty text, and had adequately explained why data on certain factors was difficult or impossible to obtain. Although the ITC relied heavily on declining trends in indicators of industrial health at the end of the period of investigation, the panel found such reliance on the most recent data to be appropriate. The panel thus approved of the ITC's general analytical approach to the case.[25]

The panel did fault the ITC, however, for basing many of its findings on questionnaire data when the response rate to the ITC questionnaires by members of the domestic industry had been exceedingly low. Questions about the financial condition of the industry yielded useable responses from producers representing only about 5% of the annual lamb crop, for example, and the ITC itself conceded in its published report that the questionnaire responses did not constitute a statistically valid sample of the domestic industry. The panel held that a violation of Article 4.1(c) arose because the data on which the ITC relied was not sufficiently representative of the "producers whose collective output . . . constitutes a major proportion" of the like or directly competitive products.[26]

The United States appealed this finding, arguing that nothing in the text of the Agreement on Safeguards imposes any requirement that data be "representative." The Appellate Body upheld the finding, however, with the qualifier that the violation should be deemed to arise under Article 4.2(a). Article 4.1(c) is simply definitional and cannot, by itself, be violated. But by relying on statistically unsound information, the United States had failed to evaluate properly all factors of an "objective and quantifiable nature" as required by Article 4.2(a).[27] Thus, *Lamb* stands squarely for the proposition that national authorities must to the extent possible base their injury determinations on statistically reliable information about the domestic industry.

Another part of the Appellate Body opinion in *Lamb* took issue with the panel's approval of the general approach to threat analysis employed by the ITC. It began by emphasizing the language of Article 4.1(b), and particularly its requirement that in threat cases, serious injury must be "clearly imminent." According to the Appellate Body, this phrase indicates "that, as a matter of fact, it must be manifest that the domestic industry is on the brink of

[25] United States—Lamb Panel paras 7.120–204. [26] Id. paras 7.208–21.
[27] United States—Lamb AB paras 128–34.

suffering serious injury."[28] The Appellate Body agreed with the panel that data from the most recent past are the most probative regarding the likely future state of the industry, but insisted that such data must be analyzed in the context of the entire investigation. "For instance, although the most recent data may indicate a decline in the domestic industry, that decline may well be a part of the normal cycle of the domestic industry rather than a precursor to clearly imminent serious injury."[29]

The Appellate Body then concluded that although the panel correctly stated the standard of review in the case (objective assessment of the facts), it did not apply it properly. The complainants made a number of specific arguments about weaknesses in the ITC analysis to which the panel did not respond. Instead, it apparently approved of the analytic approach of the ITC simply because most indicators of industrial health declined toward the end of the period of investigation, and not every indicator must decline for threat to be present.

The Appellate Body then proceeded to consider the arguments put forward before the panel by the complainants, and held that the published report of the ITC contained no reasoned and adequate response to them. For example, the ITC relied significantly in its threat finding on the fact that the prices for domestic products were "depressed" toward the end of the investigation. This finding was apparently based on a comparison of prices at the end of the period of investigation (1998) with prices during the middle of the period of investigation (1996–97). Yet, 1998 prices were in fact higher than in 1993 and 1994 at the beginning of the period of investigation, after an appropriate adjustment for inflation. The ITC did not explain why the 1996–97 prices were the proper benchmark for assessing whether prices were "depressed," rather than 1993–94 prices. On this basis, the Appellate Body found a further violation of Article 4.2(a) by the United States.

Two subsequent panel decisions again found the analysis of threat by national authorities to be deficient. In *Chile—Agricultural Products*, the panel determined that the national authorities had failed to evaluate some of the relevant factors enumerated in Article 4.2(a). Moreover, the national authorities had apparently based their finding of threat on a "counterfactual"—they concluded that if Chile's agricultural price band system was modified to ensure that it complied with Chile's bound rates of duty, producers currently protected by it would suffer injury. The panel concluded

[28] Id. para 126. [29] Id. para 138.

that a finding of threat based on such policy counterfactuals is impermissible.[30]

Argentina—Peaches also addressed a threat determination by national authorities. In addition to an apparent failure by the national authorities to evaluate one enumerated factor in Article 4.2(a), the panel determined that the authorities had made the same sort of error identified by the Appellate Body in *Lamb*—an excessive reliance on increasing imports and declining indicators of industrial health at the end of the period of investigation. The panel suggested that the apparent trends at the end of the period of investigation might have been due to an unusually bad harvest abroad a year earlier that led to exceptionally low imports and to exceptional prosperity for domestic import-competing firms. The published report of the national authorities contained no "reasoned and adequate" basis to reject this alternative interpretation of the data. Further, the national authorities had made no finding to the effect that serious injury was "clearly imminent."[31]

In sum, the decisions to date involving threat determinations by national authorities also make clear that the rather imprecise legal standard for a threat determination does not confer unlimited discretion on national authorities. As a formal matter, national authorities must evaluate all of the factors raised in the treaty text and all others raised during the course of the investigation, and make explicit findings in accordance with the standards of the Agreement on Safeguards. They must be careful not to rely on suspect or unrepresentative data. And they must clearly demonstrate, in their published reports, that they have carefully considered the arguments put forward by import interests during the investigation, and must respond to them cogently.

[30] Chile—Agricultural Products Panel paras 7.163–74.

[31] Argentina—Peaches Panel paras 7.93–124.

Chapter 8

THE CAUSATION REQUIREMENT AND "NON-ATTRIBUTION"

Article 2 of the Agreement on Safeguards permits safeguard measures only when "a product is being imported in such increased quantities, absolute or relative to domestic production, and under such conditions as to cause or threaten serious injury." Article 4.2 goes on to state:

> (a) In the investigation to determine whether increased imports have caused or are threatening to cause serious injury to a domestic industry under the terms of this Agreement, the competent authorities shall evaluate all relevant factors of an objective and quantifiable nature having a bearing on the situation of that industry, in particular, the rate and amount of the increase in imports of the product concerned in absolute and relative terms, the share of the domestic market taken by increased imports, changes in the level of sales, production, productivity, capacity utilization, profits and losses, and employment.
> (b) The determination referred to in subparagraph (a) shall not be made unless this investigation demonstrates, on the basis of objective evidence, the existence of the causal link between increased imports of the product concerned and serious injury or threat thereof. When factors other than increased imports are causing injury to the domestic industry at the same time, such injury shall not be attributed to increased imports.

The requirement of a causal link between "increased quantities" and serious injury or threat raises perhaps the most difficult and problematic issues of any posed by the Agreement on Safeguards. As briefly suggested in Chapters 1 and 2, the notion that "increased quantities" of imports are a causal variable at all is inconsistent with basic price theory. The further requirement in Article 4.2(b) that injury caused by other factors "not be attributed to increased imports" is equally intractable from an economic standpoint. The fact of the matter is that injury is never "caused" by increased imports at all—it is inevitably the case that some "other factor" is the underlying cause of both the injury and the increase in import quantities.

The problem originates with a fundamentally deficient treaty text. which borrows from the deficient standard for causation under U.S. law. Long before the Agreement on Safeguards came into existence, the U.S. ITC struggled to apply the U.S. standard and failed to develop a logically sound interpretation of it. WTO panels and the Appellate Body have done no better in interpreting WTO treaty text, and the decisions to date in the WTO dispute process repeat many of the same logical fallacies that infuse ITC opinions. The result is a morass of confused precedents that leave it quite unclear what a WTO member must do to establish "causation."

Before proceeding, note that safeguards cases are not the only cases in which national authorities must examine the cause of injury or threatened injury. In antidumping and countervailing duty cases, national authorities must determine whether dumped or subsidized imports are causing or threatening to cause "material injury" to the domestic industry. Both the

Antidumping Agreement and the Agreement on Subsidies and Countervailing Measures also contain "non-attribution" obligations, requiring national to authorities to avoid attributing injury caused by other factors to dumped or subsidized imports. I will not survey the dispute panel and Appellate Body reports bearing on the causation requirement in antidumping and countervailing duty cases in this chapter, however, in part because they are rather numerous, but in greater part because they add little conceptually to what is contained in the dispute reports for safeguards cases. Suffice it to say that a number of the points to be made here are also applicable to causation analysis in antidumping and countervailing proceedings.

Section A begins with some simple economics of the causation question, designed to clarify why increased imports cannot properly be viewed as a causal variable, and why the "non-attribution" requirement of Article 4.2(b) can become absurd. Section B then considers the history of the causation inquiry by the U.S. ITC and highlights its fundamental problems. Section C reviews decisions on the issue to date by WTO panels and the Appellate Body, lays out the emerging "test" under WTO precedent, and explains why it is deeply flawed as a conceptual matter. Section D considers possible ways out of the problem, and assesses their strengths and weaknesses.

A The Economics of "Causation"

GATT Article XIX addresses circumstances in which "unforeseen developments" and "the effect of the obligations incurred" result in increased quantities of imports that cause or threaten serious injury. The causal chain in this phrasing begins with unforeseen developments and GATT obligations, which together result in increased quantities of imports, in turn causing serious injury or threat of it. For reasons that I will explain below, an economist will object to this account of the causal chain, on the grounds that increased quantities of imports do not "cause" injury or threat even as an intermediate step in the causal chain—they arise simultaneously with injury or threat. But at least the causal chain in GATT Article XIX begins with two things that an economist can understand as causal. For example, a *change* in trade policy pursuant to GATT may have a severe competitive impact on a domestic industry, and in such cases the GATT obligation may be viewed as the cause of serious injury. When that severe impact is unexpected, one can also say that the cause of the problem is a conjunction between GATT obligations and unforeseen developments. Alternatively, one can imagine scenarios in which an unforeseen development is the precipitating cause of injury. Suppose, for example, that trade policy remains fixed, but that some other economic shock upsets the competitive relationship between imported and domestic goods leading to economic distress in an import-competing industry. The economic shock may then be deemed the "unforeseen development" that causes injury. GATT obligations may be viewed as contributing to the problem as well if, *but for* the GATT obligation, the importing nation would have changed its trade policy to abate the consequences of the shock. These two scenarios thus represent circumstances in which unforeseen developments and GATT obligations together may, in coherent fashion, be said jointly to cause injury.

As noted in Chapter 1, however, GATT practice over time came to ignore the "unforeseen developments" and "effect of obligations incurred" elements of Article XIX. U.S. law, for example, simply asked whether increased quantities of imports were causing injury. The text of the Agreement on Safeguards likewise imposes no requirement for members to draw a causal link between "unforeseen developments" or GATT obligations and injury. Although the Appellate Body has revived the unforeseen developments requirement under WTO law, as discussed at length in Chapter 5, it has yet to state in any sort of clear fashion that members desiring to employ safeguard measures must draw a causal link between injury and the "unforeseen development." Instead, like U.S. law and the Agreement on Safeguards, the Appellate Body repeatedly asks national authorities to determine whether increased quantities of imports are causing serious injury or threat, and further asks them to ensure that injury caused by other factors not be "attributed" to increased imports.

This focus on the causal connection between "increased quantities" and injury is fundamentally incoherent. So too, in large measure, is the requirement of "non-attribution" that is the emphasis of so many panel and Appellate Body decisions. This section will explain why.

I wish to emphasize that the problems that I identify below have been duly noted by others, and are quite well understood by prominent economists who have devoted attention to safeguards issues. The prior literature bearing on these issues includes Grossman (1986), Pindyck and Rotemberg (1987), Kelly (1988), Rousslang (1988), Horn and Mavroidis (2003), Sykes (2003), Sykes (2004), Grossman and Mavroidis (2005), and Grossman and Sykes (2005).

Figure 8.1

We begin with a simple diagram depicting equilibrium in a competitive market with both imported and domestic goods. The diagram assumes that the imported and domestic goods are perfect substitutes (fungible), although nothing important turns on this assumption. In Figure 8.1, total consumer demand for the good in question is *D*. The supply of imports from abroad is the curve S_i, while domestic supply is S_d. Total supply is the horizontal sum of import and domestic supply, represented by the (kinked) curve S_t. Market equilibrium occurs where total supply is equal to total demand—at the quantity q_t, and the equilibrium price *p*.

The quantities of imports and domestic production, q_i and q_d, respectively, are obtained by reading each off of its respective supply curve at the equilibrium price *p*.

Within this framework, the quantity of imports, along with the quantity of domestic production and the equilibrium price, are simultaneously determined by the interplay of supply and demand forces. It makes no more sense to say that the quantity of imports causes the quantity of domestic production than the other way around—both (along with price) are the *result* of the factors that underlie the supply and demand relationships. Those factors are the *causal* or *exogenous* variables in the system.

The factors that underlie demand are essentially three—consumer tastes (the utility or benefit that consumers derive from the good in question), consumer income (how much consumers have to spend on things that they wish to buy), and the price of substitutes and complements (goods that can be used instead of or in conjunction with the good in question). The factors that underlie supply, both for imports and domestic goods, are two—the technology available to producers of the good for making and delivering it to the consumer, and the prices of all of the inputs into the process of making and delivering the good. When any one of these underlying factors changes, some associated shift will occur in the associated demand or supply relationship. The *result* will be a new equilibrium in the market, quite likely involving different quantities of imports and domestic production, and a different price. Again, the quantity of imports, the quantity of domestic production, and the price will be simultaneously determined. None is a "cause" of the other. For this reason, it makes no sense to say that *changes* in the quantity of imports cause changes in the condition of the domestic competing industry (such as changes in its output or in the price that it receives).

To be sure, changes in underlying supply and demand factors can *result* in both an increased quantity of imports and reduction in domestic production or price. Increased quantities of imports and "serious injury" in the domestic industry may thus emerge together in time. They may thus be correlated with each other in a temporal sense even though neither is a "cause" of the other. Such scenarios provide an illustration of the fundamental difference between correlation and causation, a difference that is emphasized at great length in elementary statistics.

Perhaps it is useful to consider a few examples of how various exogenous forces may cause both increased imports and conditions of injury. Suppose, first, that some event occurs abroad that lowers the costs of production for the foreign producers that supply the imports into the market. Perhaps a serious recession abroad causes their labor costs to fall. Perhaps new energy resources are discovered abroad that lowers their energy costs. Or perhaps they discover a new technology that allows them to produce goods at lower cost, a technology that is not yet available to domestic firms for some reason. The effect of such developments is to enable foreign firms to produce a given quantity of output at lower cost. Under conditions of competition, assumed for purposes of analysis here, those cost savings will be passed onto

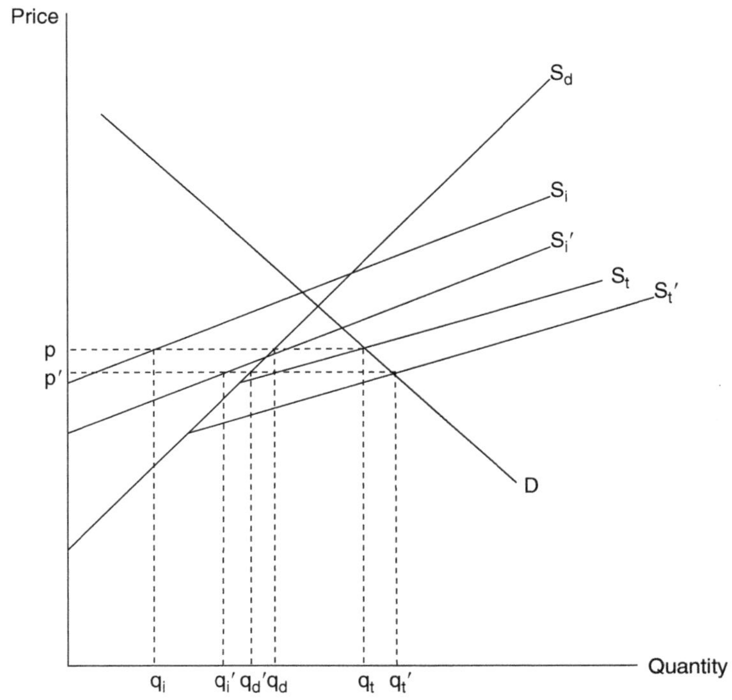

Figure 8.2

customers. The consequence is a downward (or rightward if you prefer) shift in the import supply curve in the market. This situation is depicted in Figure 8.2.

The import supply curve shifts downward from S_i to S_i'. A corresponding parallel shift occurs in total supply, from S_t to S_t'. The new equilibrium price is p'. Price has fallen, and consumer purchases increase to q_t'. Due to the lower price in equilibrium, domestic producers no longer produce as much and their output drops from q_d to q_d'. Imports have become more competitive, and the quantity of imports expands from q_i to q_i'.

The situation in Figure 8.2 plainly reflects increased quantities of imports, and perhaps the drop in domestic production and the prices received by domestic firms (likely accompanied by concomitant declines in domestic employment, capacity utilization, and so on) might be characterized as "serious injury." But the change in import quantity, and in the condition of the domestic industry, both *result* from the same underlying cause—the development(s) abroad that produce the downward shift in the import supply curve.

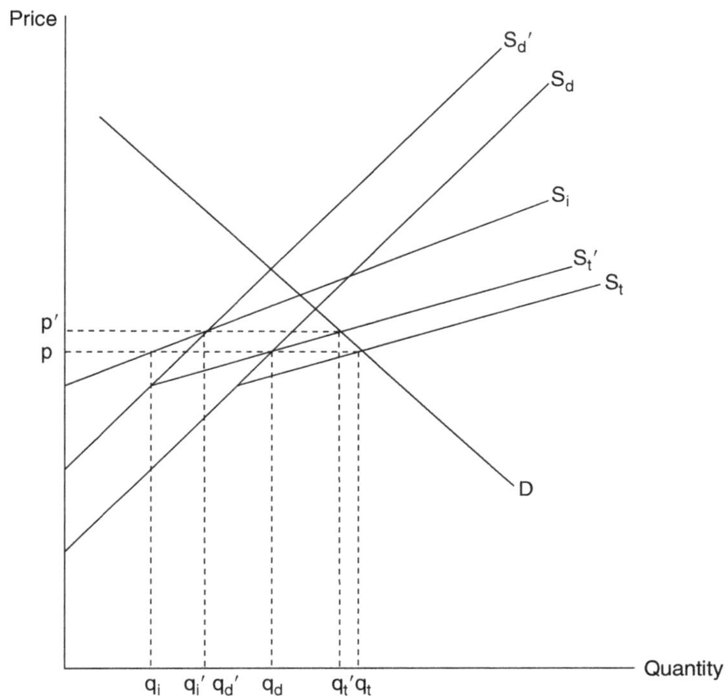

Figure 8.3

Figure 8.2 also raises a fundamental question about what it means to ensure that "other factors" causing injury are not "attributed" to increased imports, a requirement that panels and the Appellate Body have repeatedly emphasized. Suppose, for example, that the shifts in Figure 8.2 are due to a recession abroad that lowers labor costs. Can one separate and distinguish the injury caused by the recession abroad, from the injury caused by increased imports? The answer is plainly no, for the increased imports are themselves caused by the recession abroad. The task of separating the causal contribution of each to the apparent "serious injury" is logically impossible.

Figure 8.3 depicts a somewhat different situation in which the change in underlying supply and demand conditions has a domestic origin. In particular, suppose that domestic producers experience some shock to their cost structure—perhaps domestic energy prices rise dramatically, perhaps the labor supply unionizes or goes on strike, or perhaps a new government regulation raises the costs of doing business. The effect of such a cost shock is to raise the cost of each level of output by domestic firms, a cost that they must recover by charging higher prices. Starting again from the equilibrium depicted in Figure 8.1, in this case the domestic supply curve shifts upward from S_d to S_d', while the total supply curve shifts from S_t to S_t'. The new equilibrium price is again p', while the new quantities of imports, domestic production, and total consumer purchases are again q_i', q_d', and q_t', respectively. [As the Figure is drawn, q_i' and q_d' are approximately equal to one another.]

The domestic cost shock has somewhat different consequences from the shock to import supply depicted in the prior figure, because rising domestic costs lead to a higher rather than lower price in equilibrium, and to lower rather than higher total purchases by consumers. The situation is similar, however, in that domestic production has declined and the quantity of imports has increased.

Once again, increased imports arise at a time when conditions in the domestic industry have taken a turn for the worse. Domestic output has declined (probably along with closely related factors such as employment and capacity utilization). The price received by domestic firms has risen but so have their costs, and one can readily verify that the producer surplus (profit) received by domestic firms has fallen.[1] Thus, a correlation arises between increased quantities of imports and various indicia of "injury" to domestic firms. But the underlying cause of both is the domestic cost shock. Further, it is again logically impossible to disentangle the causal contribution to injury of the putative "other factor"—the cost shock—from the contribution of increased import quantities. Rather, the cost shock has caused both the increase in imports and the deterioration in the condition of the domestic industry.

As a final example, consider a change in underlying demand conditions. This possibility is best illustrated by abandoning the assumption that the imported and domestic goods are perfect substitutes, and instead supposing that they are imperfect substitutes each with their own market. Figure 8.4 depicts the two markets side by side. Each market has its own demand relation, D_i for the imported good and D_d for the domestic good. The initial equilibrium quantities and prices are q_i, p_i and q_d, p_d, for imported and domestic goods, respectively.

Now imagine that a change occurs in consumer tastes, such that some consumers no longer desire the domestic good as much, and begin to prefer

[1] For discussion of the concept of producer surplus and its depiction in a supply and demand diagram, see Chapter 3.

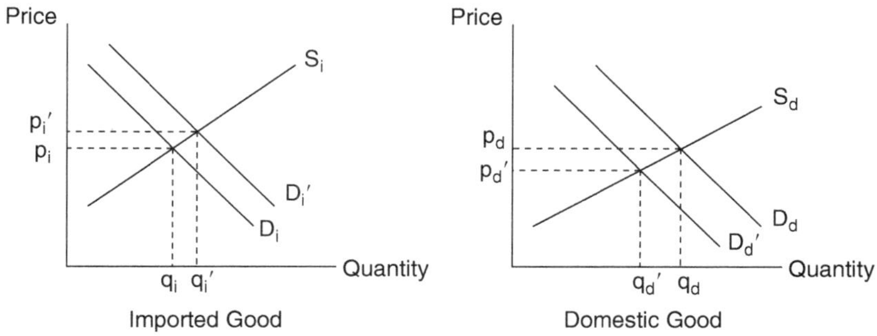

Figure 8.4

more strongly the imported good. Recall that such a change in tastes was precisely what the United States suggested had occurred in the GATT *Hatter's Fur* case as a result of the change in fashion.[2] Such a change in demand patterns may be depicted as leftward shift in the domestic demand curve to D_d', and a rightward shift in import demand curve to D_i'. In the new equilibrium, import quantity has risen to q_i', while domestic production has declined to q_d'. The new equilibrium price for imports is higher, and for domestic goods lower.

As in Figures 8.2 and 8.3, one observes that a correlation exists between increased quantities of imports and indicators of decline in the health of domestic producers. But in no sense can the relationship between the two be seen as one of cause and effect—the change in consumer tastes causes both. It would also be incoherent to suggest that a change in demand patterns is an "other factor" influencing the condition of domestic producers, the effects of which may not be "attributed" to increased imports. Once again, the "other factor" is in fact the cause of increased imports.

In sum, the analysis in this section makes two key points: (1) Increased quantities of imports cannot, as a logical matter, be viewed as a cause of injury to a domestic import-competing industry. Rather, both increased imports and injury are the *result* of changes in underlying supply and demand conditions. (2) Because increased imports are not a causal variable, it is impossible as a logical matter to ensure that their causal contribution to injury is separated from the causal contribution of "other factors," as the Appellate Body insists must be done through a "non-attribution" analysis. And when the changes in underlying supply and demand conditions that

[2] The facts of the case are noted in some detail in Chapter 5, Section C.2.

result in increased imports are labeled "other factors," it is doubly absurd to ask that their causal contribution to injury be "distinguished and separated" from the effects of imports.

I reiterate that these observations do not undermine the logic of the basic causal analysis called for by GATT Article XIX as originally drafted. Even though increased imports cannot be viewed as a causal variable, it is entirely coherent to view "unforeseen developments" and "the obligations incurred" as causal variables as discussed above. With reference to the examples developed in Figures 8.2–4, if we ask whether "unforeseen developments" and "the obligations incurred" may be said to have resulted in serious injury, one can imagine answering that question affirmatively in each case. In particular, suppose that the underlying change in supply and demand conditions in each figure can properly be labeled "unforeseen." Suppose further that the domestic industry could have prevailed upon its government to respond to the shock in question by providing it with some measure of trade protection in the absence of GATT tariff commitments. One might then say that, in each case, the injury resulted from the conjunction of unforeseen developments and GATT obligations.

But such an approach to the causal test raises another fundamental question—would the drafters of GATT, or of the Agreement on Safeguards, have meant to permit safeguard measures under all of these scenarios? Would it matter to them whether the underlying change in supply and demand conditions has a domestic or foreign origin? Or is it enough to justify safeguard measures that any unforeseen development, foreign or domestic, upsets the competitive balance to favor imports? Is the reference to "the effect of the obligations incurred" in Article XIX intended to restrict safeguard measures to cases in which some *change* in trade policy is the precipitating causal variable, as opposed to some other type of shock?

I do not know the answer to these questions (although I offer some speculations in Section D), but these are the fundamental issues that must be addressed if a coherent causal limitation on the use of safeguard measures is to be fashioned. Thus far, however, both national authorities and the WTO dispute process have assiduously avoided the fundamental issues. They instead proceed as if the pursuit of a causal link between "increased imports" and injury is logically tenable, and as if a proper "non-attribution" analysis can ensure an accurate judgment about that causal linkage. To this jumble of confused precedents we now turn, beginning with the work of the U.S. ITC.

B The Causation Test Under U.S. Law

Recall the discussion in Chapter 1, concerning the gradual demise of the unforeseen developments requirement in GATT practice. With the passage of time after the entry into force of GATT, it became increasingly unclear how properly to attribute import surges to unforeseen developments or to GATT obligations. GATT practice came to ignore these prerequisites for safeguard measures under Article XIX, a practice that continued until the Appellate Body revived them in *Korea—Dairy* and *Argentina—Footwear*.

The basic approach of the United States during the GATT years crystallized in Section 201 the Trade Act of 1974. [See Appendix 3.] That statute, which as amended remains the basis for safeguard measures under U.S. law, asks the U.S. ITC to determine "whether an article is being imported into the United States in such increased quantities as to be a substantial cause of serious injury, or the threat thereof, to the domestic industry producing an article like or directly competitive with the imported article."[3] This language parallels the language in Article 2 of the Agreement on Safeguards, with three notable differences. First, it omits the phrase "absolute or relative to domestic production." A later section of the U.S. statute, however, makes clear that "increased imports" may be found to be present when the increase is only relative to domestic production.[4] Second, the U.S. statute omits the phrase "under such conditions," an omission that probably has little legal significance under WTO law as will be noted below in Section C. Finally, and most importantly, the U.S. statute requires that increased quantities of imports be the "substantial cause" of serious injury, which it then defines as "a cause which is important and not less than any other cause."[5]

The rationale for the "substantial cause" test warrants some elaboration. U.S law takes the view that increased imports do not have to be the *sole* cause of serious injury (obviously putting to the side the fundamental question raised above as to how increased imports can be viewed as a cause at all). But the drafters of the statute were unwilling to permit safeguard measures anytime that increased imports had contributed only modestly or slightly to serious injury. Thus, they required that increased imports be an "important" cause of injury, and no less important than any other.

The structure of the U.S. statute thus requires the U.S. ITC to do three things in its causation analysis. First, it must decide how much injury

[3] 19 U.S.C. para 2252(b)(1)(A).
[4] 19 U.S.C. para 2252(c)(1)(C).
[5] 19 U.S.C. para 2252(b)(1)(B).

(or threatened injury) has been "caused" by increased imports. Second, it must decide whether the causal contribution of imports is "important." If so, it must thirdly ascertain whether the causal contribution to injury made by other "causes" is more important than the contribution of imports. Only if the answer to this last query is "no" may the ITC find that the conditions for the imposition of safeguard measures have been met.

Thus, for three decades, the ITC has been required to confront many of the puzzling questions now posed by the Agreement on Safeguards. How does one make sense of the notion that imports are a "causal" variable? How does one then measure the causal contribution of imports? What counts as an alternative "cause" of injury (akin to an "other factor" under WTO law)? How does one measure the causal contributions of other causes, for purposes of weighing them against the contribution of imports? A review of ITC practice in relation to these questions reveals for the most part an absence of careful reflection and analysis, in favor of a tendency to sweep the conceptual issues under the rug.

1 Determining the "Causal Contribution" of Increased Imports

As demonstrated in Section A, increased quantities of imports *result* from the same changes in underlying supply and demand conditions that cause economic distress to import-competing industries. The notion that one causes the other is hopelessly confused. The ITC has nevertheless been compelled to find some approach to answer the flawed causal question posed by the statute.

By far the predominant approach in ITC practice has been to cast aside the first and perhaps most basic lesson of statistical analysis—that correlation and causation are two different things. Thus, the ITC simply proceeds as if one can coherently speak of increased imports as a causal variable, and asks whether increased imports are correlated with indicia of economic distress in the domestic industry. Commissioners inquire whether rising import volumes or market share arise concurrently, or perhaps precede with a short lag, such developments as a decline in domestic prices, production, employment, profits, capacity utilization, and so on. If such a correlation is evident, the Commissioners will tend to find that imports have caused injury. Where it is lacking, they will tend to find that imports are not responsible for injury.

Consider, as but one example, the following excerpt from the ITC report in the recent safeguard investigation covering the steel industry. In discussing the causal effect of imports on conditions in the "certain carbon flat-rolled steel" industry, the ITC observed that "the dramatic increase in the volume of imports in 1998—at the midpoint of the period examined—coincided with sharp declines in the industry's condition which occurred despite growing U.S. demand."[6] The ITC proceeded to detail more generally how imports had risen, coincident with weak growth or decline in sales by domestic producers, all as a prelude to its affirmative finding on the issue of causation.

Another frequent component of the analysis by the ITC involves an examination of the relative prices of imports and domestic products and of price trends. If imports are cheaper, "underselling" the domestic goods, the ITC will tend to draw an inference that imports are causing injury.[7] Likewise, if import prices are falling, and domestic prices fall contemporaneously, an inference will tend to be drawn that imports are causing injury.[8]

Economic analysis casts great doubt on all of these approaches to the analysis of "causation." As Section A makes clear, the focus on correlation between import volumes and indicia of injury cannot show causation. A simple reliance on correlation could lead to an affirmative finding of causal connection in all of the examples developed in Figures 8.2–4 above, whether the true cause of the change in the market involves shifts in import supply conditions, domestic supply conditions, or domestic demand conditions.

A focus on the relative prices of imported and domestic goods and "underselling" is also potentially quite misleading. If imported and domestic goods are fungible, they should sell at approximately the same price at any point in time in any geographic location. If imported goods are of lower quality than domestic goods, by contrast, their equilibrium price will be lower on average, and the reverse situation will prevail if imported goods are of higher quality. An inquiry into the existence or non-existence of systematic "underselling" can thus reveal something about the relative quality of imported and domestic goods, but has no obvious bearing on any intelligible issue of "causation."

Likewise, a focus on whether the prices of imported and domestic goods tend to move up and down together reveals little of any apparent pertinence. In markets where imported and domestic goods are close substitutes, there will always be a close relationship between their prices—any large differential would produce accompanying shifts in consumer purchases until the

[6] U.S. ITC, Steel, Inv. No. TA-201–73, Pub. 3479, December, 2001, p. 59.

[7] See, e.g., id. at 62.

[8] See, e.g., id.

differential was reduced or eliminated. With reference to Figures 8.2–3, for example, one would expect more or less perfect price correlation between movements in the prices of imported and domestic goods. The absence of a close relationship between price movements, such as that depicted in Figure 8.4, simply confirms that the products are imperfect substitutes appealing to different groups of consumers.

Occasionally, Commissioners or litigants have undertaken to develop more sophisticated approaches to causation analysis that go beyond simple reliance on correlations and underselling evidence. I will return to some of these efforts in Section D.

2 Weighing the Effect of Imports Under the Substantial Cause Test

To determine whether imports are the "substantial cause" of injury, the ITC must first identify the other possible causes of injury. It is then necessary to assess their causal contribution to injury in order to weigh it against the contribution of imports. This task is similar to, although distinct from, the "non-attribution analysis" required under WTO law, and it is thus instructive to review the ITC's general approach to the substantial cause issue.

Regarding the selection of alternative "candidate causes" of injury, the general approach of the ITC has been to permit respondents to suggest them. In many (but not all) cases, the ITC uncritically accepts the respondents' list of alternative possible causes, and proceeds to evaluate their relative importance.

In deciding whether other possible causes of injury are more important than imports, the predominant approach once again is to examine their correlation with conditions of serious injury. Where possible, the ITC will assemble time series data purporting to measure the strength of the other causes, and examine the strength of the correlation between those data and indicators of industrial decline.[9] When the alternative cause is a single, discrete event, the ITC will ask whether the timing of that event is closely connected to the emergence of "serious injury" in the domestic industry.[10]

[9] For a recent illustration, see U.S. International Trade Commission, Lamb Meat, Inv. No. TA-201–68, Pub. No. 3176 (1999)(rejecting proposition that increased expenses for lamb growers were a greater cause of injury, noting that expenses had not risen dramatically during the period of investigation and had declined at the end, so they could not explain the sharp decline in industry profits).

[10] See, e.g., id. (rejecting the proposition that cessation of subsidies under National Wool Act was a greater cause of injury, noting that payments had ceased some time before the most serious injury to the domestic industry had occurred).

In some cases, an issue arises as to whether the proposed alternative cause of injury is really distinct from "increased quantities" of imports. For example, in a 1980 investigation involving the automobile industry, respondents suggested that a greater cause of injury was a shift in consumer tastes toward more fuel efficient vehicles, associated with rising gasoline prices.[11] Because imported automobiles were more fuel efficient than U.S.-produced automobiles, imports gained in sales volume and market share as domestic automobile sales declined. Note that this was much the same pattern of changes in consumer demand that was invoked to justify safeguard measures in *Hatter's Fur*, and that is depicted in Figure 8.4 above. Petitioners argued in response that a shift in tastes toward imported goods was not an alternative cause of injury, but was in fact simply the reason why imports were able to increase and cause injury. Ultimately, three of the Commissioners accepted the proposition that a shift in demand favoring imported goods was a distinct cause, and two of the three found it to be a more important cause of injury.[12]

Similar issues have arisen in other cases. In an investigation of unwrought copper imports, respondents argued that declining ore grades in domestic mines were a greater cause of injury than imports. In effect, the argument was that domestic producers had higher costs than foreign competitors for reasons entirely beyond their control, and due to a natural situation that would only worsen with time. But the Commission majority found the argument unconvincing, and in the process rejected "the notion that the Commission must determine whether the domestic industry has a comparative advantage in a product before making an affirmative determination."[13] Likewise, in an investigation of imports of rubber thread, three Commissioners expressly rejected the suggestion that a "cost advantage" for imports could be a distinct cause of injury. In so doing, they suggested that proper alternative causes were to be found "in the U.S. market or among U.S. producers, such as changes in technology or in consumer tastes, domestic competition from substitute products, plant obsolescence or poor management."[14]

[11] An economist would not label this a shift in tastes, of course, but would instead say that an increase in the price of a complementary product (gasoline)—one of the arguments in the demand function for each product—was producing a shift in the demand for each type of good.

[12] See U.S. ITC, Certain Motor Vehicles and Certain Chassis and Bodies Therefor, Inv. No. TA-201–44, Pub. No. 1110 (1980)(especially the views of Commissioners Calhoun and Stern).

[13] U.S. ITC, Unwrought Copper, Inv. No, TA-201–47, Pub. No. 1342 (1984) (views of Commissioners Eckes, Lodwick and Rohr).

[14] See U.S. ITC. Extruded Rubber Thread, Inv. No. TA-201–63, Pub. No. 2563 (1992) (views of Chairman Newquist and Commissioners Rohr and Nuzum). See also Certain Cameras,

U.S. law must also confront a question involving the proper level of "aggregation" of alternative causes. For example, should a domestic recession be viewed as a single cause, or an aggregation of various events that affect macroeconomic activity adversely? The issue is important under U.S. law because of the need to weigh the relative importance of alternative causes against the effect of imports. The more the alternative causes are "dis-aggregated," the more likely that imports will be found more important. In the aforementioned automobiles investigation, for example, three Commissioners determined that general recessionary conditions were a more important cause of injury than imports, while two dissenting Commissioners insisted that a recession was the result of a multitude of underlying causes, none of which were more important than imports. After some turnover at the ITC, the latter view carried the day in a subsequent investigation of heavy-weight motorcycle imports.[15] And in 1988, the U.S. Congress amended the statute to provide that the ITC "may not aggregate the causes of declining demand associated with a recession or economic downturn in the United States economy into a single cause."[16]

Four remarks about this analysis of "substantial causation" at the ITC are in order. First, the ITC has never articulated a clear, overall theory of what constitutes a cause of injury that is distinct from "increased quantities" of imports. The issue is relevant to WTO law as well, of course, because of the need to determine what constitutes an "other factor." Decisions in a handful of ITC cases, however, at least by some of the sitting Commissioners at the time, do suggest some possible principles. Several opinions suggest that a mere "cost advantage" for imports is not a distinct cause, unless it has a domestic origin in something like "poor management." Other cases suggest that changes in domestic demand conditions, such as recessionary conditions or even a shift in consumer preferences favoring the imperfectly substitutable imported good, may constitute distinct causes of injury. And there is the suggestion by some Commissioners that the focus in the search for other causes should be on developments in the domestic economy. Collectively, these decisions might be taken to offer some support for an interpretation of the statute that would identify the "other causes" as changes in underlying *domestic* supply and demand conditions. Likewise, changes in factors that affect *import* supply might be seen as causes not distinct from increased imports.

Inv. No. TA-201–62, Pub. No. 2315 (1990) (finding that poor management was a greater cause of injury than increased imports).

[15] See U.S. ITC, Heavyweight Motorcycles, Inv. No. TA-201–47, Pub. No. 1342 (1983) (especially views of Commissioner Eckes).

[16] 19 U.S.C. para 2252(c)(2)(A).

It is perhaps a small step from this interpretation to a construction of the statute that would assign to "increased quantities" any injury attributable to shifts in the import supply curve (recall Figure 8.2), and to "other causes" any injury attributable to shifts in domestic supply or demand curves (recall Figures 8.3–4). Indeed, two ITC Commissioners who served during the 1980s expressly embraced this view. I will return to this possibility in Section D, but suffice it to say here that many ITC Commissioners would flatly reject it. It would foreclose safeguard measures when injury was due largely to domestic macroeconomic fluctuations, for example, and would have foreclosed safeguard measures in *Hatter's Fur* even though the GATT working party accepted the U.S. justification for them in principle. Nonetheless, this approach is worthy of consideration as a possible solution to the conundrums posed by WTO treaty text.

The second remark concerns the general approach of the ITC to assessing the importance of other causes. Here, the analysis is usually much the same as it is for "increased quantities" of imports—a search for correlation between measures or events associated with the other causes and the economic indicia of serious injury or threat. One might again observe that correlation is not causation, but at least the other causes examined by the ITC are often intelligible causal variables (unlike "increased quantities" of imports). It is entirely coherent to ask what impact a domestic recession or a change in consumer tastes has had on the domestic industry, for example, or to ask how particular "bad management" decisions have affected the performance of domestic firms. The presence or absence of a correlation between such developments and indicators of industrial decline may be at least suggestive of a causal connection. Even when correlation is suggestive of causation, however, it aids little in assessing the relative importance of various causes and their quantitative contribution to injury when multiple causes of injury are present at once.

These observations too have lessons for issues that arise under the Agreement on Safeguards. National authorities seeking to comply with the Agreement must devise some method for identifying the causal contribution of "increased quantities," and for distinguishing and separating the effects of "other factors" in a proper "non-attribution" analysis. Although the decisions by the ITC might provide some useful thinking about the task of *identifying* other factors, they are quite unhelpful on the question of how to measure the effect of "increased quantities" (or even to make sense of the task), and on the question of how to distinguish and separate the effects of other factors.

The third remark is that U.S. law imposes a burden on the ITC that WTO law does not compel—the task of deciding whether other causes are more important than "increased quantities." WTO law requires that the effects of other causes not be "attributed" to imports, but does not require an assessment of their *relative* quantitative importance. The lesser requirement of WTO law avoids the problem under U.S. law of having to decide at what level of aggregation to examine other factors.

Fourth, and finally, a question arises under WTO law as to whether the substantial cause test is logically consistent with the non-attribution requirement of the Agreement on Safeguards. At one time this question was an open one, but as shall be seen in Section C, current Appellate Body jurisprudence suggests that the substantial cause test is in principle an acceptable way to proceed if the ITC can coherently and convincingly implement it.

C The Causation Test in WTO Case Law

The analysis of causation by national authorities has been challenged in every safeguards case to come before a WTO dispute panel to date. With the sole exception of *Argentina—Peaches*, in which the panel declined to reach the causation issue for reasons of judicial economy, either the panel, the Appellate Body, or both sustained the challenge, at least in part.

Although the analysis of national authorities has regularly been found inadequate, the decisions to date do not adequately point the way toward an analysis that would be found acceptable. Instead, as I will show in this section, existing precedents are confused and sometimes logically untenable. They do nothing to clarify how "increased quantities" of imports may be viewed as a causal variable, and the "non-attribution" requirement imposed by some of them asks for an analysis that is, on its face, infeasible. National authorities thus face daunting challenges if they are to fashion a causation analysis that will withstand scrutiny in future cases.

I will discuss the disputes in chronological order, followed by a brief summary and recapitulation.

1 Korea—Dairy

The panel in *Korea—Dairy* examined several claims put forward by the European Communities regarding the causal analysis by Korean authorities.

For example, in support of its affirmative finding, the report of the Korean authorities pointed to a rapid increase in imports early in the period of investigation, but also conceded that demand for the products in question had increased contemporaneously. The panel questioned how imports could be causing injury if they were merely responding to an increase in demand that domestic producers could not meet.[17] The report of the Korean authorities also acknowledged that domestic production of downstream products (such as cheese) made from the dairy products under investigation had declined, but the report did not evaluate whether decreased production of such products might be responsible for the observed injury.[18] Because the panel found the safeguard measures in question to be inconsistent with the Agreement on Safeguards on other grounds, however, it declined to make specific findings regarding a violation of the causation requirement, and the issues did not arise on appeal.

2 Argentina—Footwear

In *Footwear*, the European Communities challenged the finding of a causal link on several grounds. First, the EC argued that the Argentine authorities had simply "juxtaposed" statements in their report to the effect that imports had risen with statements about declining conditions in the domestic industry, without providing a reasoned opinion as to the causal connection between the two. Second, although the Argentine authorities had asserted in their report that imports had caused injury "owing to their lower price," the EC claimed that the authorities had in fact conducted no competent analysis of the prices of imports compared to domestic products.[19] The EC further argued that the phrase "under such conditions" in Article 2.1 constitutes a distinct analytical requirement for national authorities, who must demonstrate that the "conditions" are such as to allow imports to cause injury. In this regard, the EC suggested that the required analysis of "conditions" includes a comparison of the prices of imports to domestic goods, which Argentina allegedly had failed to do.

In evaluating these claims, the panel addressed the general question of how to establish a causal link at some length. The panel noted the language in Article 4.2 requiring national authorities to consider the "rate and amount" of the increase in imports, and "changes" in the level of domestic sales,

17 Korea—Dairy Panel para 7.92.

18 Id. paras 7.94–95.

19 Argentina—Footwear Panel 8.234–35.

production, and so on. The panel inferred from this language that "*trends*—in both injury factors and the imports—matter as much as their absolute levels." It proceeded to state: "In the particular context of causation analysis, we also believe that this provision means that it is the *relationship* between the movements in imports (volume and market share) and the movements in injury factors that must be central to a causation analysis and determination . . . [I]f causation is present, an increase in imports normally should coincide with a decline in the relevant injury factors. While such a coincidence cannot prove causation . . . its absence would create serious doubts as to the existence of a causal link, and would require a *very* compelling analysis of why causation is still present."[20]

Thus, much like the historical practice at the U.S. ITC, the panel suppressed the problem of how to conceptualize increased imports as a causal variable, and simply presumed that it is coherent to treat them as causal. It then held that the best evidence of causation is "coincidence" of trends in imports and injury factors. The irony of the phrasing is glaring—the Merriam-Webster dictionary defines "coincidence" as "the occurrence of events that happen at the same time by accident but seem to have some connection."[21] The *Footwear* panel would thus enshrine the principle that causation is best established through temporal simultaneity, a confusion that has a long pedigree in safeguards investigations to be sure.

Regarding the suggestion by the EC that the phrase "under such conditions" requires a price comparison, the panel found no textual support for that proposition. Instead, it held that the phrase "under such conditions" indicates "the need to analyse the *conditions of competition* between the imported product and the domestic like or directly competitive product." The panel did not say exactly what that analysis requires, and simply noted that products may compete with each other along a variety of dimensions in addition to price.[22]

Having set out these general principles, the panel proceeded to hold that Argentina's causation analysis was deficient. First, it found a lack of coincidence between imports and injury factors. Although imports declined toward the end of the period of investigation, injury factors continued to show decline as well.[23] Second, the panel found that there was no evidence in the record to support Argentina's claim that imports were cheaper, and that Argentine authorities failed to reconcile their findings with evidence that the

20 Id. paras 8.237–38.

21 See <http://www.m-w.com/dictionary/coincidence>.

22 Argentina—Footwear Panel paras 8.250–51.

23 Id. para 8.243.

unit value of imports had been increasing during the period of investigation.[24] Finally, the panel determined that Argentina had failed to establish that "other factors"—particularly its own domestic recession—were not causing injury that had inappropriately been "attributed" to imports. Although the report of the Argentine authorities asserted that it had ruled out this possibility, the panel held that its assertions were unpersuasive and that "an analysis separating the effects of the recession from those of imports would have been necessary."[25]

Argentina appealed the panel's findings regarding its causation analysis, but the Appellate Body affirmed the panel's core findings across the board. In particular, it agreed with the panel that "in an analysis of causation, 'it is the *relationship* between the *movements* in imports (volume and market share) and the *movements* in injury factors that must be central to a causation analysis and determination.' Furthermore, with respect to a 'coincidence' between an increase in imports and a decline in the relevant injury factors, we note that the Panel simply said that this should 'normally' occur if causation is present."[26] Hence, in its first important statement on the subject, the Appellate Body endorses the notion that "coincidence analysis" is a centerpiece of causation analysis. Like the panel, the Appellate Body seems unaware of (or untroubled by) the profound conceptual difficulty in conflating correlation with causation in a context where the ostensible "causal" variable is in fact endogenous.

3 United States—Wheat Gluten

In the first challenge to a determination by the U.S. ITC to reach the panel stage, *United States—Wheat Gluten*, the panel embraced the analytical approach set forth in *Footwear*. In particular, it stated that a reviewing panel should ascertain whether national authorities have properly determined: "(i) whether an upward trend in imports coincides with downward trends in the injury factors, and if not, whether an adequate, reasoned and reasonable explanation is provided as to why nevertheless the data show causation; (ii) whether the conditions of competition between the imported and domestic product as analyzed demonstrate the existence of the causal link between the imports and any injury; and (iii) whether other relevant factors have been analyzed and whether it is established that injury caused by factors other than imports has not been attributed to

[24] Id. para 8.258–59. [25] Id. para 8.269. [26] Argentina—Footwear AB para 144.

imports."[27] This three-stage description of the required analysis has now become standard.

With respect to the coincidence analysis in item (i), the panel noted that imports had generally increased over the period of investigation while most injury factors declined, and thus found "overall" coincidence in trends to be present. Regarding the conditions of competition analysis in item (ii), the panel found the ITC's analysis to be acceptable here as well, noting, *inter alia*, evidence in the record that European imports had undersold domestic wheat gluten.[28]

As for the non-attribution analysis required in item (iii), the EC argued that the ITC had failed to consider a possible cause of injury other than imports, namely, fluctuations in the protein content of the domestic wheat crop that affect the demand for what gluten. The panel ruled, however, that this factor had not been clearly raised before the ITC by the respondents in the domestic investigation. Accordingly, the ITC was not obliged to consider it.[29]

The panel nevertheless found the "non-attribution" analysis by the United States to be deficient because, in the panel's view, the substantial cause test under U.S. law was inadequate to meet the non-attribution requirement. In particular, the panel read Article 4.2(b)—which requires a "casual link between increased imports . . . and serious injury or threat thereof"—to impose an obligation on national authorities to demonstrate that "increased imports . . . *in and of themselves*, cause *serious* injury."[30] That is, in the view of the panel, once the effects of other factors on the domestic industry have been separated and not "attributed" to imports, the remaining quantum of injury attributable solely to imports must be "serious." Under the substantial cause test in U.S. law, by contrast, the ITC simply determines whether serious injury is present, and whether increased imports are an important cause and no less important than any other cause. This test could be satisfied, the panel concluded, even if increased imports by themselves were insufficient to cause serious injury. Because the U.S. ITC had acknowledged that at least one other factor had caused some injury, the panel held that its analysis of causation did not satisfy the non-attribution requirement of Article 4.2(b).[31]

On appeal, several key findings of the panel were reversed. The Appellate Body first held that the panel erred in concluding that national authorities need only consider "other factors" clearly raised by the respondents in the

[27] United States—Wheat Gluten Panel para 8.91.
[28] Id. paras 8.95–118.
[29] Id. paras 8.121–27.
[30] Id. para 8.138.
[31] Id. paras 8.151–53.

domestic investigation. Instead, the obligation to conduct an "investigation" and to evaluate "all relevant factors" imposes on national authorities a duty to identify possible other factors on their own. Whenever the authorities "consider" that a factor "may be relevant," they have a duty to investigate it.[32] Having overruled the panel on this point, however, the Appellate Body concluded that the ITC had in fact given adequate consideration to the effects of fluctuations in the protein content of the wheat crop.

The Appellate Body then turned to the finding by the panel that increased imports must be sufficient, in and of themselves, to cause serious injury or threat. It reviewed the textual requirements for causal linkage between increased imports and injury, and saw nothing in text that requires imports alone to be the cause of serious injury. Rather, according to the Appellate Body, the text contemplates that other factors might also be the cause of serious injury, and simply requires that injury caused by other factors not be attributed to imports. Thus, concluded the Appellate Body, the panel erred in holding that increased imports by themselves must suffice to cause serious injury, and in concluding that the substantial cause test under U.S. law was inadequate to fulfill the non-attribution requirement. It is enough if increased quantities of imports make some causal contribution to serious injury, as long as injury due to other factors is not attributed to imports.[33]

This reading of the Agreement is at first blush puzzling. If increased imports need not suffice to cause serious injury (putting aside what it means for them to "cause" anything), but must simply have made some contribution to injury, what is the point of the non-attribution requirement? It would seem enough for national authorities to show that imports had contributed some injury, and superfluous to require them also to separate and distinguish the injury caused by other factors. To make sense of the Appellate Body's interpretation, one must imagine that the Appellate Body is concerned about situations in which increased imports have not made any causal contribution whatsoever to serious injury, and where a casual connection is nevertheless found because of an erroneous attribution of injury caused by other factors. Alternatively, the concern might relate to the question of how restrictive the safeguard measure can be—if it can only address the injury caused by imports, and not that caused by other factors, then it becomes necessary to know how much injury is "attributable" to each. This issue will be discussed further in Chapter 9 concerning the permissible extent of safeguard measures.

32 United States—Wheat Gluten AB paras 52–56. This ruling is also discussed in Chapter 3, along with the issue of whether it creates opportunities for strategic behavior by respondents in the national investigation.

33 Id. paras 66–79.

Note further that under the Appellate Body's ruling, safeguard measures are permissible whenever "increased quantities" have made *any* demonstrable contribution to serious injury. The only proviso is that injury due to other factors must be "separated and distinguished" in the non-attribution portion of the analysis. This principle seemingly opens the door to safeguard measures in a large universe of cases so long as the non-attribution analysis can be done in a manner that withstands scrutiny.

In any event, having reversed the panel on this issue, the Appellate Body proceeded to complete the analysis regarding the adequacy of the non-attribution analysis by the ITC. The facts were as follows. During the five-year period of investigation employed by the ITC, the volume of imports had risen 38 percent. Over the same period, U.S. productive capacity had grown 68 percent. Capacity utilization at U.S. firms had fallen considerably along with profits, and the U.S. ITC stated in its report that had imports not risen as they did, capacity utilization rates would have been considerably higher and would have allowed the U.S. industry to operate more profitably. Thus, the Appellate Body inferred, injury was directly linked to declining rates of capacity utilization.[34] The Appellate Body then noted that had U.S. capacity not risen over the period of investigation, its capacity utilization rate would have fallen only modestly even with the increased volume of imports. Further, had imports maintained their market share over the period of investigation (instead of increasing their share), capacity utilization rates still would have fallen significantly due to the increased domestic capacity brought on line.[35] In the face of this evidence, the Appellate Body concluded that the U.S. ITC had not "adequately evaluated the complexities of this issue," and had not demonstrated that injury caused by the increase in U.S. capacity had not been attributed to imports.[36]

The reasoning here is problematic in a number of respects. First, at the risk of seeming a broken record, it does nothing to help with the question of how to conceptualize imports as a causal variable. Second, taking seriously for a moment the notion that imports are "causal," the facts would suggest that the problems suffered by U.S. producers were caused by two factors—rising imports, and investment in new capacity that proved unnecessary. In the absence of either factor, U.S. producers would have been considerably more profitable. Why, then, is it inappropriate to attribute at least part of the "serious injury" to imports? Indeed, as the United States had argued, much of the increase in capacity was put in place before imports began to increase.

[34] Id. paras 81, 84. [35] Id. paras 85–86. [36] Id. para 91.

The sequence of events thus suggested that U.S. producers had invested in new capacity in anticipation of growth opportunities, but that imports had captured those growth opportunities and rendered the new investment uneconomical. It could thus be argued that the unexpected import competition was the real "problem," and that investments in capacity were not a conceptually distinct cause of injury, but rather a background predicate for the injury caused by imports. To this line of argument, the Appellate Body responded: "[T]he relevance of an 'other factor', under Article 4.2(b), depends on whether that 'other factor' was, or was not, 'causing injury' 'at the same time' as increased imports. Therefore, the possible relevance of the increases in capacity added during the period of investigation does not depend on the moment in time when the increases in capacity occurred, but on when the effects of those increases are felt, and whether they are 'causing injury' 'at the same time' as increased imports."[37] This response simply begs the question as to why domestic investments in new capacity should be considered an "other factor" distinct from imports, if indeed the anticipated recoupment on those investments was frustrated by an unexpected import surge.

More generally, *Wheat Gluten* illustrates a fundamental logical problem with the requirement of non-attribution. The conjunction of new capacity investment by U.S. firms, and unexpectedly vigorous import competition, resulted in a steep decline in domestic profitability. One might thus say that the two factors were joint causes of the injury, under circumstances where neither factor alone would have caused the problem. It is then logically impossible to say that one factor caused some portion of the problem while the other factor caused the rest—any such allocation of causal responsibility is utterly arbitrary. By insisting that the effects of capacity utilization be separated and distinguished, the Appellate Body asks national authorities to embark upon an impossible task.

4 United States—Lamb

The *Lamb* panel focused on an issue that was also central in *Wheat Gluten*—whether the substantial cause test under U.S. law was adequate to meet the non-attribution requirement of Article 4.2(b). The *Lamb* panel issued its decision after the panel decision in *Wheat Gluten*, but before the Appellate Body decision. Like the *Wheat Gluten* panel, the *Lamb* panel concluded that

[37] Id. para 88.

imports must be sufficient by themselves to cause serious injury or threat. Because the U.S. ITC had not ruled out the possibility that various other factors had contributed somewhat to serious injury, the panel held that the finding of substantial cause under U.S. law was logically insufficient to establish that imports, by themselves, had caused serious injury.

Consistent with its findings in *Wheat Gluten*, the Appellate Body overruled the panel on the proposition that imports must, in themselves, cause serious injury or threat.[38] And as in *Wheat Gluten*, the Appellate Body proceeded to complete the analysis as to whether the United States had complied with the non-attribution requirement. Once again, it found the analysis of the ITC to be deficient on other grounds.

The U.S. ITC had considered six factors other than increased imports that might have contributed to serious injury: "the cessation of subsidy payments under the National Wool Act of 1954; competition from other meat products, such as beef, pork and poultry; increased input costs; overfeeding of lambs; concentration in the packing segment of the industry; and a failure to develop and maintain an effective marketing program for lamb meat."[39] The Appellate Body accepted these "other factors" as the proper ones, without discussion, and simply inquired whether the United States had done enough to ensure that injury caused by them had not been "attributed" to imports. It acknowledged that the substantial cause test under U.S. law required the ITC to weigh the various factors, and thus to ascertain the importance of each, but in the view of the Appellate Body the ITC had done little to explain how it had performed this task. Instead, its analysis consisted of little more than conclusory assertions: "In the absence of any meaningful explanation of the nature and extent of the injurious effects of these six 'other' factors, it is impossible to determine whether the USITC properly separated the injurious effects of these other factors from the injurious effects of the increased imports."[40]

Although I do not wish to defend the proposition that the U.S. ITC is a model of analytic rigor, the Appellate Body again fails to appreciate the logical problems raised by the non-attribution requirement. If, indeed, the six factors above had caused injury, some of them would also be among the causes of increased imports. For example, suppose that the cessation of Wool Act payments, increased input costs, overfeeding of lambs, concentration in the U.S. packing industry that slaughters domestic lambs, and

[38] United States—Lamb AB paras 165–71.

[39] Id. para 182, n. 138.

[40] Id. para 186.

failure to develop and maintain an effective marketing program had injured U.S. lamb producers by raising their costs or reducing the demand by packers for American-grown lamb meat. These developments would then *lead* to increased imports from abroad. The notion that the effects of these factors can be "properly separated... from the injurious effects of the increased imports" is simply logical *non sequitur*.

5 United States—Line Pipe

The decision in *Line Pipe* closely parallels the Appellate Body's treatment of the U.S. ITC's analysis in *Lamb*. In the investigation before the ITC, Korea advanced a number of "other factors" that it contended were responsible for the injury experienced by U.S. producers, one of which was a decline in oil and gas drilling and production. The U.S. ITC "considered" the importance of this factor, and concluded that it was not a more important cause of injury than increased imports. Both the panel and the Appellate Body concluded, however, that the ITC offered no clear explanation as to how it had reached this conclusion, or what method of analysis had been employed to separate the effects of a decline in drilling and production from the effects of increased imports—the "cited parts of the USITC Report do not *establish explicitly*, with a *reasoned and adequate explanation*, that injury caused by factors other than the increased imports was not attributed to increased imports. The passage on page I-30 of the USITC Report highlighted by the United States is but a mere assertion that injury caused by other factors is not attributed to increased imports."[41]

6 Chile—Agricultural Products

The panel decision in *Agricultural Products*, which was not appealed, briefly addresses the adequacy of Chile's causation analysis. It notes that the analysis by the Chilean authorities was quite cursory, and did not discuss the effects of other factors that Argentina had raised, such as the effects of a severe domestic drought.[42] Not surprisingly, the panel then held that the analysis was inadequate to meet the requirements of Article 4.2(b).

Along the way, the panel made one notable claim. It stated that "Chile's analysis of causality was strictly limited to its statement that international

41 United States—Line Pipe AB para 220.
42 Chile—Agricultural Products Panel para 7.179.

prices, import prices and domestic prices are linked . . . injury must be caused or threatened by increased imports, not decreasing international prices."[43]

From an economic perspective, the suggestion that injury must be caused by increased imports, and not by declining international prices, is backwards. As Figure 8.2 illustrates, a decline in world market prices is a potential cause of increased imports. Such a decline may occur because of declining demand in foreign markets, or cost reductions abroad due to falling input prices or to the use of more efficient technology. Such developments can be viewed as causal variables, the effects of which will be transmitted to the market of the importing country through falling international prices (or, more precisely, a shift in the import supply curve). The *result* will be an increase in the quantity of imports.

Likewise, if the importing nation is small in relation to the world market for the good in question, it may be a price taker for that good. In such cases, the import price may be taken to be an exogenous or causal variable, even though the quantity of imports cannot be. See Grossman (1986). The panel's suggestion that injury must be caused by increased imports, and not by falling international prices, is thus fundamentally at odds with a proper economic understanding of import markets.

7 United States—Steel

The steel case encompassed ten "industries." The dispute panel found fault with the ITC analysis of causation in nine of the ten. In each instance, the panel held that the ITC failed to demonstrate a causal link between increased imports and injury, that it failed to ensure that injury caused by other factors was not "attributed" to imports, or both.

A complete review of all of the analysis for each of the ten industries would involve us in an unnecessarily lengthy exercise, and many of the important legal and analytical issues have already been addressed in connection with the earlier cases. Accordingly, I will confine attention here to a few highlights that introduce or reinforce some key points.

(a) Demonstrating the Causal Link to Imports

Taking its cue from prior decisions, the *Steel* panel suggested that a causal linkage between increased imports and injury might be established in one of two ways: through a "coincidence" analysis, or through an analysis of the

[43] Id. para 7.177.

conditions of competition. A coincidence analysis examines the "temporal relationship between the movements in imports and the movements in injury factors."[44] Such coincidence is "normally" evident "if causation is present,"[45] although the panel allowed that a temporal lag may exist between import increases and injury "in certain cases."[46] Where a clear coincidence exists, "no further analysis is required of the competent authority," save for a careful non-attribution analysis.[47] Where coincidence is lacking or an analysis of coincidence has not been undertaken, by contrast, the panel would require the competent authority to explain its absence and to show causation convincingly through other means.

An analysis of the conditions of competition, according to the panel, requires the competent authority to consider the factors enumerated in Article 4.2(a) of the Safeguards Agreement: changes in import volume, import market share, domestic sales, production, productivity, capacity utilization, profits and losses, and employment. Other unenumerated factors may also be relevant.[48] Further, "price . . . in the Panel's view, is an important, if not the most important, factor in analysing the conditions of competition in a particular market . . . we consider that relative price trends as between imports and domestic products will often be a good indicator of whether injury is being transmitted to the domestic industry . . . given that price changes have an immediate effect on profitability, all other things being equal."[49]

Against this backdrop, the panel proceeded to consider the analysis of the U.S. ITC as to each of the challenged measures. In the important category of certain carbon flat-rolled steel (CCFRS), for example, it found "that there was no coincidence between, on the one hand, import trends and the situation of the domestic industry of CCFRS, as reflected in data for production, net commercial sales, productivity and capacity utilization of the domestic CCFRS. We have also found that there was a lack of coincidence between import trends and declines in domestic operating margin . . . We did discern coincidence, albeit lagged, between increased imports, on the one hand, and employment, on the other hand . . . Having taken into consideration all of the foregoing, in the Panel's view, overall, coincidence did not exist."[50] "Given a lack of coincidence between import trends and the injury factors, it was for USITC to provide a compelling explanation as to why a causal link was considered, nevertheless, to exist."[51]

[44] United States Steel Panel para 10.299. [45] Id. para 10.300. [46] Id. para 10.310.
[47] Id. para 10.307. [48] Id. para 10.318. [49] Id. para 10.320.
[50] Id. paras 10.374–75. [51] Id. para 10.376.

The ITC's analysis of the conditions of competition for CCFRS was then found deficient as well. The panel first suggested that the product category might be too broad for such an analysis to be undertaken at all in convincing fashion. Further, the ITC apparently relied heavily on evidence of import underselling and downward price trends for both imports and domestic products for two sub-products in the CCFRS category, without explaining "why pricing data for the other three items that constituted CCFRS were not specifically considered." And, "while some of the domestically produced constituent items were undersold by the import counterparts at particular points during the period of investigation, this was not necessarily the case for the entire period of investigation."[52] Thus, the conditions of competition analysis failed to support the existence of a causal link between increased imports and injury in the view of the panel.

For some other product lines, the panel found the ITC's analysis more convincing. As to fittings, flanges, and tool joints (FFTJ), the panel examined the relation between imports and indicators of injury, and noted that "clear coincidence exists between the upward trend in imports and the downward trend in the injury factors, except for productivity." Because the ITC report had not analyzed this coincidence in detail, however, the panel also found that a conditions of competition analysis was required to support the ITC's finding of a causal link.[53] In that regard, the panel reviewed data assembled by the ITC showing that imported products significantly undersold domestic products during the period of investigation, and on that basis concluded that the conditions of competition analysis supported the existence of a causal link.

In the case of hot-rolled bar, the panel noted that the ITC had not undertaken a coincidence analysis. But as part of its analysis of the conditions of competition, the ITC assembled data on market penetration by imports along with import and domestic prices. The data were presented in the following graph, which I denote Figure 8.5.

Based on these data, the panel concurred that a causal link was present—"[t]he USITC explained that domestic prices declined in an effort to mitigate the erosion of market share . . . On the basis of the foregoing, overall, we find that the USITC's conditions of competition analysis was compelling."[54]

It would be unfair to fault the panel for following the analytic lead of the Appellate Body on these issues, but its analysis is nonetheless deeply flawed for reasons that have been noted previously. The panel insists that the

[52] Id. para 10.379. [53] Id. para 10.516. [54] Id. paras 10.429–30.

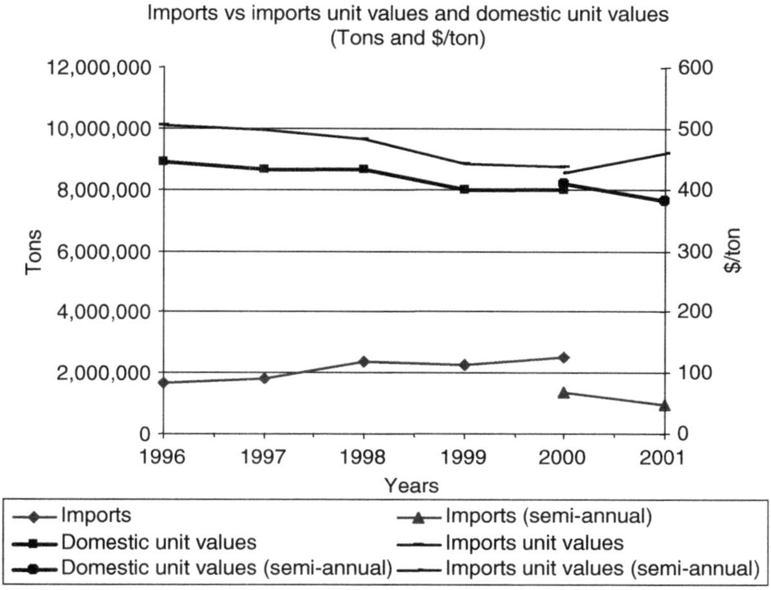

Figure 8.5

linchpin in the search for *causation* is a search for *coincidence*. Although it is not disreputable to examine correlation as an aid to an exploration of causation in some settings, one can only do so when one variable is a logical candidate for the cause of the other. But import quantities simply do not *cause* anything.

The "conditions of competition" analysis that serves as an alternative to coincidence analysis is no more comforting. Evidence of import "underselling" is typically the foundation for an inference of causation here, but such evidence simply suggests that imports are of lower perceived quality than domestic products, and says nothing about any causal linkage. And to the degree that a high degree of correlation between the price series for imported and domestic goods lie at the heart of a "conditions of competition" analysis, that fact simply suggests that the goods are reasonably close substitutes in consumption. Again, no inference of "causation" is supported, as indeed there is no intelligible causal variable under examination.

To be sure, cases will arise in which "coincidence" is relatively stronger or weaker. Cases will arise in which imported goods undersell domestic goods, and many cases will arise in which import and domestic price trends are highly correlated. It will thus be possible for importing nations to demonstrate "causation" with some regularity using the tests that the panel applies.

But if any relationship exists between that set of cases, and the set of cases in which safeguard measures are appropriate on some principled basis, it will arise only by "coincidence."

(b) Non-Attribution Analysis

As with earlier panels, the *Steel* panel simply accepted at face value the "other factors" put forth by the respondents, with no discussion as to how or why they were appropriate or inappropriate. The panel then checked to see whether the ITC had convincingly distinguished the injury attributable to the factor in question, and ensured that such injury was not attributed to imports. For a number of industries, the panel found the ITC's non-attribution analysis to be lacking.

I offer one illustrative example of the analysis. In the case of hot-rolled bar, the panel had accepted the ITC's analysis of the conditions of competition as a basis for finding a causal link between increased imports and injury. But the respondents argued before the ITC that injury was caused, *inter alia*, by increased input costs for domestic producers, what the panel termed increases in the costs of goods sold (COGS). The ITC acknowledged that COGS had risen during part of the period of investigation, but argued that import competition had suppressed prices and prevented domestic firms from recouping their higher costs. On that basis, the ITC concluded that imports were the more important cause of injury. The panel evidently considered this analysis too cursory, falling short of a "reasoned and adequate" explanation. The panel hinted, however, that if the ITC had gone further in its analysis, it might have been able to defend its conclusion. In particular, the panel noted that there was a general lack of "coincidence" between changes in COGS and operating margins for domestic producers. Had changes in COGS "played a significant role in the situation of the domestic industry, one would have expected operating margins to increase while COGS was decreasing."[55]

The panel's analysis suffers from the same logical flaws noted in other cases. An increase in input costs for domestic firms will lead them to institute price increases if they can. But, as may have been the case in the hot-rolled bar market, import competition may prevent such price increases, or lead domestic firms to lose sales as a result of them. The price increases that are instituted or attempted by domestic firms, due to rising COGS, are then the *cause* of greater import volumes. While the panel insists that the injury attributed to rising COGS must be distinguished from the injury attributed

[55] Id. para 10.440.

to imports, the above discussion makes clear that this task is logically impossible.

The panel's suggestion that one can analyze the causal importance of COGS by looking at the coincidence between changes in COGS and operating margins is also silly. Other things being equal, increases in COGS will surely tend to lower operating margins, but many other factors in the market are variable over time, and the absence of a "coincidence" between changes in COGS and operating margins simply indicates that other things are happening simultaneously—a clear demonstration of why "coincidence" and causation are two different things. Obviously, the presence of other factors varying simultaneously cannot negate the fact that increases in input costs, other things being equal, are disadvantageous for domestic producers.

The ultimate issue raised by this example is simply this—should safeguard measures be permitted when the cause of injury to a domestic industry, and the cause of rising imports, is a shock to the cost structure of domestic firms? There may be good reasons to answer this question yes or no, but the analysis of the panel merely masks and confuses it.

The Appellate Body decision in *Steel* did not address the panel's analysis. Having upheld the findings that the United States measures violated the Agreement on Safeguards on various other grounds, the Appellate Body exercised judicial economy to avoid the causation questions.

8 Summary

The panel and Appellate Body decisions to date on the causal analysis required by the Safeguards Agreement suggest that national authorities must undertake three tasks: (a) search for coincidence or correlation between rising import volumes and market share and indicators of decline in the domestic industry; (b) analyze the "conditions of competition" between imported and domestic goods, which may include a search for evidence of import underselling and of a correlation between the prices of imported and domestic goods; and (c) identify the "other factors" that may have contributed to injury, and establish by a "reasoned and adequate explanation" that injury caused by those factors has not been attributed to increased imports.

Each of these requirements is logically flawed if a goal of the Agreement on Safeguards is to limit safeguard measures to circumstances in which injury results from some intelligible causal sequence relating to import competition. Increased quantities of imports are no more a cause of injury than injury is a cause of increased imports—they are both, simultaneously, the product of underlying changes in supply and demand conditions. Accordingly, increased quantities of imports cannot cause injury, and any correlation between import trends and indicators of injury is inherently spurious.

The typical "conditions of competition" analysis is no more useful. Underselling by imports, and/or correlation between the prices of imported and domestic goods, offer some basis for an inference about the degree to which imported and domestic goods are close substitutes, but add nothing to an analysis of causation *per se*.

Finally, the non-attribution analysis required by panels and the Appellate Body regularly asks national authorities to separate and distinguish the effects of "other factors" from increased imports when such separation is logically impossible because the "other factors" in question are themselves the cause of increased imports. The non-attribution requirement thus raises a fundamental question as to what is even meant by the notion of a "cause" distinct from imports, and the decisions to date do not even recognize this problem, let alone point the way toward a resolution of it. As long as the case law continues to call for an analysis that is infeasible even in principle, the non-attribution requirement threatens to stand as an insuperable barrier to WTO-legal safeguard measures.

Critics of safeguards policies may welcome this development, an observation that returns us to the central normative issue of Chapter 2—do safeguard measures have a useful role to play in the WTO system? To those who believe that the answer to this question is or may be yes, however, the current state of affairs may be seen as quite unsatisfactory.

D Possible Solutions

I now turn to the tough question—if the analysis of "causation" in WTO case law to date is largely incoherent, what is to be done? Do logically sound alternatives exist that can be reconciled with the treaty text, and that have appeal as a policy matter?

Commentators have wrestled with these questions in relation to U.S. law and its substantial cause test for a number of years. This section will draw on that literature. WTO law is different in important particulars, however, so that the emphasis of the analysis must shift. I proceed by delineating several options, and discussing the merits of each.

1 Sweep the Issues Under the Rug

The current drift in the WTO system shows remarkable parallel to the historical practice at the U.S. ITC, which has generally been to ignore the fact that much of its analysis is economically fallacious. One can simply pretend that correlation and causation are the same, that price underselling and price correlation are interesting indicators of "causation," and that the best way to determine whether some "other factor" is causing injury is to see whether it too is closely correlated with injury indicators. The *Steel* panel suggested that such an approach might well suffice both to show the causal link between injury and imports, and to establish "non-attribution." A virtue of this approach is that it is consistent with existing WTO case law, therefore, and it may require little additional work by national authorities.

The obvious disadvantage of this approach is that the opportunity to use WTO-legal safeguard measures becomes largely random. Whenever the right confluence of meaningless correlations (or non-correlations) and price movements come together, safeguard measures are permissible but not otherwise. To the degree that the drafters of GATT Article XIX, and of the Agreement on Safeguards, had any well-defined set of circumstances in mind for which safeguard measures were thought to be appropriate, this approach has little hope of identifying them. One might just as well ask national authorities to roll a pair of dice, and say that the causal standard is met whenever they roll a seven.

Another potential disadvantage of this approach is that it is by definition lacking in logical rigor, so that it will always be possible to say that national authorities have failed to offer a "reasoned and adequate" explanation for their findings. A complaining member can argue before a WTO dispute panel, for example, that a simple search for correlation between injury factors and imports on the one hand, and injury factors and "other factors" on the other, does not satisfactorily "separate and distinguish" the effects of other factors, and ensure that they have not been "attributed" to imports. National authorities will have a hard time responding persuasively to this criticism, since it is correct. Findings of causation resting on this approach to "analysis" are thus inherently vulnerable to attack before a dispute panel.

To the degree that national authorities can address the domestic political pressures for safeguards adequately with measures that need not last much longer than the length of time required for complainants to obtain an adverse ruling at the WTO, of course, the prospect of an unfavorable ruling may not be of great concern. What some commentators term the "three-year free pass," owing to the delays inherent in WTO dispute resolution, may in some cases render the WTO legality of safeguard measures a near afterthought. In these instances, the conceptually flawed approach to causal analysis that has prevailed to date may remain the path of least resistance.

2 Focus on the Unforeseen Developments

Chapter 5 considered at some length the question whether the drafters of the Agreement on Safeguards intended to revive the first clause of Article XIX regarding "unforeseen developments." That prerequisite for safeguard measures had long lay dormant in GATT practice, and its omission from the text of the Agreement on Safeguards strongly hints that the drafters did not seek to resurrect it. One can thus quarrel with the decisions by the Appellate Body in *Korea—Dairy* and in *Argentina—Footwear* requiring anew that national authorities demonstrate unforeseen developments.

A potential consequence of a revived unforeseen developments requirement, however, is that a coherent exogenous variable might resurface for purposes of causal analysis. One asks not whether "increased imports" have caused injury in the abstract, a question that makes little sense for the reasons given in Section A, but asks instead whether particular unforeseen developments have caused injury via their effect on the relative competitive position of imported and domestic goods.

The problem of "non-attribution" might also appear to become more tractable. One might say that as long as the unforeseen developments have resulted in a shift in competitive advantage toward imported goods, in turn resulting in increased imports and in injury or threat to domestic firms, then by definition injury has not been "attributed" to any factor other than imports. The task of identifying the "other factors" to which import-related injury must not be "attributed," and of assessing their impact, would then take on much less importance.

This approach has the dual virtue of being reconcilable with the treaty text as interpreted by the Appellate Body, and of being economically intelligible. Nevertheless, its implementation raises a number of difficulties, some conceptual and some practical.

The fundamental conceptual question is what "counts" as an unforeseen development? This question actually has two components—what is meant by "unforeseen," and what is the difference between an "unforeseen development" and an "other factor"?

As to the first component, the discussion in Chapter 5 suggests that the focus of dispute panels will be on the reasonable expectations of trade negotiators during the prior negotiating round. Events that occur after that point in time may benefit from a rebuttable presumption that they are unforeseen. Horn and Mavroidis (2003) offer some other possible limitations on what should be deemed "unforeseen" such as, for example, the principle that the event in question must be beyond the control of the government of the importing nation.

The second component of the conceptual inquiry is perhaps more difficult. Imagine, for example, an "unforeseen" shock to the costs of domestic firms, such as a sudden jump in energy prices or a labor strike. The result is an upward shift in the domestic supply curve, resulting in increased imports, and declining production and profitability at domestic firms (the situation depicted in Figure 8.3 earlier). Are safeguard measures to be permitted here, on the grounds that an "unforeseen development" has produced increased imports and injury, even though the "development" is a domestic supply shock? Or is the supply shock an "other factor," the effects of which may not be "attributed" to imports? One could ask the same sort of question about the demand shifts in Figure 8.4—is a change in consumer tastes favoring imports an "unforeseen development" that can justify safeguard measures as the United States argued over half a century ago in *Hatter's Fur*, or is it an "other factor"? One might even ask whether some of the events that can shift the import supply curve (Figure 8.2) should be treated as "other factors" (such as macroeconomic developments that alter exchange rates).

The reader will no doubt note that these issues closely parallel the issues raised above regarding the conundrums of non-attribution analysis. If one shifts the inquiry from whether increased imports have caused injury to whether unforeseen developments have caused injury, while retaining the requirement of non-attribution, one still confronts the task of delineating the "other factors" that are conceptually distinct from the eligible set of unforeseen developments. WTO decisions to date afford little help with such matters, and the treaty text provides no guidance. The unanswered questions are much the same as before—later parts of this section will suggest some possible answers, but none are firmly grounded in the treaty text.

Even if the conceptual issues can be overcome satisfactorily, a formidable practical task remains. How does one confidently establish the increase in imports and the injury attributable to the unforeseen development? Recall, for example, the questions that arose in *United States—Steel*. The United States claimed that unforeseen developments such as the Asian financial crisis and the dissolution of the Soviet Union had contributed to a surge of U.S. steel imports. It was certainly plausible that such developments might have led steel exporters to divert sales toward the U.S. market (i.e., to offer steel for sale to the United States at a lower price than otherwise, effectively shifting the import supply curve). But exactly how much did these developments affect steel supply to the United States? It may be impossible to ascertain the answer to such a question with a high degree of confidence, and difficult even to make an informed guess without a mathematical model of global steel trade. Such models can be quite costly and time consuming to construct. Reliable econometric estimates or informed assumptions about relevant parameters may be difficult to come by as well, especially in the relatively brief time frame typically employed by national authorities in safeguards investigations. The problem may be compounded for less prominent, smaller industries for which little pre-existing data exist. And, of course, even in industries on which substantial data may be found, the data may or may not correspond to the proper "industry definition(s)" for purposes of a safeguards investigation.

In sum, the practical difficulties involved in constructing a "reasoned and adequate" account of the causal chain running from unforeseen developments to injury may be enormous. I note that the small amount of careful empirical work done on safeguards issues to date, work that I will address in a moment, does not attempt to start with "unforeseen developments" and to trace their effects, but in one way or another takes a simper approach.

3 Focus on the Import Supply Curve

A number of economic commentators have addressed the question of how to operationalize the substantial cause test under U.S. law. Several of these commentators, including Grossman (1986), Kelly (1988), and Irwin (2003), favor an approach that would decompose the injury suffered by an import-competing industry into three general components—injury due to shifts in the import supply curve, injury due to shifts in the domestic supply curve, and injury due to shifts in the domestic demand curve. Only the first component of injury would be deemed injury due to "increased imports." Injury due to domestic supply and demand shifts (or to the various underlying factors that induce such shifts) would be considered injury due to other causes. These commentators also suggest methods for estimating the injury due to each factor.

This approach to analysis can readily be adapted to the causation requirement under WTO law. One might say that all injury attributable to an import supply shift is injury due to "increased quantities" of imports. Injury attributable to domestic supply and demand shifts might be deemed injury due to "other factors." Under WTO law, there is no need to weigh the relative contribution of each factor as under the U.S. substantial cause test, but one can still use this framework to "separate and distinguish" the effects of the "other factors" in a non-attribution analysis. As long as serious injury (or threat) is present, and as long as an import supply shift has made some contribution to it (recall *Wheat Gluten* and *Lamb* state that increased imports need not suffice to cause serious injury by themselves), the importing nation might be deemed to meet the causation requirement of the Agreement on Safeguards by showing the extent of the causal contribution from the import supply shift and by identifying the contribution made by the other factors. The importing nation might use the same framework to ascertain the permissible extent of a safeguard measure, as discussed in the next chapter.

Would such an approach to the causation analysis by importing nations be legally permissible? Would it be desirable as a policy matter? It is difficult to answer either question definitively.

As to the legality of an approach that equated the effects of "increased quantities" with shifts in the import supply curve, panels and the Appellate Body have repeatedly stated that the text does not compel any particular method of analysis. If an importing nation were to proceed by carefully delineating the effects of import supply, domestic supply and domestic demand shifts, treating the first as the effect of "increased quantities" and the second and third as "other factors," one might argue that the analysis is at least permissible. A literalist might respond, however, that a showing of injury due to import supply shifts is not the same as a showing of injury caused by "increased quantities," a showing which, of course, is logically problematic as demonstrated in Section A. The text of the Agreement on Safeguards also requires national authorities to consider the volume and market share of imports, factors that play little direct role in an analysis that seeks to identify the consequences of shifting supply and demand curves. Finally, it might be argued that existing WTO case law clearly requires both a "coincidence" analysis and a "conditions of competition" analysis, neither of which is to be found in a causation analysis that focuses exclusively on shifts in demand and supply curves. Given the foolishness of the existing precedents on these points, one might hope that they could somehow be put to the side, but it is difficult to say with confidence how a future dispute panel would rule.

As to the broader policy question, it is by no means clear that safeguard measures should be permitted whenever, and only when, injury is attributable to shifts in the import supply curve. Consider once again the facts of the old *Hatter's Fur* case under GATT. The United States argued that the import surge resulted from a change in domestic consumer tastes favoring the imported good over the domestic good (akin to the shift depicted in Figure 8.4 above), and the GATT working party seemed to accept this justification in principle. To be sure, the United States had also made a recent tariff concession that shifted the import supply curve. But implicit in the U.S. position was that the tariff change itself would have caused no great distress absent the subsequent change in consumer tastes—the precipitating cause of serious injury was the change in domestic demand conditions. An emphasis on import supply shifts as the cause of injury would rule out safeguard measures under these conditions—would that outcome be at odds with what the drafters of GATT intended? One can also wonder whether safeguard measures should routinely be ruled out when domestic supply shocks cause serious distress to import-competing firms (the situation depicted in Figure 8.3).

To address such issues, one requires a coherent theory of when safeguard measures should be permitted, but there is certainly no consensus on such a theory. The account of safeguard measures put forward by Bagwell and Staiger (1990, 2002) and discussed in Chapter 2, for example, emphasizes that certain economic shocks may create a temptation for nations to cheat on the GATT bargain to improve their terms of trade. This account seemingly does not justify limiting safeguard measures only to cases where the import supply curve has shifted. Domestic supply and demand shocks (such as those depicted in Figures 8.3–4) could also create the temptation to cheat.

If one believes that safeguard measures are needed to restore the competitiveness of beleaguered industries, or to promote structural adjustment (views that I suggest are mistaken in Chapter 2), it is also quite unclear whether injury due to an import supply shift should be necessary, or sufficient, for the use of safeguards. It is difficult to see why import supply shocks make out a better case for restoring competitiveness than domestic shocks, or why the need for structural adjustment is any greater with an import supply shock.

Sykes (1991, 2003) suggests that the implicit logic of Article XIX may be to permit temporary trade protection when economic shocks produce circumstances in which exporters experience greater prosperity than they reasonably expected or bargained for, and in which import-competing firms experience severe economic distress. In other words, the purpose of safeguard measures may be to "rebalance" the bargain temporarily in response to such shocks. The argument draws heavily on the contractarian explanation for safeguard measures discussed in Chapter 2, and the political economy analysis that accompanies it. If this proposition about the proper role of safeguards is correct, it would follow that safeguard measures should be allowed under some conditions where injury is *not* caused by shifts in the import supply curve (such as perhaps under the facts in *Hatter's Fur*). Likewise, this interpretation suggests that safeguard measures may be inappropriate in some cases where injury *is* due to shifts in the import supply curve. For example, if macroeconomic conditions abroad lead to recession, and exporters lower their prices because of the recessionary conditions in their home or third country markets, the import supply curve will shift but the circumstances would not correspond to a situation where exporters were experiencing unexpected prosperity. (Recall that recessionary conditions abroad were the "unforeseen developments" that the United States pointed to in *Steel*.)

Grossman (1986) also offers some reason to doubt the wisdom of safeguard measures in response to every possible shift of the import supply curve. Suppose, for example, that the import supply curve is denominated in the currency of the importing country, and that its currency appreciates. The price of imports in domestic currency will fall, shifting the import supply curve and perhaps causing serious injury to import-competing firms. Grossman notes, however, that trade protection in response to such a general shift in the exchange rate may be quite undesirable, as it will result in further exchange rate movements that cause injury in other industries (such as domestic exporting industries) that have already been injured by the prior appreciation of the domestic currency.

In sum, the suggestion by some economic commentators that injury due to "increased quantities" of imports should be equated with injury due to shifts in the import supply curve lacks clear grounding in the policies that underlie the Agreement on Safeguards. Because those policies are quite murky, however, it is also difficult to say with confidence that any particular approach is inconsistent with them.

If the legal and policy concerns can be overcome, certain practical considerations remain. In particular, although the task of quantifying the effects of shifts in demand and supply curves in the importing country is perhaps less daunting in many cases than the challenge of tracing the effects of "unforeseen developments" throughout global markets, it can still represent a considerable empirical undertaking. I thus conclude this section by reviewing some efforts to operationalize this approach in the past.

Grossman (1986) uses a structural model of the domestic industry to obtain a "reduced form" equation that allows a relevant injury factor to be expressed as a function of exogenous variables. He applies this approach to the U.S. steel industry, focusing on total industry employment as the relevant injury factor (although the approach could easily be adapted to encompass other injury factors as well, an adaptation that would be compelled by current WTO law). Under the assumptions of his structural model, employment in the steel industry is a function of the real domestic price of energy, the real domestic price of iron, the real wage of domestic workers,[56] the real price of imported steel in foreign currency, the exchange rate, the tariff on imported steel, domestic industrial production, and a time trend. The first three factors capture domestic supply considerations, the second three capture factors that affect the price of imports to U.S. consumers (the position of the import supply curve), the seventh is a factor capturing shifts in domestic demand, and the time trend captures a variety of additional factors that may relate to technology trends, demand trends, and the like. Grossman uses the real price of imports as an exogenous variable on the assumption that the import supply curve is perfectly elastic (the supply curve is horizontal at the prevailing price). Otherwise, it would be necessary to treat import prices as endogenous and to include in the model other exogenous variables that shift the import supply curve.

Grossman obtained (monthly) time series for all of the variables and estimated the reduced form equation econometrically, experimenting with lag structures to obtain a reasonable fit with the data. The multiple regression technique used for this purpose allows the researcher to estimate the effects of each exogenous variable individually, holding constant the effects of changes in the other variables. Using the resulting parameter estimates, it is then possible to simulate the effects of different time paths for the various exogenous variables on developments in the industry. Grossman could inquire, for example, how much higher steel industry employment would have been had all the factors affecting import prices to consumers (exchange rates, the price of steel in foreign currency, and tariff rates) remained unchanged over some period of time. He could compare this effect to the effect on steel industry employment of such factors as declining U.S. industrial production or rising energy prices. On the basis of such analysis, Grossman questioned whether import-related factors were the substantial cause of the loss of employment in the steel industry, although he acknowledged that the time frame over which that question was asked could prove quite important to the answer (the baseline issue in the terminology of Chapter 6).

[56] He also estimates an alternative model in which the wage is taken to be endogenous and omitted as an explanatory variable.

Grossman's basic approach could be adapted to causation analysis under the Agreement on Safeguards. A structural model could be used to derive reduced form equations for all of the relevant injury factors. The parameters in these equations could be estimated econometrically, and the effects on all injury factors of the exogenous variables that affect the import supply curve could then be calculated. The effects of the "other factors" could also be calculated, to show that they had not been "attributed" to imports.

The greatest impediment to such an exercise in practice will often be the task of assembling the necessary data. Grossman did the analysis for one injury factor (employment), and for the steel "industry" in the aggregate. This approach allowed him to obtain the necessary data to construct a monthly time series for all of the relevant variables. Imagine, by contrast, undertaking the analysis for every injury factor listed in Article 4.2 of the Agreement on Safeguards, and doing it for each of two dozen or so steel "industries" defined by the ITC in the recent *Steel* investigation. Or imagine undertaking the analysis for a smaller or less studied industry for which little or no publicly available data exist. To assemble enough data for statistically sound econometric results, national authorities (or parties to the investigation) would often have to gather the data themselves and ensure its statistical soundness, often within an unrealistically tight time frame. The costs of such an undertaking could be exceedingly high.

Because of this important practical problem with Grossman's econometric approach, Kelly (1988) and Irwin (2003) advocate an alternative that relies on educated judgments about key parameters. Kelly considers three stylized market settings—a competitive market in which imported and domestic goods are perfect substitutes, a competitive market in which imported and domestic goods are imperfect substitutes, and a market in which the domestic firm is a "dominant firm" (with market power) and the suppliers of imported goods act as a competitive fringe. Starting from simple linear models, he shows that in each case it is possible to decompose the change in domestic production into three components—a change due to a shift in import supply, a change due to a shift in domestic demand, and a change due to a shift in domestic supply (or cost in the dominant firm case). In turn, each of these three components can be expressed as a function of observable variables (such as changes in prices, domestic production, import quantities, market shares, and total consumption) plus certain elasticities of supply and demand (domestic and import demand elasticities, domestic and import supply elasticities, and cross-price elasticities of demand). Kelly then suggests that the effect of each shift on domestic production can be estimated using data on the observable variables coupled with informed judgments about the relevant elasticities. That is, instead of estimating the relevant elasticities econometrically, Kelly suggests that a fact finder can obtain qualitative information allowing an educated judgment about each of them. Indeed, U.S. ITC reports often contain assessments of various elasticities derived from qualitative assessments.

Like Grossman, Kelly employs his framework to assess whether changes in the import supply curve are the substantial cause of injury under U.S. law. But his framework too can be adapted to address the issues that arise under WTO law. One can use the framework directly to estimate the effects of import supply shifts and "other factors" (domestic demand and supply or cost shifts) on domestic production for purposes of a non-attribution analysis. The framework can also be used with minor modification to estimate the effects of shifts in the various curves on price, and with additional assumptions it might be adapted to estimate the effects of the shifts on other injury factors.

The advantage of the framework endorsed by Kelly and Irwin is that it does not require any econometric estimation, and relies wholly on data that are routinely gathered in safeguards investigations along with informed guesses about pertinent elasticities. A disadvantage, of course, is precisely that it requires subjective judgments about key parameters. Oftentimes considerable uncertainty and controversy will exist about these parameters, resulting in a fairly wide range of plausible values. Sensitivity analyses drawing on different assumptions can produce widely varying results. In addition, the Kelly framework has not yet been adapted to address injury factors other than production (and implicitly price), and the additional information requirements to address other injury factors are not yet clear.

Note that a rough equivalent to Kelly's approach was briefly embraced by two U.S. ITC Commissioners in the 1980s. Consider, as an illustration of their analysis, an investigation involving imports of wooden roofing products from Canada.[57] In their opinion in that case, the two Commissioners observed that over the period of investigation, imports had risen considerably, domestic production had fallen by a roughly equivalent quantity, total domestic consumption had fallen slightly and real prices had fallen. The fact that imports had risen in the face of a declining real price established that the import supply curve had shifted. But the import supply shift was not the sole

[57] See U.S. ITC, Wood Shakes and Shingles, Inv. No. TA 201–56 (1986) (views of Vice Chairman Liebeler and Commissioner Brunsdale).

cause of developments in the market, because an import supply shift alone would have led to an increased level of domestic consumption. The Commissioners further argued (perhaps erroneously, see Kelly (1988)), that domestic supply had not shifted because technology had not changed and the price of the most important input product had remained steady. They thus concluded that the drop in consumption must be due to a leftward shift of domestic demand. The question then became whether the demand shift or the import supply shift was the "substantial cause" of the distress experienced by domestic firms. The Commissioners concluded that the demand shift was a more important cause of injury than the import supply shift on the theory that demand was highly elastic, and hence price would not be much affected by an import supply shift—had the import supply shift occurred without the demand shift, demand would have grown to absorb additional imports with only a modest reduction in price and an accordingly modest impact on domestic firms. Most of the harm to domestic firms, therefore, must have resulted from the demand shift. Kelly's quantitative analysis of the case tends to confirm that a demand shift was the primary cause of injury, at least over the full period of investigation.

Irwin (2003) offers further illustrations of how Kelly's framework can be applied, using information on elasticities from ITC reports to analyze a number of recent safeguards cases in the United States. He concludes that an import supply shift was the dominant cause of injury in both *Wheat Gluten* and *Line Pipe*, for example, while a domestic supply shift was the dominant cause of injury in *Lamb*.

Of course, WTO law does not require that increased imports be the "substantial cause" of injury, but as noted the framework devised by Kelly could be adapted to the task of "non-attribution" analysis under WTO law. It can also be used to delimit the permissible extent of a safeguard measure as discussed in the next chapter. The ultimate wisdom of such an approach turns heavily on the harder issue raised earlier—whether the drafters of GATT Article XIX and the Agreement on Safeguards would wish to equate injury due to "increased quantities" with a shift in import supply.

4 Focus on Hypothetical Quantitative Restrictions

Another possible approach to causal analysis is to attribute injury to "increased quantities" of imports if, and to the extent that, a counterfactual quantitative restriction on imports would have averted or ameliorated injury. For example, suppose that imports have risen from 10,000 units annually to

15,000 units during the period of investigation, and that the import-competing industry experiences serious injury contemporaneously with this increase. One might say that the quantum of injury attributable to increased imports is the quantum of injury that would have been *avoided* if, counterfactually, the importing nation had imposed a quantitative restriction during the period of investigation that restricted imports to the initial annual level of 10,000. One could of course select other baselines—one might consider the effects of a counterfactual quantitative restriction that limited import growth to some historical average rate, for example, or that prevented imports from gaining a market share above some baseline value.

This approach to causal analysis differs importantly from the focus on import supply curve shifts in the last section. To see how, consider Figure 8.6. [See also Rousslang (1988).] The figure assumes for simplicity, contrary to the prior figures in this chapter, that import supply is perfectly elastic (horizontal) and given by the curve S_i. Domestic demand is *D*, and domestic

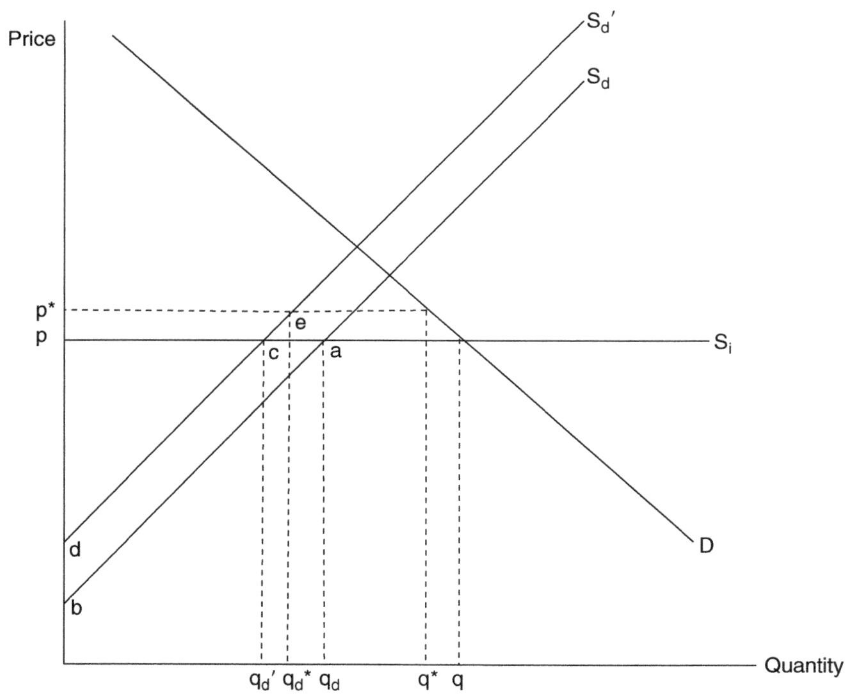

Figure 8.6

supply is initially S_d. In the initial equilibrium, domestic production is q_d, total consumption is *q* and imports are equal to the difference, $q - q_d$. Let us now imagine a domestic supply shock that raises the costs of domestic firms and shifts domestic supply upward to S_d'. As a result, domestic production declines to q_d', while total consumption remains the same (because of the constant import price) and imports increase to $q - q_d'$.

If injury due to "increased quantities" of imports is deemed to exist only when the cause is a shift in the import supply curve, as in the discussion of subsection 4, then no import-related injury arises at all in Figure 8.6. The import supply curve has not shifted.

If instead, however, we define the injury attributable to imports as the harm caused by the absence of a counterfactual import restraint limiting imports to their initial level $(q - q_d)$, import-related injury is present. A quantitative restriction limiting imports to $q - q_d$ would, following the domestic supply shift, cause price to rise to p^*. The market will then clear with reduced total consumption of q^* increased domestic production at q_d^*, and imports equal to $q^* - q_d^*$ $(= q - q_d)$. The quantity $q_d^* - q_d'$ thus represents the loss of domestic production that would have been averted had a quantitative restriction been in place limiting imports to their initial value following the domestic supply shock. The remaining diminution in domestic production, $q_d - q_d^*$, is the loss of production that would have occurred because of the domestic supply shift even if the quantitative restriction had been in place. Thus, under this approach to causal analysis, $q_d^* - q_d'$ is the injury attributable to increased quantities of imports, while $q_d - q_d^*$ is the injury attributable to "other factors."

The figure also shows how the loss of profit to domestic producers can be allocated between "increased quantities" of imports and "other factors." Initial domestic producer surplus (profit) is given by the area of the triangle *pab*. After the supply shock, profit falls to the area *pcd*. Had a quantitative restriction been in place restricting imports to their initial value, profit after the supply shift would have been *p*ed*. Thus, of the total loss of profit by domestic producers due to the supply shift, and captured by area *abdc*, an amount equal to area *p*ecp* would have been averted by the quantitative restriction and would be deemed import-related injury. The remaining loss, equal to the difference between these two areas, would be attributed to "other factors."

A similar approach to causal analysis, known as "shift-share analysis," has occasionally been employed by some Commissioners at the U.S. ITC. This technique decomposes injury into two components—injury attributable to

Table 8.1

	Consumption	Imports	Domestic Production	Import Share
Base year	1,000,000	300,000	700,000	30%
Current year	800,000	320,000	480,000	40%

an increase in the market share of imports, and injury attributable to declining domestic consumption. ITC Commissioners employing shift-share analysis would compare these two components of injury, and find that increased imports were the "substantial cause" of injury if the component due to the increased market share of imports was larger.[58]

To illustrate, consider Table 8.1 in which the entries represent quantity units of some arbitrary good. The table reflects declining domestic consumption of the good in question between the base year and the current year, and a rising market share of imports. Shift share analysis traditionally focuses on domestic production as the key injury factor, and asks how much of the decline in domestic production would have been averted if imports had retained their original market share. Here, had the import share remained 30% while consumption declined from 1,000,000 units to 800,000 units, imports would have fallen from 300,000 units to 240,000 units. Subtracting this amount from total consumption in the current year, domestic production would have been 560,000 units in the counterfactual scenario. Thus, of the decline in domestic production from 700,000 units to 480,000 units, a decline of 80,000 units (560,000–480,000) is attributed to the rising market share of imports. The remainder of the decline in domestic production, 140,000 units (700,000–560,000), is attributed to the decline in consumption and would have occurred even if the market share of imports had remained constant. On these facts, ITC Commissioners embracing shift-share analysis would conclude that the decline in consumption was a more important cause of injury than increased imports (imports are not the "substantial cause" of injury).[59] Of course, one might also apply this technique while holding constant the quantity of imports rather than the market

[58] A useful illustration of this approach may be found in U.S. ITC, Certain Motor Vehicles, Inv. No. TA-201–44 (1980) (Views of Chairman Alberger).

[59] Shift-share analysis fell out of favor at the ITC, in significant part because petitioners (and Congress) objected to the notion that declining "consumption" is a single cause of injury to be weighed against imports under the substantial cause test. Although ITC Commissioners often speak of "consumption" as a measure of demand, it is in fact simply the quantity at which supply and

share—by that reasoning, only 20,000 units of the decline in domestic production would be attributable to increased imports.

The general approach to causal analysis reflected in Figure 8.6 and in shift-share analysis can also be adapted to the non-attribution exercise under WTO law. Using the same baseline that national authorities employ to establish "increased imports" (the subject of Chapter 6), one might investigate what portion of the serious injury or threat to the domestic industry would have been averted had imports been constrained to their initial quantity or market share. That quantum of injury becomes the injury attributed to "increased quantities," while the remaining injury is attributed to "other factors." The exercise is particularly simple when, as in the illustrations above, domestic production is the injury factor of interest and imports are perfect substitutes for domestic products—one can simply assume that imports displace domestic production on a one-for-one basis. The analysis is more complex when imports and domestic goods are imperfect substitutes, and when injury factors other than domestic production are considered. Nevertheless, economists have the theoretical tools to undertake such analysis, and the main impediments are likely to be data limitations.

A statistically sophisticated attempt to implement this approach was undertaken by the Chilean respondents in an investigation of unwrought copper imports before the U.S. ITC. The work of the consulting experts in that case led to the subsequent publication of Pindyck and Rotemberg (1987). Pindyck & Rotemberg developed reduced form equations for two types of injury factors in the domestic copper industry—domestic production and employment. They posited that these factors depend on real domestic GNP (capturing demand conditions), relative wages in the U.S. copper-mining industry (capturing an important factor affecting domestic supply), a time trend (capturing miscellaneous changes in the market such as environmental regulations and productivity growth), and the quantity of imports. Their use of imports as an exogenous variable is driven by the premise that an objective of the analysis is to capture the effects of a hypothetical quantitative restriction on imports—in a counterfactual environment in which imports were subject to a binding quantitative restriction during the period of investigation, the quantity of imports would indeed be exogenous.

demand balance at the prevailing price. It is thus determined by both supply and demand factors. Moreover, petitioners routinely argue that declining demand by itself is the product of multiple causes.

The difficulty with assuming imports to be exogenous for purposes of statistical estimation, however, is that in reality the quantity of imports is endogenous for the reasons given in Section A of this chapter. Their value will generally be correlated with the error terms in multiple regressions estimating the reduced form equations, producing biased estimates of their effects. To address this potential problem with their approach, Pindyck & Rotemberg undertook some additional statistical procedures.[60]

Pindyck and Rotemberg estimated their reduced form equations using annual data for a 34-year period, and then used the parameter estimates to simulate the effects of various counterfactual assumptions about imports, GNP growth, and wages. Their simulations suggested that rising imports—or more precisely, the absence of a quota to restrain them—were a less important cause of declining production and employment than recessionary conditions in the U.S. economy at the time and the high rate of relative wage growth in copper mining.

Is this general approach to causal analysis a suitable way to assess causation under the Agreement on Safeguards, from a legal, policy or practical standpoint? The answers are again somewhat unclear.

As to the legal issue, one might argue (as do Pindyck and Rotemberg) that an approach to analysis that focuses on the impact of a counterfactual quantitative restriction fits nicely with the textual requirement of a causal linkage between "increased quantities" of imports and injury—it seems natural to say that increased quantities of imports cause injury to the extent that a quantitative restriction preventing the increase in imports would avert injury. Further, if the injurious effects due to the absence of the hypothetical quantitative restriction can be demonstrated with reasonable care, national authorities can "attribute" all remaining injury to "other factors" in accordance with their non-attribution obligation. If it remains necessary to "separate and distinguish" the effect of each "other factor," that task can be undertaken in principle using the reduced form statistical technique employed by Pindyck and Rotemberg.

But there are some potential obstacles to this approach as well. The most obvious is again the body of existing precedent requiring national authorities to conduct an analysis of "coincidence" and "conditions of competition." A focus on the impact of a hypothetical quantitative restriction pays little

60 In particular, Pindyck and Rotemberg estimated their reduced form equations using instrumental variables, a standard technique for addressing bias associated with an endogenous independent variable, and also ran "Granger-Sims" causality regressions testing for a causal connection between imports and the injury factors.

attention to such matters. Further, the conceptual problems of "non-attribution" analysis remain an issue. Suppose, for example, that a nation imposes a safeguard measure in response to the developments in Figure 8.6. A complaining nation then argues before a WTO dispute panel that the importing nation has improperly attributed to imports injury caused by a domestic supply shock. Who wins? Given the confusion that prevails in the non-attribution decisions to date, one cannot answer that question with any confidence.

From a policy standpoint, an approach that focuses on the effect of counterfactual quantitative restrictions is more troublesome, especially in light of the Appellate Body decisions in *Wheat Gluten* and *Lamb*. Recall that those decisions held that increased imports need not be sufficient, in themselves, to cause serious injury, but must merely contribute to it. Yet, in virtually any imaginable case in which serious injury is present, a counterfactual quantitative restriction on imports would confer *some* benefit on the domestic import-competing industry. It follows almost inexorably, therefore, that in every case where both serious injury and increased imports are present, this approach to causal analysis would find that the serious injury was at least partly attributable to increased imports. Thus, safeguard measures would always be allowable in the presence of serious injury and increased imports regardless of the nature of the shocks that have precipitated economic distress in the import-competing industry, subject of course to some limits on the extent of the safeguard measures that will be discussed in Chapter 9. It is perhaps difficult to imagine that the drafters of GATT and the Agreement on Safeguards would have wanted to open the door to safeguard measures so widely. The problem would be less acute if the Appellate Body were to reverse itself on the question whether increased imports must in themselves cause serious injury, but there is little basis to suppose that such a reversal is likely.

On the practical side, careful implementation of this approach in a fashion that would allow all of the injury factors in the Agreement on Safeguards to be addressed, and that would allow the effects of all "other factors" to be "separated and distinguished," could pose a daunting empirical challenge. Pindyck and Rotemberg conducted their analysis for only two types of injury factors, and had the luxury of working with an industry for which much publicly-available data already existed. Their approach in other contexts would likely encounter the same data problems that would arise under the approach of Grossman (1986), discussed above. The shift-share analysis approach of the U.S. ITC avoids the data issues, but is vulnerable to the additional objection that it does not conduct an adequate non-attribution analysis—respondents in investigations before national authorities are likely to raise a wide range of "other factors" besides declining total consumption.

5 Summary and Implications

The causation requirement for the use of safeguard measures is deeply confused and unsatisfactory, and it is impossible to discern from the treaty text the set of circumstances in which the drafters intended to permit the use of such measures. The problem begins with the original text of GATT Article XIX, which poses a logically coherent question—whether "unforeseen developments" and changes in trade policy have caused injury—but does not specify the types of "unforeseen developments" that may serve as a predicate for safeguards. One might infer that *any* unforeseen development will do, but if so the opportunity to use safeguard measures becomes extremely broad, particularly if (as the Appellate Body has suggested) the requirement of a linkage to a change in trade policy is no longer an important hurdle (see Chapter 5). The Agreement on Safeguards confuses matters further by merely asking for a causal linkage between injury and "increased quantities" of imports. Because conditions of injury and increased imports result simultaneously from changes in underlying supply and demand factors, it makes no sense to say that one causes the other.

Previous economic commentators have suggested two ways to make sense of the situation. One is to equate injury due to "increased quantities" of imports with injury due to shifts in the import supply curve; the other is to attribute injury to "increased quantities" of imports to the degree that a counterfactual quantitative restriction equal to some baseline level of imports would have averted injury. I have offered a third possibility here—a return to the approach of GATT Article XIX, and to the question whether some exogenous "unforeseen development" has caused injury. All of these options are logically intelligible, yet none of them are clearly desirable as a policy matter, and each poses considerable practical challenges to implementation.

The dispute process thus far has failed to acknowledge these conceptual problems. Existing precedents require national authorities to search for "coincidence" between import trends and injury factors, and to analyze "conditions of competition." For the reasons given in this chapter, neither line of analysis bears any useful relation to questions of causation. If these two analytical steps were all that existing precedent required, however, cases would no doubt arise in which safeguard measures would be permissible.

But the third strand of analysis required under existing precedents—"non-attribution" analysis—requires national authorities to "separate and distinguish" the effects of all "other factors" to ensure that injury due to them is not "attributed" to imports. This task is not only difficult as a practical matter, but often becomes logically impossible because the "other factor" at issue is among the *causes* of increased imports. An analysis to separate the causal contribution of "imports" and the "other factors" in such cases simply cannot be undertaken in convincing fashion. The legal requirement of a "reasoned and adequate" non-attribution analysis then becomes an insurmountable hurdle, both in theory and in practice. In this regard, it is noteworthy that no finding of causation heretofore examined in the dispute process has been upheld.

The predictable effect of this state of affairs is to discourage the use of safeguard measures. For example, the United States undertook nine safeguards investigations in the first five years after the conclusion of the Uruguay Round, but it has undertaken no new investigations in the past five years (since *Steel*). Commentators who view safeguard measures as wasteful protectionism may welcome this state of affairs. But as Chapter 2 argued, safeguard measures have a plausibly useful role to play in the system. Further, protectionist pressures may simply be diverted elsewhere, as into antidumping and countervailing duty actions. To the degree that these "unfair" trade cases are not an adequate substitute for safeguard measures, pressures may re-emerge for the use of grey-area measures. It is at least unclear, therefore, whether the substantial present impediments to WTO-legal safeguard measures are in the best interest of the trading system.

The ideal solution to the current problems would be a renegotiation of the Agreement on Safeguards to specify more clearly the circumstances under which safeguard measures are believed to be appropriate by WTO members, and to conform the causation requirement accordingly. At this writing, however, the prospects for such a renegotiation do not appear bright.

A possible alternative might be for the Appellate Body to take the lead in fashioning a more coherent causal standard, embracing one or more theories of the proper role of safeguard measures in the system. If the Appellate Body errs in such initiatives, WTO members might then renegotiate to correct the problem. Whatever the potential merits of such an approach, however, the Appellate Body generally avoids such "activism" and weds itself closely to treaty text. That strategy cannot hope to resolve the current dilemmas given the fundamental deficiencies in the text as currently written.

A third possible route to a coherent causation standard might be for some importing nation to take the lead in fashioning a sensible approach to the causal inquiry, and then to push hard for ratification of its approach in the dispute process. Although dispute panels will likely resist and preach fidelity to precedent, perhaps a forceful appeal could persuade the Appellate Body to deemphasize the requirements for "coincidence" and "conditions of competition" analysis and to accept a logically intelligible "non-attribution" analysis even in the face of some statistical challenges. Of course, the danger would arise that the importing nation would not select the most sensible interpretation of the causal inquiry from a systemic perspective. That danger returns us full circle to the need for some collectively negotiated solution.

Chapter 9

PERMISSIBLE MEASURES AND THEIR DURATION

The last several chapters focus on the legal prerequisites for the use of safeguard measures. Even if those prerequisites are met, safeguard measures must obey a number of additional restrictions on their scope and duration. These principles are the subject of this chapter.

I begin with perhaps the most fundamental question—to what extent may a safeguard measure restrict trade in the affected goods? An examination of this question leads to some general principles, and to some more specific rules applicable to safeguard measures that involve quantitative restrictions. I then turn to one of the core issues in the Uruguay Round negotiations on safeguards, and one that has recurred often in safeguards disputes—the discriminatory application of safeguard measures, or "selectivity." The rules concerning the permissible duration and interim review of safeguard measures come next, followed by a brief discussion of provisional measures and the special rules applicable to developing countries.

A "To the Extent Necessary"

Article 5.1 of the Agreement on Safeguards provides:

> A Member shall apply safeguard measures only to the extent necessary to prevent or remedy serious injury and to facilitate adjustment. If a quantitative restriction is used, such a measure shall not reduce the quantity of imports below the level of a recent period which shall be the average of imports in the last three representative years for which statistics are available, unless clear justification is given that a different level is necessary to prevent or remedy serious injury. Members should choose measures most suitable for the achievement of these objectives.

This text raises several obvious issues. How does a member establish that a measure is applied "only to the extent necessary to prevent or remedy serious injury and to facilitate adjustment?" Must a showing to that effect be made at the time the safeguard measure is applied, or is it required only in the event of a challenge in the dispute resolution process? What if some of the "serious injury" has been attributed to factors other than increased imports—can a safeguard measure nevertheless remediate all of the injury, or must it be confined to the import-related injury? If the latter, and in light of the discussion in Chapter 8 regarding the challenges of distinguishing import-related injury from that caused by "other factors," how can a member demonstrate that only the "import-related injury" has been addressed? Finally, with reference to sentence two, what is meant by a "representative year," and how might one devise a "clear justification" for a more restrictive measure?

1 Justification for the Measure: The Timing Issue

The second question above was raised squarely in *Korea—Dairy*. The European Communities argued that Korea's published report did nothing to demonstrate that the measure chosen was the "most suitable" one to remedy or prevent serious injury. Likewise, Korea made no showing in its report that the measure was "necessary" for that purpose. Korea argued that Article 5.1 imposed no obligation to make such a showing prior to the application of a measure, except in the case of a quantitative restriction reducing imports below their average level in the three most recent representative years, as described in sentence two. The panel sided with Europe: "[I]t must be possible for a panel to evaluate, in accordance with the applicable standard of review, whether a member has acted in accordance with Article 5.1. Therefore, the member applying the measure must provide a reasoned explanation as to how the authorities reached the conclusion that the particular measure in question satisfies all the requirements of Article 5.1."[1]

The Appellate Body reversed. It agreed with the panel that Article 5.1 imposes a binding obligation, but disagreed that members must always provide a showing of compliance with Article 5.1 in their published report. Instead, Article 5.1, second sentence, requires a "clear justification" only when a quantitative restriction reduces imports below the average level in the "last three representative years." In other cases, there is no requirement for prior justification as to the extent of the measure. The Appellate Body reaffirmed this principle later in *United States—Line Pipe*: "Article 5.1 does not establish a general procedural obligation to demonstrate compliance with Article 5.1, first sentence, at the time a measure is applied."[2]

2 Injury Attributable to "Other Factors"

The question of how much "injury" a measure may "remedy" was also addressed in *United States—Line Pipe*. The parties to the dispute agreed that in addition to injury caused by imports, the U.S. industry had been injured by a decline in activity in the oil and gas industry. Korea alleged that the safeguard measure adopted by the United States was tailored to alleviate not only the injury caused by imports, but also the injury attributable to the decline in oil and gas activity. The United States offered two responses. First, it disputed the factual proposition that its measure was intended to address more than the injury caused by imports. Second, it argued that the text imposed no such limitation on safeguard measures in any event—a measure may remedy the "serious injury" found to exist, whatever its cause. The panel accepted the first argument, concluding that Korea had failed to carry the burden of showing that the measure was intended to address more than just the injury caused by imports. Accordingly, the panel found it unnecessary to rule on the second argument.[3]

[1] Korea—Dairy Panel para 7.101. [2] United States—Line Pipe AB para 234.
[3] United States—Line Pipe Panel para 7.110.

Korea appealed, and the United States again argued that the first sentence of Article 5.1 permits a measure that remedies all of the "serious injury." The argument proceeded from the absence of any textual limitation to the contrary in Article 5.1. In addition, as the Appellate Body had ruled in *United States—Wheat Gluten*, safeguard measures are permissible whenever increased quantities of imports have contributed along with other factors to serious injury—they need not be sufficient, in and of themselves, to cause serious injury. And in a case where imports alone have not caused serious injury, Article 5.1 nevertheless allows a member to remedy "serious injury." *A fortiori*, it must be allowable for measures to address more than just the injury caused by increased imports.

The Appellate Body disagreed, and held that a measure may address only that portion of the "serious injury" attributable to increased quantities of imports. It based its conclusion on three arguments. First, it pointed to the non-attribution requirement of Article 4.2(b). It would be "illogical," according to the Appellate Body, for the Agreement on Safeguards to require members to distinguish the injurious effects of other factors in their causation analysis, and at the same time to allow them to apply measures addressing all injury, whatever the cause.[4] Second, the Appellate Body drew support from the remedy allowable in antidumping and subsidies cases. GATT Article VI (along with the Antidumping and Subsidies Codes) limits countermeasures in such cases to an amount that offsets the amount of dumping or subsidization. The Appellate Body argued that it would be peculiar to limit countermeasures against unfairly traded imports to the amount that offsets the margin of unfairness, while allowing a safeguard "countermeasure" against fairly traded imports to offset injury caused by other factors.[5] Finally, the Appellate Body pointed to the general principle of "proportionality" governing countermeasures in international law, and argued that it supported a limitation of safeguard measures to a level addressing only the injury caused by imports.[6]

One can certainly quibble with the Appellate Body's reasoning on these points. The absence of any textual limitation in Article 5.1 on the degree of "serious injury" that safeguard measures may address might well be taken to support the U.S. position on the issue. The drafters could have inserted a clear limitation had they so desired. The U.S. argument proceeding from *Wheat Gluten* also has some force. In addition, the Appellate Body's reliance on the principles governing countermeasures seems misplaced.

[4] United States—Line Pipe AB para 252. [5] Id. para 257. [6] Id. para 258.

Countermeasures are intended to offset or redress some breach of an international obligation, and safeguard measures are simply not countermeasures.

The structure of Article 5.1 of the Agreement on Safeguards, with its rules regarding the extent of any quantitative restriction, also seems at odds to a degree with the Appellate Body's reasoning. Article 5.1 permits quantitative restrictions that eliminate the recent import surge. But if they do more, by reducing imports below their average levels in the three most recent "representative years," the member employing such measures must provide "clear justification . . . that a different level is necessary to prevent or remedy serious injury." The notion that a member can in principle justify measures that do more than eliminate the recent import surge because they are "necessary to prevent or remedy serious injury" perhaps casts further doubt on the Appellate Body's conclusion—why would a measure restricting imports below their "representative" level ever be necessary to remedy only the import-related injury?

In any event, having ruled that a safeguard measure must be limited to redressing import-related injury, the Appellate Body turned to the question whether Korea had established a *prima facie* case that the U.S. measure was excessive. It held that because Korea had earlier established a violation of the non-attribution requirement of Article 4.2, it had also established a *prima facie* case that the measure exceeded what was necessary to address the injury caused by imports.[7]

Whatever its merits, the Appellate Body ruling in *Line Pipe* has the effect of importing into Article 5.1 all of the messy and unresolved issues associated with non-attribution analysis. As argued in Chapter 8, the Appellate Body has offered no clear conception of what it means to say that injury is "caused" by imports. It has offered no clear conception of what constitutes an "other factor" causing injury distinct from imports. Indeed, it (along with panels) has regularly failed to appreciate that some of the "other factors" it has discussed are in fact themselves the cause of increased imports! The requirements of "non-attribution analysis" thus seem profoundly muddled, as argued previously, and it is quite unclear what sort of analysis would be deemed sufficient to satisfy the non-attribution requirement. Because inadequate non-attribution analysis also establishes a *prima facie* violation of Article 5.1 after *Line Pipe*, it is now equally unclear how a member can establish that its safeguard measure does not exceed the permissible level.

For possible solutions to the confusion surrounding the non-attribution requirement, I refer the reader back to Chapter 8. As indicated there, I am

[7] Id. paras 261–62.

rather pessimistic that any coherent solution to the confusion will emerge without a careful renegotiation of the Agreement.

I conclude this section by noting a possible alternative approach to judging the permissible extent of a safeguard measure, although it would require some modification of the *Line Pipe* ruling. Article 5.1 suggests that in most cases quantitative restrictions should not reduce imports below the levels in the three most recent representative years. GATT Article XIX, as originally drafted and applied, contemplated the revocation of a trade concession that had caused an unforeseen and sufficiently injurious import surge. Both provisions suggest that the drafters were willing to tolerate measures that constrain imports to recent "representative" or pre-concession levels, but that stiffer measures are suspect. Drawing on this logic, one might imagine a sort of "safe harbor" for measures that do not reduce the volume of trade below its level prior to the import surge that triggered the safeguards investigation. Any more stringent measure would require "clear justification," putting aside the hard question of what kind of justification might suffice. Such a test would give clearer guidance to members wishing to employ safeguard measures. It could also be squared with the Appellate Body ruling in *Line Pipe* if one embraced the "hypothetical quantitative restriction" approach to causation analysis discussed in the last chapter (I do not mean to endorse that approach particularly, only to note the relationship here). Under that approach to causal analysis, import-related injury is precisely the injury that would have been avoided by a hypothetical quantitative restriction holding imports to their baseline level. A safeguard measure which did so, and no more, would thus address only import-related injury under this view and would comport with the Appellate Body holding in *Line Pipe*.

3 The Adjustment Issue

The text of Article 5.1 refers both to preventing or remedying serious injury, and to "facilitating adjustment." The cases thus far, as noted, are focused on "remedying injury," and on ensuring that only import-related injury is "remedied." But the text of Article 5.1, and the conjunction "and" between the remediation of injury and the facilitation of adjustment, suggests that an additional limitation on measures may exist—could a measure be necessary to prevent or remedy serious injury, yet be unnecessary to facilitate adjustment? Logically, the answer would seem to be yes. In the absence of a safeguard measure, perhaps import competition will contribute to serious injury (in some intelligible sense of causation as discussed in Chapter 8).

Yet, market forces may lead the beleaguered industry to "adjust" quite well, as by transferring resources to other pursuits, without any trade intervention. When challenged in the dispute process, therefore, must a nation that employs a safeguard measure also demonstrate its necessity to some process of adjustment?

Thus far, no complainant in a safeguard dispute has yet made an argument along these lines. It thus remains unclear whether the facilitation of adjustment requirement adds anything of substance to Article 5.1.

The one issue that has arisen is a procedural one. In *Korea—Dairy*, the European Communities argued that Article 5.1 requires investigating authorities to obtain and consider an adjustment plan prior to implementing a safeguard measure, which Korea had not done. The panel rejected this argument, finding no textual basis for it.[8]

4 Article 5.1, Sentence Two

Recall the language from Article 5.1: "If a quantitative restriction is used, such a measure shall not reduce the quantity of imports below the level of a recent period which shall be the average of imports in the last three representative years for which statistics are available, unless clear justification is given that a different level is necessary to prevent or remedy serious injury." This text poses two key issues, neither of which has yet been addressed in the dispute resolution process. First, what is meant by a "representative year?" The use of the term "representative" implies that the most recent years need not be "representative" in all cases, but why not? The answer likely relates back to some of the issues discussed in Chapter 6 regarding the baseline for assessing the presence of "increased quantities." Importing nations may suggest that a recent year was unrepresentative because imports were aberrantly high because of unusual events, such as a domestic labor strike. Exporting nations may argue that a recent year was unrepresentative because imports were aberrantly low because of unusual events, such as a crop failure in a major exporting nation (recall *Argentina—Peaches*). In the first instance, national authorities may determine what they consider to be "representative," and complaining nations in a dispute will presumably have the burden to show that national authorities acted inappropriately.

The second, murkier issue concerns the possibility of a "clear justification" for a quantitative restriction that reduces imports below the average level in

[8] Korea—Dairy Panel para 7.108.

the three most recent representative years. If, indeed, "representative years" have been chosen, when would a more restrictive measure be "necessary to prevent or remedy serious injury?" As noted earlier, one possibility is that serious injury has arisen for reasons other than the import surge, and that an import restriction doing more than simply reversing the surge is needed to address it. But such a measure would seemingly run afoul of the holding in *Line Pipe* that safeguard measures may not address injury due to "other factors." With the *Line Pipe* holding in mind, therefore, the question becomes, when is a quantitative restriction reducing imports below their "representative" level nevertheless necessary to address import-related injury? I do not know the answer to that question and decline to offer speculation.

B Selectivity

Discrimination in the use of safeguard measures, or what came to be known as "selectivity" in the later years of GATT, was a central concern of the negotiators during the Uruguay Round. Lee (2005) states that "the issue of selectivity remained the most difficult and important one throughout the negotiations."

1 Economic Note

Selectivity is but one species of trade discrimination, whereby some trading partners are afforded more favorable access to a market than others. Such discrimination reduces the conventional measure of economic welfare, other things being equal. The reason is that discrimination can cause the problem known to economists as "trade diversion." Holding constant the volume of imports, global economic welfare will be greater if they are supplied by the lowest-cost or most "efficient" producers of them, which will be the case in competitive equilibrium with a non-discriminatory (most-favored-nation) tariff. Under such a tariff, the seller(s) who can offer the lowest price (or the best combination of price and quality) will make the sale. With discriminatory tariffs or with quantitative restrictions that fail to replicate what would happen with a non-discriminatory tariff, sales may be made by higher cost producers who are the beneficiaries of the more favorable tariff or who are allocated import rights under the quantitative restriction despite their higher cost. The costs of shifting production from lower cost to higher cost producers because of trade discrimination constitute the welfare loss from trade diversion.

The "other things being equal" caveat to the proposition that trade discrimination reduces economic welfare relates to the possibility that trade discrimination may also result in "trade creation." To the degree that discrimination lowers barriers to trade with *efficient* suppliers of the importing nation, it will expand trade in a constructive way. Thus, for example, if NAFTA lowers tariffs on imports into the United States from Canada and Mexico and if those countries are low-cost suppliers for the U.S. market, the growth in trade with Canada and Mexico will increase economic welfare for the reasons considered in Chapter 2. The classic reference is Viner (1950).

This observation affords a possible defense of provisions such as GATT Article XXIV, which allows the formation of customs unions and free trade areas. Perhaps trade liberalization is at times politically easier on a regional or "smaller numbers" basis than on a global basis. If the liberalization that occurs under the auspices of Article XXIV is not politically feasible on a most-favored-nation basis, and if the parties to Article XXIV arrangements are by-and-large efficient suppliers to each other so that the degree of trade diversion is not too great, then such arrangements can raise economic welfare relative to an environment in which the most-favored-nation principle is always observed.

It is perhaps difficult to make a comparable argument for discriminatory safeguard measures. The analogous argument would have to take the following form: If safeguard measures were required to be nondiscriminatory, the measures chosen would be more restrictive of trade than if the measures could be discriminatory, and on balance the discriminatory measures are more trade-creating than trade-diverting relative to the non-discriminatory baseline. It is logically possible that this might be true, but hard to imagine why it would be true in any systematic fashion.

Nevertheless, one can easily understand why political pressures might arise for discriminatory safeguard measures, and why officials in importing nations may be largely indifferent to the problem of trade diversion. Nations have relationships with other nations that span many issues. Discriminatory safeguard measures can be used to reward friendlier or more cooperative nations, and to punish less friendly or cooperative nations. Likewise, measures that target only the most successful foreign supplier countries may be enough to placate the domestic constituency favoring safeguards while offending as few trading partners as possible. In addition, note that the costs of trade diversion will be borne heavily by domestic consumers who pay higher prices and by low cost foreign suppliers who lose business to higher cost foreign suppliers. The consumers may be too poorly organized to weigh in politically, and foreign suppliers may have little influence on domestic political officials. The actors primarily harmed by trade diversion, therefore, may be politically ineffective at resisting it.

In the context of a trade negotiation, however, exporters threatened by trade diversion can weigh in to push their representatives to negotiate measures that will reduce it. Further, the exporters who *benefit* from trade diversion will tend to be less vigorous in resisting such measures because they have higher costs which dissipate those benefits to a considerable degree. This concededly crude sketch of the political dynamic suggests that trade agreements may tend to discourage practices that cause trade diversion, at least if those practices do not also generate significant trade creation.

Even if discriminatory safeguard measures are not likely to be trade creating to any great extent, however, it would be a mistake to expect that the political equilibrium will necessarily prohibit them. The countervailing consideration relates back to the discussion in Chapter 3 regarding the reason why declining industries tend to invest more political resources to secure protection than prosperous ones—prosperous industries might expect any rents from protection to be dissipated by competitive entry, while declining industries can retain the rents created by protection as long as their rate of return remains below the level that would attract competitive entry. For the same reasons, declining industries may invest more political resources to avert measures that harm their exports than prosperous industries.[9] If so, prosperous exporters may be somewhat more tolerant of measures that target their exports than weaker exporters. With this background, I return to a discussion of the legal principles.

2 The Core Obligation: Article 2.2

During the Uruguay Round, many developing countries sought to establish a tight non-discrimination obligation for safeguards. They believed that formal safeguard measures as well as grey-area measures had regularly discriminated against them in the past, a belief that provided much of the impetus for the safeguards negotiations. The United States and especially Europe, however, sought to retain the flexibility to use safeguards on a selective basis. The eventual result was, not surprisingly, something of a compromise.

[9] To be sure, if the declining industry has especially high costs and earns little profit on export sales, it will invest little to protect them.

The basic obligation is contained in Article 2.2: "Safeguard measures shall be applied to a product being imported irrespective of its source." This language imposes some level of non-discrimination obligation, although it leaves open precisely what it means to "apply" measures to all sources, that is, to what extent might such "application" nevertheless entail some degree of discrimination. Other sections of the Agreement make clear that a degree of selectivity is permissible under some circumstances, as when imports from a particular supplier country have increased disproportionately (discussed in the next subsection), and when some of the imports come from developing countries (discussed later in this chapter).

Another issue that was anticipated during the negotiations, but on which no clear consensus was reached, concerned the use of safeguard measures by and within customs unions and free trade areas. In particular, could the members of such an arrangement apply safeguard measures to outsiders only? This issue will receive considerable attention below, as will the rather peculiar doctrine of "parallelism" that it has begotten in the course of WTO dispute resolution.

3 Selective Quantitative Restrictions

Safeguard measures often take the form of tariffs. Indeed, of the 31 definitive safeguard measures in place as of November 3, 2005, 26 entailed tariff increases, tariff surcharges, or specific duties.[10]

Nothing in the Agreement on Safeguards specifically requires non-discriminatory tariffs, although as noted the general obligation of Article 2.2 is to apply measures to every product "irrespective of its source." Perhaps this language alone is sufficient to prohibit any tariff discrimination as part of a safeguard measure. Even if it is not, GATT Article I almost certainly applies to safeguard measures, just as the Appellate Body has held that GATT Article XIX remains applicable. A discriminatory tariff as part of a safeguard measure would then run afoul of the obligation in GATT Article I to apply all "customs duties and other charges" in a nondiscriminatory fashion.

GATT Article I does not apply to quantitative restrictions, however, and instead GATT has a separate article on "non-discriminatory administration of quantitative restrictions" (Article XIII). Some of the principles embodied in Article XIII were transplanted into the Agreement on Safeguards, while

[10] See Report (2005) of the Committee on Safeguards to the Council for Trade in Goods, G/L/761, 8 November 2005, Annex 3.

others were not. Thus, the rules regarding selective quantitative restrictions may be found in both places, assuming (I think correctly) that GATT Article XIII applies to actions governed by the Agreement on Safeguards. I will begin with this last point, and then turn to specific principles applicable to quantitative restrictions.

In *United States—Line Pipe*, Korea alleged that the U.S. safeguard measure violated several of the requirements contained in GATT Article XIII. The United States argued in response that Article XIII did not apply to safeguard measures. It noted, *inter alia*, that the Agreement on Safeguards made no mention of Article XIII. It also noted that some of the obligations contained in Article XIII had been incorporated into the Agreement on Safeguards while others had not, thus supporting an inference in the view of the United States that the drafters intended the omitted obligations to be inapplicable.

The panel rejected the proposition that Article XIII was inapplicable. In so doing, it embraced much of the reasoning that the Appellate Body had developed in *Korea—Dairy* and *Argentina—Footwear* in support of the proposition that GATT obligations are cumulative with those of the Agreement on Safeguards. The failure of the Agreement to mention GATT Article XIII did not support an inference that Article XIII was inapplicable, nor did the existence of some redundancy between the provisions of Article XIII and the Agreement.[11]

The Appellate Body decisions in *Dairy* and *Footwear* indeed provide strong support for the panel's conclusion. The United States did not pursue this particular issue on appeal, and one strongly suspects that it would have lost before the Appellate Body had it raised the matter. The issue has not come up in more recent safeguards disputes. Thus, although the Appellate Body has not squarely ruled on the issue, it seems likely that any quantitative measure falling within the terms of GATT Article XIII must obey its strictures, as well as the more limited restrictions in the Agreement on Safeguards. I now turn to those rules.

The one principle that is found in both GATT Article XIII and the Agreement on Safeguards is contained in the latter's Article 5.2(a):

> In cases in which a quota is allocated among supplying countries, the Member applying the restrictions may seek agreement with respect to the allocation of shares in the quota with all other Members having a substantial interest in supplying the product concerned. In cases in which this method is not reasonably practicable, the Member concerned shall allot to Members having a substantial interest in supplying

[11] United States—Line Pipe Panel paras 7.30–50.

> the product shares based upon the proportions, supplied by such Members during a previous representative period, of the total quantity or value of imports of the product, due account being taken of any special factors which may have affected or may be affecting the trade in the product.

Though not identical, this language closely parallels the first two sentences of GATT Art. XIII(2)(d) (the third sentence being omitted from the language in the Agreement).

As is clear from the text, no obligation exists to allocate quota shares among supplier countries. But various problems may arise in the absence of such allocations. If the opportunity to import is captured by the importers who are first in line, substantial resources may be expended in pursuit of being first. Likewise, nations may be excluded altogether from the opportunity to supply under an unallocated quota if their production cycle places them at the end of the line (a particular issue with agricultural products that have different growing seasons in different countries). In addition, it may be quite unclear when the quota will be exhausted, and the danger arises that goods will be shipped and then denied entry because no quota is left. Supplier countries may thus have good reason to prefer an allocated quota.

But the allocation process introduces a great risk of discrimination, as was clearly recognized in GATT Art. XIII. The solution transplanted into the Agreement on Safeguards is to encourage negotiation over quota shares. Negotiations may be difficult and unsuccessful, however, particularly when the number of supplier countries is substantial, and so the alternative is to allocate shares based on each country's market share during a "previous representative period." This standard raises the issue noted earlier of how one determines what is "representative." Neither the Agreement on Safeguards nor GATT Art. XIII defines the term. Both simply suggest that "due account" be taken of "special factors" that may be affecting trade in the product. Art. XIII(4) also states that the importing nation shall "initially" select the representative period, but imposes on the importing nation an obligation to consult on the matter with "substantial" suppliers who request consultations.

Although squabbles may arise over the "representative period," the approach in Article 5.2(a) represents a sensible way to minimize the degree of trade discrimination from the introduction of an allocated quota. As long as the "representative period" was itself free of trade discrimination, market shares during that period probably represent a reasonable prediction of what they would have been going forward in many cases. To be sure, in dynamic industries where market shares change significantly and quickly, an allocation of shares based on historical information may be quite imperfect, but a workable alternative may be difficult to devise.

The obligation in Article 5.2(a) is subject to an important exception in Article 5.2(b), which provides:

> A Member may depart from the provisions in subparagraph (a) provided that consultations under paragraph 3 of Article 12 are conducted under the auspices of the Committee on Safeguards provided for in paragraph 1 of Article 13 and that clear demonstration is provided to the Committee that (*i*) imports from certain Members have increased in disproportionate percentage in relation to the total increase of imports of the product concerned in the representative period, (*ii*) the reasons for the departure from the provisions in subparagraph (a) are justified, and (*iii*) the conditions of such departure are equitable to all suppliers of the product concerned. The duration of any such measure shall not be extended beyond the initial period under paragraph 1 of Article 7. The departure referred to above shall not be permitted in the case of threat of serious injury.

This section has no parallel in GATT Art. XIII, and creates new legal authority for selective measures under the specified conditions. The key condition lies in item (i), and its reference to situations where "imports from certain Members have increased in disproportionate percentage in relation to the total increase of imports of the product concerned in the representative period." In other words, selective measures may be permissible if the import surge that motivates the safeguard measure has come primarily from "certain Members." If so, the importing member may be able to justify allocating a smaller quota to those members than their market share during the "representative period" would otherwise suggest. Interestingly, this authority suggests that a safeguard measure may impose a disproportionate reduction in exports on the most rapidly growing exporters, consistent with the political economy notion developed earlier that more prosperous exporters may resist export restrictions somewhat less vigorously than less prosperous exporters.

The opportunity to employ selective measures in these circumstances is subject to oversight, however, by the Committee on Safeguards. A member proposing to proceed in this fashion must provide "clear demonstration" to the Committee that all three conditions in Article 5.2(b) are satisfied. Condition (i) is reasonably clear, but the second and third conditions—that a departure from Article 5.2(a) is "justified," and that the details of the departure are "equitable to all suppliers"—are quite open-ended. To date, the Committee has provided little guidance as to precisely what these standards require. The text also limits these measures to the initial period under

Article 7 (a maximum of four years), and prohibits them when the injury finding is based only on threat.

GATT Art. XIII contains a number of additional provisions with which safeguard measures must comply if they take the form of quantitative restrictions (or a tariff-rate quota, which sets a tariff that varies according to the quantity imported). I will not undertake a thorough exposition of Article XIII, as it is a generally applicable provision of GATT that is treated in detail elsewhere in references on GATT. See Jackson (1969) and Mavroidis (2005). As an illustration of some of the issues that may arise, however, I will briefly sketch the facts of the dispute over the measure in *United States—Line Pipe* and its resolution before the panel.

The *Line Pipe* dispute resulted from a measure that imposed a tariff-rate quota on line pipe imports into the United States. Existing tariffs would apply to imports from any supplier country up to a total of 9,000 short tons, while imports above that amount would be subject to an additional *ad valorem* tariff of 19% (falling to 15% in the second year and 11% in the third).

Korea first alleged that the measure violated the "chapeau" of Article XIII(2), which states that in applying quantitative restrictions, "parties shall aim at a distribution of trade in such product approaching as closely as possible the shares which the various contracting parties might be expected to obtain in the absence of such restrictions." Although the United States argued elsewhere that a tariff-rate quota was not a quantitative restriction, Article XIII(2) was nevertheless applicable because of Article XIII(5), which states that "the provisions of this Article shall apply to any tariff quota." The panel found that the 9,000 short ton exemption for every supplier, regardless of its historical volume of trade in line pipe, bore no relation to the likely shares that each supplier would have obtained in the absence of the restriction, and hence that the chapeau to Article XIII(2) had indeed been violated.[12] The United States did not appeal this finding.

Korea next argued that the measure violated Article XIII(2)(a), which states that "[w]herever practicable, quotas representing the total amount of permitted imports should be fixed." Korea claimed that the 9,000 per supplier exemption was not equivalent to "fixing" a quota, because it was altogether uncertain how many supplier nations would avail themselves of the exemption. The United States argued in response that these provisions did not apply to tariff rate quotas, and that in any event it was not practicable

[12] United States—Line Pipe Panel paras 7.53–55.

to "fix" a limit as Korea argued. The panel sided with Korea. It held that Article XIII(2) applied to tariff-rate quotas by virtue of Article XIII(5), and that the proper interpretation of it required the United States to "fix" the quantity of imports that would be exempt from the higher tariffs. The fact that the 9,000 short ton per supplier exemption created a theoretical upper bound on exempt imports did not create the degree of certainty that a "fixed" limit would afford. As to the claim that "fixing" the limit was not practicable, the panel saw no reason why the United States had to structure the measure as it did. The United States did not appeal this finding either.

Korea also challenged the measure on the grounds that the United States had not negotiated with Korea over its allocation, as it asserted was required by Article XII(2)(d), and that it had not provided proper notice of the measure as required by Article XIII(3)(b). The panel did not reach these issues on grounds of judicial economy.

Line Pipe clearly illustrates how GATT Article XIII adds to a complainant's arsenal in cases where a safeguard measure takes the form of a quantitative restriction or tariff-rate quota, assuming the panel to have been correct in holding that Article XIII applies to safeguard measures. The myriad of additional obligations attached to the use of such measures perhaps explains why tariff measures are far more popular to date.

Interestingly, there is no parallel to Article XIII(5) in the Agreement on Safeguards. Hence, the requirements of Article 5 for quantitative restrictions are arguably inapplicable to tariff-rate quotas, as was held by the panel in *Line Pipe*.[13] If the panel ruling is correct on that point, the somewhat peculiar situation arises where a tariff-rate quota can be challenged as discriminatory under GATT Art. XIII (by virtue of XIII(5)), but not under the parallel language of Article 5 in the Agreement on Safeguards.

4 The Doctrine of Parallelism

Members of customs unions and free trade areas may wish to exempt other members from safeguard measures that they employ under WTO auspices. Indeed, in some cases, they are under a treaty obligation to provide such an exemption. NAFTA Art. 802, for example, requires NAFTA members taking action pursuant to GATT Article XIX to exempt imports from other NAFTA members unless "(a) imports from a Party, considered individually, account for a substantial share of total imports; and (b) imports from a Party,

[13] See United States—Line Pipe Panel paras 7.66–75.

considered individually, or in exceptional circumstances imports from Parties considered collectively, contribute importantly to the serious injury, or threat thereof, cause by imports." Exemptions along these lines are plainly discriminatory vis-à-vis other WTO members, and the question whether this form of selectivity is permissible under WTO law has been a subject of considerable controversy.

The core question, which I shall postpone to the next subsection and which is as yet unresolved, is whether the legal authority for the discrimination that inheres in the formation of customs unions and free trade areas—GATT Article XXIV—extends so far as to permit selective safeguards that exempt other members of such entities. To date, the Appellate Body has avoided ruling on that difficult question by devising instead a doctrine of "parallelism." Parallelism requires, in essence, a strict correspondence between the imports that are found to be a "cause" of serious injury or threat, and the imports that are restricted by a safeguard measure. Violations of this requirement have been found on numerous occasions, and they have allowed the Appellate Body to escape the ultimate question regarding Article XXIV.

I shall first sketch the genesis and history of the parallelism doctrine in the cases, and note the ways in which it has been found to have been violated. I then offer some thoughts about the wisdom and logic of the doctrine.

Parallelism in WTO Disputes. The term parallelism was introduced by the panel in *Argentina—Footwear.*[14] Argentina is a member of MERCOSUR. In its footwear investigation, the Argentine government conducted its injury analysis on the basis of imports from all sources, including MERCOSUR countries. But the safeguard measure that it eventually applied excluded MERCOSUR imports. The European Communities took the position that the exclusion of MERCOSUR imports from an Argentine safeguard measure was in principle permissible on the basis of GATT Art. XXIV, but only if those imports were also excluded from the injury analysis.

Argentina sought to defend its analysis on the basis of footnote 1 to the Agreement on Safeguards, which states:

> A customs union may apply a safeguard measure as a single unit or on behalf of a member State. When a customs union applies a safeguard measure as a single unit, all the requirements for the determination of serious injury or threat thereof under this Agreement shall be based on the conditions existing in the customs union as a whole. When a safeguard measure is applied on behalf of a member State, all the requirements for the determination of serious injury or threat thereof shall be based

[14] Argentina—Footwear Panel para 8.87.

on the conditions existing in that member State and the measure shall be limited to that member State. Nothing in this Agreement prejudges the interpretation of the relationship between Article XIX and paragraph 8 of Article XXIV of GATT 1994.

The panel noted that the Argentine measure was applied only to imports into Argentina, not into MERCOSUR as a whole, and thus considered the third sentence to be the starting point for analysis. It requires that the injury test be satisfied based on conditions in the Member State applying the safeguard measure, and that the measure be limited to imports into that Member State. But the panel saw nothing in sentence three to suggest that the Member State could exempt imports from other Member States. Thus, it felt that the case was governed in the first instance by Article 2.2 requiring that safeguard measures be applied to every import "irrespective of its source."[15]

The exemption of MERCOSUR imports from the measure violated Article 2.2, in the view of the panel, unless the violation could be excused by GATT Article XXIV. On this point, the panel took note of sentence four in the footnote, which reserves the issue of the relationship between Article XIX and Article XXIV. The panel then proceeded to consider the implications of Article XXIV, and concluded that it did not provide a defense for Argentina[16] (I will return to this part of the analysis in the next subsection.)

On appeal, the Appellate Body disagreed with the panel's reasoning in important respects. It began by questioning the panel's focus on sentence three of footnote one. Sentence one refers to cases in which a "customs union may apply a safeguard measure," and notes that the customs union may apply the measure on behalf of the entire union or a Member State. Sentences two and three consider each possibility. In *Footwear*, by contrast, the measure was applied by Argentina, not by MERCOSUR. The Appellate Body thus concluded that the first three sentences of the footnote were irrelevant to the case.[17] It also reversed the panel's findings regarding the applicability of Article XXIV, on the (rather dubious) grounds that Argentina had not argued to the panel that it was relying on Article XXIV as a defense.[18]

The Appellate Body then picked up on the panel's suggestion that there is an implied "parallelism between the scope of a safeguard investigation and the scope of the application of safeguard measures." In a peculiarly abbreviated passage, the Appellate Body simply quoted Article 2.2, noted that Argentina's injury investigation had encompassed imports from all sources, and then asserted that "[i]n applying safeguard measures on the basis of the

[15] Id. paras 8.76–92. [16] Id. paras 8.93–102.
[17] Argentina—Footwear AB para 108. [18] Id. paras 109–10.

investigation in this case, Argentina was also required under Article 2.2 to apply those measures to imports from all sources, including from other MERCOSUR member States.[19]" No other reasoning was offered, and the Appellate Body noted that it had not decided the issue whether, "as a general principle, a member of a customs union can exclude other members of that customs union from the application of a safeguard measure."[20]

A similar issue surfaced in *United States—Wheat Gluten*. The U.S. ITC found that the injury test was satisfied based on imports from all sources. It then examined imports from Canada and Mexico separately, based on statutory procedures relating to NAFTA Article 802. Imports from Mexico were nil, and thus not a "substantial share" under the statutory test. Imports from Canada were substantial, but the ITC found that they were "not contributing importantly to the serious injury." Accordingly, and in accordance with the NAFTA treaty obligation, the United States excluded Canada and Mexico from its safeguard measure.

The European Communities claimed that the United States had violated the parallelism principle established in *Footwear*. The panel agreed, reasoning that the United States finding of injury was based on imports from all sources, and that when Canadian imports were excluded it was no longer clear that the remaining imports sufficed to cause serious injury. In the view of the panel, the United States should have examined imports from all sources excluding Canada in its injury analysis—the separate analysis by the ITC of Canadian imports standing alone was insufficient to establish that imports from *sources other than Canada* sufficed to cause serious injury.[21]

The panel's finding was grounded in its belief that the imports under investigation must, "in and of themselves," suffice to cause or threaten serious injury. This finding was overruled by the Appellate Body as noted in Chapter 8. Somewhat oddly, however, the Appellate Body took no note of this fact in addressing the parallelism issue on appeal. It simply reiterated the parallelism requirement that it had introduced in *Footwear*. In so doing, it suggested that its textual basis lay in the fact that the phrase "product . . . being imported" appears in both Article 2.1 and Article 2.2. Hence, according to the Appellate Body, Article 2.2 requires that any safeguard measure be applied to the same "product . . . being imported" that served as the basis for the injury investigation. It then further noted, as had the panel, that the United States had made no explicit finding that imports from all

[19] Id. para 112. [20] Id. para 114.
[21] United States—Wheat Gluten Panel paras 8.171–77.

sources excluding Canada had caused or threatened to cause serious injury. The absence of such a finding was enough to establish a violation.[22]

The question of parallelism arose anew in *United States—Line Pipe*. This time around, the U.S. ITC again based most of its analysis on imports from all sources, but included in its report a short footnote stating that "we would have reached the same result had we excluded imports from Canada and Mexico from our analysis," followed by a short recitation of the purported basis for this statement. The panel held that Korea had failed to make a showing that the ITC footnote was deficient, and thus found for the United States on the parallelism question.[23] The Appellate Body reversed, however, holding in essence that the footnote to the ITC opinion was largely conclusory, and that it failed to provide a "reasoned and adequate explanation" for the finding that non-NAFTA imports caused or threatened serious injury.[24]

A final wrinkle was added in *United States—Steel*. The U.S. ITC had once again based its initial injury analysis on imports from all sources. But prior to the implementation of the steel safeguard measures by the United States, the ITC issued a supplemental report that undertook among other things to redo the original causation analysis by excluding imports from Canada, Mexico, Israel, and Jordan, which were to be exempted from the measures. The panel reviewed the analysis measure-by-measure for the various steel "industries," and found a number of difficulties with it. For example, in the view of the panel, the ITC had not given adequate consideration to the fact that imports from the non-excluded countries were smaller in quantity than the volume of imports considered in the original causation analysis.[25] In addition, the revised ITC analysis made reference at a number of points to "non-NAFTA imports," while the imports to be excluded also included those from Israel and Jordan.[26]

More importantly, the supplemental ITC report did not redo the "non-attribution analysis." The panel held that this aspect of the causation analysis had to be redone, because the imports being considered were smaller in quantity and their effects in comparison to "other factors" would not be the same.[27] The panel thus held, in effect, that the excluded imports became an

[22] United States—Wheat Gluten AB paras 95–98.

[23] United States—Line Pipe Panel paras 7.169–71.

[24] United States—Line Pipe AB paras 185–97.

[25] See, e.g., United States—Steel Panel para 10.603.

[26] See, e.g., id. para 10.607–08.

[27] See, e.g., id. para 10.604–06.

"other factor" that had to be accounted for as part of the non-attribution analysis.

The Appellate Body affirmed the panel, underscoring even more clearly that the excluded imports are an "other factor" that must be included in non-attribution analysis—their effects must be "separated and distinguished" from the effects of the included imports, and the ITC had not done so in its supplemental report.[28] The Appellate Body also upheld the panel's finding that the ITC had not made clear findings based on the exclusion of imports from Mexico, Canada, Israel, and Jordan.

Is the Parallelism Doctrine Sound? The doctrine of parallelism surely has some surface appeal. It seems inappropriate to base an injury finding on one group of imports, and then to exclude some of those imports from the measure intended to remediate injury. Pauwelyn (2004) is nonetheless rather critical of the parallelism doctrine. He suggests, among other things, that it has no strong textual basis and that it was invented by the Appellate Body to enable it to duck the fundamental issue of whether safeguard measures excluding imports from fellow members of customs unions and free trade areas are allowable pursuant to GATT Article XXIV.

I concur in these criticisms to a considerable extent. I would also add that fidelity to parallelism seems quite pointless when the underlying approach to injury analysis in all cases is so deeply flawed, as argued in Chapter 8. Consider the *Steel* case. In the interest of parallelism, both the panel and the Appellate Body would have the ITC revise its import data, and then undertake the same conceptually flawed analyses of coincidence, conditions of competition, and non-attribution. The excluded imports would become an "other factor" to which injury from the included imports could not be attributed. Such exercises are no more meaningful or coherent with the revised data than with the original.

Were the parallelism issue to be approached in an economically intelligible fashion, one of the alternative approaches to injury analysis sketched in Chapter 8 might be employed to inquire whether developments relating to some subset of import suppliers had caused injury. Such an inquiry would further increase the complexity of the economic analysis required in these cases, but is at least possible in principle. Until a logically sound approach to the question of causation is articulated by the Appellate Body or in a renegotiated Safeguards Agreement, however, the requirement of parallelism seems little more than a sideshow.

[28] United States—Steel AB para 450.

5 The Ultimate Question: Article XXIV and Selective Safeguards

The Appellate Body held in *Line Pipe* that the question whether GATT Article XXIV affords a defense of selective safeguard measures "becomes relevant" only if the doctrine of parallelism has been satisfied in the course of injury analysis.[29] A dispute raising the Article XXIV issue in the absence of any violation of parallelism has not yet arisen, and thus the Appellate Body has dodged the Article XXIV issue thus far. Some panels have addressed the applicability of Article XXIV, however, as have commentators. This section draws on the discussion elsewhere to offer some thoughts on the possible resolution of the issue. A more exhaustive legal treatment, with which I agree in considerable part but not in its entirety, is that of Pauwelyn (2004).

At the policy level, one might begin with the following query—if the WTO is willing to tolerate the discrimination that inheres in customs unions and free trade areas generally, why not also allow selective safeguard measures exempting other members of such entities? Are the costs of such measures somehow greater or more worrisome than the costs of other forms of discrimination? I am not aware of any economic argument that would yield an affirmative answer to this last question. Further, footnote 1 to the Agreement on Safeguards seems to make clear that a customs union as a whole may apply safeguard measures to outsiders only, as long as the injury test is satisfied for the customs union as a whole. If such discrimination against outsiders is permissible on behalf of the entire customs union, why not also on behalf of an individual member? Perhaps some subtle economic issues arise that I am not addressing, but an initial cut at the question suggests no obvious reason why this type of selectivity by a member of a customs union or free-trade area should be especially worrisome.

Turning to the legal question, GATT Article XXIV(5) provides that "the provisions of this Agreement shall not prevent, as between the territories of contracting parties, the formation of a customs union or a free-trade area or the adoption of an interim agreement necessary for the formation of a customs union or of a free-trade area." Article XXIV(8)(a) defines a customs union as "the substitution of a single customs territory for two or more customs territories, so that (i) duties and other restrictive regulations of commerce (except, where necessary, those permitted under [GATT] Articles XI, XII, XIII, XIV, XV and XX) are eliminated with respect to substantially

[29] United States—Line Pipe AB para 198.

all the trade between the constituent territories . . . ,and (ii) . . . substantially the same duties and other regulations of commerce are applied by each of the members of the union to the trade of territories not included in the union." Under Article XXIV(8)(b), "[a] free-trade area shall be understood to mean a group of two or more customs territories in which the duties and other restrictive regulations of commerce (except, where necessary, those permitted under [GATT] Articles XI, XII, XIII, XIV, XV and XX) are eliminated on substantially all the trade between the constituent territories in products originating in such territories."

Recall as well the last sentence of footnote 1 to the Agreement on Safeguards: "Nothing in this Agreement prejudges the interpretation of the relationship between Article XIX and paragraph 8 of Article XXIV of GATT 1994." Here, the drafters clearly acknowledge the possible interconnection between Article XXIV and selective safeguard measures, and suggest that they have deliberately left the issue open.

Within this legal framework, can one justify safeguard measures that exclude imports from members of a customs union or free trade area? To answer this question one must confront a series of three sub-questions.

First, does Article XXIV *require* the members of a customs union or free trade area to eliminate the possibility of applying safeguard measures to trade among themselves? An argument to that effect was advanced by Argentina in *Argentina—Footwear*. Argentina reasoned that the requirement to eliminate "duties and other restrictive regulations of commerce" on "substantially all trade" among members of a customs union or free-trade area was subject only to the enumerated exceptions for GATT Articles XI, XII, XIII, XIV, XV, and XX. Because Article XIX is not listed among those exceptions, the proper inference in Argentina's view was that Article XIX measures within a customs union or free trade area are impermissible. If that is right, the argument runs, an exception to Article 2.2 of the Agreement on Safeguards should be found—the non-discrimination requirement of Article 2.2 should not be construed to compel WTO members to violate GATT Article XXIV.

The *Footwear* panel rejected this argument for several reasons,[30] and rightly so in my view. The simplest argument is that even if Article XIX is omitted from the list of enumerated exceptions in Article XXIV(8), the obligation in XXIV(8) merely requires the elimination of duties and other restrictions on *substantially all* trade, not *all* trade. This text clearly contemplates that certain other restrictions will remain even if they are not

[30] See Argentina—Footwear Panel paras 8.93–102.

among the enumerated exceptions. It is difficult to imagine, for example, that the drafters of Article XXIV intended to preclude the possibility of national security measures pursuant to GATT Article XXI within a customs union or free trade area. Likewise, occasional internal safeguard measures under Article XIX, limited in duration and to specific products, should not violate the obligation to eliminate barriers on *substantially all* internal trade.

If that is correct, and Article XXIV does not *require* members of customs unions and free trade areas to eschew safeguard measures on trade amongst themselves, might it nevertheless *permit* them to adopt such a policy? The first hurdle to overcome if one is to reach an affirmative conclusion relates to the fact that, as written, Article XXIV only affords an exception to the obligations of GATT ("this Agreement"), not to those of other WTO agreements. Also, footnote 1 to the Agreement on Safeguards refers to the relationship "between Article XIX and paragraph 8 of Article XXIV," not to the relationship between the Agreement on Safeguards and Article XXIV. A narrow reading of the pertinent text might thus lead to the conclusion that Article XXIV cannot afford a defense to a violation of the Agreement on Safeguards, only to a violation of GATT. Indeed, precisely that suggestion arose in *United States—Wheat Gluten*, and the parties seemed to dance around the question in their arguments.[31] We thus come to the second sub-question—can Article XXIV ever justify a derogation from the Agreement on Safeguards?

The Appellate Body confronted this class of issues in *Turkey—Textiles*, a case involving restrictions imposed by Turkey on imports from certain third countries that were purportedly necessary to facilitate Turkey's entry into the EU.[32] In that case, the Appellate Body suggested that Article XXIV might provide a defense to violations of WTO Agreements other than GATT if Article XXIV had been "incorporated" into the other agreement (in that case the Agreement on Textiles and Clothing was at issue, which was found to incorporate GATT Article XXIV in its Article 2.4).[33]

The mention of Article XXIV in footnote 1 of the Agreement on Safeguards provides some foundation for an argument that it has been "incorporated." Further, taking a slightly different tack, the panel in *United States—Line Pipe* emphasized the "close interrelation between Article XIX and the Safeguards Agreement," pointing to Article 1 of the Agreement which states: "safeguard measures . . . shall be understood to mean those

[31] See United States—Wheat Gluten Panel paras 8.178–81.

[32] Turkey—Restrictions on Imports of Textile and Clothing Products, WT/DS34/AB/R (hereafter Turkey—Textiles AB).

[33] See Turkey—Textiles AB para 45 & n. 13.

measures provided for in Article XIX of GATT." In light of this interrelationship, the panel thought it "incongruous" to hold that Article XXIV could justify a derogation from Article XIX but not from the Agreement on Safeguards.[34] In effect, the panel found that the Agreement on Safeguards incorporated Article XIX, along with applicable defenses to any violation of Article XIX. This finding seems a sensible construction of the legal framework as a whole.

Even if Article XXIV can in principle afford a defense to violations of both GATT and the Agreement on Safeguards, however, it remains to consider whether the defense is a good one in the present context. Thus, we come to the third and final sub-question—are safeguard measures that exclude imports from other members of a customs union or free trade area within the scope of what is authorized by Article XXIV?

As Pauwelyn (2004) notes, existing Appellate Body jurisprudence suggests that the answer is no. In *Turkey—Textiles*, the Appellate Body focused on the chapeau to Article XXIV(5): "the provisions of this Agreement shall not prevent . . . the formation of a customs union or free trade area." The Appellate Body ultimately concluded that this text would afford a defense to a violation of GATT only if a failure to adopt the measure at issue would literally "prevent" the customs union or free trade area from coming into being. That test is satisfied, the Appellate Body held, only if "the party claiming the benefit of this defence [can] demonstrate that the measure at issue is introduced upon the formation of a customs union that fully meets the requirements of sub-paragraphs 8(a) and 5(a) of Article XXIV. And, second, that party must demonstrate that the formation of that customs union would be prevented if it were not allowed to introduce the measure at issue."[35] Thus, the measure must satisfy a timing requirement (introduced upon formation) and a test of necessity to the formation of the preferential trading arrangement.

It is questionable whether a safeguard measure introduced *after* the formation of a customs union (or free trade area) could ever meet this test. Perhaps it might be argued that a treaty commitment to eschew internal safeguards (such as NAFTA Article 802) meets the test because it was introduced upon formation, and that measures subsequently adopted pursuant to the treaty commitment should qualify as well,[36] but the matter is unclear. Even if such a manoeuver would satisfy the Appellate Body on the

[34] United States—Line Pipe Panel para 7.150.

[35] Turkey—Textiles AB para 58.

[36] The Line Pipe panel accepted this view. See United States—Line Pipe Panel para 7.141, n. 128.

timing issue, however, it is also questionable whether the absence of such a treaty commitment would have *prevented* the formation of the customs union or free trade area. For the reasons given earlier, it seems unlikely that Article XXIV prohibits safeguard measures internal to a customs union or free trade area.

Pauwelyn (2004) is highly critical of the reasoning in *Turkey—Textiles*. He makes the point, *inter alia*, that if the reasoning is correct, it would be illegal for a customs union that had abolished tariffs on substantially all internal trade at the time of its formation to later abolish all remaining tariffs, a result that Pauwelyn considers an absurdity. The *Line Pipe* panel also noted the problem, and suggested that perhaps the above standard from *Turkey—Textiles* should be read only to apply to a measure that increases barriers to trade with outsiders (as in the *Textiles* case), and not to measures that *liberalize* internal trade.[37]

Pauwelyn and the *Line Pipe* panel thus favor a more liberal construction of the measures authorized by Article XXIV. Safeguard measures exempting imports from other members of a customs union or free trade area would be allowable under their reading of Article XXIV, which in turn would afford a defense to violations of GATT Article XIX or Article 2.2 of the Agreement on Safeguards.

In conclusion, existing Appellate Body precedent casts doubt on the availability of an Article XXIV defense for safeguard measures that exclude imports from fellow members of customs unions and free trade areas, even if the importing nation respects the doctrine of parallelism in its injury analysis. Some wiggle room exists in the law for a decision in the other direction, but the willingness of the Appellate Body to permit that outcome remains untested.

C Duration and Review

Article 7 of the Agreement on Safeguards contains a number of provisions respecting the duration and review of safeguard measures. In this section, I sketch the basic requirements of Article 7, noting a few ambiguities as well as the small amount of academic work that touches on its structure. The obligations may be divided into roughly three components: general limitations on the duration of safeguard measures, requirements for progressive

[37] United States—Line Pipe Panel para 7.148.

liberalization; and restrictions on the use of safeguard measures in industries previously protected by them.

1 Limits on Duration

Paragraphs 1–3 of Article 7 provide:

1. A Member shall apply safeguard measures only for such period of time as may be necessary to prevent or remedy serious injury and to facilitate adjustment. The period shall not exceed four years, unless it is extended under paragraph 2.
2. The period mentioned in paragraph 1 may be extended provided that the competent authorities of the importing Member have determined, in conformity with the procedures set out in Articles 2, 3, 4 and 5, that the safeguard measure continues to be necessary to prevent or remedy serious injury and that there is evidence that the industry is adjusting, and provided that the pertinent provisions of Articles 8 and 12 are observed.
3. The total period of application of a safeguard measure including the period of application of any provisional measure, the period of initial application and any extension thereof, shall not exceed eight years.

Paragraph 1 imposes a four year limit on safeguard measures, subject to the possibility of an extension under paragraph 2. Paragraph 1 also limits measures to the time "necessary" to prevent or remedy serious injury or to facilitate adjustment, although it is difficult to imagine an importing nation being challenged on this issue as a practical matter. Paragraph 3 adds an upper bound of eight years on the duration of a safeguard measure, even if an extension has been duly made.

In addition to the eight-year upper bound, the other key feature of the system is that a member desiring to employ safeguard measures beyond the initial four year window must conduct another investigation pursuant to the procedural requirements of Articles 2–5 (most importantly the notice and publication requirements). The substantive inquiry in such an investigation is, of course, somewhat different from that of the original investigation. Rather than asking whether increased import quantities have caused or threatened to cause serious injury, the focus will be on whether the safeguard measure continues to be necessary to prevent or remedy injury.[38] Secondly, there must be "evidence that the industry is adjusting."

[38] The language of the U.S. statute, for example, closely parallels the wording of Article 7.2. See 19 U.S.C. para 2254(c)(1).

The first of these inquiries is roughly the mirror image of the causal inquiry that one would undertake if using the "hypothetical quantitative restriction" approach to causation analysis as described in Chapter 8. Rather than asking how much such a restriction would have benefited the domestic industry, one instead asks how much the removal of an existing restriction (whether a tariff or a quantitative measure) would hurt the industry. If the measure is at all substantial, and if the condition of the industry continues to exhibit "significant overall impairment," it will no doubt be easy to conclude that the measure remains "necessary." Only if the industry is prospering, and that prosperity would not be seriously jeopardized by the removal of the measure, would the investigation likely conclude that the measure was no longer required.

It is somewhat unclear what is needed to satisfy the second conceptual inquiry—whether there is "evidence that the industry is adjusting." Is evidence of renewed or improving prosperity necessary? Is it sufficient? Must the industry be investing in new capital projects? Or is it enough to show that the industry is contracting and moving resources to alternative uses? The concept of "adjustment" in the safeguards area seems to encompass all of the above—adjustment could be an improvement in the competitiveness of protected firms, or an orderly contraction of those firms.[39] And if evidence of "adjustment" exists whether the industry is exhibiting renewed prosperity or continued contraction, then this hurdle seems a minimal one. One therefore doubts that importing nations will find the need to provide evidence of "adjustment" a serious impediment to the extension of safeguard measures.

For the above reasons, importing nations desiring to extend safeguard measures will likely conclude in most cases that an extension is legally permissible. The bright-line limit of eight years in Article 7.3, one suspects, may do considerably more to limit the duration of safeguard measures than the re-investigation requirement in Article 7.2.

2 Progressive Liberalization

Article 7.4 provides:

In order to facilitate adjustment in a situation where the expected duration of a safeguard measure as notified under the provisions of paragraph 1 of Article 12 is over one year, the Member applying the measure shall progressively liberalize it at regular intervals during the period of application. If the duration of the measure exceeds three

[39] See, e.g., 19 U.S.C. para 2251(b) ("positive adjustment" may occur through the restoration of competitiveness or through orderly contraction).

years, the Member applying such a measure shall review the situation not later than the mid-term of the measure and, if appropriate, withdraw it or increase the pace of liberalization. A measure extended under paragraph 2 shall not be more restrictive than it was at the end of the initial period, and should continue to be liberalized.

This is a relatively straightforward provision that requires essentially two things. First, measures lasting over one year must be liberalized at "regular intervals." The interval implicitly suggested by this text is one year, and in practice national authorities often liberalize annually.[40] Second, for any measure that exceeds three years, a mid-term review is required to consider whether the measure remains necessary at all, and whether its extent may be reduced.

The requirement for progressive liberalization is commonly justified by the notion that safeguard measures should facilitate adjustment. If a substantial measure is maintained without any liberalization, the argument runs, and is then suddenly withdrawn, the economic shock to the protected industry might well produce serious injury and dislocation all over again. This reasoning is not completely persuasive, since firms in the protected industry can presumably anticipate the change in policy and prepare themselves for it. Still, to the degree that the abrupt discontinuation of a measure might at times involve a substantial contraction in output and employment, the ability of the measure to facilitate adjustment might indeed be called into question.

A related explanation for progressive liberalization is the desire of WTO members to impose time limits on safeguard measures. Absent progressive liberalization, the removal of a measure might lead quickly to a substantial import surge, creating anew the conditions that justified the safeguard measure in the first instance. Political pressure to impose a new measure may emerge in response. The rules governing previously protected industries, addressed immediately below, also address this potential problem of "serial safeguards" in troubled industries.

3 Previously Protected Industries

Paragraphs 5 and 6 of Article 7 provide:

5. No safeguard measure shall be applied again to the import of a product which has been subject to such a measure, taken after the date of entry into force of the

[40] See, e.g., United States—Wheat Gluten Panel para 2.8 (reference to annual increase in U.S. quota limit); United States—Line Pipe Panel para 2.5 (reference to annual reduction in duty under tariff-rate quota).

WTO Agreement, for a period of time equal to that during which such measure had been previously applied, provided that the period of non-application is at least two years.

6. Notwithstanding the provisions of paragraph 5, a safeguard measure with a duration of 180 days or less may be applied again to the import of a product if:
   (a) at least one year has elapsed since the date of introduction of a safeguard measure on the import of that product; and
   (b) such a safeguard measure has not been applied on the same product more than twice in the five-year period immediately preceding the date of introduction of the measure.

Subject to the caveat in Article 7.6, the general rule in Article 7.5 is that if an industry has been protected by a safeguard measure for X years, then it cannot be protected by a new measure for X years after the expiration of the first measure or for two years after expiration, whichever is greater.

These rules plug an obvious loophole that would otherwise exist in the system. Even if a "measure" cannot extend more than eight years under Article 7.3, WTO members could in the absence of Article 7.5 simply start a new investigation of an industry upon the expiration of any safeguard measure that protects it. Because the expiration of a measure will often be followed by an increase in imports, and by some attendant hardships for domestic firms, the distinct possibility arises that the injury test will be satisfied anew and that a new "measure" could be justified. Article 7.5 prevents such serial application of safeguard measures.

Bagwell and Staiger (2005) advance an interesting defense of this mechanism, within a framework closely connected to their general explanation for safeguard measures as discussed in Chapter 2. They posit that WTO members have a lot of "private information" about their political situation and the attendant pressures to deviate from trade commitments, information that they cannot credibly reveal to outsiders. Accordingly, it may be difficult for outsiders (including a dispute resolution process) to determine whether a safeguard mechanism is being abused. One response to this problem is to have a rule prohibiting the use of safeguard measures when they have been used by the same party to protect the same industry in the recent past. Such a rule encourages parties to trade agreements not to use safeguard measures unless "they really need them" to address domestic pressures to deviate from commitments—if they use them when they are not needed, they may lose the opportunity to use them in the future when they are.

D Provisional Measures

Article 6 of the Agreement on Safeguards provides:

In critical circumstances where delay would cause damage which it would be difficult to repair, a Member may take a provisional safeguard measure pursuant to a preliminary determination that there is clear evidence that increased imports have caused or are threatening to cause serious injury. The duration of the provisional measure shall not exceed 200 days, during which period the pertinent requirements of Articles 2 through 7 and 12 shall be met. Such measures should take the form of tariff increases to be promptly refunded if the subsequent investigation referred to in paragraph 2 of Article 4 does not determine that increased imports have caused or threatened to cause serious injury to a domestic industry. The duration of any such provisional measure shall be counted as a part of the initial period and any extension referred to in paragraphs 1, 2 and 3 of Article 7.

The obvious function of this provision is to permit a time-limited measure to be imposed before the completion of a thorough injury investigation, as long as there is "clear evidence" that the injury test will be satisfied and "delay" will cause irreparable damage. Any such measure must take the form of a tariff, refundable in the event that the complete injury investigation does not support the preliminary determination.

A review of the notifications to the Committee on Safeguards indicates that provisional measures are reasonably common. Such measures were notified to the Committee on Safeguards 47 times between the entry into force of the Agreement on Safeguards and November 2005.[41] Some WTO members permit such measures regardless of the type of product at issue. Others, like the United States, limit provisional relief to particular industries where delay in the implementation of a measure is said to raise a particular risk of irreparable harm, namely, industries that produce perishable agricultural or citrus products.[42]

The text raises a few issues. For example, what suffices as "clear evidence" that the injury test will be met, in the absence of a thorough injury investigation? Presumably, a stark increase in imports coupled with some compelling evidence of great economic distress in the pertinent industry is needed. Likewise, when can it be said that "delay will cause damage which it would be difficult to repair?" The emphasis on perishable products in the U.S. statute suggests one possibility, where domestic producers cannot hold

[41] See the discussion in Chapter 2. [42] See 19 U.S.C. para 2252(d).

their production in inventory until the completion of a full investigation. For non-perishable products, the issue is a more open one.

As a practical matter, however, these issues are unlikely to be at the center of any WTO dispute. By the time that a panel can be constituted to examine them, either the provisional measures will have been replaced by definitive measures, or the provisional measures will simply have expired.

E Special Rules for Developing Countries

Article 9 of the Agreement on Safeguards contains two special principles relating to developing countries, one relating to the application of safeguard measures to their exports, and the other concerning the application of safeguard measures to their imports. The first is contained in Article 9.1:

> Safeguard measures shall not be applied against a product originating in a developing country Member as long as its share of imports of the product concerned in the importing Member does not exceed 3 per cent, provided that developing country Members with less than 3 per cent import share collectively account for not more than 9 per cent of total imports of the product concerned.

The 3% threshold for the exclusion of developing imports is sometimes referred to as the *de minimis* threshold.

Footnote 2 of the Agreement on Safeguards imposes a further obligation to notify any action taken under this paragraph "immediately" to the Committee on Safeguards. Accordingly, the annual reports of the Committee regularly list various notifications of decisions not to apply safeguard measures to developing country members.

This provision was at issue in *United States—Line Pipe*. Although Korea's own exports exceeded the 3% threshold, Korea nevertheless challenged the U.S. measure for its failure to exclude from the coverage of the measure imports from developing countries below the threshold. Korea's standing to raise this argument was not challenged.

Recall the structure of the U.S. measure in *Line Pipe*—it excluded from the additional tariff under the tariff-rate quota the first 9,000 short tons of line pipe imported from any country, developing or not. The United States argued that this structure satisfied Article 9.1 because 9,000 short tons represented 2.7% of imports before application of the measure, and that after application of the measure total imports would decline so that 9,000 short tons would exceed 3% of imports. Accordingly, any nation supplying less than 3% of imports would be exempt from the application of the measure.

The panel held that the measure violated Article 9.1 for two reasons. First, because the measure did not specifically exclude developing countries below the 3% threshold by enumerating them, the measure "applied" to them even if they would not actually pay the higher tariff rate. Second, the panel found that the U.S. argument regarding the relationship between the 3% threshold and the 9,000 short ton limit was conjectural—it was possible to envision a scenario in which imports did not decline enough to render 9,000 short tons equal to 3% or more of total imports.[43]

The Appellate Body disagreed with the panel on the first point, noting that no textual requirement exists for members to exclude developing countries from a measure by name. Nevertheless, it agreed that a measure can "apply" to an exporting country even if it does not operate in practice to restrain its exports. It further agreed with the panel that even if the United States expected the 9,000 short ton limit to exceed the 3% threshold, those expectations might be wrong. Accordingly, the measure violated Article 9.1.[44]

Line Pipe creates a rather exacting standard, in that a violation of Article 9.1 apparently arises if the measure is structured in such a way as to make it *possible* for it to apply to *de minimis*, developing country exporters, even if that possibility is an unlikely one. The difficulty, of course, is that import volumes are often uncertain, and it may not be clear *ex ante* which exporting nations will fall below the *de minimis* level. An importing nation might best respond to the *Line Pipe* ruling by expressly excluding all developing countries that might plausibly fall below the threshold, which is precisely what the United States undertook to do subsequently in structuring the measures at issue in *United States—Steel.*

The other special provisions for developing country members, contained in Article 9.2, provides them with limited exemptions from Article 7. In particular, developing country members may apply safeguard measures for up to ten years, rather than eight as specified in Article 7.3. Further, contrary to the general rule in Article 7.5, developing country members may apply a new measure to an industry previously protected by a measure if no measure has been in effect for *half* the time that the previous measure was in effect, or two years, whichever is greater.

[43] United States—Line Pipe Panel paras 7.172–81.
[44] United States—Line Pipe AB paras 120–33.

All of these provisions raise the question of what constitutes a "developing country." This issue cuts through many areas of WTO law regarding special and differential treatment, and has never been thoroughly addressed in the dispute process. I am unaware of any dispute to date in the WTO raising the question whether a member has wrongly been denied status as a "developing country" member, or has wrongly claimed such status. The issue did come before a panel in a 1958 GATT case involving the right of Ceylon (now Sri Lanka) to invoke special privileges under GATT Article XVIII which, among other things, permits developing countries to engage in infant industry protection. In finding that Ceylon qualified as a developing country, the panel relied on the interpretive notes to Article XVIII, which led them to focus on development indicators such as per capita GNP and the share of manufacturing, mining, and construction in GNP.[45]

[45] See Report of the Panel on Article XVIII Applications by Ceylon, GATT, 6th Supp. BISD 14, 112 (1958).

Chapter 10

COMPENSATION, RETALIATION AND THE PROHIBITION OF GREY-AREA MEASURES

As discussed in Chapter 1 at some length, the proliferation of trade restrictions outside the formal ambit of GATT Article XIX—so-called grey-area measures—provided much of the impetus for the Uruguay Round negotiations on safeguards. A substantial constituency within GATT sought the elimination of such measures. To this end, the final Agreement on Safeguards introduced two modifications relative to the old GATT system. First, in Article 8, it softened the GATT rules on compensation and retaliation with the aim of making formal safeguard measures more palatable to importing nations. Second, in Article 11, it introduced a prohibition on grey-area measures. These developments are the focus of this chapter. Economic commentary on these general issues may be found in Chapter 1, discussing the rise of grey-area measures and the movement to suppress them, as well as Chapter 2, discussing the economics of safeguard measures when accompanied by compensation or retaliation. Here, I will focus mainly on the legal issues raised by Articles 8 and 11.

A The New Rules on Compensation and Retaliation

Recall the basic structure of GATT Article XIX. Under paragraph 2, members employing safeguard measures were obliged to consult with affected trading partners, with the objective of negotiating "compensation" for the trade benefits lost due to the imposition of a safeguard measure. If those negotiations failed to reach an accord, affected trading partners had the right under paragraph 3 to withdraw "substantially equivalent concessions." Under Article XIX, therefore, an importing nation that employed a safeguard measure would always pay a price—it had to choose between offering alternative trade concessions as compensation, or suffering retaliation through a withdrawal of substantially equivalent concessions. The evident purpose of this system was to preserve the basic balance of concessions that had been negotiated under GATT auspices, and also to discourage undue resort to Article XIX measures.

Article 8 of the Agreement on Safeguards, which of course prevails over conflicting provisions of Article XIX, provides instead as follows:

1. A Member proposing to apply a safeguard measure or seeking an extension of a safeguard measure shall endeavour to maintain a substantially equivalent level of concessions and other obligations to that existing under GATT 1994 between it and the exporting Members which would be affected by such a measure, in accordance with the provisions of paragraph 3 of Article 12. To achieve this objective, the Members concerned may agree on any adequate means of trade compensation for the adverse effects of the measure on their trade.
2. If no agreement is reached within 30 days in the consultations under paragraph 3 of Article 12, then the affected exporting Members shall be free, not later than 90 days after the measure is applied, to suspend, upon the expiration of 30 days from the day on which written notice of such suspension is received by the Council for Trade in Goods, the application of substantially equivalent concessions or other obligations under GATT 1994, to the trade of the Member applying the safeguard measure, the suspension of which the Council for Trade in Goods does not disapprove.
3. The right of suspension referred to in paragraph 2 shall not be exercised for the first three years that a safeguard measure is in effect, provided that the safeguard measure has been taken as a result of an absolute increase in imports and that such a measure conforms to the provisions of this Agreement.

Paragraphs 1 and 2 restate the basic rules of Article XIX, rephrased slightly. The new wrinkle appears in paragraph 3, which suspends the right of retaliation for three years, "provided that" the safeguard measure follows an absolute increase in imports (as opposed to a mere increase in the market share of imports) and that it "conforms to the provisions" of the Agreement.

From an economic standpoint, Article 8 changes the "threat point" in bargaining over compensation as long as the conditions of paragraph 3 are satisfied. The importing member applying a safeguard measure can make a less generous offer of compensation, secure in the knowledge that if the offer is rejected, the affected trading partners will nevertheless be unable to retaliate for three years. Indeed, one might argue that there is little incentive for the importing nation to make any serious offer of compensation under these circumstances, at least for the period covered by the first three years.

Before concluding that no *bona fide* offer of compensation is required, however, note the language of Article 8.1, which states that a member "shall endeavour" to maintain an equivalent level of concessions. This phrasing might be taken to require bargaining in good faith, accompanied by a serious and genuine offer. An argument hinting at such a standard was advanced by the European Communities in *United States—Wheat Gluten*, where the EC argued that because of the absence of meaningful consultations prior to the implementation of the measure, the United States had not made a "genuine endeavour" to comply with Article 8.1, and had not demonstrated that it "actively and concretely offered adequate compensation" that was rejected.[1] The panel did not address the implicit question of whether and to what extent a general obligation to bargain in good faith exists, and instead held simply that the failure of the United States to offer "adequate opportunity for prior consultations," as required by Article 12.3 (see the discussion in Chapter 4), was also sufficient to establish a violation of Article 8.1, particularly in light of the explicit linkage to Article 12.3 in the text of Article 8.1. The Appellate Body affirmed on this point,[2] and in *Line Pipe* it reiterated that a failure to comply with the consultations requirement of Article 12.3 also establishes a violation of Article 8.1.[3] The question whether some greater obligation to bargain in good faith exists has not yet been addressed.

Two other issues raised by the text warrant mention. First, suppose that an exporting nation harmed by a safeguard measure retaliates by invoking its rights under Article 8.2. Suppose further that the Council for Trade in Goods does not disapprove the level of retaliation. The member targeted by retaliation nonetheless claims that the retaliatory suspension of concessions is excessive, going beyond what is "substantially equivalent." May that member raise a claim to this effect in the dispute resolution process, or is it precluded from doing so by the fact that the Council did not disapprove the level of retaliation? I do not know the answer to this question, although the best

[1] United States—Wheat Gluten Panel para 8.213.
[2] United States—Wheat Gluten AB paras 144–46.
[3] United States—Line Pipe AB paras 114–19.

approach may be to allow the claim to be brought. Inaction by the Council, in the form of its failure to "disapprove," does not necessarily establish that the level of retaliation was appropriate. The Council will not necessarily have all the data bearing on "equivalence" that would be gathered and examined by a dispute panel, and its members may disagree on the question before it. A case can be made for allowing the matter to proceed to the sort of binding arbitral process afforded by the Dispute Settlement Understanding.

Finally, with reference to Article 8.3, suppose that a dispute arises over whether the safeguard measure in question "conforms to the provisions of the Agreement," or whether it follows an "absolute increase in imports." Can a right to retaliate arise on the basis that a measure is non-conforming prior to a dispute settlement finding to that effect? The issue arose during the course of the *Steel* dispute. Complaining nations challenged, *inter alia*, the industry definitions employed by the United States in its injury analysis. Under the alternative industry definitions put forward by the complainants, some of the industries covered by the challenged measures may not have exhibited an "absolute increase in imports," which is required by Article 8.3 if the right of retaliation is to be suspended. The European Communities suggested informally that it had a right to retaliate immediately on this basis, while the United States argued that there could be no retaliation until the dispute process upheld the claim that there had been no absolute increase in imports.

The United States had the better argument, in my view. Article 23(2)(a) of the WTO dispute Settlement Understanding provides that "Members shall not make a determination to the effect that a violation has occurred... except through reference to dispute settlement." A determination by the European Communities that no absolute increase in imports was present would have amounted to a unilateral finding that the industry definitions employed by the United States violated the Agreement on Safeguards. The issue never came to a head, however, as the European Communities eventually relented on the threat to retaliate without a dispute settlement finding.

To be sure, given the delays that inhere in the WTO dispute resolution process, something approaching a three-year period may elapse before the process yields a definitive judgment about the conformity of a measure. That problem inheres in all cases, however, and the "three-year free pass" for violators is by no means limited to safeguards disputes.

B The Prohibition of Grey-Area Measures

The goal of prohibiting grey-area measures, and of bringing all safeguard-like measures under formal legal discipline, was the central objective of many safeguards negotiators during the Uruguay Round. Article 11 of the Agreement on Safeguards, concerning the "prohibition and elimination of certain measures," is thus the crowning achievement of the Agreement in the view of many observers.

Its structure is simple. Article 11.1 contains a prohibition on the introduction of any new "certain measures," defined in a manner to be discussed in a moment. Article 11.2 requires a phase-out of all existing such measures, to be completed by the end of 1999. Article 11.3 prohibits members from any behavior that would "encourage or support" non-governmental measures equivalent to those covered by Article 11.1.

The key challenge in drafting Article 11 was to take the concept of a "grey-area measure," a colloquial term from the days of GATT, and to give it some legal precision. Article 11 thus defines the "certain measures" to be prohibited with reference to three principles. First, according to Article 11.1(a), any "emergency action on imports of particular products as set forth in Article XIX of GATT" is a measure covered by Article 11. Such measures must be taken in a manner that "conforms with the provisions of that Article applied in accordance with this Agreement."

Second, under Article 11.1(b), members are prohibited from seeking, taking, or maintaining any "voluntary export restraints, orderly marketing agreements, or any other similar measures on the import or export side." "Voluntary export restraints" and "orderly marketing agreements" are terms that were often used to refer to negotiated arrangements between an importing nation and an exporting nation(s) whereby exports would be limited to levels below those produced by ordinary market forces. The arrangements were commonly administered by the exporting nation, which would impose some mechanism for restricting its exports to the agreed level. It was also possible to have such arrangements administered or enforced by the importing nation. The text makes clear that these arrangements are now prohibited regardless of who administers them. Further, they are prohibited whether pursuant to "agreements, arrangements and understandings entered into by two or more Members," or whether they are actions nominally undertaken by a "single Member."

Footnote 4 to the Agreement offers some "examples" of the "similar measures" that are also prohibited. It mentions "export moderation, export-price or import-price monitoring systems, export or import surveillance, compulsory import cartels and discretionary export or import licensing schemes, any of which afford protection." The fact that these are just "examples" indicates that the list is not exhaustive. The sweep of the term "similar measures" is broad indeed, therefore, and might be taken to encompass virtually any non-tariff import- or export-related measure that operates to afford protection.

Third, and finally, Article 11.1(c) makes clear that it does not prohibit measures that are taken "pursuant to" provisions of GATT other than Article XIX, or to other WTO Agreements. Likewise, footnote 3 to the Agreement states that a quantitative safeguard measure taken in conformity with GATT Article XIX and the Agreement on Safeguards may be administered by the exporting nation without violating Article 11.

The reference to measures "on the import or export side" in Article 11.1(b) further suggests by implication that the prohibition in Article 11 is not aimed at domestic regulatory measures that may have an adverse impact on imports. Such measures may, to be sure, run afoul of other WTO obligations (such as those contained in GATT Article III or the technical barriers agreements, for example).

Putting all of these pieces together, one might summarize the domain of the prohibited "certain measures" as follows:

—non-tariff measures (tariffs are governed by GATT Article II bindings)
—that operate specifically on imports or exports
—that afford protection
—and that are not authorized by some GATT provision other than Article XIX, or by some other WTO agreement or understanding.

Beyond the question of what measures are covered, one can imagine a few potential controversies as to the scope or applicability of Article 11. In particular, controversy may arise as to whether a measure potentially prohibited by Article 11 has been taken "pursuant to" another provision of WTO law. For example, consider an "undertaking" by an exporter or exporting nation ostensibly pursuant to Article 8 of the WTO Antidumping Agreement or Article 18 of the WTO Agreement on Subsidies and Countervailing Measures. Such "undertakings" are entered to avoid the imposition of antidumping or countervailing duties, "settling the case" in a sense. If such an undertaking were to be entered in a manner that did not comport with the requirements of the pertinent Agreement, one might argue that it is not "pursuant to" that Agreement, and potentially subject to Article 11.

Controversy might also arise as to the applicability of Article 11.3, which concerns non-governmental measures. The question of what sort of non-governmental measure would be "equivalent to" the measures prohibited by Article 11.1 is an entirely open one. Further, it may be quite unclear whether the government of a WTO member has done something to "encourage or support" a non-governmental measure.

To date, however, no disputes have arisen relating to Article 11 that have yielded dispute settlement findings. I am also unaware of any other substantial controversies regarding its implementation or interpretation. Further, the obligation to phase out existing measures covered by Article 11 seems to have been taken quite seriously, and the annual reports of the Committee on Safeguards regularly reported progress in that regard up through the 1999 deadline. Hence, by all appearances, Article 11 seems to have worked well up to this writing. There is some cause for concern about the long run, however, given the great difficulty that WTO members now face in utilizing safeguard measures that will withstand legal challenge. I develop that theme further in my concluding remarks.

Concluding Remarks

This book has surveyed the legal and economic issues associated with the use of safeguard measures in the WTO system. Clearly, many important and interesting questions remain unanswered. We do not yet have, in my opinion, a fully convincing account of the WTO rules as a matter of political economy. Likewise, the role of safeguard measures remains controversial from a normative perspective, and scholars will no doubt continue to debate the wisdom of such measures from a public policy standpoint. Finally, many central legal questions remain open. The most important, in my opinion, are associated with the requirements of "causation" and "non-attribution" under Article XIX and the Agreement on Safeguards, and related requirements concerning the permissible scope of safeguard measures. As I hope I have made clear, the interpretation of these requirements to date in WTO case law is confused and logically flawed. It is unclear what questions are being asked, let alone how to answer them. The requirement of "unforeseen developments," and of a linkage between those developments and the import surge, also raises daunting conceptual and practical issues.

The legal uncertainty associated with safeguard measures presents a substantial hurdle for any WTO member that wishes to use them without fear of successful legal challenge. At this writing, every safeguard measure that has been examined by the dispute settlement system has been found illegal, on multiple grounds. It is quite unclear on many issues what refinements to the analysis of national authorities will allow it to pass muster, and one can make a strong argument that renegotiation of the Agreement on Safeguards is needed to clarify some of the core obligations. At this writing, however, the prospects for such a renegotiation appear minimal.

Safeguard measures in the WTO system thus operate in something of a legal limbo. As Appendices 6–7 suggest, many nations employ safeguard measures without any challenge being brought to them, even though a successful legal challenge would likely be possible if some WTO member were to devote the necessary resources. If major players such as the United States and the EC employ safeguard measures, however, legal challenge is quite likely and the odds of a successful challenge are high (so far, 100%). The result, roughly speaking, is that smaller countries can employ safeguard measures without having to worry *too much* about the legal details. Larger countries must worry much more, although they can still take advantage of the "three-year free pass" to utilize safeguard measures until such time as the dispute process declares them illegal.

We thus confront a striking irony. As the book has documented, a principal impetus for the safeguards negotiations during the Uruguay Round was a desire by many nations to eliminate "grey-area" measures—measures that were similar to safeguard measures in many respects but that escaped formal legal discipline under GATT. Yet, safeguard measures in the new system are regularly "illegal" as well, even if they are not always challenged, and the road to lawful measures is not well-lit.

For better or worse, the result is that the major players are discouraged from using safeguard measures. The United States appears to have given up on safeguard measures for the time being, with no new domestic investigations since the *Steel* case. The European Communities did institute some measures relating to imports of salmon in 2005, but abandoned them quickly after a challenge was brought by Chile and Norway. Larger trading nations are thus being pushed to seek out substitutes for safeguard measures, the most obvious being antidumping duties. Some danger exists of a return to negotiated, managed trade arrangements as well, although there are few signs of that problem at this writing.

Commentators who view safeguard measures nothing more than wasteful protectionism may find this state of affairs quite satisfactory. Others who believe that safeguard measures have a useful role to play in the trading system, for any of the reasons explored in Chapter 2, may find the situation more worrisome. I remain quite agnostic, and hope only that this book helps to crystallize and illuminate the outstanding issues.

References

Alchian, Armen A. (1970). "Information Costs, Pricing, and Resource Unemployment," in Edmund S. Phelps, (ed.) *Microeconomic Foundations of Employment and Inflation Theory* (New York: Norton).

Bagwell, Kyle and Robert W. Staiger (1990). "A Theory of Managed Trade," *American Economic Review* 80: 779–795.

Bagwell, Kyle and Robert W. Staiger (2002). *The Economics of the World Trading System* (Cambridge MA: The MIT Press).

Bagwell, Kyle and Robert W. Staiger (2003). "Protection and the Business Cycle," *Advances in Economic Analysis and Policy* 3, Issue 1, Article 3.

Bagwell, Kyle and Robert W. Staiger (2005). "Enforcement, Private Political Pressure, and the General Agreement on Tariffs and Trade/World Trade Organization Escape Clause," *Journal of Legal Studies* 471–512.

Baldwin, Robert E. (1982). "The Political Economy of Protectionism," in Jagdish N. Bhagwati (ed.), *Import Competition and Response* (Chicago: University of Chicago Press).

Barton, John H and Bart S. Fisher (1986). *International Trade and Investment* (Boston: Little, Brown).

Becroft, Ross (2005). "The Standard of Review Strikes Back: the U.S.—Korea DRAMs Appeal" (mimeo).

Bhagwati, Jagdish (1988). *Protectionism* (Cambridge MA: The MIT Press).

Bown, Chad P. (2002). "Why are Safeguards Under the WTO so Unpopular?," *World Trade Review* 1: 47–62.

Buchanan, James M. and Gordon Tullock (1962). *The Calculus of Consent* (Ann Arbor, MI: University of Michigan Press).

Cline, William R. (1990). *The Future of World Trade in Textiles and Apparel*, 2d ed. (Washington: Institute for International Economics).

Cooper, Richard N. (1987). "Trade Policy and Foreign Policy," in Robert M. Stern (ed.), *Trade Policies in a Changing World Economy* (Cambridge, MA: MIT Press).

Corden, W. Max (1974). *Trade Policy and Economic Welfare* (Oxford: Clarendon Press).

Croley, Stephen P. and John H. Jackson (1996). "WTO Dispute Procedures, Standard of Review, and Deference to National Governments," *American Journal of International Law* 90: 193–213.

Dam, Kenneth W. (1970). *The GATT: Law and International Economic Organization* (Chicago: University of Chicago Press).

Deardorff, Alan (1987). "Safeguards Policy and the Conservative Social Welfare Function," in Henryk Kierzkowski (ed.), *Protection and Competition in International Trade: Essays in Honor of W. M. Corden* (Oxford: Blackwell).

Dixit, Avinash K. and Victor Norman (1980). *Theory of International Trade* (Cambridge, UK: Cambridge University Press).

Durling, James P. and Thomas J. Prusa (2003). "Using Safeguard Protection to Raise Domestic Rivals' Costs," *Japan and the World Economy* 15: 47–68.

Ethier, Wilfred (1984). "Higher Dimensional Issues in Trade Theory," in R. Jones & P. Kenen (eds)., *Handbook of International Economics*, Vol. 1 (Amsterdam: North-Holland).

Grossman, Gene M. (1986). "Imports as a Cause of Injury: The Case of the U.S. Steel Industry," *Journal of International Economics* 20: 201–222.

Grossman, Gene M. and Petros C. Mavroidis (2005). "United States—Definitive Safeguard Measures on Imports of Circular Welded Carbon Quality Line Pipe from Korea," in H. Horn & P. C. Mavroidis (eds.), *The WTO Case Law of 2002*, American Law Institute Reporters Series (Cambridge UK: Cambridge University Press).

Grossman. Gene M. and Alan O. Sykes (2005). "United States—Definitive Safeguard Measures on Certain Steel Products," in H. Horn & P.C. Mavroidis (eds.), *The WTO Case Law of 2003*, American Law Institute Reporters Series (Cambridge UK: Cambridge University Press, forthcoming).

Helpman, Elhanan and Paul R. Krugman (1989). *Trade Policy and Market Structure* (Cambridge, MA: MIT Press).

Hillman, Arye L. (1982). "Declining Industries and Political Support Protectionist Motives," *American Economic Review* 72: 1180–87.

Horn, Henrik and Petros C. Mavroidis (2003). "United States—Safeguard Measures on Imports of Fresh, Chilled or Frozen Lamb Meat from New Zealand and Australia: What Should be Required of a Safeguard Investigation?", in H. Horn & P.C. Mavroidis (eds.), *The WTO Case Law of 2001*, American Law Institute Reporters Series (Cambridge UK: Cambridge University Press).

Hufbaner, Gary Clyde and Howard F. Rosen (1986). *Trade Policy for Troubled Industries* (Washington: Institute for International Economics).

Irwin, Douglas (2003). "Causing Problems? The WTO Review of Causation and Injury Attribution in U.S. Section 201 Cases," *World Trade Review* 2: 297–325.

Jackson, John H. (1969). *World Trade and the Law of GATT* (New York: Bobbs Merrill).

Jackson, John H. (1997). *The World Trading System* 2d ed. (Cambridge MA: MIT Press).

Jackson, John H., William J. Davey and Alan O. Sykes (2002). *Legal Problems of International Economic Relations* 4th ed. (St. Paul, MN: West Publishing).

Johnson, Harry (1971). *Aspects of the Theory of Tariffs* (Cambridge, MA: Harvard University Press).

Kelly, Kenneth (1988). "The Analysis of Causality in Escape Clause Cases," *Journal of Industrial Economics* 37: 187–207.

Krugman, Paul R. (1986). *Strategic Trade Policy and the New International Economics* (Cambridge, MA: MIT Press).

Krugman, Paul R. and Maurice Obstfeld (2003). *International Economics*, 6th ed. (Boston, MA: Addison-Wesley).

Lawrence, Robert Z. and Robert E. Litan (1986). *Saving Free Trade* (Washington: Brookings Institution).

Lee, Yong-Shik (2005). *Safeguard Measures in World Trade: The Legal Analysis* 2d ed. (The Hague: Kluwer Law International).

Magee, Stephen P. and Leslie Young (1987). "Endogenous Protection in the United States, 1900–1984," in Robert M. Stern, (ed.), *U.S. Trade Policies in a Changing World Economy* (Cambridge, MA: MIT Press).

Mavroidis, Petros (2005). *The General Agreement on Tariffs and Trade* (Oxford UK: Oxford University Press).

McGovern, Edmond (1986). *International Trade Regulation*, 2d ed. (London: Gobefield).

Olson, Jr., Mancur (1965). *The Logic of Collective Action: Public Goods and the Theory of Groups* (Cambridge, MA: Harvard Press).

Osech, Matthias (2003). "Standards of Review in WTO Dispute Resolution," *Journal of International Economic Law* 6: 635–659.

Pauwelyn, Joost (2004). "The Puzzle of WTO Safeguards and Regional Trade Agreements," *Journal of International Economic Law* 7: 109–142.

Pindyck, Robert & Julio Rotemberg. (1987). "Are Imports to Blame?: Attribution of Injury under the 1974 Trade Act," *Journal of Law and Economics* 30: 101–122.

Rasmussen, Eric (2001). *Games and Information*. 3d ed. (Oxford UK: Blackwell).

Richardson, J. David (1982). "Trade Adjustment Assistance Under the United States Trade Act of 1974: An Analytical Examination and Worker Survey," in Jagdish N. Bhagwati, (ed.), *Import Competition and Response* (Chicago,: University of Chicago Press).

Rosendorff, B. Peter and Helen V. Milner (2001). "The Optimal Design of International Trade Institutions: Uncertainty and Escape," *International Organization* 55: 829–857.

Rousslang, Donald J. (1988). "Import Injury in U.S. Trade Law: An Economic View," *International Review of Law and Economics* 8:177–182.

Samuelson, Paul A. (1973). *Economics*, 9th ed. (New York: McGraw Hill).

Shavell, Steven (1980). "Damage Measures for Breach of Contract," *Bell Journal of Economics* 11: 466–490.

Smith, Alasdair and Anthony J. Venables (1991). "Counting the Cost of Voluntary Export Restraints in the European Car Market," in E. Helpman & A. Razin (eds.), *International Trade and Trade Policy* (Cambridge, MA: MIT Press).

Srinivasan, T.N. (2005). "The Dispute Settlement System of the WTO: A Brief History and Evaluation from Economic, Contractarian and Legal Perspectives" (mimeo).

Stewart, Terence P. (1993). *The GATT Uruguay Rounds: A Negotiating History*. (The Hague: Kluever Law and Taxation).

Sykes, Alan O. (1990). "Safeguards Reform: The Injury Test," in Michael J. Trebilcock & Robert York, *Fair Exchange: Reforming the Trade Remedy Laws* (Toronto: C.D. Howe Institute).

Sykes, Alan O. (1991). "Protectionism as a 'Safeguard': A Positive Analysis of the GATT 'Escape Clause' with Normative Speculations," *University of Chicago Law Review* 58: 255–305.

Sykes, Alan O. (2003). "The Safeguards Mess: A Critique of Appellate Body Jurisprudence," *World Trade Review* 2: 261–295.

Sykes, Alan O. (2004). "The Persistent Puzzles of Safeguards: Lessons from the Steel Dispute," *Journal of International Economic Law* 7: 523–564.

Tarr, David G. (1989). *A General Equilibrium Analysis of the Welfare and Employment Effects of U.S. Quotas in Textiles, Autos and Steel* (Washington: Federal Trade Commission).

Tarr, David G. and Morris Morkre (1984). *Aggregate Costs to the United States of Tariffs and Quotas on Imports* (Washington: Federal Trade Commission).

Trebilcock, Michael J., Marsha A. Chandler and Robert Howse (1990). *Trade and Transitions: A Comparative Analysis of Adjustment Policies* (London: Routledge).

Varian, Hal R. (1992). *Microeconomic Analysis* 3d ed. (New York: Norton).

Viner, Jacob (1950). *The Customs Union Issue* (New York: Carnegie Endowment for International Peace, and London: Stevens & Sons).

Willig, Robert D. (1976). "Consumer's Surplus Without Apology," *American Economic Review* 66: 587–597.

APPENDICES

APPENDIX 1
General Agreement on Tariffs and Trade

Article XIX. Emergency Action on Imports of Particular Products

1. (*a*) If, as a result of unforeseen developments and of the effect of the obligations incurred by a contracting party under this Agreement, including tariff concessions, any product is being imported into the territory of that contracting party in such increased quantities and under such conditions as to cause or threaten serious injury to domestic producers in that territory of like or directly competitive products, the contracting party shall be free, in respect of such product, and to the extent and for such time as may be necessary to prevent or remedy such injury, to suspend the obligation in whole or in part or to withdraw or modify the concession.

(*b*) If any product, which is the subject of a concession with respect to a preference, is being imported into the territory of a contracting party in the circumstances set forth in subparagraph (*a*) of this paragraph, so as to cause or threaten serious injury to domestic producers of like or directly competitive products in the territory of a contracting party which receives or received such preference, the importing contracting party shall be free, if that other contracting party so requests, to suspend the relevant obligation in whole or in part or to withdraw or modify the concession in respect of the product, to the extent and for such time as may be necessary to prevent or remedy such injury.

2. Before any contracting party shall take action pursuant to the provisions of paragraph 1 of this Article, it shall give notice in writing to the CONTRACTING PARTIES as far in advance as may be practicable and shall afford the CONTRACTING PARTIES and those contracting parties having a substantial interest as exporters of the product concerned an opportunity to consult with it in respect of the proposed action. When such notice is given in relation to a concession with respect to a preference, the notice shall name the contracting party which has requested the action. In critical circumstances, where delay would cause damage which it would be difficult to repair, action under paragraph 1 of this Article may be taken provisionally without prior consultation, on the condition that consultation shall be effected immediately after taking such action.

3. (*a*) If agreement among the interested contracting parties with respect to the action is not reached, the contracting party which proposes to take or continue the action shall, nevertheless, be free to do so, and if such action is taken or continued, the affected contracting parties shall then be free, not later than ninety days after such action is taken, to suspend, upon the expiration of thirty days from the

day on which written notice of such suspension is received by the CONTRACTING PARTIES, the application to the trade of the contracting party taking such action, or, in the case envisaged in paragraph 1 (*b*) of this Article, to the trade of the contracting party requesting such action, of such substantially equivalent concessions or other obligations under this Agreement the suspension of which the CONTRACTING PARTIES do not disapprove.

(*b*) Notwithstanding the provisions of subparagraph (*a*) of this paragraph, where action is taken under paragraph 2 of this Article without prior consultation and causes or threatens serious injury in the territory of a contracting party to the domestic producers of products affected by the action, that contracting party shall, where delay would cause damage difficult to repair, be free to suspend, upon the taking of the action and throughout the period of consultation, such concessions or other obligations as may be necessary to prevent or remedy the injury.

APPENDIX 2

The WTO Agreement on Safeguards

Members,

Having in mind the overall objective of the Members to improve and strengthen the international trading system based on GATT 1994;

Recognizing the need to clarify and reinforce the disciplines of GATT 1994, and specifically those of its Article XIX (Emergency Action on Imports of Particular Products), to re-establish multilateral control over safeguards and eliminate measures that escape such control;

Recognizing the importance of structural adjustment and the need to enhance rather than limit competition in international markets; and

Recognizing further that, for these purposes, a comprehensive agreement, applicable to all Members and based on the basic principles of GATT 1994, is called for;

Hereby *agree* as follows:

Article 1. General Provision

This Agreement establishes rules for the application of safeguard measures which shall be understood to mean those measures provided for in Article XIX of GATT 1994.

Article 2. Conditions

1. A Member[1] may apply a safeguard measure to a product only if that Member has determined, pursuant to the provisions set out below, that such product is being imported into its territory in such increased quantities, absolute or relative to domestic production, and under such conditions as to cause or threaten to cause serious injury to the domestic industry that produces like or directly competitive products.

2. Safeguard measures shall be applied to a product being imported irrespective of its source.

[1] A customs union may apply a safeguard measure as a single unit or on behalf of a member State. When a customs union applies a safeguard measure as a single unit, all the requirements for the determination of serious injury or threat thereof under this Agreement shall be based on the conditions existing in the customs union as a whole. When a safeguard measure is applied on behalf of a member State, all the requirements for the determination of serious injury or threat thereof shall be based on the conditions existing in that member State and the measure shall be limited to that member State. Nothing in this Agreement prejudges the interpretation of the relationship between Article XIX and paragraph 8 of Article XXIV of GATT 1994.

Article 3. Investigation

1. A Member may apply a safeguard measure only following an investigation by the competent authorities of that Member pursuant to procedures previously established and made public in consonance with Article X of GATT 1994. This investigation shall include reasonable public notice to all interested parties and public hearings or other appropriate means in which importers, exporters and other interested parties could present evidence and their views, including the opportunity to respond to the presentations of other parties and to submit their views, *inter alia*, as to whether or not the application of a safeguard measure would be in the public interest. The competent authorities shall publish a report setting forth their findings and reasoned conclusions reached on all pertinent issues of fact and law.

2. Any information which is by nature confidential or which is provided on a confidential basis shall, upon cause being shown, be treated as such by the competent authorities. Such information shall not be disclosed without permission of the party submitting it. Parties providing confidential information may be requested to furnish non-confidential summaries thereof or, if such parties indicate that such information cannot be summarized, the reasons why a summary cannot be provided. However, if the competent authorities find that a request for confidentiality is not warranted and if the party concerned is either unwilling to make the information public or to authorize its disclosure in generalized or summary form, the authorities may disregard such information unless it can be demonstrated to their satisfaction from appropriate sources that the information is correct.

Article 4. Determination of Serious Injury or Threat Thereof

1. For the purposes of this Agreement:
   (a) "serious injury" shall be understood to mean a significant overall impairment in the position of a domestic industry;
   (b) "threat of serious injury" shall be understood to mean serious injury that is clearly imminent, in accordance with the provisions of paragraph 2. A determination of the existence of a threat of serious injury shall be based on facts and not merely on allegation, conjecture or remote possibility; and
   (c) in determining injury or threat thereof, a "domestic industry" shall be understood to mean the producers as a whole of the like or directly competitive products operating within the territory of a Member, or those whose collective output of the like or directly competitive products constitutes a major proportion of the total domestic production of those products.

2. (a) In the investigation to determine whether increased imports have caused or are threatening to cause serious injury to a domestic industry under the terms of this Agreement, the competent authorities shall evaluate all relevant factors of an objective and quantifiable nature having a bearing on the situation of that industry, in particular, the rate and amount of the increase

in imports of the product concerned in absolute and relative terms, the share of the domestic market taken by increased imports, changes in the level of sales, production, productivity, capacity utilization, profits and losses, and employment.

(b) The determination referred to in subparagraph (a) shall not be made unless this investigation demonstrates, on the basis of objective evidence, the existence of the causal link between increased imports of the product concerned and serious injury or threat thereof. When factors other than increased imports are causing injury to the domestic industry at the same time, such injury shall not be attributed to increased imports.

(c) The competent authorities shall publish promptly, in accordance with the provisions of Article 3, a detailed analysis of the case under investigation as well as a demonstration of the relevance of the factors examined.

Article 5. Application of Safeguard Measures

1. A Member shall apply safeguard measures only to the extent necessary to prevent or remedy serious injury and to facilitate adjustment. If a quantitative restriction is used, such a measure shall not reduce the quantity of imports below the level of a recent period which shall be the average of imports in the last three representative years for which statistics are available, unless clear justification is given that a different level is necessary to prevent or remedy serious injury. Members should choose measures most suitable for the achievement of these objectives.

2. (a) In cases in which a quota is allocated among supplying countries, the Member applying the restrictions may seek agreement with respect to the allocation of shares in the quota with all other Members having a substantial interest in supplying the product concerned. In cases in which this method is not reasonably practicable, the Member concerned shall allot to Members having a substantial interest in supplying the product shares based upon the proportions, supplied by such Members during a previous representative period, of the total quantity or value of imports of the product, due account being taken of any special factors which may have affected or may be affecting the trade in the product.

(b) A Member may depart from the provisions in subparagraph (a) provided that consultations under paragraph 3 of Article 12 are conducted under the auspices of the Committee on Safeguards provided for in paragraph 1 of Article 13 and that clear demonstration is provided to the Committee that (*i*) imports from certain Members have increased in disproportionate percentage in relation to the total increase of imports of the product concerned in the representative period, (*ii*) the reasons for the departure from the provisions in subparagraph (a) are justified, and (*iii*) the conditions of such departure are equitable to all suppliers of the product concerned. The duration of any such measure shall not be extended beyond the initial period under paragraph 1 of Article 7. The departure referred to above shall not be permitted in the case of threat of serious injury.

Article 6. Provisional Safeguard Measures

In critical circumstances where delay would cause damage which it would be difficult to repair, a Member may take a provisional safeguard measure pursuant to a preliminary determination that there is clear evidence that increased imports have caused or are threatening to cause serious injury. The duration of the provisional measure shall not exceed 200 days, during which period the pertinent requirements of Articles 2 through 7 and 12 shall be met. Such measures should take the form of tariff increases to be promptly refunded if the subsequent investigation referred to in paragraph 2 of Article 4 does not determine that increased imports have caused or threatened to cause serious injury to a domestic industry. The duration of any such provisional measure shall be counted as a part of the initial period and any extension referred to in paragraphs 1, 2 and 3 of Article 7.

Article 7. Duration and Review of Safeguard Measures

1. A Member shall apply safeguard measures only for such period of time as may be necessary to prevent or remedy serious injury and to facilitate adjustment. The period shall not exceed four years, unless it is extended under paragraph 2.

2. The period mentioned in paragraph 1 may be extended provided that the competent authorities of the importing Member have determined, in conformity with the procedures set out in Articles 2, 3, 4 and 5, that the safeguard measure continues to be necessary to prevent or remedy serious injury and that there is evidence that the industry is adjusting, and provided that the pertinent provisions of Articles 8 and 12 are observed.

3. The total period of application of a safeguard measure including the period of application of any provisional measure, the period of initial application and any extension thereof, shall not exceed eight years.

4. In order to facilitate adjustment in a situation where the expected duration of a safeguard measure as notified under the provisions of paragraph 1 of Article 12 is over one year, the Member applying the measure shall progressively liberalize it at regular intervals during the period of application. If the duration of the measure exceeds three years, the Member applying such a measure shall review the situation not later than the mid-term of the measure and, if appropriate, withdraw it or increase the pace of liberalization. A measure extended under paragraph 2 shall not be more restrictive than it was at the end of the initial period, and should continue to be liberalized.

5. No safeguard measure shall be applied again to the import of a product which has been subject to such a measure, taken after the date of entry into force of the WTO

Agreement, for a period of time equal to that during which such measure had been previously applied, provided that the period of non-application is at least two years.

6. Notwithstanding the provisions of paragraph 5, a safeguard measure with a duration of 180 days or less may be applied again to the import of a product if:

(a) at least one year has elapsed since the date of introduction of a safeguard measure on the import of that product; and

(b) such a safeguard measure has not been applied on the same product more than twice in the five-year period immediately preceding the date of introduction of the measure.

Article 8. Level of Concessions and Other Obligations

1. A Member proposing to apply a safeguard measure or seeking an extension of a safeguard measure shall endeavour to maintain a substantially equivalent level of concessions and other obligations to that existing under GATT 1994 between it and the exporting Members which would be affected by such a measure, in accordance with the provisions of paragraph 3 of Article 12. To achieve this objective, the Members concerned may agree on any adequate means of trade compensation for the adverse effects of the measure on their trade.

2. If no agreement is reached within 30 days in the consultations under paragraph 3 of Article 12, then the affected exporting Members shall be free, not later than 90 days after the measure is applied, to suspend, upon the expiration of 30 days from the day on which written notice of such suspension is received by the Council for Trade in Goods, the application of substantially equivalent concessions or other obligations under GATT 1994, to the trade of the Member applying the safeguard measure, the suspension of which the Council for Trade in Goods does not disapprove.

3. The right of suspension referred to in paragraph 2 shall not be exercised for the first three years that a safeguard measure is in effect, provided that the safeguard measure has been taken as a result of an absolute increase in imports and that such a measure conforms to the provisions of this Agreement.

Article 9. Developing Country Members

1. Safeguard measures shall not be applied against a product originating in a developing country Member as long as its share of imports of the product concerned in the importing Member does not exceed 3 per cent, provided that developing country Members with less than 3 per cent import share collectively account for not more than 9 per cent of total imports of the product concerned.[2]

2. A developing country Member shall have the right to extend the period of application of a safeguard measure for a period of up to two years beyond the maximum period provided for in paragraph 3 of Article 7. Notwithstanding the

[2] A Member shall immediately notify an action taken under paragraph 1 of Article 9 to the Committee on Safeguards.

provisions of paragraph 5 of Article 7, a developing country Member shall have the right to apply a safeguard measure again to the import of a product which has been subject to such a measure, taken after the date of entry into force of the WTO Agreement, after a period of time equal to half that during which such a measure has been previously applied, provided that the period of non-application is at least two years.

Article 10. Pre-existing Article XIX Measures

Members shall terminate all safeguard measures taken pursuant to Article XIX of GATT 1947 that were in existence on the date of entry into force of the WTO Agreement not later than eight years after the date on which they were first applied or five years after the date of entry into force of the WTO Agreement, whichever comes later.

Article 11. Prohibition and Elimination of Certain Measures

1. (a) A Member shall not take or seek any emergency action on imports of particular products as set forth in Article XIX of GATT 1994 unless such action conforms with the provisions of that Article applied in accordance with this Agreement.
   (b) Furthermore, a Member shall not seek, take or maintain any voluntary export restraints, orderly marketing arrangements or any other similar measures on the export or the import side.[3,4] These include actions taken by a single Member as well as actions under agreements, arrangements and understandings entered into by two or more Members. Any such measure in effect on the date of entry into force of the WTO Agreement shall be brought into conformity with this Agreement or phased out in accordance with paragraph 2.
   (c) This Agreement does not apply to measures sought, taken or maintained by a Member pursuant to provisions of GATT 1994 other than Article XIX, and Multilateral Trade Agreements in Annex 1A other than this Agreement, or pursuant to protocols and agreements or arrangements concluded within the framework of GATT 1994.

2. The phasing out of measures referred to in paragraph 1(b) shall be carried out according to timetables to be presented to the Committee on Safeguards by the Members concerned not later than 180 days after the date of entry into force of the

[3] An import quota applied as a safeguard measure in conformity with the relevant provisions of GATT 1994 and this Agreement may, by mutual agreement, be administered by the exporting Member.

[4] Examples of similar measures include export moderation, export-price or import-price monitoring systems, export or import surveillance, compulsory import cartels, and discretionary export or import licensing schemes, any of which afford protection.

WTO Agreement. These timetables shall provide for all measures referred to in paragraph 1 to be phased out or brought into conformity with this Agreement within a period not exceeding four years after the date of entry into force of the WTO Agreement, subject to not more than one specific measure per importing Member,[5] the duration of which shall not extend beyond 31 December 1999. Any such exception must be mutually agreed between the Members directly concerned and notified to the Committee on Safeguards for its review and acceptance within 90 days of the entry into force of the WTO Agreement. The Annex to this Agreement indicates a measure which has been agreed as falling under this exception.

3. Members shall not encourage or support the adoption or maintenance by public and private enterprises of non-governmental measures equivalent to those referred to in paragraph 1.

Article 12. Notification and Consultation

1. A Member shall immediately notify the Committee on Safeguards upon:
   (a) initiating an investigatory process relating to serious injury or threat thereof and the reasons for it;
   (b) making a finding of serious injury or threat thereof caused by increased imports; and
   (c) taking a decision to apply or extend a safeguard measure.

2. In making the notifications referred to in paragraphs 1(b) and 1(c), the Member proposing to apply or extend a safeguard measure shall provide the Committee on Safeguards with all pertinent information, which shall include evidence of serious injury or threat thereof caused by increased imports, precise description of the product involved and the proposed measure, proposed date of introduction, expected duration and timetable for progressive liberalization. In the case of an extension of a measure, evidence that the industry concerned is adjusting shall also be provided. The Council for Trade in Goods or the Committee on Safeguards may request such additional information as they may consider necessary from the Member proposing to apply or extend the measure.

3. A Member proposing to apply or extend a safeguard measure shall provide adequate opportunity for prior consultations with those Members having a substantial interest as exporters of the product concerned, with a view to, *inter alia*, reviewing the information provided under paragraph 2, exchanging views on the measure and reaching an understanding on ways to achieve the objective set out in paragraph 1 of Article 8.

4. A Member shall make a notification to the Committee on Safeguards before taking a provisional safeguard measure referred to in Article 6. Consultations shall be initiated immediately after the measure is taken.

[5] The only such exception to which the European Communities is entitled is indicated in the Annex to this Agreement.

5. The results of the consultations referred to in this Article, as well as the results of mid-term reviews referred to in paragraph 4 of Article 7, any form of compensation referred to in paragraph 1 of Article 8, and proposed suspensions of concessions and other obligations referred to in paragraph 2 of Article 8, shall be notified immediately to the Council for Trade in Goods by the Members concerned.

6. Members shall notify promptly the Committee on Safeguards of their laws, regulations and administrative procedures relating to safeguard measures as well as any modifications made to them.

7. Members maintaining measures described in Article 10 and paragraph 1 of Article 11 which exist on the date of entry into force of the WTO Agreement shall notify such measures to the Committee on Safeguards not later than 60 days after the date of entry into force of the WTO Agreement.

8. Any Member may notify the Committee on Safeguards of all laws, regulations, administrative procedures and any measures or actions dealt with in this Agreement that have not been notified by other Members that are required by this Agreement to make such notifications.

9. Any Member may notify the Committee on Safeguards of any non-governmental measures referred to in paragraph 3 of Article 11.

10. All notifications to the Council for Trade in Goods referred to in this Agreement shall normally be made through the Committee on Safeguards.

11. The provisions on notification in this Agreement shall not require any Member to disclose confidential information the disclosure of which would impede law enforcement or otherwise be contrary to the public interest or would prejudice the legitimate commercial interests of particular enterprises, public or private.

Article 13. Surveillance

1. A Committee on Safeguards is hereby established, under the authority of the Council for Trade in Goods, which shall be open to the participation of any Member indicating its wish to serve on it. The Committee will have the following functions:

- (a) to monitor, and report annually to the Council for Trade in Goods on, the general implementation of this Agreement and make recommendations towards its improvement;
- (b) to find, upon request of an affected Member, whether or not the procedural requirements of this Agreement have been complied with in connection with a safeguard measure, and report its findings to the Council for Trade in Goods;
- (c) to assist Members, if they so request, in their consultations under the provisions of this Agreement;

(d) to examine measures covered by Article 10 and paragraph 1 of Article 11, monitor the phase-out of such measures and report as appropriate to the Council for Trade in Goods;

(e) to review, at the request of the Member taking a safeguard measure, whether proposals to suspend concessions or other obligations are "substantially equivalent", and report as appropriate to the Council for Trade in Goods;

(f) to receive and review all notifications provided for in this Agreement and report as appropriate to the Council for Trade in Goods; and

(g) to perform any other function connected with this Agreement that the Council for Trade in Goods may determine.

2. To assist the Committee in carrying out its surveillance function, the Secretariat shall prepare annually a factual report on the operation of this Agreement based on notifications and other reliable information available to it

Article 14. Dispute Settlement

The provisions of Articles XXII and XXIII of GATT 1994 as elaborated and applied by the Dispute Settlement Understanding shall apply to consultations and the settlement of disputes arising under this Agreement.

Annex

Members concerned	Product	Termination
EC/Japan	Passenger cars, off road vehicles, light commercial vehicles, light trucks (up to 5 tonnes), and the same vehicles in wholly knocked-down form (CKD sets).	31 December 1999

Exception Referred to in Paragraph 2 of Article 11

APPENDIX 3
U.S. National Legislation

SECTIONS 201–204 OF THE TRADE ACT OF 1974, CODIFIED AS 19 U.S.C. PARAS 2251–54

PARA 2251. ACTION TO FACILITATE POSITIVE ADJUSTMENT TO IMPORT COMPETITION

(a) Presidential action

If the United States International Trade Commission (hereinafter referred to in this part as the "Commission") determines under section 2252(b) of this title that an article is being imported into the United States in such increased quantities as to be a substantial cause of serious injury, or the threat thereof, to the domestic industry producing an article like or directly competitive with the imported article, the President, in accordance with this part, shall take all appropriate and feasible action within his power which the President determines will facilitate efforts by the domestic industry to make a positive adjustment to import competition and provide greater economic and social benefits than costs.

(b) Positive adjustment to import competition

(1) For purposes of this part, a positive adjustment to import competition occurs when—

(A) the domestic industry—

(i) is able to compete successfully with imports after actions taken under section 2254 of this title terminate, or

(ii) the domestic industry experiences an orderly transfer of resources to other productive pursuits; and

(B) dislocated workers in the industry experience an orderly transition to productive pursuits.

(2) The domestic industry may be considered to have made a positive adjustment to import competition even though the industry is not of the same size and composition as the industry at the time the investigation was initiated under section 2252(b) of this title.

Para 2252. Investigations, Determinations, and Recommendations by Commission

(a) Petitions and adjustment plans

(1) A petition requesting action under this chapter [19 USCS paras 2251 et seq.] for the purpose of facilitating positive adjustment to import competition may be filed with the Commission by an entity, including a trade association, firm, certified or recognized union, or group of workers, which is representative of an industry.

(2) A petition under paragraph (1)—

(A) shall include a statement describing the specific purposes for which action is being sought, which may include facilitating the orderly transfer of resources to more productive pursuits, enhancing competitiveness, or other means of adjustment to new conditions of competition; and

(B) may—

(i) subject to subsection (d)(1)(C)(i), request provisional relief under subsection (d)(1); or

(ii) request provisional relief under subsection (d)(2).

(3) Whenever a petition is filed under paragraph (1), the Commission shall promptly transmit copies of the petition to the Office of the United States Trade Representative and other Federal agencies directly concerned.

(4) A petitioner under paragraph (1) may submit to the Commission and the United States Trade Representative (hereafter in this chapter [19 USCS paras 2251 et seq.] referred to as the "Trade Representative"), either with the petition, or at any time within 120 days after the date of filing of the petition, a plan to facilitate positive adjustment to import competition.

(5) (A) Before submitting an adjustment plan under paragraph (4), the petitioner and other entities referred to in paragraph (1) that wish to participate may consult with the Trade Representative and the officers and employees of any Federal agency that is considered appropriate by the Trade Representative, for purposes of evaluating the adequacy of the proposals being considered for inclusion in the plan in relation to specific actions that may be taken under this chapter [19 USCS paras 2251 et seq.].

(B) A request for any consultation under subparagraph (A) must be made to the Trade Representative. Upon receiving such a request, the Trade Representative shall confer with the petitioner and provide such assistance, including publication of appropriate notice in the Federal Register, as may be practicable in obtaining other participants in the consultation. No consultation may occur under subparagraph (A) unless the Trade Representative, or his delegate, is in attendance.

(6) (A) In the course of any investigation under subsection (b), the Commission shall seek information (on a confidential basis, to the extent appropriate) on

actions being taken, or planned to be taken, or both, by firms and workers in the industry to make a positive adjustment to import competition.

(B) Regardless whether an adjustment plan is submitted under paragraph (4) by the petitioner, if the Commission makes an affirmative determination under subsection (b), any—

(i) firm in the domestic industry;

(ii) certified or recognized union or group of workers in the domestic industry;

(iii) State or local community;

(iv) trade association representing the domestic industry; or

(v) any other person or group of persons,

may, individually, submit to the Commission commitments regarding actions such persons and entities intend to take to facilitate positive adjustment to import competition.

(7) Nothing in paragraphs (5) and (6) may be construed to provide immunity under the antitrust laws.

(8) The procedures concerning the release of confidential business information set forth in section 332(g) of the Tariff Act of 1930 [19 USCS para 1332(g)] shall apply with respect to information received by the Commission in the course of investigations conducted under this chapter [19 USCS paras 2251 et seq.], part 1 of title III of the North American Free Trade Agreement Implementation Act, title II of the United States-Jordan Free Trade Area Implementation Act [19 USCS para 2112 note], title III of the United States-Chile Free Trade Agreement Implementation Act [19 USCS para 3805 note], title III of the United States-Singapore Free Trade Agreement Implementation Act [19 USCS para 3805 note], title III of the United States-Australia Free Trade Agreement Implementation Act [19 USCS para 3805 note], and title III of the United States-Morocco Free Trade Agreement Implementation Act [19 USCS para 3805 note]. The Commission may request that parties providing confidential business information furnish nonconfidential summaries thereof or, if such parties indicate that the information in the submission cannot be summarized, the reasons why a summary cannot be provided. If the Commission finds that a request for confidentiality is not warranted and if the party concerned is either unwilling to make the information public or to authorize its disclosure in generalized or summarized form, the Commission may disregard the submission.

(b) Investigations and determinations by Commission

(1) (A) Upon the filing of a petition under subsection (a), the request of the President or the Trade Representative, the resolution of either the Committee on Ways and Means of the House of Representatives or the Committee on Finance of the Senate, or on its own motion, the Commission shall promptly make an investigation to determine whether an article is

being imported into the United States in such increased quantities as to be a substantial cause of serious injury, or the threat thereof, to the domestic industry producing an article like or directly competitive with the imported article.

(B) For purposes of this section, the term "substantial cause" means a cause which is important and not less than any other cause.

(2) (A) Except as provided in subparagraph (B), the Commission shall make the determination under paragraph (1) within 120 days (180 days if the petition alleges that critical circumstances exist) after the date on which the petition is filed, the request or resolution is received, or the motion is adopted, as the case may be.

(B) If before the 100th day after a petition is filed under subsection (a)(1) the Commission determines that the investigation is extraordinarily complicated, the Commission shall make the determination under paragraph (1) within 150 days (210 days if the petition alleges that critical circumstances exist) after the date referred to in subparagraph (A).

(3) The Commission shall publish notice of the commencement of any proceeding under this subsection in the Federal Register and shall, within a reasonable time thereafter, hold public hearings at which the Commission shall afford interested parties and consumers an opportunity to be present, to present evidence, to comment on the adjustment plan, if any, submitted under subsection (a), to respond to the presentations of other parties and consumers, and otherwise to be heard.

(c) Factors applied in making determinations

(1) In making determinations under subsection (b), the Commission shall take into account all economic factors which it considers relevant, including (but not limited to)—

(A) with respect to serious injury—

(i) the significant idling of productive facilities in the domestic industry,

(ii) the inability of a significant number of firms to carry out domestic production operations at a reasonable level of profit, and

(iii) significant unemployment or underemployment within the domestic industry;

(B) with respect to threat of serious injury—

(i) a decline in sales or market share, a higher and growing inventory (whether maintained by domestic producers, importers, wholesalers, or retailers), and a downward trend in production, profits, wages, productivity, or employment (or increasing underemployment) in the domestic industry,

(ii) the extent to which firms in the domestic industry are unable to generate adequate capital to finance the modernization of their domestic plants and equipment, or are unable to maintain existing levels of expenditures for research and development,

(iii) the extent to which the United States market is the focal point for the diversion of exports of the article concerned by reason of restraints on exports of such article to, or on imports of such article into, third country markets; and

(C) with respect to substantial cause, an increase in imports (either actual or relative to domestic production) and a decline in the proportion of the domestic market supplied by domestic producers.

(2) In making determinations under subsection (b), the Commission shall—

(A) consider the condition of the domestic industry over the course of the relevant business cycle, but may not aggregate the causes of declining demand associated with a recession or economic downturn in the United States economy into a single cause of serious injury or threat of injury; and

(B) examine factors other than imports which may be a cause of serious injury, or threat of serious injury, to the domestic industry.

The Commission shall include the results of its examination under subparagraph (B) in the report submitted by the Commission to the President under subsection (e).

(3) The presence or absence of any factor which the Commission is required to evaluate in subparagraphs (A) and (B) of paragraph (1) is not necessarily dispositive of whether an article is being imported into the United States in such increased quantities as to be a substantial cause of serious injury, or the threat thereof, to the domestic industry.

(4) For purposes of subsection (b), in determining the domestic industry producing an article like or directly competitive with an imported article, the Commission—

(A) to the extent information is available, shall, in the case of a domestic producer which also imports, treat as part of such domestic industry only its domestic production;

(B) may, in the case of a domestic producer which produces more than one article, treat as part of such domestic industry only that portion or subdivision of the producer which produces the like or directly competitive article; and

(C) may, in the case of one or more domestic producers which produce a like or directly competitive article in a major geographic area of the United States and whose production facilities in such area for such article constitute a substantial portion of the domestic industry in the United States and primarily serve the market in such area, and where the imports are concentrated in such area, treat as such domestic industry only that segment of the production located in such area.

(5) In the course of any proceeding under this subsection, the Commission shall investigate any factor which in its judgment may be contributing to increased imports of the article under investigation. Whenever in the course of its investigation

the Commission has reason to believe that the increased imports are attributable in part to circumstances which come within the purview of subtitles A and B of title VII [19 USCS paras 1671 et seq. and 1673 et seq.] or section 337 of the Tariff Act of 1930 [19 USCS para 1337], or other remedial provisions of law, the Commission shall promptly notify the appropriate agency so that such action may be taken as is otherwise authorized by such provisions of law.

(6) For purposes of this section:

(A) (i) The term "domestic industry" means, with respect to an article, the producers as a whole of the like or directly competitive article or those producers whose collective production of the like or directly competitive article constitutes a major proportion of the total domestic production of such article.

(ii) The term "domestic industry" includes producers located in the United States insular possessions.

(B) The term "significant idling of productive facilities" includes the closing of plants or the underutilization of production capacity.

(C) The term "serious injury" means a significant overall impairment in the position of a domestic industry.

(D) The term "threat of serious injury" means serious injury that is clearly imminent.

(d) Provisional relief

(1) (A) An entity representing a domestic industry that produces a perishable agricultural product or citrus product that is like or directly competitive with an imported perishable agricultural product or citrus product may file a request with the Trade Representative for the monitoring of imports of that product under subparagraph (B). Within 21 days after receiving the request, the Trade Representative shall determine if—

(i) the imported product is a perishable agricultural product or citrus product; and

(ii) there is a reasonable indication that such product is being imported into the United States in such increased quantities as to be, or likely to be, a substantial cause of serious injury, or the threat thereof, to such domestic industry.

(B) If the determinations under subparagraph (A)(i) and (ii) are affirmative, the Trade Representative shall request, under section 332(g) of the Tariff Act of 1930 [19 USCS para 1332(g)], the Commission to monitor and investigate the imports concerned for a period not to exceed 2 years. The monitoring and investigation may include the collection and analysis of information that would expedite an investigation under subsection (b).

(C) If a petition filed under subsection (a)—

(i) alleges injury from imports of a perishable agricultural product or citrus product that has been, on the date the allegation is included in the petition, subject to monitoring by the Commission under subparagraph (B) for not less than 90 days; and

(ii) requests that provisional relief be provided under this subsection with respect to such imports;

the Commission shall, not later than the 21st day after the day on which the request was filed, make a determination, on the basis of available information, whether increased imports (either actual or relative to domestic production) of the perishable agricultural product or citrus product are a substantial cause of serious injury, or the threat thereof, to the domestic industry producing a like or directly competitive perishable product or citrus product, and whether either—

(I) the serious injury is likely to be difficult to repair by reason of perishability of the like or directly competitive agricultural product; or

(II) the serious injury cannot be timely prevented through investigation under subsection (b) and action under section 203 [19 USCS para 2253].

(D) At the request of the Commission, the Secretary of Agriculture shall promptly provide to the Commission any relevant information that the Department of Agriculture may have for purposes of making determinations and findings under this subsection.

(E) Whenever the Commission makes an affirmative preliminary determination under subparagraph (C), the Commission shall find the amount or extent of provisional relief that is necessary to prevent or remedy the serious injury. In carrying out this subparagraph, the Commission shall give preference to increasing or imposing a duty on imports, if such form of relief is feasible and would prevent or remedy the serious injury.

(F) The Commission shall immediately report to the President its determination under subparagraph (C) and, if the determination is affirmative, the finding under subparagraph (E).

(G) Within 7 days after receiving a report from the Commission under subparagraph (F) containing an affirmative determination, the President, if he considers provisional relief to be warranted and after taking into account the finding of the Commission under subparagraph (E), shall proclaim such provisional relief that the President considers necessary to prevent or remedy the serious injury.

(2) (A) When a petition filed under subsection (a) alleges that critical circumstances exist and requests that provisional relief be provided under this subsection with respect to imports of the article identified in the petition,

the Commission shall, not later than 60 days after the petition containing the request was filed, determine, on the basis of available information, whether—

(i) there is clear evidence that increased imports (either actual or relative to domestic production) of the article are a substantial cause of serious injury, or the threat thereof, to the domestic industry producing an article like or directly competitive with the imported article; and

(ii) delay in taking action under this chapter would cause damage to that industry that would be difficult to repair.

(B) If the determinations under subparagraph (A)(i) and (ii) are affirmative, the Commission shall find the amount or extent of provisional relief that is necessary to prevent or remedy the serious injury. In carrying out this subparagraph, the Commission shall give preference to increasing or imposing a duty on imports, if such form of relief is feasible and would prevent or remedy the serious injury.

(C) The Commission shall immediately report to the President its determinations under subparagraph (A)(i) and (ii) and, if the determinations are affirmative, the finding under subparagraph (B).

(D) Within 30 days after receiving a report from the Commission under subparagraph (C) containing an affirmative determination under subparagraph (A)(i) and (ii), the President, if he considers provisional relief to be warranted and after taking into account the finding of the Commission under subparagraph (B), shall proclaim, for a period not to exceed 200 days, such provisional relief that the President considers necessary to prevent or remedy the serious injury. Such relief shall take the form of an increase in, or the imposition of, a duty on imports, if such form of relief is feasible and would prevent or remedy the serious injury.

(3) If provisional relief is proclaimed under paragraph (1)(G) or (2)(D) in the form of an increase, or the imposition of, a duty, the President shall order the suspension of liquidation of all imported articles subject to the affirmative determination under paragraph (1)(C) or paragraph (2)(A), as the case may be, that are entered, or withdrawn from warehouse for consumption, on or after the date of the determination.

(4) (A) Any provisional relief implemented under this subsection with respect to an imported article shall terminate on the day on which—

(i) if such relief was proclaimed under paragraph (1)(G) or (2)(D), the Commission makes a negative determination under subsection (b) regarding injury or the threat thereof by imports of such article;

(ii) action described in section 203(a)(3)(A) or (C) [19 USCS para 2253(a)(3)(A) or (C)] takes effect under section 203 [19 USCS para 2253] with respect to such article;

(iii) a decision by the President not to take any action under section 203(a) [19 USCS para 2253(a)] with respect to such article becomes final; or

(iv) whenever the President determines that, because of changed circumstances, such relief is no longer warranted.

(B) Any suspension of liquidation ordered under paragraph (3) with respect to an imported article shall terminate on the day on which provisional relief is terminated under subparagraph (A) with respect to the article.

(C) If an increase in, or the imposition of, a duty that is proclaimed under section 203 [19 USCS para 2253] on an imported article is different from a duty increase or imposition that was proclaimed for such an article under this section, then the entry of any such article for which liquidation was suspended under paragraph (3) shall be liquidated at whichever of such rates of duty is lower.

(D) If provisional relief in the form of an increase in, or the imposition of, a duty is proclaimed under this section with respect to an imported article and neither a duty increase nor a duty imposition is proclaimed under section 203 [19 USCS para 2253] regarding such article, the entry of any such article for which liquidation was suspended under paragraph (3) may be liquidated at the rate of duty that applied before provisional relief was provided.

(5) For purposes of this subsection:

(A) The term "citrus product" means any processed oranges or grapefruit, or any orange or grapefruit juice, including concentrate.

(B) A perishable agricultural product is any agricultural article, including livestock, regarding which the Trade Representative considers action under this section to be appropriate after taking into account—

(i) whether the article has—

(I) a short shelf life,

(II) a short growing season, or

(III) a short marketing period,

(ii) whether the article is treated as a perishable product under any other Federal law or regulation; and

(iii) any other factor considered appropriate by the Trade Representative.

The presence or absence of any factor which the Trade Representative is required to take into account under clause (i), (ii), or (iii) is not necessarily dispositive of whether an article is a perishable agricultural product.

(C) The term "provisional relief" means—

(i) any increase in, or imposition of, any duty;

(ii) any modification or imposition of any quantitative restriction on the importation of an article into the United States; or

(iii) any combination of actions under clauses (i) and (ii).

(e) Commission recommendations

(1) If the Commission makes an affirmative determination under subsection (b)(1), the Commission shall also recommend the action that would address the serious injury, or threat thereof, to the domestic industry and be most effective in facilitating the efforts of the domestic industry to make a positive adjustment to import competition.

(2) The Commission is authorized to recommend under paragraph (1)—

(A) an increase in, or the imposition of, any duty on the imported article;

(B) a tariff-rate quota on the article;

(C) a modification or imposition of any quantitative restriction on the importation of the article into the United States;

(D) one or more appropriate adjustment measures, including the provision of trade adjustment assistance under chapter 2 [19 USCS paras 2271 et seq.]; or

(E) any combination of the actions described in subparagraphs (A) through (D).

(3) The Commission shall specify the type, amount, and duration of the action recommended by it under paragraph (1). The limitations set forth in section 203(e) [19 USCS para 2253(e)] are applicable to the action recommended by the Commission.

(4) In addition to the recommendation made under paragraph (1), the Commission may also recommend that the President—

(A) initiate international negotiations to address the underlying cause of the increase in imports of the article or otherwise to alleviate the injury or threat; or

(B) implement any other action authorized under law that is likely to facilitate positive adjustment to import competition.

(5) For purposes of making its recommendation under this subsection, the Commission shall—

(A) after reasonable notice, hold a public hearing at which all interested parties shall be provided an opportunity to present testimony and evidence; and

(B) take into account—

(i) the form and amount of action described in paragraph (2)(A), (B), and (C) that would prevent or remedy the injury or threat thereof,

(ii) the objectives and actions specified in the adjustment plan, if any, submitted under subsection (a)(4),

(iii) any individual commitment that was submitted to the Commission under subsection (a)(6),

(iv) any information available to the Commission concerning the conditions of competition in domestic and world markets, and likely developments affecting such conditions during the period for which action is being requested, and

(v) whether international negotiations may be constructive to address the injury or threat thereof or to facilitate adjustment.

(6) Only those members of the Commission who agreed to the affirmative determination under subsection (b) are eligible to vote on the recommendation required to be made under paragraph (1) or that may be made under paragraph (3). Members of the Commission who did not agree to the affirmative determination may submit, in the report required under subsection (f), separate views regarding what action, if any, should be taken under section 203 [19 USCS para 2253].

(f) Report by Commission

(1) The Commission shall submit to the President a report on each investigation undertaken under subsection (b). The report shall be submitted at the earliest practicable time, but not later than 180 days (240 days if the petition alleges that critical circumstances exist) after the date on which the petition is filed, the request or resolution is received, or the motion is adopted, as the case may be.

(2) The Commission shall include in the report required under paragraph (1) the following:

(A) The determination made under subsection (b) and an explanation of the basis for the determination.

(B) If the determination under subsection (b) is affirmative, the recommendations for action made under subsection (e) and an explanation of the basis for each recommendation.

(C) Any dissenting or separate views by members of the Commission regarding the determination and any recommendation referred to in subparagraphs (A) and (B).

(D) The findings required to be included in the report under subsection (c)(2).

(E) A copy of the adjustment plan, if any, submitted under section 201(b)(4) [19 USCS para 2251(b)(4)].

(F) Commitments submitted, and information obtained, by the Commission regarding steps that firms and workers in the domestic industry are taking, or plan to take, to facilitate positive adjustment to import competition.

(G) A description of—

(i) the short- and long-term effects that implementation of the action recommended under subsection (e) is likely to have on the petitioning domestic industry, on other domestic industries, and on consumers, and

(ii) the short- and long-term effects of not taking the recommended action on the petitioning domestic industry, its workers and the communities where production facilities of such industry are located, and on other domestic industries.

(3) The Commission, after submitting a report to the President under paragraph (1), shall promptly make it available to the public (with the exception of the confidential information obtained under section 202(a)(6)(B) [subsec. (a)(6)(B) of this section] and any other information which the Commission determines to be confidential) and cause a summary thereof to be published in the Federal Register.

(g) Expedited consideration of adjustment assistance petitions

If the Commission makes an affirmative determination under subsection (b)(1), the Commission shall promptly notify the Secretary of Labor and the Secretary of Commerce of the determination. After receiving such notification—

(1) the Secretary of Labor shall give expedited consideration to petitions by workers in the domestic industry for certification for eligibility to apply for adjustment assistance under chapter 2 [19 USCS paras 2271 et seq.]; and

(2) the Secretary of Commerce shall give expedited consideration to petitions by firms in the domestic industry for certification of eligibility to apply for adjustment assistance under chapter 3 [19 USCS paras 2341 et seq.].

(h) Limitations on investigations

(1) Except for good cause determined by the Commission to exist, no investigation for the purposes of this section shall be made with respect to the same subject matter as a previous investigation under this chapter [19 USCS paras 2251 et seq.], unless 1 year has elapsed since the Commission made its report to the President of the results of such previous investigation.

(2) No new investigation shall be conducted with respect to an article that is or has been the subject of an action under section 203(a)(3)(A), (B), (C), or (E) [19 USCS para 2253(a)(3)(A), (B), (C), or (E)] if the last day on which the President could take action under section 203 [19 USCS para 2253] in the new investigation is a date earlier than that permitted under section 203(e)(7) [19 USCS para 2253(e)(7)].

(3) (A) Not later than the date on which the Textiles Agreement enters into force with respect to the United States, the Secretary of Commerce shall publish in the Federal Register a list of all articles that are subject to the Textiles Agreement. An investigation may be conducted under this section concerning imports of any article that is subject to the Textiles Agreement only if the United States has integrated that article into GATT 1994 pursuant to the Textiles Agreement, as set forth in notices published in the Federal Register by the Secretary of Commerce, including the notice published under section 331 of the Uruguay Round Agreements Act [19 USCS para 3591].

(B) For purposes of this paragraph:

(i) The term "Textiles Agreement" means the Agreement on Textiles and Clothing referred to in section 101(d)(4) of the Uruguay Round Agreements Act [19 USCS para 3511(d)(4)].

(ii) The term "GATT 1994" has the meaning given that term in section 2(1)(B) of the Uruguay Round Agreements Act [19 USCS para 3501(1)(B)].

(i) Limited disclosure of confidential business information under protective order

The Commission shall promulgate regulations to provide access to confidential business information under protective order to authorized representatives of interested parties who are parties to an investigation under this section.

Para 2253. Action by President after Determination of Import Injury

(a) In general

(1) (A) After receiving a report under section 202(f) [19 USCS para 2252(f)] containing an affirmative finding regarding serious injury, or the threat thereof, to a domestic industry, the President shall take all appropriate and feasible action within his power which the President determines will facilitate efforts by the domestic industry to make a positive adjustment to import competition and provide greater economic and social benefits than costs.

(B) The action taken by the President under subparagraph (A) shall be to such extent, and for such duration, subject to subsection (e)(1), that the President determines to be appropriate and feasible under such subparagraph.

(C) The interagency trade organization established under section 242(a) of the Trade Expansion Act of 1962 [19 USCS para 1872(a)] shall, with respect to each affirmative determination reported under section 202(f) [19 USCS para 2252(f)], make a recommendation to the President as to what action the President should take under subparagraph (A).

(2) In determining what action to take under paragraph (1), the President shall take into account—

(A) the recommendation and report of the Commission;

(B) the extent to which workers and firms in the domestic industry are—

(i) benefitting from adjustment assistance and other manpower programs, and

(ii) engaged in worker retraining efforts;

(C) the efforts being made, or to be implemented, by the domestic industry (including the efforts included in any adjustment plan or commitment submitted to the Commission under section 202(a) [19 USCS para 2252(a)]) to make a positive adjustment to import competition;

(D) the probable effectiveness of the actions authorized under paragraph (3) to facilitate positive adjustment to import competition;

(E) the short- and long-term economic and social costs of the actions authorized under paragraph (3) relative to their short- and long-term economic and social benefits and other considerations relative to the position of the domestic industry in the United States economy;

(F) other factors related to the national economic interest of the United States, including, but not limited to—

(i) the economic and social costs which would be incurred by taxpayers, communities, and workers if import relief were not provided under this chapter [19 USCS paras 2251 et seq.],

(ii) the effect of the implementation of actions under this section on consumers and on competition in domestic markets for articles, and

(iii) the impact on United States industries and firms as a result of international obligations regarding compensation;

(G) the extent to which there is diversion of foreign exports to the United States market by reason of foreign restraints;

(H) the potential for circumvention of any action taken under this section;

(I) the national security interests of the United States; and

(J) the factors required to be considered by the Commission under section 202(e)(5) [19 USCS para 2252(e)(5)].

(3) The President may, for purposes of taking action under paragraph (1)—

(A) proclaim an increase in, or the imposition of, any duty on the imported article;

(B) proclaim a tariff-rate quota on the article;

(C) proclaim a modification or imposition of any quantitative restriction on the importation of the article into the United States;

(D) implement one or more appropriate adjustment measures, including the provision of trade adjustment assistance under chapter 2 [19 USCS paras 2271 et seq.],

(E) negotiate, conclude, and carry out agreements with foreign countries limiting the export from foreign countries and the import into the United States of such article;

(F) proclaim procedures necessary to allocate among importers by the auction of import licenses quantities of the article that are permitted to be imported into the United States;

(G) initiate international negotiations to address the underlying cause of the increase in imports of the article or otherwise to alleviate the injury or threat thereof;

(H) submit to Congress legislative proposals to facilitate the efforts of the domestic industry to make a positive adjustment to import competition;

(I) take any other action which may be taken by the President under the authority of law and which the President considers appropriate and feasible for purposes of paragraph (1); and

(J) take any combination of actions listed in subparagraphs (A) through (I).

(4) (A) Subject to subparagraph (B), the President shall take action under paragraph (1) within 60 days (50 days if the President has proclaimed provisional relief under section 202(d)(2)(D) [19 USCS para 2252(d)(2)(D)] with respect to the article concerned) after receiving a report from the Commission containing an affirmative determination under section 202(b)(1) [19 USCS para 2252(b)(1)] (or a determination under such section which he considers to be an affirmative determination by reason of section 330(d) of the Tariff Act of 1930 [19 USCS para 1330(d)]).

(B) If a supplemental report is requested under paragraph (5), the President shall take action under paragraph (1) within 30 days after the supplemental report is received, except that, in a case in which the President has proclaimed provisional relief under section 202(d)(2)(D) [19 USCS para 2252(d)(2)(D)] with respect to the article concerned, action by the President under paragraph (1) may not be taken later than the 200th day after the provisional relief was proclaimed.

(5) The President may, within 15 days after the date on which he receives a report from the Commission containing an affirmative determination under section 202(b)(1) [19 USCS para 2252(b)(1)], request additional information from the Commission. The Commission shall, as soon as practicable but in no event more than 30 days after the date on which it receives the President's request, furnish additional information with respect to the industry in a supplemental report.

(b) Reports to Congress

(1) On the day the President takes action under subsection (a)(1), the President shall transmit to Congress a document describing the action and the reasons for taking the action. If the action taken by the President differs from the action required to be recommended by the Commission under section 202(e)(1) [19 USCS para 2252(e)(1)], the President shall state in detail the reasons for the difference.

(2) On the day on which the President decides that there is no appropriate and feasible action to take under subsection (a)(1) with respect to a domestic industry, the President shall transmit to Congress a document that sets forth in detail the reasons for the decision.

(3) On the day on which the President takes any action under subsection (a)(1) that is not reported under paragraph (1), the President shall transmit to Congress a document setting forth the action being taken and the reasons therefor.

(c) Implementation of action recommended by Commission

If the President reports under subsection (b)(1) or (2) that—

(1) the action taken under subsection (a)(1) differs from the action recommended by the Commission under section 202(e)(1) [19 USCS para 2252(e)(1)]; or

(2) no action will be taken under subsection (a)(1) with respect to the domestic industry;

the action recommended by the Commission shall take effect (as provided in subsection (d)(2)) upon the enactment of a joint resolution described in section 152(a)(1)(A) [19 USCS para 2192(a)(1)(A)] within the 90-day period beginning on the date on which the document referred to in subsection (b)(1) or (2) is transmitted to the Congress.

(d) Time for taking effect of certain relief

(1) Except as provided in paragraph (2), any action described in subsection (a)(3)(A), (B), or (C), that is taken under subsection (a)(1) shall take effect within 15 days after the day on which the President proclaims the action, unless the President announces, on the date he decides to take such action, his intention to negotiate one or more agreements described in subsection (a)(3)(E) in which case the action under subsection (a)(3)(A), (B), or (C) shall be proclaimed and take effect within 90 days after the date of such decision.

(2) If the contingency set forth in subsection (c) occurs, the President shall, within 30 days after the date of the enactment of the joint resolution referred to in such subsection, proclaim the action recommended by the Commission under section 202(e)(1) [19 USCS para 2252(e)(1)].

(e) Limitations on actions

(1) (A) Subject to subparagraph (B), the duration of the period in which an action taken under this section may be in effect shall not exceed 4 years. Such period shall include the period, if any, in which provisional relief under section 202(d) [19 USCS para 2252(d)] was in effect.

(B) (i) Subject to clause (ii), the President, after receiving an affirmative determination from the Commission under section 204(c) [19 USCS para 2252(c)] (or, if the Commission is equally divided in its determination, a determination which the President considers to be an affirmative determination of the Commission), may extend the effective period of any action under this section if the President determines that—

(I) the action continues to be necessary to prevent or remedy the serious injury; and

(II) there is evidence that the domestic industry is making a positive adjustment to import competition.

(ii) The effective period of any action under this section, including any extensions thereof, may not, in the aggregate, exceed 8 years.

(2) Action of a type described in subsection (a)(3)(A), (B), or (C) may be taken under subsection (a)(1), under section 202(d)(1)(G) [19 USCS para 2252(d)(1)(G)], or under section 202(d)(2)(D) [19 USCS para 2252(d)(2)(D)] only to the extent the

cumulative impact of such action does not exceed the amount necessary to prevent or remedy the serious injury.

(3) No action may be taken under this section which would increase a rate of duty to (or impose a rate) which is more than 50 percent ad valorem above the rate (if any) existing at the time the action is taken.

(4) Any action taken under this section proclaiming a quantitative restriction shall permit the importation of a quantity or value of the article which is not less than the average quantity or value of such article entered into the United States in the most recent 3 years that are representative of imports of such article and for which data are available, unless the President finds that the importation of a different quantity or value is clearly justified in order to prevent or remedy the serious injury.

(5) An action described in subsection (a)(3)(A), (B), or (C) that has an effective period of more than 1 year shall be phased down at regular intervals during the period in which the action is in effect.

(6) (A) The suspension, pursuant to any action taken under this section, of—
  (i) subheadings 9802.00.60 or 9802.00.80 of the Harmonized Tariff Schedule of the United States with respect to an article; and
  (ii) the designation of any article as an eligible article for purposes of title V;
  shall be treated as an increase in duty.

(B) No proclamation providing for a suspension referred to in subparagraph (A) with respect to any article may be made by the President, nor may any such suspension be recommended by the Commission under section 202(e) [19 USCS para 2252(e)], unless the Commission, in addition to making an affirmative determination under section 202(b)(1) [19 USCS para 2252(b)(1)], determines in the course of its investigation under section 202(b) [19 USCS para 2252(b)] that the serious injury, or threat thereof, substantially caused by imports to the domestic industry producing a like or directly competitive article results from, as the case may be—
  (i) the application of subheading 9802.00.60 or subheading 9802.00.80 of the Harmonized Tariff Schedule of the United States; or
  (ii) the designation of the article as an eligible article for the purposes of title V.

(7) (A) If an article was the subject of an action under subparagraph (A), (B), (C), or (E) of subsection (a)(3), no new action may be taken under any of those subparagraphs with respect to such article for—
  (i) a period beginning on the date on which the previous action terminates that is equal to the period in which the previous action was in effect, or
  (ii) a period of 2 years beginning on the date on which the previous action terminates,
  whichever is greater.

(B) Notwithstanding subparagraph (A), if the previous action under subparagraph (A), (B), (C), or (E) of subsection (a)(3) with respect to an article was in effect for a period of 180 days or less, the President may take a new action under any of those subparagraphs with respect to such article if—
   (i) at least 1 year has elapsed since the previous action went into effect; and
   (ii) an action described in any of those subparagraphs has not been taken with respect to such article more than twice in the 5-year period immediately preceding the date on which the new action with respect to such article first becomes effective.

(f) Certain agreements

(1) If the President takes action under this section other than the implementation of agreements of the type described in subsection (a)(3)(E), the President may, after such action takes effect, negotiate agreements of the type described in subsection (a)(3)(E), and may, after such agreements take effect, suspend or terminate, in whole or in part, any action previously taken.

(2) If an agreement implemented under subsection (a)(3)(E) is not effective, the President may, consistent with the limitations contained in subsection (e), take additional action under subsection (a).

(g) Regulations

(1) The President shall by regulation provide for the efficient and fair administration of all actions taken for the purpose of providing import relief under this chapter [19 USCS paras 2251 et seq.].

(2) In order to carry out an international agreement concluded under this chapter [19 USCS paras 2251 et seq.], the President may prescribe regulations governing the entry or withdrawal from warehouse of articles covered by such agreement. In addition, in order to carry out any agreement of the type described in subsection (a)(3)(E) that is concluded under this chapter [19 USCS paras 2251 et seq.] with one or more countries accounting for a major part of United States imports of the article covered by such agreement, including imports into a major geographic area of the United States, the President may issue regulations governing the entry or withdrawal from warehouse of like articles which are the product of countries not parties to such agreement.

(3) Regulations prescribed under this subsection shall, to the extent practicable and consistent with efficient and fair administration, insure [ensure] against inequitable sharing of imports by a relatively small number of the larger importers.

Para 2254. Monitoring, Modification, and Termination of action

(a) Monitoring

(1) So long as any action taken under section 203 [19 USCS para 2253] remains in effect, the Commission shall monitor developments with respect to the domestic industry, including the progress and specific efforts made by workers and firms in the domestic industry to make a positive adjustment to import competition.

(2) If the initial period during which the action taken under section 203 [19 USCS para 2253] is in effect exceeds 3 years, or if an extension of such action exceeds 3 years, the Commission shall submit a report on the results of the monitoring under paragraph (1) to the President and to the Congress not later than the date that is the mid-point of the initial period, and of each such extension, during which the action is in effect.

(3) In the course of preparing each report under paragraph (2), the Commission shall hold a hearing at which interested persons shall be given a reasonable opportunity to be present, to produce evidence, and to be heard.

(4) Upon request of the President, the Commission shall advise the President of its judgment as to the probable economic effect on the industry concerned of any reduction, modification, or termination of the action taken under section 203 [19 USCS para 2253] which is under consideration.

(b) Reduction, modification, and termination of action

(1) Action taken under section 203 [19 USCS para 2253] may be reduced, modified, or terminated by the President (but not before the President receives the report required under subsection (a)(2)(A)) if the President—

(A) after taking into account any report or advice submitted by the Commission under subsection (a) and after seeking the advice of the Secretary of Commerce and the Secretary of Labor, determines, on the basis that either—

(i) the domestic industry has not made adequate efforts to make a positive adjustment to import competition, or

(ii) the effectiveness of the action taken under section 203 [19 USCS para 2253] has been impaired by changed economic circumstances,

that changed circumstances warrant such reduction, or termination; or

(B) determines, after a majority of the representatives of the domestic industry submits to the President a petition requesting such reduction, modification, or termination on such basis, that the domestic industry has made a positive adjustment to import competition.

(2) Notwithstanding paragraph (1), the President is authorized to take such additional action under section 203 [19 USCS para 2253] as may be necessary to eliminate any circumvention of any action previously taken under such section.

(3) Notwithstanding paragraph (1), the President may, after receipt of a Commission determination under section 129(a)(4) of the Uruguay Round Agreements Act [19 USCS para 3538(a)(4)] and consulting with the Committee on Ways and Means of the House of Representatives and the Committee on Finance of the Senate, reduce, modify, or terminate action taken under section 203 [19 USCS para 2253].

(c) Extension of action

(1) Upon request of the President, or upon petition on behalf of the industry concerned filed with the Commission not earlier than the date which is 9 months, and not later than the date which is 6 months, before the date any action taken under section 203 [19 USCS para 2253] is to terminate, the Commission shall investigate to determine whether action under section 203 [19 USCS para 2253] continues to be necessary to prevent or remedy serious injury and whether there is evidence that the industry is making a positive adjustment to import competition.

(2) The Commission shall publish notice of the commencement of any proceeding under this subsection in the Federal Register and shall, within a reasonable time thereafter, hold a public hearing at which the Commission shall afford interested parties and consumers an opportunity to be present, to present evidence, and to respond to the presentations of other parties and consumers, and otherwise to be heard.

(3) The Commission shall transmit to the President a report on its investigation and determination under this subsection not later than 60 days before the action under section 203 [19 USCS para 2253] is to terminate, unless the President specifies a different date.

(d) Evaluation of effectiveness of action

(1) After any action taken under section 203 [19 USCS para 2253] has terminated, the Commission shall evaluate the effectiveness of the actions in facilitating positive adjustment by the domestic industry to import competition, consistent with the reasons set out by the President in the report submitted to the Congress under section 203(b) [19 USCS para 2253(b)].

(2) During the course of the evaluation conducted under paragraph (1), the Commission shall, after reasonable public notice, hold a hearing on the effectiveness of the action. All interested persons shall have the opportunity to attend such hearing and to present evidence or testimony at such hearing.

(3) A report on the evaluation made under paragraph (1) and the hearings held under paragraph (2) shall be submitted by the Commission to the President and to the Congress by no later than the 180th day after the day on which the actions taken under section 203 [19 USCS para 2253] terminated.

(e) Other provisions

(1) Action by the President under this chapter [19 USCS para 2251 et seq.] may be taken without regard to the provisions of section 126(a) of this Act [19 USCS para 2136(a)] but only after consideration of the relation of such actions to the international obligations of the United States.

(2) If the Commission treats as the domestic industry production located in a major geographic area of the United States under section 202(c)(4)(C) [19 USCS para 2252(c)(4)(C)], then the President shall take into account the geographic concentration of domestic production and of imports in that area in taking any action authorized under paragraph (1).

APPENDIX 4

EC Legislation (Council Regulation (EC) No 3285/94 of 22 December 1994)

[Note: Additional European Regulations governing safeguard measures affecting imports from certain countries have been omitted. These include Council Regulation (EC) 519/94 concerning state trading and former state trading nations, and Council Regulation (EC) 517/94 concerning textile imports from certain third countries.]

COUNCIL REGULATION (EC) No 3285/94 of 22 December 1994 on the common rules for imports and repealing Regulation (EC) No 518/94

THE COUNCIL OF THE EUROPEAN UNION,

Having regard to the Treaty establishing the European Community, and in particular Article 113 thereof,

Having regard to the instruments establishing the common organization of agricultural markets and the instruments concerning processed agricultural products, in particular in so far as they provide for derogation from the general principle that quantitative restrictions or measures having equivalent effect may be replaced solely by the measures provided for in the said instruments,

Having regard to the proposal from the Commission,

Having regard to the opinion of the European Parliament, (1)

Whereas the common commercial policy should be based on uniform principles; whereas Council Regulation (EC) No 518/94 of 7 March 1994 on common rules for imports and repealing Regulation (EEC) No 288/82 (2) is an important part of the policy;

Whereas due account was taken when Regulation (EC) No 518/94 was adopted from the Community's international obligations, particularly those deriving from Article XIX of the General Agreement on Tariffs and Trade (GATT);

Whereas the completion of the Uruguay Round has led to the foundation of the World Trade Organization (WTO); whereas Annex 1A to the Agreement establishing the WTO contains inter alia the General Agreement on Tariffs and Trade 1994 (GATT 1994) and an Agreement on Safeguards;

Whereas the Agreement on Safeguard meets the need to clarify and reinforce the disciplines of GATT 1994, and specifically those of Article XIX; whereas that Agreement requires the elimination of safeguard measures which escape those rules, such as voluntary export restraints, orderly marketing arrangements and any other similar import or export arrangements;

Whereas the Agreement on Safeguards also covers ECSC products; whereas the common rules for imports, especially as regards safeguard measures, therefore also applies to those products without prejudice to any possible measures to apply an agreement specifically concerning ECSC products;

Whereas in the light of these new multilateral rules the common rules for imports should be made clearer and if necessary amended, particularly where the application of safeguard measures is concerned;

Whereas the starting point for the common rules for imports is liberalization of imports, namely the absence of any quantitative restrictions;

Whereas the Commission should be informed by the Member States of any danger created by trends in imports which might call for Community surveillance or the application of safeguard measures;

Whereas in such instances the Commission should examine the terms and conditions under which imports occur, the trend in imports, the various aspects of the economic and trade situations and, where appropriate, the measures to be applied;

Whereas if Community surveillance is applied, release for free circulation of the products concerned should be made subject to presentation of an import document meeting uniform criteria; whereas that document should, on simple application by the importer, be endorsed by the authorities of the Member States within a certain period but without the importer thereby acquiring any right to import; whereas the document should therefore be valid only during such period as the import rules remain unchanged;

Whereas the Member States and the Commission should exchange the information resulting from Community surveillance as fully as possible;

Whereas it falls to the Commission and the Council to adopt the safeguard measures required by the interests of the Community; whereas those interests should be considered as a whole and should in particular encompass the interest of Community producers, users and consumers;

Whereas safeguard measures against a Member of the WTO may be considered only if the product in question is imported into the Community in such greatly increased quantities and on such terms or conditions as to cause, or threaten to cause, serious injury to Community producers of like or directly competing products, unless international obligations permit derogation from this rule;

Whereas the terms 'serious injury', 'threat of serious injury' and 'Community producers' should be defined and more precise criteria for determining injury be established;

Whereas an investigation must precede the application of any safeguard measure, subject to the reservation that the Commission be allowed in urgent cases to apply provisional measures;

Whereas there should be more detailed provisions on the opening of investigations, the checks and inspections required, access by exporter countries and interested parties to the information gathered, hearings for the parties involved and the opportunities for those parties to submit their views;

Whereas the provisions on investigations introduced by this Regulation are without prejudice to Community or national rules concerning professional secrecy;

Whereas it is also necessary to set time limits for the initiation of investigations and for determinations as to whether or not measures are appropriate, with a view to ensuring that such determinations are made quickly, in order to increase legal certainty for the economic operators concerned;

Whereas in cases in which safeguard measures take the form of a quota the level of the latter should be set in principle no lower than the average level of imports over a representative period of at least three years;

Whereas in cases in which a quota is allocated among supplier countries each country's quota may be determined by agreement with the countries themselves or by taking as a reference the level of imports over a representative period; whereas derogations from these rules should nevertheless be possible where there is serious injury and a disproportionate increase in imports, provided that due consultation under the auspices of the WTO Committee on Safeguards takes place;

Whereas the maximum duration of safeguard measures should be determined and specific provisions regarding extension, progressive liberalization and reviews of such measures be laid down;

Whereas the circumstances in which products originating in a developing country Member of the WTO should be exempt from safeguard measures should be established;

Whereas surveillance or safeguard measures confined to one or more regions of the Community may prove more suitable than measures applying to the whole Community; whereas, however, such measures should be authorized only exceptionally and where no alternative exists; whereas it is necessary to ensure that such measures are temporary and cause the minimum of disruption to the operation of the internal market;

Whereas in the interests of uniformity in rules for imports, the formalities to be carried out by importers should be simplified and made identical regardless of the place where the goods clear customs; whereas it is therefore desirable to provide that any formalities should be carried out using forms corresponding to the specimen annexed to the Regulation;

Whereas import documents issued in connection with Community surveillance measures should be valid throughout the Community irrespective of the Member State of issue;

Whereas the textile products covered by Council Regulation (EC) No 517/94 of 7 March 1994 on common rules for imports of textile products from certain third countries not covered by bilateral agreements, protocols or other arrangements, or by other specific Community import rules (3) are subject to special treatment at Community and international level, except for the products listed in Annex II which are integrated into GATT 1994; whereas they should therefore be excluded from the scope of this Regulation;

Whereas the provisions of this Regulation are applicable without prejudice to Articles 77, 81, 244, 249 and 280 of the Act of Accession of Spain and Portugal;

Whereas national restrictions with respect to products falling under the ECSC Treaty will be progressively dismantled in accordance with the provisions of the WTO;

Whereas Regulation (EC) No 518/94 should consequently be repealed,

HAS ADOPTED THIS REGULATION

Title I. General Principles

Article 1

1. This Regulation applies to imports of products originating in third countries, except for:

- — textile products covered by Regulation (EC) No 517/94, other than the products listed in Annex II in so far as those products originate in a country which is a member of the WTO,
- — the products originating in certain third countries listed in Council Regulation (EC) No 519/94 on common rules for imports from certain third countries (4).

2. The products referred to in paragraph 1 shall be freely imported into the Community and accordingly, without prejudice to the safeguard measures which may be taken under Title V, shall not be subject to any quantitative restrictions.

Title II. Community Information and Consultation Procedure

Article 2

The Commission shall be informed by the Member States should trends in imports appear to call for surveillance or safeguard measures. This information shall contain the evidence available, as determined on the basis of the criteria laid down in Article 10. The Commission shall immediately pass this information on to all the Member States.

Article 3

Consultations may be held either at the request of a Member State or on the initiative of the Commission. They shall take place within eight working days of the Commission receiving the information provided for in Article 2 and, in any event, before the introduction of any Community surveillance or safeguard measure.

Article 4

1. Consultation shall take place within an Advisory Committee, hereinafter called 'the Committee', made up of representatives of each Member State with a representative of the Commission as chairman.

2. The Committee shall meet when convened by its chairman. He shall provide the Member States with all relevant information as promptly as possible.

3. Consultations shall cover in particular:
   - terms and conditions of import, import trends and the various aspects of the economic and commercial situation with regard to the product in question,
   - the measures, if any, to be taken.

4. Consultations may be conducted in writing if necessary. The Commission shall in this event inform the Member States, which may express their opinion or request oral consultations within a period of five to eight working days, to be decided by the Commission.

Title III. Community Investigation Procedure

Article 5

1. Without prejudice to Article 8, the Community investigation procedure shall be implemented before any safeguard measure is applied.

2. Using as a basis the factors described in Article 10, the investigation shall seek to determine whether imports of the product in question are causing or threatening to cause serious injury to the Community producers concerned.

3. The following definitions shall apply:

(a) 'serious injury' means a significant overall impairment in the position of Community producers,

(b) 'threat of serious injury' means serious injury that is clearly imminent;

(c) 'Community producers' means the producers as a whole of the like or directly competing products operating within the territory of the Community, or those whose collective output of the like or directly competing products constitutes a major proportion of the total Community production of those products.

Article 6

1. Where after consultations referred to in Article 3, it is apparent to the Commission that there is sufficient evidence to justify the initiation of an investigation, the Commission shall:

(a) initiate an investigation within one month of receipt of information from a Member State and publish a notice in the Official Journal of the European Communities; such notice shall give a summary of the information received, and stipulate that all relevant information is to be communicated to the

Commission; it shall state the period within which interested parties may make known their views in writing and submit information, if such views and information are to be taken into account during the investigation; it shall also state the period within which interested parties may apply to be heard orally by the Commission in accordance with paragraph 4;

(b) commence the investigation, acting in cooperation with the Member States.

2. The Commission shall seek all information it deems to be necessary and, where it considers it appropriate, after consulting the Committee, endeavour to check this information with importers, traders, agents, producers, trade associations and organizations.

The Commission shall be assisted in this task by staff of the Member State on whose territory these checks are being carried out, provided that Member State so wishes.

Interested parties which have come forward pursuant to paragraph 1 (a) and representatives of the exporting country may, upon written request, inspect all information made available to the Commission in connection with the investigation other than internal documents prepared by the authorities of the Community or its Member States, provided that that information is relevant to the presentation of their case and not confidential within the meaning of Article 9 and that it is used by the Commission in the investigation.

Interested parties which have come forward may communicate their views on the information in question to the Commission; those views may be taken into consideration where they are backed by sufficient evidence.

3. The Member States shall supply the Commission, at its request and following procedures laid down by it, with the information at their disposal on developments in the market of the product being investigated.

4. The Commission may hear the interested parties. Such parties must be heard where they have made a written application within the period laid down in the notice published in the Official Journal of the European Communities, showing that they are actually likely to be affected by the outcome of the investigation and that there are special reasons for them to be heard orally.

5. When information is not supplied within the time limits set by this Regulation or by the Commission pursuant to this Regulation, or the investigation is significantly impeded, findings may be made on the basis of the facts available. Where the Commission finds that any interested party or third party has supplied it with false or misleading information, it shall disregard the information and may make use of facts available.

6. Where it appears to the Commission, after the consultation referred to in Article 3, that there is insufficient evidence to justify an investigation, it shall inform the Member States of its decision within one month of receipt of the information from the Member States.

Article 7

1. At the end of the investigation, the Commission shall submit a report on the results to the Committee.

2. Where the Commission considers, within nine months of the initiation of the investigation, that no Community surveillance or safeguard measures are necessary, the investigation shall be terminated within a month, the Committee having first been consulted. The decision to terminate the investigation, stating the main conclusions of the investigation and a summary of the reasons therefor, shall be published in the Official Journal of the European Communities.

3. If the Commission considers that Community surveillance or safeguard measures are necessary, it shall take the necessary decisions in accordance with Titles IV and V, no later than nine months from the initiation of the investigation. In exceptional circumstances, this time limit may be extended by a further maximum period of two months; the Commission shall then publish a notice in the Official Journal of the European Communities setting forth the duration of the extension and a summary of the reasons therefor.

Article 8

1. The provisions of this Title shall not preclude the use, at any time, of surveillance measures in accordance with Articles 11 to 15 or provisional safeguard measures in accordance with Articles 16, 17 and 18.

Provisional safeguard measures shall be applied:

— in critical circumstances where delay would cause damage which it would be difficult to repair, making immediate action necessary, and

— where a preliminary determination provides clear evidence that increased imports have caused or are threatening to cause serious injury.

2. The duration of such measures shall not exceed 200 days.

3. Provisional safeguard measures should take the form of an increase in the existing level of customs duty (whether the latter is zero or higher) if such action is likely to prevent or repair the serious injury.

4. The Commission shall immediately conduct whatever investigation measures are still necessary.

5. Should the provisional safeguard measures be repealed because no serious injury or threat of serious injury exists, the customs duties collected as a result of the provisional measures shall be automatically refunded as soon as possible. The procedure laid down in Article 235 et seq of Council Regulation (EEC) No 2913/92 of 12 October 1992 establishing the Community Customs Code (5) shall apply.

Article 9

1. Information received pursuant to this Regulation shall be used only for the purpose for which it was requested.

2. (a) Neither the Council, nor the Commission, nor the Member States, nor the officials of any of these shall reveal any information of a confidential nature received pursuant to this Regulation, or any information provided on a confidential basis without specific permission from the supplier of such information.

   (b) Each request for confidentiality shall state the reasons why the information is confidential.

However, if it appears that a request for confidentiality is unjustified and if the supplier of the information wishes neither to make it public nor to authorize its disclosure in general terms or in the form of a summary, the information concerned may be disregarded.

3. Information shall in any case by considered to be confidential if its disclosure is likely to have a significantly adverse effect upon the supplier or the source of such information.

4. The preceding paragraphs shall not preclude reference by the Community authorities to general information and in particular to reasons on which decisions taken pursuant to this Regulation are based. The said authorities shall, however, take into account the legitimate interest of legal and natural persons concerned that their business secrets should not be divulged.

Article 10

1. Examination of the trend of imports, of the conditions in which they take place and of serious injury or threat of serious injury to Community producers resulting from such imports shall cover in particular the following factors:

(a) the volume of imports, in particular where there has been a significant increase, either in absolute terms or relative to production or consumption in the Community;

(b) the price of imports, in particular where there has been a significant price undercutting as compared with the price of a like product in the Community;

(c) the consequent impact on Community producers as indicated by trends in certain economic factors such as:

— production,
— capacity utilization,
— stocks,
— sales,
— market share,
— prices (i.e. depression of prices or prevention of price increases which would normally have occurred),
— profits,
— return on capital employed,
— cash flow,
— employment;

— factors other than trends in imports which are causing or may have caused injury to the Community producers concerned.

2. Where a threat of serious injury is alleged, the Commission shall also examine whether it is clearly foreseeable that a particular situation is likely to develop into actual injury. In this regard account may be taken of factors such as:

(a) the rate of increase of the exports to the Community;

(b) export capacity in the country of origin or export, as it stands or is likely to be in the foreseeable future, and the likelihood that that capacity will be used to export to the Community.

TITLE IV. SURVEILLANCE

Article 11

1. Where the trend in imports of a product originating in a third country covered by this Regulation threatens to cause injury to Community producers, and where the interests of the Community so require, import of that product may be subject, as appropriate, to:

(a) retrospective Community surveillance carried out in accordance with the provisions laid down in the decision referred to in paragraph 2,

(b) prior Community surveillance carried out in accordance with Article 12.

2. The decision to impose surveillance shall be taken by the Commission according to the procedure laid down in Article 16 (7) and (8).

3. The surveillance measures shall have a limited period of validity. Unless otherwise provided, they shall cease to be valid at the end of the second six-month period following the six months in which the measures were introduced.

Article 12

1. Products under prior Community surveillance may be put into free circulation only on production of an import document. Such document shall be endorsed by the competent authority designated by Member States, free of charge, for any quantity requested and within a maximum of five working days of receipt by the national competent authority of a declaration by any Community importer, regardless of his place of business in the Community. This declaration shall be deemed to have been received by the national competent authority no later than three working days after submission, unless it is proven otherwise.

2. The import document and the declaration by the importer shall be made out on a form corresponding to the model in Annex I.

Additional information to that provided for in the aforementioned form may be required. Such information shall be specified in the decision to impose surveillance.

3. The import document shall be valid throughout the Community, regardless of the Member State of issue.

4. A finding that the unit price at which the transaction is effected exceeds that indicated in the import document by less than 5 % or that the total value or quantity of the products presented for import exceeds the value or quantity given in the import document by less than 5 % shall not preclude the release for free circulation of the product in question. The Commission, having heard the opinions expressed in the Committee and taking account of the nature of the products and other special features of the transactions concerned, may fix a different percentage, which, however, should not normally exceed 10 %.

5. Import documents may be used only for such time as arrangements for liberalization of imports remain in force in respect of the transactions concerned. Such import documents may not in any event be used beyond the expiry of a period which shall be laid down at the same time and by means of the same procedure as the imposition of surveillance, and shall take account of the nature of the products and other special features of the transactions.

6. Where the decision taken pursuant to Article 11 so requires, the origin of products under Community surveillance must be proved by a certificate of origin. This paragraph shall not affect other provisions concerning the production of any such certificate.

7. Where the product under prior Community surveillance is subject to regional safeguard measures in a Member State, the import authorization granted by that Member State may replace the import document.

Article 13

Where import of a product has not been made subject to prior Community surveillance within eight working days of the end of consultations, the Commission, in accordance with Article 18, may introduce surveillance confined to imports into one or more regions of the Community.

Article 14

1. Products under regional surveillance may be put into free circulation in the region concerned only on production of an import document. Such document shall be endorsed by the competent authority designated by the Member State(s) concerned, free of charge, for any quantity requested and within a maximum of five working days of receipt by the national competent authority of a declaration by any Community importer, regardless of his place of business in the Community. This declaration shall be deemed to have been received by the national competent authority no later than three working days after submission, unless it is proven otherwise. Import documents may be used only for such time as arrangements for imports remain liberalized in respect of the transactions concerned.

2. The import document and the declaration by the importer shall be made out on a form corresponding to the model in Annex I.

Additional information to that provided in the aforementioned form may be required. Such particulars shall be specified in the decision to impose surveillance.

Article 15

1. Member States shall communicate to the Commission within the first 10 days of each month in the case of Community or regional surveillance:

(a) in the case of prior surveillance, details of the sums of money (calculated on the basis of cif prices) and quantities of goods in respect of which import documents were issued or endorsed during the preceding period;
(b) in every case, details of imports during the period preceding the period referred to in subparagraph (a).

The information supplied by Member States shall be broken down by product and by country.

Different provisions may be laid down at the same time and by the same procedure as the surveillance arrangements.

2. Where the nature of the products or special circumstances so require, the Commission may, at the request of a Member State or on its own initiative, amend the timetables for submitting this information.

3. The Commission shall inform the Member States accordingly.

TITLE V. SAFEGUARD MEASURES

Article 16

1. Where a product is imported into the Community in such greatly increased quantities and/or on such terms or conditions as to cause, or threaten to cause, serious injury to Community producers, the Commission, in order to safeguard the interests of the Community, may, acting at the request of a Member State or on its own initiative:.

(a) limit the period of validity of import documents within the meaning of Article 12 to be endorsed after the entry into force of this measure;
(b) alter the import rules for the product in question by making its release for free circulation conditional on production of an import authorization, the granting of which shall be governed by such provisions and subject to such limits as the Commission shall lay down

The measures referred to in (a) and (b) shall take effect immediately.

2. As regards Members of the WTO, the measures referred to in paragraph 1 shall be taken only when the two conditions indicated in the first subparagraph of that paragraph are met.

3. (a) If establishing a quota, account shall be taken in particular of:
— the desirability of maintaining, as far as possible, traditional trade flows,

— the volume of goods exported under contracts concluded on normal terms and conditions before the entry into force of a safeguard measure within the meaning of this Title, where such contracts have been notified to the Commission by the Member State concerned,

— the need to avoid jeopardizing achievement of the aim pursued in establishing the quota.

(b) Any quota shall not be set lower than the average level of imports over the last three representative years for which statistics are available unless a different level is necessary to prevent or remedy serious injury.

4. (a) In cases in which a quota is allocated among supplier countries, allocation may be agreed with those of them having a substantial interest in supplying the product concerned for import into the Community.

Failing this, the quota shall be allocated among the supplier countries in proportion to their share of imports into the Community of the product concerned during a previous representative period, due account being taken of any specific factors which may have affected or may be affecting the trade in the product.

(b) Provided that its obligation to see that consultations are conducted under the auspices of the WTO Committee on Safeguards is not disregarded, the Community may nevertheless depart from this method of allocation in case of serious injury if imports originating in one or more supplier countries have increased in disproportionate percentage in relation to the total increase of imports of the product concerned over a previous representative period.

5. (a) The measures referred to in this Article shall apply to every product which is put into free circulation after their entry into force. In accordance with Article 18 they may be confined to one or more regions of the Community.

(b) However, such measures shall not prevent the release for free circulation of products already on their way to the Community provided that the destination of such products cannot be changed and that those products which, pursuant to Articles 11 and 12, may be put into free circulation only in production of an import document are in fact accompanied by such a document.

6. Where intervention by the Commission has been requested by a Member State, the Commission shall take a decision within a maximum of five working days of receipt of such a request.

7. Any decision taken by the Commission pursuant to this Article shall be communicated to the Council and to the Member States. Any Member State may, within one month following the day of such communication, refer the decision to the Council.

8. If a Member State refers the Commission's decision to the Council, the Council, acting by a qualified majority, may confirm, amend or revoke that decision

If, within three months of the referral of the matter to the Council, the Council has not taken a decision, the decision taken by the Commission shall be deemed revoked.

Article 17

Where the interests of the Community so require, the Council, acting by a qualified majority on a proposal from the Commission drawn up in accordance with the terms of Title III, may adopt appropriate measures to prevent a product being imported into the Community in such greatly increased quantities and/or on such terms or conditions as to cause, or threaten to cause, serious injury to Community producers of like or directly competing products.

Article 16

(2), (3), (4) and (5) shall apply.

Article 18

Where it emerges, primarily on the basis of the factors referred to in Article 10, that the conditions laid down for the adoption of measures pursuant to Articles 11 and 16 are met in one or more regions of the Community, the Commission, after having examined alternative solutions, may exceptionally authorize the application of surveillance or safeguard measures limited to the region(s) concerned if it considers that such measures applied at that level are more appropriate than measures applied throughout the Community.

These measures must be temporary and must disrupt the operation of the internal market as little as possible.

The measures shall be adopted in accordance with the provisions laid down in Articles 11 and 16 respectively.

Article 19

No safeguard measure may be applied to a product originating in a developing country Member of the WTO as long as that country's share of Community imports of the product concerned does not exceed 3 %, provided that developing country Members with less than a 3 % import share collectively account for not more than 9 % of total Community imports of the product concerned.

Article 20

1. The duration of safeguard measures must be limited to the period of time necessary to prevent or remedy serious injury and to facilitate adjustment on the part of Community producers. The period should not exceed four years, including the duration of any provisional measure.

2. Such initial period may be extended, except in the case of the measures referred to in Article 16 (4) (b), provided it is determined that:

— the safeguard measure continues to be necessary to prevent or remedy serious injury,

— and there is evidence that Community producers are adjusting.

3. Extensions shall be adopted in accordance with the terms of Title III and using the same producers as the initial measures. A measure so extended shall not be more restrictive than it was at the end of the initial period.

4. If the duration of the measure exceeds one year, the measure must be progressively liberalized at regular intervals during the period of application, including the period of extension.

5. The total period of application of a safeguard measure, including the period of application of any provisional measures, the initial period of application and any prorogation thereof, may not exceed eight years.

Article 21

1. While any surveillance or safeguard measure applied in accordance with Titles IV and V is in operation, consultations shall be held within the Committee, either at the request of a Member State or on the initiative of the Commission. If the duration of a safeguard measure exceeds three years, the Commission shall seek such consultations no later than the mid-point of the period of application of that measure. The purpose of such consultations shall be:

(a) to examine the effects of the measure;
(b) to determine whether and in what manner it is appropriate to accelerate the pace of liberalization;
(c) to ascertain whether its application is still necessary.

2. Where, as a result of the consultations referred to in paragraph 1, the Commission considers that any surveillance or safeguard measure referred to in Articles 11, 13, 16, 17 and 18 should be revoked or amended, it shall proceed as follows:

(a) where the measure was enacted by the Council, the Commission shall propose to the Council that it be revoked or amended. The Council shall act by a qualified majority;
(b) in all other cases, the Commission shall amend or revoke Community safeguard and surveillance measures.

Where the decision relates to regional surveillance measures, it shall apply from the sixth day following that of its publication in the Official Journal of the European Communities.

Article 22

1. Where imports of a product have already been subject to a safeguard measure no further such measure shall be applied to that product until a period equal to the

duration of the previous measure has elapsed. Such period shall not be less than two years.

2. Notwithstanding paragraph 1, a safeguard measure of 180 days or less may be reimposed for a product if:

(a) at least one year has elapsed since the date of introduction of a safeguard measure on the import of that product; and

(b) such a safeguard measure has not been applied to the same product more than twice in the five-year period immediately preceding the date of introduction of the measure.

Title VI. Final Provisions

Article 23

Where the interests of the Community so require, the Council, acting by a qualified majority on a proposal from the Commission, may adopt appropriate measures to allow the rights and obligations of the Community or of all its Member States, in particular those relating to trade in commodities, to be exercised and fulfilled at international level.

Article 24

1. This Regulation shall not preclude the fulfilment of obligations arising from special rules contained in agreements concluded between the Community and third countries.

2. (a) Without prejudice to other Community provisions, this Regulation shall not preclude the adoption or application by Member States:

(i) of prohibitions, quantitative restrictions or surveillance measures on grounds of public morality, public policy or public security; the protection of health and life of humans, animals or plants, the protection of national treasures possessing artistic, historic or archaeological value, or the protection of industrial and commercial property;

(ii) of special formalities concerning foreign exchange;

(iii) of formalities introduced pursuant to international agreements in accordance with the Treaty.

(b) The Member States shall inform the Commission of the measures or formalities they intend to introduce or amend in accordance with this paragraph. In the event of extreme urgency, the national measures or formalities in question shall be communicated to the Commission immediately upon their adoption.

Article 25

1. This Regulation shall be without prejudice to the operation of the instruments establishing the common organization of agricultural markets or of Community or

national administrative provisions derived therefrom or of the specific instruments applicable to goods resulting from the processing of agricultural products; it shall operate by way of complement to those instruments.

2. However, in the case of products covered by the instruments referred to in paragraph 1, Articles 11 to 15 and 22 shall not apply to those in respect of which the Community rules on trade with third countries require the production of a licence or other import document.

Articles 16, 18 and 21 to 24 shall not apply to those products in respect of which such rules provide for the application of quantitative import restrictions.

Article 26

1. Residual national restrictions relating to products covered by the ECSC Treaty shall be progressively dismantled in accordance with the provisions of the WTO.

2. Until 31 December 1995, Spain and Portugal may maintain the quantitative restrictions on agricultural products referred to in Articles 77, 81, 244, 249 and 280 of the Act of Accession.

Article 27

Regulation (EC) No 518/94 is hereby repealed. References to the repealed Regulation shall be understood as referring to this Regulation.

Article 28

This Regulation shall enter into force on 1 January 1995.

This Regulation shall be binding in its entirety and directly applicable in all Member States.

APPENDIX 5

National Legislation Notified to the Committee on Safeguards

[Note: excerpted from Report (2005) of the Committee on Safeguards to the Council for Trade in Goods, Annex 1, 8 November 2005.]

Safeguards Legislative Notifications[1]

Member	Notification Provided
Albania	G/SG/N/1/ALB/1 (*)
Angola	None
Antigua and Barbuda	None
Argentina	G/SG/N/1/ARG/3 + Suppl.1 (*)
Armenia	G/SG/N/1/ARM/1
Australia	G/SG/N/1/AUS/2
Bahrain	G/SG/N/1/BHR/1 (*)
Bangladesh	G/SG/N/1/BGD/1
Barbados	G/SG/N/1/BRB/1 (*)
Belize	None
Benin	G/SG/N/1/BEN/1 + Corr.1 (Corr.1—French only) (*)
Bolivia	G/SG/N/1/BOL/1 + Suppl.1 (*)
Botswana	G/SG/N/1/BWA/1 (*)
Brazil	G/SG/N/1/BRA/3 + Suppl.1
Brunei Darussalam	G/SG/N/1/BRN/1 (*)
Bulgaria	G/SG/N/1/BGR/1
Burkina Faso	None
Burundi	G/SG/N/1/BUR/1 (*)
Cambodia	None
Cameroon	None
Canada	G/SG/N/1/CAN/3
Central African Republic	None

[1] The 25 member states of the European Communities are not indicated individually in this table and are counted as 1 under the entry "European Communities" for the purpose of this table.

Safeguards Legislative Notifications (*cont.*)

Member	Notification Provided
Chad	G/SG/N/1/TCD/1 (*)
Chile	G/SG/N/1/CHL/2
China	G/SG/N/1/CHN/2 + Suppl.1–4
Colombia	G/SG/N/1/COL/2
Congo	None
Congo, Dem. Republic	None
Costa Rica	G/SG/N/1/CRI/3
Côte d'Ivoire	G/SG/N/1/CIV/1 (*)
Croatia	G/SG/N/1/HRV/2 + Add. 1
Cuba	G/SG/N/1/CUB/1
Djibouti	None
Dominica	G/SG/N/1/DMA/1 (*)
Dominican Republic	G/SG/N/1/DOM/2 + Corr.1 (Corr.1—Spanish only)
Ecuador	G/SG/N/1/ECU/3
Egypt	G/SG/N/1/EGY/2
El Salvador	G/SG/N/1/SLV/2
European Communities	G/SG/N/1/EEC/1 + Suppl.1&2
Fiji	G/SG/N/1/FJI/1 (*)
Former Yugoslav Republic of Macedonia	G/SG/N/1/MKD/1 + Corr.1 + Suppl.1
Gabon	None
Gambia, The	None
Georgia	G/SG/N/1/GEO/1 (*)
Ghana	G/SG/N/1/GHA/1 (*)
Grenada	None
Guatemala	G/SG/N/1/GTM/2
Guinea Bissau	None
Guinea, Republic of	G/SG/N/1/GIN/1 (*)
Guyana	None
Haiti	G/SG/N/1/HTI/1 (*)
Honduras	G/SG/N/1/HND/2
Hong Kong, China	G/SG/N/1/HKG/1 (*)
Iceland	G/SG/N/1/ISL/1 (*)
India	G/SG/N/1/IND/2 + Suppl.1
Indonesia	G/SG/N/1/IDN/2

(*cont.*)

Member	Notification Provided
Israel	G/SG/N/1/ISR/1 + Corr. 1
Jamaica	G/SG/N/1/JAM/2 + Corr. 1
Japan	G/SG/N/1/JPN/2 + Corr.1 & Suppl.1 G/SG/N/1/JPN/3
Jordan	G/SG/N/1/JOR/2 + Corr. 1&2
Kenya	G/SG/N/1/KEN/1 (*)
Korea	G/SG/N/1/KOR/5
Kuwait	None
Kyrgyz Republic	G/SG/N/1/KGZ/1
Lesotho	G/SG/N/1/LSO/1 (*)
Liechtenstein	G/SG/N/1/LIE/1 (*)
Macao, China	G/SG/N/1/MAC/2
Madagascar	G/SG/N/1/MDG/1 (*)
Malawi	G/SG/N/1/MWI/1 (*)
Malaysia	G/SG/N/1/MYS/1 (*)
Maldives	G/SG/N/1/MDV/1 (*)
Mali	None
Mauritania	None
Mauritius	G/SG/N/1/MUS/1 (*)
Mexico	G/SG/N/1/MEX/1 + Suppl.1 & Corr.1
Moldova	G/SG/N/1/MDA/1
Mongolia	G/SG/N/1/MNG/1 (*)
Morocco	G/SG/N/1/MAR/1 (*)
Mozambique	None
Myanmar	G/SG/N/1/MYM/1 (*)
Namibia	G/SG/N/1/NAM/2 (*)
Nepal	None
New Zealand	G/SG/N/1/NZL/1
Nicaragua	G/SG/N/1/NIC/1
Niger	None
Nigeria	G/SG/N/1/NGA/1 (*)
Norway	G/SG/N/1/NOR/3
Oman	G/SG/N/1/OMN/1 (*)
Pakistan	G/SG/N/1/PAK/3
Panama	G/SG/N/1/PAN/1
Papua New Guinea	None
Paraguay	G/SG/N/1/PRY/2

Safeguards Legislative Notifications (*cont.*)

Member	Notification Provided
Peru	G/SG/N/1/PER/2 + Suppl. 1 & 2
Philippines	G/SG/N/1/PHL/2
Qatar	G/SG/N/1/QAT/1 (*)
Romania	G/SG/N/1/ROM/1
Rwanda	None
Saint Kitts & Nevis	None
Saint Lucia	G/SG/N/1/LCA/1 (*)
Saint Vincent & Grenadines	None
Senegal	G/SG/N/1/SEN/1 (*)
Sierra Leone	None
Singapore	G/SG/N/1/SGP/1 (*)
Solomon Islands	None
South Africa	G/SG/N/1/ZAF/1 + ZAF/2
Sri Lanka	G/SG/N/1/LKA/1 (*)
Suriname	G/SG/N/1/SUR/1 (*)
Swaziland	None
Switzerland	G/SG/N/1/CHE/1 (*)
Separate Customs Territory of Taiwan, Penghu, Kinmen and Matsu	G/SG/N/1/TPKM/2 + Suppl.1
Tanzania	None
Thailand	G/SG/N/1/THA/2
Togo	None
Trinidad and Tobago	G/SG/N/1/TTO/1 (*)
Tunisia	G/SG/N/1/TUN/2
Turkey	G/SG/N/1/TUR/3
Uganda	G/SG/N/1/UGA/1 (*)
United Arab Emirates	G/SG/N/1/ARE/1 (*)
United States	G/SG/N/1/USA/1
Uruguay	G/SG/N/1/URY/1 + Supp.1 & Corr.1 (Corr.1—Spanish only)
Venezuela	G/SG/N/1/VEN/2
Zambia	G/SG/N/1/ZMB/1 (*)
Zimbabwe	G/SG/N/1/ZWE/2 (*)

—*Notification* accompanied with the mark (*) is a "nil" notification.
—*"None"* means that no notification has been submitted.

APPENDIX 6

Safeguard Measures Notified to the Committee on Safeguards Since the Inception of the WTO

[Note: excerpted from annual reports of the Committee on Safeguards to the Council for Trade in Goods, 2000–2005.]

SUMMARY OF NOTIFICATIONS OF INITIATIONS AND OUTCOMES OF SAFEGUARD INVESTIGATIONS AND OF APPLICATION OF SAFEGUARD MEASURES 1 JANUARY 1995–9 NOVEMBER 2000

Member & Investigation	Initiation date	Effective date of provisional measure, if any	Outcome of injury investigation	Decision on applying definitive measure	Effective date and type of definitive measure, if any	Termination
Argentina						
Footwear	25.02.97 (G/SG/N/6/ARG/1 & Corr.1 & Suppl.1)	25.02.97 (G/SG/N/7/ARG/1 & Corr.1 & Suppl.1)	Affirmative (G/SG/N/8/ARG/1 /Suppl.1 & Suppl.2)	Affirmative (G/SG/N/10/ARG/1 & Corr.1 & Suppl.1 & Suppl.2 & Suppl.3 & Suppl.4 & Suppl.5)	13.09.97 Tariff increase 16.11.98 Converted to tariff rate quota. Extended in July 2000 (G/SG/N/10/ARG/1/Suppl.5)	

Summary of Notifications of Safeguard Investigations and of Safeguard Measures 1 January 1995–9 November 2000 (*cont.*)

Member & Investigation	Initiation date	Effective date of provisional measure, if any	Outcome of injury investigation	Decision on applying definitive measure	Effective date and type of definitive measure, if any	Termination
Toys	03.02.98 (G/SG/N/6/ARG/2 & Suppl.1)	N/A	Ongoing	N/A	N/A	
Motorcycles	22.07.2000 (G/SG/N/6/ARG/3 & Suppl.1)	N/A	Ongoing	N/A	N/A	
Australia						
Swine meat	26.06.98 (G/SG/N/6/AUS/1 & Suppl.1)	N/A	Affirmative (G/SG/N/8/AUS/1)	Negative	N/A	Investigation terminated (G/SG/N/9/AUS/1)
Brazil						
Toys	18.06.96 (G/SG/N/6/BRA/1)	After 18.06.96 (G/SG/N/7/BRA/1)	Affirmative (G/SG/N/8/BRA/1)	Affirmative (G/SG/N/10/BRA/1 & (G/SG/N/10/BRA/2)	10.01.97 Tariff increase. Extended in December 1999 (G/SG/N/10/ BRA/2/Suppl.1)	
Chile						
Tyres	30.08.99 (G/SG/N/6/CHL/1)	N/A	Negative	Negative	N/A	Investigation terminated (G/SG/N//9/CHL/1)
Wheat, wheat flour, cane/beet sugar, edible vegetable oils	30.09.99(G/SG/N/ 6/CHL/2& Suppl.1)	26.11.99 (G/SG/N/7/CHL/2 & Suppl.1)	Affirmative (G/SG/N/8/CHL/1)	Affirmative (G/SG/N/10/CHL/1 & Suppl.1)	22.01.2000 Tariff increase	

Socks (synthetic and cotton)	09.02.2000 (G/SG/N/6/CHL/3)	07/2000 Synthetic socks only (G/SG/N/7/CHL/4)	N/A	Negative	N/A	Investigation on cotton socks terminated (G/SG/N/9/CHL/2)
Liquid & powdered milk	21.06.2000(G/SG/N/6/CHL/4)	13.07.2000 (G/SG/N/7/CHL/3 & Suppl.1)	Ongoing	N/A	N/A	
Colombia						
Taxis	28.06.99 (G/SG/N/6/COL/1)	N/A	N/A	Negative	N/A	Investigation terminated 29.02.2000 (G/SG/N/9/COL/1)
Czech Republic						
Cane/Beet sugar	03.03.99 (G/SG/N/6/CZE/1 & Suppl.1)	12.03.99 (G/SG/N/7/CZE/1 & Suppl.1)	Affirmative (G/SG/N/8/CZE/1 & Corr.1 & Suppl.1)	Affirmative (G/SG/N/10/CZE/1 & Corr.1 & Suppl.1)	20.09.99 Tariff rate quota	
Ecuador						
Sandals	12.01.99 (G/SG/N/6/ECU/1)	N/A	Ongoing	N/A	N/A	
Matches	28.10.99 (G/SG/N/6/ECU/2)	N/A	Ongoing	N/A	N/A	
Egypt						
Safety matches	05.08.98 (G/SG/N/6/EGY/1)	After 05.08.98 (G/SG/N/7/EGY/1)	Affirmative (G/SG/N/8/EGY/1)	Affirmative (G/SG/N/10/EGY/1)	19.02.99 Tariff increase	
Common fluorescent lamps	19.09.99 (G/SG/N/6/EGY/2)	N/A	Affirmative (G/SG/N/8/EGY/2 & Suppl.1)	Affirmative (G/SG/N/10/EGY/2 & Suppl.1)	27.02.2000 Tariff increase	
Powdered milk	25.09.2000 (G/SG/N/6/EGY/3)	26.09.2000 (G/SG/N/7/EGY/2)	Ongoing	N/A	N/A	
El Salvador						
Pork	19.01.2000 (G/SG/N/6/SLV/1)	N/A	Ongoing	N/A	N/A	
Rice	26.06.2000 (G/SG/N/6/SLV/2)	N/A	Ongoing	N/A	N/A	

Summary of Notifications of Safeguard Investigations and of Safeguard Measures 1 January 1995–9 November 2000 (*cont.*)

Member & Investigation	Initiation date	Effective date of provisional measure, if any	Outcome of injury investigation	Decision on applying definitive measure	Effective date and type of definitive measure, if any	Termination
India						
Acetylene black	28.11.97 (G/SG/N/6/IND/1)	N/A	Affirmative (G/SG/N/8/IND/1)	Affirmative (G/SG/10/IND/1 & Suppl.1)	10.12.98 Tariff increase	
Carbon black	05.02.98 (G/SG/N6/IND/2)	N/A	Affirmative (G/SG/N/8/IND/2)	Affirmative (G/SG/N/10/IND/2)	28.02.99 Tariff increase	
Slabstock polyol	26.02.98 (G/SG/N/6/IND/3)	N/A	Affirmative (G/SG/N/8/IND/5)	Affirmative (G/SG/N/10/IND/3 & Suppl.1)	24.12.98 Tariff increase	
Propylene glycol	26.02.98 (G/SG/N/6/IND/4)	N/A	Affirmative (G/SG/N/8/IND/4)	Affirmative (G/SG/N/10/IND/4 & Suppl.1)	24.12.98 Tariff increase	
Hardboard	24.05.98 (G/SG/N/6/IND/5)	N/A	Affirmative (G/SG/N/8/IND/3)	Negative	N/A	Investigation terminated 12.11.99 (G/SG/N/9/IND/2)
Styrene butadiene rubber	19.01.98 (G/SG/N/6/IND/6)	N/A	N/A	Negative	N/A	Investigation terminated 01.05.98 (G/SG/N/6/IND/1)
Phenol	02.02.99 (G/SG/N/6/IND/7)	N/A	Affirmative (G/SG/N/8/IND/6)	Affirmative (G/SG/N/10/IND/5)	30.06.99 Tariff increase	
Acetone	16.06.99 (G/SG/N/6/IND/8)	N/A	Affirmative (G/SG/N/8/IND/8)	Affirmative (G/SG/N/10/IND/6)	27.01.2000 Tariff increase	
White/yellow phosphorus	15.09.99 (G/SG/N/6/IND/9)	N/A	N/A	Negative	N/A	Investigation terminated 17.01.2000 (G/SG/N/9/IND/3)

Gamma ferric oxide/magnetic iron oxide	06.07.2000 (G/SG/N/6/IND/10)	N/A	Ongoing	N/A	N/A	
Methylene chloride	17.07.2000 (G/SG/N/6/IND/11 + Corr.1)	N/A	Ongoing	N/A	N/A	
Korea						
Soybean oil	30.08.95 (G/SG/N/6/KOR & Suppl.1)	N/A	Affirmative	Negative	N/A	Investigation terminated (G/SG/N/6/KOR/Suppl.1)
Dairy products	28.05.96 (G/SG/N/6/KOR/2)	N/A	Affirmative (G/SG/N/8/KOR/1)	Affirmative (G/SG/N/10/KOR/1 & Corr.1 & Suppl.1 & Suppl.1/Corr.1)	01.03.97 Import quota	Measure terminated 20.05.2000
Bicycles and parts	27.08.96 (G/SG/N/6/KOR/3)	N/A	Affirmative (G/SG/N/8/KOR/2 & Corr.1)	Negative	N/A	Investigation terminated (G/SG/N/9/KOR/1 & Corr.1)
Garlic	16.10.99 (G/SG/N/6/KOR/4)	13.11.99 (G/SG/N/7/KOR/4)	Affirmative (G/SG/N/8/KOR/3)	Affirmative(G/SG/N/10/KOR/2 + Suppl.1)	01.06.2000 Tariff increase	
Latvia						
Swine meat	20.05.99 (G/SG/N/6/LVA/1)	01.06.99 (G/SG/N/7/LVA/1)	Affirmative (G/SG/N/8/LVA/1)	Affirmative (G/SG/N/10/LVA/1 & Suppl.1)	18.12.99 Variable customs duty	Measure terminated 01.06.2000 (G/SG/N/10/LVA/2)
Morocco						
Bananas	26.06.2000 (G/SG/N/6/MAR/1)	N/A	Ongoing	N/A	N/A	
Slovak Republic						
Swine meat	05.05.99 (G/SG/N/6/SVK/1)	21.05.99 (G/SG/N/7/SVK/1)	N/A	Negative	N/A	Investigation terminated 19.11.99 (G/SG/N/9/SVK/1)
Sugar	20.10.2000 (G/SG/N/6/SVK/2)	N/A	Ongoing	N/A	N/A	

Summary of Notifications of Safeguard Investigations and of Safeguard Measures 1 January 1995–9 November 2000 (*cont.*)

Member & Investigation	Initiation date	Effective date of provisional measure, if any	Outcome of injury investigation	Decision on applying definitive measure	Effective date and type of definitive measure, if any	Termination
Slovenia						
Swine meat	15.10.98 (G/SG/N/6/SVN/1)	27.11.98 (G/SG/N/7/SVN/1 & Suppl.1) 16.01.99 prov. measure terminated	Ongoing	N/A	N/A	
United States						
Tomatoes	29.03.95 (G/SG/N/6/USA/2)	N/A	Negative	Negative	N/A	Investigation terminated 12.08.96 (G/SG/N/9/USA/1)
Brooms	04.03.96 (G/SG/N/6/USA/2)	N/A	Affirmative (G/SG/N/8/USA/1)	Affirmative (G/SG/N/10/USA/1)	28.11.96 Tariff increase	Measure terminated 03.12.98 (G/SG/N/10/USA/1 /Suppl.1)
Tomatoes & peppers	11.03.96 (G/SG/N/6/USA/3)	N/A	Negative (G/SG/N/9/USA/1)	N/A	N/A	Investigation terminated
Wheat gluten	01.10.97 (G/SG/N/6/USA/4)	N/A	Affirmative (G/SG/N/8/USA/2 & Rev.1 & Rev1/Suppl.1)	Affirmative (G/SG/N/10/USA/2 & Suppl.1 + Corr.1)	01.06.98 QR	
Lamb meat	07.10.98 (G/SG/N/6/USA/5)	N/A	Affirmative (G/SG/N/8/ USA/3 + Corr.1,2)	Affirmative (G/SG/N/10/USA/3 & Suppl.1)	22.07.99 Tariff quota	

Steel wire rod	12.01.99 (G/SG/N/6/USA/6 + Corr.1)	N/A	Affirmative (G/SG/N/8/USA/4 & Suppl.1 & Suppl.2)	Affirmative (G/SG/N/10/USA/4)	01.03.2000 Tariff quota	
Line pipe	29.07.99 (G/SG/N/6/USA/7)	N/A	Affirmative (G/SG/N/8/USA/ 7 + Add.1 & Suppl.1)	Affirmative (G/SG/N/10/USA/5)	01.03.2000 Tariff increase	
Crabmeat	15.03.2000 (G/SG/N/6/USA/8)	N/A	Negative	Negative	N/A	Investigation terminated 11.07.2000 (G/SG/N/9/USA/2)
Extruded rubber thread	15.06.2000 (G/SG/N/6/USA/9)	N/A	Negative	Negative	N/A	Investigation terminated 03.10.2000 (G/SG/N/9/USA/3)
Venezuela, Bolivarian Republic of						
Cold-rolled steel	28.01.2000 (G/SG/N/6/VEN/1)	N/A	N/A	Negative	N/A	Investigation terminated 12.05.2000 (G/SG/N/9/VEN/1)
Hot-rolled steel	28.01.2000 (G/SG/N/6/VEN/2)	N/A	N/A	Negative	N/A	Investigation terminated 12.05.2000 (G/SG/N/9/VEN/2)
Tyres	08.03.2000 (G/SG/N/6/VEN/3)	N/A	Ongoing	N/A	N/A	

SUMMARY OF NOTIFICATIONS OF INITIATIONS, PRELIMINARY MEASURES, DEFINITIVE MEASURES, AND TERMINATIONS FROM 10 NOVEMBER 2000–29 OCTOBER 2001

Reporting Member	Safeguard investigations initiated	Preliminary safeguard measures imposed	Definitive safeguard measures imposed	Safeguard investigations terminated
Argentina	Peaches; 12/01/2001; G/SG/N/6/ARG/4	Peaches; 12/01/2001; G/SG/N/7/ARG/2	Peaches; 08/08/2001; G/SG/N/10/ARG/3 Motorcycles; 22/06/2001; G/SG/N/10/ARG/2	
Brazil	Coconuts; 10/08/2001; G/SG/N/6/BRA/2			
Bulgaria	Non-aqueous ammonium nitrate; 10/11/2000; G/SG/N/6/BGR/1	Non-aqueous ammonium nitrate; 28/11/2000; G/SG/N/7/BGR/1		
Chile	Lighters; 31/08/2001 G/SG/N/6/CHL/6		Liquid/powdered milk; 10/01/2001; G/SG/N/10/CHL/3	
	Mixed oils; 19/12/2000; G/SG/N/6/CHL/5	Mixed Oils; 13/01/2001; G/SG/N/7/CHL/5/Suppl.1		Mixed oils; 25/04/2001; G/SG/N/9/CHL/3
Czech Republic	Isoglucose; 20/12/2000; G/SG/N/6/CZE/3	Isoglucose; 10/01/2001; G/SG/N/7/CZE/2	Isoglucose; 26/07/2001; G/SG/N/10/CZE/2	
	Footwear; 01/11/2000; G/SG/N/6/CZE/2			Footwear; 25/07/2001; G/SG/N/9/CZE/1

Ecuador		Matches; 12/2000; G/SG/N/7/ECU/1		
Egypt			Powdered milk; 12/04/2001; G/SG/N/10/EGY/4	
El Salvador	Fertilizers; 08/11/2000; G/SG/N/6/SLV/3			Rice; 31/05/2001; G/SG/N/9/SLV/2 Pigmeat; 09/02/2001; G/SG/N/9/SLV/1
Japan	Tatami-Omote; 22/12/2000; G/SG/N/6/JPN/1 Welsh onions; 22/12/2000; G/SG/N/6/JPN/1 Shiitake mushrooms; 22/12/2000; G/SG/N/6/JPN/1	Tatami-Omote; 23/04/2001; G/SG/N/7/JPN/1 Welsh onions; 23/04/2001; G/SG/N/7/JPN/1 Shiitake mushrooms; 23/04/2001; G/SG/N/7/JPN/1		
Jordan	Biscuits/chocolates; 10/12/2000; G/SG/N/6/JOR/1		Biscuits; 01/09/2001; G/SG/N/10/JOR/1	Chocolate; 14/06/2001; G/SG/N/9/JOR/1
Morocco	Rubber plates & sheets; 05/12/2001; G/SG/N/6/MAR/2		Bananas; 04/2001; G/SG/N/10/MAR/1	
Philippines	Ceramic tiles; 28/05/2001; G/SG/N/6/PHL/2 Cement; 28/05/2001; G/SG/N/6/PHL/1			
Poland	Potassium nitrate; 22/12/2000; G/SG/N/6/POL/1			
Slovak Republic	Sugar; 20/10/2000; G/SG/N/6/SVK/2		Sugar; 01/05/2001; G/SG/N/10/SVK/1	
United States	Steel; 28/06/2001; G/SG/N/6/USA/10			

SUMMARY OF NOTIFICATIONS OF INITIATIONS, PRELIMINARY MEASURES, DEFINITIVE MEASURES, AND TERMINATIONS FROM 30 OCTOBER 2001–28 OCTOBER 2002

Reporting Member	Safeguard investigations initiated	Preliminary safeguard measures imposed	Definitive safeguard measures imposed	Safeguard investigations terminated
Brazil			Coconuts; 01/09/2002; G/SG/N/10/BRA/3	
Bulgaria	Crown Corks; 25/10/2001; G/SG/N/6/BGR/2	Ammonium nitrate; 01/07/2002; G/SG/N/7/BGR/2		
	Ammonium Nitrate; 16/01/2001; G/SG/N/6/BGR/3			
	Urea; 14/05/2002; G/SG/N/6/BGR/4			
	Steel; 08/07/2002; G/SG/N/6/BGR/5			
Canada	Steel; 25/03/2002; G/SG/N/6/CAN/1			
Chile	Steel; 28/12/2001; G/SG/N/6/CHL/7	Fructose; 07/ 2002; G/SG/N/7/CHL/6	Steel; 07/2002; G/SG/N/10/CHL/4	Steel; 26/03/2002; G/SG/N/9/CHL/5
	Steel; 05/04/2002; G/SG/N/6/CHL/8		Fructose; 30/08/2002; G/SG/N/10/CHL/5	Lighters; 09/01/2002; G/SG/N/9/CHL/4
	Lighters; 31/08/2001; G/SG/N/6/CHL/6			Glucose; 05/07/2002; G/SG/N/9/CHL/6
	Fructose/Glucose; 08/06/2002; G/SG/N/6/CHL/9			
Costa Rica	Rice; 11703/2002; G/SG/N/6/CRI/1	Rice; 12/03/2002; G/SG/N/7/CRI/1		
Czech Republic	Cocoa Powder; 15/11/2001; G/SG/N/6/CZE/4	Cocoa Powder; 30/11/2001; G/SG/N/7/CZE/3	Cocoa Powder; 14/06/2002; G/SG/N/10/CZE/3	
	Citric Acid; 30/01/2002; G/SG/N/6/CZE/5			

	Wire, Ropes and Cables; 27/02/2002; G/SG/N/6/CZE/6 Tubes and pipes; 06/03/2002; G/SG/N/6/CZE/7 Ammonium nitrate; 14/08/2002; G/SG/N/6/CZE/8 Steel; 28/08/2002; G/SG/N/6/CZE/9			
Ecuador			Matches; 24/10/2002; G/SG/N/10/ECU/1	
European Communities	Steel; 28/03/2002; G/SG/N/6/EEC/1	Steel; 29/03/2002; G/SG/N/7/EEC/1	Steel; 29/09/2002; G/SG/N/10/EEC/1/Suppl.1	
Hungary	Steel; 22/05/2002; G/SG/N/6/HUN/1	Steel; 03/06/2002; G/SG/N/7/HUN/1		
India	Epichlorohydrin (ECH); 14/03/2002; G/SG/N/6/IND/12 Industrial Sewing Machine Needles; 13/08/2002; G/SG/N/6/IND/14 Vegetable oil; 27/05/2002; G/SG/N/6/IND/13		Gamma Ferric Oxide (GFO)/Magnetic Iron Oxide (MIO); 24 January 2001; G/SG/N/10/IND/7	
Japan				Tatami-omote, welsh onion and shiitake mushrooms; 21/12/2001; G/SG/N/9/JPN/1
Jordan	Magnetic tapes; 24/01/2002; G/SG/N/6/JOR/2 Ceramic sinks; 27/05/2002; G/SG/N/6/JOR/7 Ceramic tiles; 29/05/2002; G/SG/N/6/JOR/4 Cooking appliances; 29/05/2002; G/SG/N/6/JOR/5	Magnetic tapes; 01–02/2002; G/SG/N/7/JOR/1	Magnetic tapes; 01/05/2002; G/SG/N/10/JOR/2	

Summary of Notifications of Initiations, Preliminary Measures, Definitive Measures, and Terminations from 30 October 2001–28 October 2002 (*cont.*)

Reporting Member	Safeguard investigations initiated	Preliminary safeguard measures imposed	Definitive safeguard measures imposed	Safeguard investigations terminated
	Cooking appliances; 29/05/2002; G/SG/N/6/JOR/8 Electric accumulators; 29/05/2002; G/SG/N/6/JOR/6 Pasta; 18/05/2002; G/SG/N/6/JOR/3			
Latvia	Live pigs and pork; 01/07/2002; G/SG/N/6/LVA/2			
Lithuania			Pastry yeast; 01/03/2002; G/SG/N/10/LTU/1	
Mexico	Plywood panels; 15/08/2002; G/SG/N/6/MEX/1			
Morocco				Rubber; 27/06/2001; G/SG/N/9/MAR/1
People's Republic of China	Steel; 20/05/2002; G/SG/N/6/CHN/1	Steel; 24/05/2002; G/SG/N/7/CHN/1		

Philippines		Grey portland cement; 07/11/2001; G/SG/N/7/PHL/1 Ceramic floor and wall tiles; 26/11/2001; G/SG/N/7/PHL/2	Ceramic floor and wall tiles; 11/04/2002 ; G/SG/N/10/PHL/1	Tomato paste; 26/12/2001; G/SG/N/9/PHL/1
Poland	Calcium Carbide; 18/02/2002; G/SG/N/6/POL/2 Steel; 08/06/2002; G/SG/N/6/POL/4 Water heaters; 28/05/2002; G/SG/N/6/POL/3	Steel; 19/08/2002; G/SG/N/7/POL/1		
El Salvador				Fertilizer; 19/10/2001; G/SG/N/9/SLV/3
Slovak Republic	Ammonium nitrate; 14 October 2002; G/SG/N/6/SVK/3			
United States			Certain steel products; 20/03/2002; G/SG/N/10/USA/6	Certain steel products; 22/11/2001; G/SG/N/9/USA/4
Venezuela	Paper; 16/10/2001; G/SG/N/6/VEN/4 Iron/steel U sections; 01/11/2001; G/SG/N/6/VEN/5			

SUMMARY OF NOTIFICATIONS OF INITIATIONS, PRELIMINARY MEASURES, DEFINITIVE MEASURES, AND TERMINATIONS FROM 29 OCTOBER 2002–15 OCTOBER 2003

Reporting Member	Safeguard investigations initiated	Preliminary safeguard measures imposed	Definitive safeguard measures imposed	Safeguard investigations terminated
Bulgaria	Iron and steel; 30 April 2003; G/SG/N/6/BGR/6		Crown corks; 14 January 2003; G/SG/N/10/BGR/1	Urea; 14 March 2003; G/SG/N/9/BGR/1
			Ammonium nitrate; 3 February 2003; G/SG/N/10/BGR/2	Steel; 23 September 2003; G/SG/N/9/BGR/2
Chile			Fructose; 27 February 2003; G/SG/N/10/CHL/5/Suppl. 2	Glucose; 27 February 2003; G/SG/N/9/CHL/6/Suppl. 3
Czech Republic		Ammonium nitrate; 19 February 2003; G/SG/N/7/CZE/4	Sugar; 25 February 2003; G/SG/N/10/CZE/4	Wire, ropes and cables; 5 March 2003; G/SG/N/9/CZE/3
			Tubes and pipes; 28 February 2003; G/SG/N/10/CZE/5	Citric acid; 5 November 2002; G/SG/N/9/CZE/2
			Ammonium nitrate; 4 September 2003; G/SG/N/10/CZE/6	Steel; 19 May 2003; G/SG/N/9/CZE/4
Ecuador	Fibreboard; 20 February 2003; G/SG/N/6/ECU/3	Smooth ceramics; 10 October 2003; G/SG/N/7/ECU/2	Fibreboard; 8 October 2003; G/SG/N/10/ECU/2/Suppl.1	
	Smooth ceramics; 28 July 2003; G/SG/N/6/ECU/4	Fibreboard; 26 February 2003; G/SG/N/10/ECU/2		

	Ceramics and porcelains; 17 September 2003; G/SG/N/6/ECU/5			
Estonia	Swine meat; 15 April 2003; G/SG/N/6/EST/1			
European Communities	Mandarins; 28 July 2003; G/SG/N/6/EEC/2			
Hungary	Ammonium nitrate; 27 January 2003; G/SG/N/6/HUN/2	Ammonium nitrate; 5 February 2003; G/SG/N/7/HUN/2	Steel; 7 April 2003; G/SG/N/10/HUN/1	Steel; 4 April 2003; G/SG/N/9/HUN/1
	White sugar; 28 July 2003; G/SG/N/6/HUN/3	White sugar; 28 July 2003; G/SG/N/7/HUN/3	Ammonium nitrate; 20 June 2003; G/SG/N/10/HUN/2	Ammonium nitrate; 20 June 2003; G/SG/N/9/HUN/2 (Partial termination)
India	Bisphenol A; 14 March 2003; G/SG/N/6/IND/15		Epichlorohydrin; 18 December 2002; G/SG/N/10/IND/8	
Jordan	Aerated water; 20 September 2002; G/SG/N/6/JOR/9		Sanitary Ware Products; 21 February 2003; G/SG/N/10/JOR/4 Pasta; 24 February 2003; G/SG/N/10/JOR/3	Aerated water; 9 September 2003; G/SG/N/9/JOR/6 Ceramic tiles; 31 October 2002; G/SG/N/9/JOR/2 Electric accumulators; 31 October 2002; G/SG/N/9/JOR/3 Cooking appliances; 31 October 2002; G/SG/N/9/JOR/4 and 31 October 2002; G/SG/N/9/JOR/5
Latvia			Live pig and pork; 23 June 2003; G/SG/N/10/LVA/3	
Moldova	Sugar; 30 September 2003; G/SG/N/6/MDA/1		Sugar; 30 September 2003; G/SG/N/10/MDA/1	

Summary of Notifications of Initiations, Preliminary Measures, Definitive Measures, and Terminations from 29 October 2002–15 October 2003 (*cont.*)

Reporting Member	Safeguard investigations initiated	Preliminary safeguard measures imposed	Definitive safeguard measures imposed	Safeguard investigations terminated
People's Republic of China			Steel; 5 November 2002; G/SG/N/10/CHN/1	
Philippines	Glass mirrors; 8 May 2003; G/SG/N/6/PHL/3	Glass mirrors; 13 October 2003; G/SG/N/7/PHL/3	Cement; 10 July 2003; G/SG/N/10/PHL/2	
	Figured glass; 8 May 2003; G/SG/N/6/PHL/4	Figured glass; 13 October 2003; G/SG/N/7/PHL/4		
	Float glass; 23 May 2003; G/SG/N/6/PHL/5	Float glass; 13 October 2003; G/SG/N/7/PHL/5		
Poland	Matches; 23 May 2003; G/SG/N/6/POL/5		Steel; 27 March 2003; G/SG/N/10/POL/1 Calcium carbide; 28 August 2003; G/SG/N/10/POL/3 Water heaters; 14 August 2003; G/SG/N/10/POL/2	
Slovak Republic			Ammonium nitrate; 14 April 2003; G/SG/N/10/SVK/2	
United States				Steel wire rod; 24 March 2003; G/SG/N/10/USA/4/Suppl. 2 Line pipe; 24 March 2003; G/SG/N/10/USA/5/Rev.1/Suppl.1
Venezuela	Footwear; 21 November 2002; G/SG/N/6/VEN/6	Iron/steel U sections; 5 November 2002; G/SG/N/7/VEN/1		

SUMMARY OF VARIOUS NOTIFICATIONS BETWEEN 15 OCTOBER 2003–18 OCTOBER 2004

Reporting Member	Safeguard investigations initiated	Provisional safeguard measures	Definitive safeguard measures	Safeguard investigations terminated without measures	Expired or terminated measures[1]
Argentina	coloured television sets; 16 July 2004; G/SG/N/6/ARG/5				
Brazil	toys; 14 November, 2003; G/SG/N/6/BRA/1/suppl.1		Toys; 19 December, 2003; G/SG/N/10/BRA/2/ suppl.2		
Bulgaria				certain steel products; 15 July, 2004; G/SG/N/9/BGR/3	
Canada				certain steel products; 15 October, 2003; G/SG/N/9/CAN/1	
China					certain steel products; 4 February, 2004; G/SG/N/10/CHN/1/Suppl. 1
Colombia	electric smoothing irons; 2 March, 2004; G/SG/N/6/COL/2				
Ecuador	paper and paperboard; 16 December, 2003; G/SG/N/6/ECU/6			paper and paperboard; 15 March, 2004; G/SG/N/9/ECU/2	
Ecuador			smooth ceramics; 25 February, 2004; G/SG/N/10/ECU/3		
Ecuador	pneumatic tyres of rubber; 17 December, 2003; G/SG/N/6/ECU/7			pneumatic tyres of rubber; 17 March, 2004; G/SG/N/9/ECU/1	

[1] This column includes only those that were notified in writing.

Summary of Various Notifications between 15 October 2003–18 October 2004 (*Cont.*)

Reporting Member	Safeguard investigations initiated	Provisional safeguard measures	Definitive safeguard measures	Safeguard investigations terminated without measures	Expired or terminated measures
European Communities					certain steel products; 19 December, 2004 G/SG/N/10/EEC/1/Suppl.2
European Communities		mandarins; 6 November, 2003; G/SG/N/7/EEC/2	mandarins; 16 March, 2004; G/SG/N/10/EEC/2 + Suppl. 1		
European Communities	salmon; 17 March, 2004; G/SG/N/6/EEC/3	salmon; 16 August, 2004; G/SG/N/7/EEC/3			
Hungary[2]			white sugar; 28 November, 2003; G/SG/N/10/HUN/3		
India	starch, modified starches and manioc based sago; 4 August, 2004; G/SG/N/6/IND/16				
Jamaica	cement; 25 February, 2004; G/SG/N/6/JAM/1	cement; 25 February, 2004; G/SG/N/7/JAM/1	cement; 23 April, 2004; G/SG/N/10/JAM/1 + Corr. 1		cement; 15 September, 2004; G/SG/N/9/JAM/1
Moldova	cosmetic and perfumery products; 13 July, 2004; G/SG/N/6/MDA/2 + Corr. 1				
Peru	certain textiles; 30 August 2004; G/SG/N/6/PER/1				
Philippines			Grey Portland cement; 18 March, 2004; G/SG/N/10/PHL/2/Suppl.1		

Philippines		float glass; 26 May, 2004; G/SG/N/10/PHL/3 + Corr.1	
Philippines		figured glass; 26 May, 2004; G/SG/N/10/PHL/4	
Philippines		glass mirrors; 26 May, 2004; G/SG/N/10/PHL/5	
Poland[3]		matches; 9 December, 2003; G/SG/N/10/POL/4	
Turkey	thermometers; 26 July, 2004; G/SG/N/6/TUR/1		
Turkey	active earth and clays; 26 July, 2004; G/SG/N/6/TUR/2		
Turkey	certain glassware; 27 July, 2004; G/SG/N/6/TUR/3		
Turkey	unframed glass mirrors; 27 July, 2004; G/SG/N/6/TUR/4		
Turkey	certain voltmeters and ammeters; 27 July, 2004; G/SG/N/6/TUR/5		
United States			certain steel products; 12 December, 2004 G/SG/N/10/USA/6/Suppl.8

[2] EC stated in the meeting of 25 October 2004 that this measure has been terminated at the end of April 2004. (Hungary acceded to the European Union on 1 May 2004.)

[3] EC stated in the meeting of 25 October 2004 that this measure has been terminated at the end of April 2004. (Poland acceded to the European Union on 1 May 2004.)

SUMMARY OF VARIOUS NOTIFICATIONS BETWEEN 26 OCTOBER 2004–3 NOVEMBER 2005

Reporting Member	Safeguard investigations initiated	Provisional safeguard measures	Definitive safeguard measures (including recommendations of imposition)	Safeguard investigations terminated without measures	Expired or terminated measures[4]
Canada (bicycles)	10/02/2005 (G/SG/N/6/CAN/2)				
Chile (wheat flour)	10/12/2004 (G/SG/N/6/CHL/10 + Suppl.1)	10/12/2004 (G/SG/N/7/CHL/7 + Suppl.1)	04/03/2005 (G/SG/N/10/CHL/6 + Suppl.1&2)		
Colombia (domestic blenders)	26/01/2004 (G/SG/N/6/COL/3)			17/08/2004 (G/SG/N/9/COL/3)	
Colombia (electric smoothing irons)				17/08/2004 (G/SG/N/9/COL/3)	
European Communities (strawberries)	06/07/2005 (G/SG/N/6/EEC/4 + Corr.1)				
European Communities (salmon)			06/02/2005 (G/SG/N/10/EEC/3 + Suppl.1–3)		27/04/2005 G/SG/N/10/EEC/3/Suppl.3
Indonesia (lighters)	28/07/2005 (G/SG/N/6/IDN/2)				
Indonesia (ceramic tableware)	19/10/2004 (G/SG/N/6/IDN/1)		10/05/2005 (G/SG/N/10/IDN/1)		

Jordan (insecticides)	16/01/2005 (G/SG/N/6/JOR/10)		16/10/2005 (G/SG/N/10/JOR/5 + Suppl.1)	
Moldova (cosmetics and perfumery products)		(n.a.)[5] G/SG/N/7/MDA/1		
Morocco (ceramic tiles)	24/01/2005 (G/SG/N/6/MAR/3)		01/09/2005 (G/SG/N/10/MAR/2) (The measure is not imposed as of 3 November 2005.)	
Pakistan (footwear)	10/05/2005 (G/SG/N/6/PAK/1)			15/08/2005 (G/SG/N/9/PAK/1)
Peru (certain textiles)		14/10/2004 (G/SG/N/7/PER/1, + Suppl.1&2)		04/05/2005 (G/SG/N/9/PER/1)
Turkey (thermometers)				04/03/2005 (G/SG/N/9/TUR/2)
Turkey (active earth and clays)			08/07/2005 (G/SG/N/10/TUR/1 + Corr.1)	
Turkey (certain glassware)				18/01/2005 (G/SG/N/9/TUR/1)
Turkey (unframed glass mirrors)				03/05/2005 (G/SG/N/9/TUR/3)
Turkey (certain voltmeters and ammeters)			12/08/2005 (G/SG/N/10/TUR/2)	

4 This column includes only those that were notified in writing.

5 The notification does not specify the date from which the provisional measure will enter into force.

APPENDIX 7

Active Safeguard Investigations and Existing Safeguard Measures in Place as of November 3, 2005

[excerpted from Report (2005) of the Committee on Safeguards to the Council for Trade in Goods]

Member & Investigation	Initiation date	Effective date of provisional measure, if any[1]	Effective date and type of definitive measure, if any
Brazil			
Toys	06.10.03[2] (G/SG/N/6/BRA/ 1/Suppl.1)		01.01.04 Tariff surcharge (G/SG/N/10/BRA/2/ Suppl.2)
Coconuts	10.08.01 (G/SG/N/6/BRA/2)		09.02 Quantitative restriction (G/SG/N/10/BRA/3 & Suppl.1 & Suppl.2)
Bulgaria			
Crown corks	25.10.01 (G/SG/N/6/BGR/2)		19.11.02 Specific duty (G/SG/N/10/BGR/1)
Ammonium nitrate	16.01.02 (G/SG/N/6/BGR/3)		29.12.02 Tariff quota (G/SG/N/10/BGR/2)
Canada			
Bicycles	10.02.05 (G/SG/N/6/CAN/2)		
Chile			
Wheat flour	10.12.04 (G/SG/N/6/CHL/10 & Suppl.1)	10.12.04 (G/SG/N/7/CHL/7 & Suppl.1)	04.03.05 Tariff increase (G/SG/N/10/CHL/6 + Suppl.1&2)
Costa Rica			
Rice	04.03.02 (G/SG/N/6/CRI/1)	12.03.02 (G/SG/N/7/CRI/1 & Suppl.1)	N/A
Egypt			
Safety matches	05.08.98 (G/SG/N/6/EGY/1)		19.02.99 Tariff increase (G/SG/N/10/EGY/1)

[1] Only those provisional measures that are in force as of 3 November 2005 are included in this table.

[2] This is a notification on initiation of a review of the safeguard measure. The original measure was imposed on 1 January 1997 (G/SG/N/10/BRA/1).

(Table *cont.*)

Member & Investigation	**Initiation date**	**Effective date of provisional measure, if any**[1]	**Effective date and type of definitive measure, if any**
Common fluorescent lamps	19.09.99 (G/SG/N/6/EGY/2)		27.02.00 Tariff increase (G/SG/N/10/EGY/2 & Suppl.1) 27.02.01 extended (G/SG/N/10/EGY/3)
Powdered milk	25.09.00 (G/SG/N/6/EGY/3)		12.04.01 Tariff increase (G/SG/N/10/EGY/4)
European Communities			
Mandarins	11.07.03 (G/SG/N/6/EEC/2)		11.04.04 Tariff rate quotas (G/SG/N/10/EEC/2)
Strawberries	06.07.05 (G/SG/N/6/EEC/4 & Corr.1)		
India			
Acetylene black	28.11.97 (G/SG/N/6/IND/1)		10.12.98 Tariff increase (G/SG/N/10/IND/1 & Suppl.1)
Carbon black	05.02.98 (G/SG/N/6/IND/2)		28.02.99 Tariff increase (G/SG/N/10/IND/2)
Slabstock polyol	26.02.98 (G/SG/N/6/IND/3)		24.12.98 Tariff increase (G/SG/N/10/IND/3 & Suppl.1)
Propylene glycol	26.02.98 (G/SG/N/6/IND/4)		24.12.98 Tariff increase (G/SG/N/10/IND/4 & Suppl.1)
Phenol	02.02.99 (G/SG/N/6/IND/7)		30.06.99 Tariff increase (G/SG/N/10/IND/5)
Acetone	16.06.99 (G/SG/N/6/IND/8)		27.01.2000 Tariff increase (G/SG/N/10/IND/6)
Gamma ferric oxide/ magnetic iron oxide	06.07.2000 (G/SG/N/6/IND/10)		23.01.02 Tariff increase (G/SG/N/10/IND/7)
Methylene chloride	17.07.2000 (G/SG/N/6/IND/11 & Corr.1)		N/A
Epichloro-hydrin	14.03.02 (G/SG/N/6/IND/12)		30.10.02 Tariff increase (G/SG/N/10/IND/8)
Vegetable oil	27.05.02 (G/SG/N/6/IND/13)		N/A

[1] Only those provisional measures that are in force as of 3 November 2005 are included in this table.

(Table *cont.*)

Member & Investigation	Initiation date	Effective date of provisional measure, if any[1]	Effective date and type of definitive measure, if any
Bisphenol A	06.03.03 (G/SG/N/6/IND/15)		N/A
Starch, modified starches and manioc based sago	07.07.04 (G/SG/N/6/IND/16)		N/A
Indonesia			
Ceramic tableware	19.10.04 (G/SG/N/6/IDN/1)		10.05.05 Specific duty (G/SG/N/10/IDN/1)
Lighters	28.07.05 (G/SG/N/6/IDN/2)		
Jordan			
Biscuits/ chocolates	10.12.00 (G/SG/N/6/JOR/1)		01.09.01 Specific customs duty (G/SG/N/10/JOR/1) *Partial termination (chocolates) (G/SG/N/9/JOR/1)*
Insecticides	16.01.05 (G/SG/N/6/JOR/10)		16.10.05 Tariff increase (G/SG/N/10/JOR/5 + Suppl.1)
Magnetic tapes	24.01.02 (G/SG/N/6/JOR/2)		01.05.02 Specific customs duty (G/SG/N/10/JOR/2)
Pasta	18.05.02 (G/SG/N/6/JOR/3)		Tariff surcharge (G/SG/N/10/JOR/3)
Tiles	29.05.02 (G/SG/N/6/JOR/4)		N/A *Partial termination (CN 6907.1 & 6908.1) (G/SG/N/9/JOR/2)*
Sinks	27.05.02 (G/SG/N/6/JOR/7)		Tariff surcharge (G/SG/N/10/JOR/4)
Mexico			
Plywood panels	15.08.02 (G/SG/N/6/MEX/1)		N/A
Moldova			
Sugar	21.05.03 (G/SG/N/6/MDA/1)		01.01.04 Tariff increase (G/SG/N/10/MDA/1)
Cosmetic and perfumery products	18.06.03 (G/SG/N/6/MDA/2)	(n.a.)[3] G/SG/N/7/MDA/1	N/A

[1] Only those provisional measures that are in force as of 3 November 2005 are included in this table.

[3] The notification does not specify the date from which the provisional measure will enter into force.

(Table *cont.*)

Member & Investigation	Initiation date	Effective date of provisional measure, if any[1]	Effective date and type of definitive measure, if any
Morocco			
Ceramic tiles	24.01.05 (G/SG/N/6/MAR/3)		(The measure proposed in G/SG/N/10/MAR/2 is not imposed as of 3 November 2005)
Philippines			
Grey Portland cement	28.05.01 (G/SG/N/6/PHL/1)		10.12.01 Tariff surcharge (G/SG/N/10/PHL/2)
Ceramic floor tiles	28.05.01 (G/SG/N/6/PHL/2)		11.04.02 Tariff surcharge (G/SG/N/10/PHL/1)
Glass mirrors	16.04.03 (G/SG/N/6/PHL/3)		13.10.03 Tariff surcharge (G/SG/N/10/PHL/5)
Figured glass	16.04.03 (G/SG/N/6/PHL/4)		13.10.03 Tariff surcharge (G/SG/N/10/PHL/4)
Float glass	21.05.03 (G/SG/N/6/PHL/5)		13.10.03 Tariff surcharge (G/SG/N/10/PHL/3)
Turkey			
Active earth and clays	17.07.04 (G/SG/N/6/TUR/2)		08.07.05 Quantitative restriction (G/SG/N/TUR/1 & Corr.1)
Certain voltmeters and ammeters	17.07.04 (G/SG/N/6/TUR/5)		12.08.05 Quantitative restriction (G/SG/N/10/TUR/2)
Venezuela			
Tyres	08.03.00 (G/SG/N/6/VEN/3)		N/A
Paper	16.10.01 (G/SG/N/6/VEN/4)		N/A
Iron/steel U sections	01.11.01 (G/SG/N/6/VEN/5)	12.12.02 (G/SG/N/7/VEN/ 1/Suppl.1)	N/A
Footwear	23.09.02 (G/SG/N/6/VEN/6)		N/A

[1] Only those provisional measures that are in force as of 3 November 2005 are included in this table.

Index

The manufacturer's authorised representative in the EU for product safety is Oxford University Press España S.A. of el Parque Empresarial San Fernando de Henares, Avenida de Castilla, 2 – 28830 Madrid (www.oup.es/en or product.safety@oup.com). OUP España S.A. also acts as importer into Spain of products made by the manufacturer.

www.ingramcontent.com/pod-product-compliance
Ingram Content Group UK Ltd.
Pitfield, Milton Keynes, MK11 3LW, UK
UKHW021136160926
475595UK00020B/102
9780199277407